Financial First Aid

Financial First Aid

Smart Remedies for Hundreds of Curable Money Ailments

Mary L. Sprouse

JOHN WILEY & SONS, INC.

New York • Chichester • Weinheim • Brisbane • Singapore • Toronto

Copyright © 1998 by Mary L. Sprouse.
Published by John Wiley & Sons, Inc.

Library of Congress Cataloging-in-Publication Data:

Sprouse, Mary L.
    Financial first aid : smart remedies for hundreds of curable money
ailments / Mary L. Sprouse.
        p.   cm.
    Includes index.
    ISBN 0-471-19340-2 (alk. paper)
    1. Finance, Personal.   I. Title.
HG179.S5577   1998
332.024—dc21   97-17934

Printed in the United States of America

10 9 8 7 6 5 4 3 2 1

For Maya,
often neglected, but always loved

Acknowledgments

This book would not have been possible without the assistance of certain individuals. The author wishes to thank Rebekah Verdon, CLU, CFC, of Balanced Financials in Beverly Hills, California, for generously giving her time to ensure that much of the information on insurance in Chapter 5 was factually accurate.

The author would also like to thank Sharon Remer for her dedication to facts and dogged persistence in ferreting out sources of information.

Nor would this book have been published without the efforts of my agent, Henry Dunow, whose ability to keep a concept alive borders on the miraculous.

Finally, the author thanks Maya, whose fifth year of life passed almost unnoticed while her mother was absorbed in putting words on paper.

M.L.S.

Contents

Contents

Introduction

Flat broke. Uninsured. Out of work. Homeless. These are just a few of the fears that keep honest, hardworking Americans awake at night. The specter of financial failure is even more frightening because it can strike through no fault of your own. A spectacular run of bad luck can land even a tycoon on the streets.

Not all financial ailments have dire consequences, however. Our modern world wreaks minor fiscal havoc daily—with "snafus," "computer glitches," "human error," and "the fine print."

Of course, some of us also suffer from self-inflicted financial wounds. Haste, carelessness, lack of knowledge, and plain gullibility can easily lay our assets low.

Whatever their cause, no matter how serious they are, one must deal with financial ailments. Otherwise, they will grow worse, until the finest financial doctors may not be able to restore you.

No one is immune to financial problems. Even the most diligent money managers can fall victim to an ailing economy, tax maladies, damaged credit, or computer viruses. The remedy may be as minor as a Band-Aid or as urgent as critical care. You have to seek treatment, though. And that is where this book can help you. In the chapters that follow, you will find a prescription for almost every financial affliction, including what to do:

- To correct bank errors.

- To manage your debt.

- To raise a home down payment.

- To file a consumer complaint.

- To resolve warranty disputes.

- To preserve your assets when serious illness strikes.

- To avoid being turned down for insurance.

- To obtain the best insurance rates available.

- If you are refused a loan.

- If your credit report is wrong.

- If you are audited.

- If you owe federal or state tax.

- To overturn tax penalties.

- To fight a property tax overassessment.

- To dispute erroneous bills and credit card charges.

- To protect yourself when buying a home.

- If your stock loses value or becomes worthless.

- If you do not have an employer retirement or health plan or the plan is terminated or goes broke.

- If your bank, brokerage firm, or insurance company goes under.

- If your home value declines until you have a negative equity.

- If you are threatened with foreclosure.

- If you are pursued by debt collectors.

- If you lose bonds or stock certificates.

- To ensure your financial privacy.

- If your health plan refuses to pay for services.

- If your Social Security earnings record is wrong.

- If your credit cards are lost or stolen.

- To make sure your family is financially secure if you die.

- To avoid probate.

The answers to these and a plague of other topics that might ail you are grouped in chapters dealing with banking, borrowing and credit cards, consumer problems, home ownership, insurance, investments, divorce, taxes, retirement and pension plans, and estate planning and death.

This is not a book for professional problem solvers. If you have been stricken with an ailment only lawyers can cure, you should seek legal help as soon as you have an elementary grasp of the basic remedies outlined in these pages. Most readers, however, will find relief for their troubles by following the over-the-counter advice dispensed in this book.

Step-by-step instructions for treating each disorder are presented. If there are several forms of relief, they are all discussed in detail. Where appropriate, names, addresses, and telephone numbers of regulatory agencies or helpful organizations are included, along with sample letters you can use to state your case, demand a remedy, initiate an investigation, or involve third parties. Finally, where applicable, the book provides tips to prevent fiscal upsets before they occur.

Keep this book handy. It is an all-inclusive reference work for many financial irritations, mishaps, and disasters. Use it the same way you would use any first aid book, such as the *Physicians' Desk Reference* or *The American Medical Association Family Medical Guide*. Sooner or later, unfortunately, you are likely to come down with some financial malady.

It is easy to blithely charge hundreds, even thousands of dollars without feeling as if you have spent so much as a cent. It is much harder to shell out a dollar bill. Parting with a dollar makes us feel poorer.

Maybe that is why a financial crisis involving cash invokes our most primal fears. Losing your credit card is inconvenient; losing your last dime is terrifying.

Fortunately, few of our cash and banking maladies are the stuff of nightmares. And with the advice in this chapter, they can be quickly corrected. Some of the afflictions are mild—earning a low savings rate or not knowing how to balance a checkbook. Some are nuisances, such as mix-ups with electronic bill paying. And, if you are ever stranded in a strange city with no money, you can find help in these pages for that emergency, too.

■ CASH

AILMENT

I need to send cash to a relative in a hurry.

℞ No need to panic. It is fairly simple, although hardly cheap, to get money where it is needed. Here are your options:

Western Union. If you have a credit card and a telephone, you can hire Western Union to deliver cash for pickup at any of 16,000 locations in the United States and overseas. Inside the United States, you can use MasterCard or Visa to charge transfers of up to $2000 by phone. If you need to send more than $2000, you will have to go to a Western Union office. If you go in person, Western Union will accept MasterCard or Visa, a cashier's check, or cash.

Western Union charges from $15 for a $50 transfer to $203 to send $5000. Whether you will pay more for an overseas transfer depends in part on where the money is going. There is no surcharge on Western Union transfers to London or Paris, for example, but you will pay an extra $52 to send the same amount to Barcelona.

Moneygram.   Moneygram is Western Union's chief rival in the money-moving business. To send cash, you will have to go to a Moneygram office. However, Moneygram will accept telephone orders for an extra fee if you have a MasterCard, Visa, or Discover card. Moneygram does not accept the American Express card.

Moneygram charges $13 to transfer up to $100. Sending $300 costs $20; $1000 costs $49; $2000 costs $79; and transferring $5000 costs $199. There is an extra charge for foreign transfers of $2000 or less, but no surcharge for larger amounts.

For locations, call Western Union at 800-225-5227 and Moneygram at 800-926-9400. Use the same numbers to order a cash transfer by phone.

Bank wire transfer.   The best bargain when sending money is to use a bank or savings and loan to make a wire transfer of funds—to another bank or thrift near the person who needs cash. The more money you are moving, the more you will save.

Unlike the sliding-scale fees used by Western Union and Moneygram, banks generally charge a flat fee—usually $25 or less. The transfer takes less than an hour to complete in the United States. Overseas transfers usually cost around $30 and take longer because business days do not coincide. Most banks also charge the recipient of the cash a small fee ($15 or more).

Even if you are not near your own bank, you can use your MasterCard or Visa to get a cash advance at almost any other bank. Then use that cash to fund a wire transfer.

Delivery services.   The most obvious way to get money from one pocket to another is overnight mail. But it is unwise. Sure, you can slip a wad of bills into an envelope. But the major overnighters, such as Federal Express and United Parcel Service, will not accept a package they know contains cash. The U.S. Postal Service does not prohibit mailing cash, but it advises against it. And no delivery service will pay a claim for the money if the envelope gets lost.

AILMENT

AILMENT

I am away from home and need cash.

R If you are stuck without a credit card, you could ask someone to wire you what you need (see previous discussion). Or, if you are carrying plastic, you could wire yourself money by calling Western Union or Moneygram and charging the transfer to a credit card. But there are easier—and cheaper—options.

If you can scrape by with $500 or less, your best bet may be an automated teller machine (ATM). Most ATMs in the United States and an increasing number overseas are linked to one of two national networks: Cirrus and Plus. The result: The same card you slip into your hometown machine will produce instant cash in Peoria or Paris.

Cirrus and Plus now honor most members of regional networks, too. Look for the logos of the systems they honor plastered on the ATM. The odds are that wherever you are an ATM machine will recognize your ATM card and dispense cash. There may be a nominal transaction fee, most often $2 or less.

ATMs have drawbacks, though. You usually cannot withdraw more than $500 a day. And ATMs are not always reliable—systems go down, individual machines run out of cash, and sometimes there is trouble getting through to your home bank.

If your ATM card is not accepted by a particular cash machine, your credit card probably will be. MasterCard, Visa, American Express, and Discover work in most ATMs. Just make sure you know your personal identification number (PIN) when you travel.

During banking hours, you can withdraw cash up to your credit limit if you take your credit card inside. But whether you get cash inside or outside the bank, you start paying interest from the day you get the advance. The exception: The Discover card charges a transaction fee equal to $2\frac{1}{2}\%$ of the cash advance (a minimum of $2.50 and no maximum) and gives you an interest-free grace period as long as you pay your bill in full each month. American Express customers have other options depending on which card you have.

AILMENT

I have forgotten the personal identification number (PIN) for one of my bank cards and cannot withdraw cash.

R Call your credit card issuer and explain this common problem. You will typically be asked to supply such personal data as your mother's maiden name and one of your most recent charges as proof you are not an impostor. After the issuer is sure you are who you claim to be, you will be given a new PIN over the phone. Write it down right away, so you will not forget it before you have a chance to use it.

☐ Prevention

Every financial expert warns against carrying your PIN around with you. This is sound advice, but not much use on a street corner. Most of us have several credit and ATM cards, all with different and in no way memorable PINs. A more useful suggestion is to write your PINs without identifying them as such on a scrap piece of paper and place it in a separate compartment or pocket from your ATM and credit cards. If you cannot remember which PIN belongs to which card, code each number some way that will not be readily obvious to a stranger—maybe an S for Visa, instead of a V. Use your ingenuity.

■ BANKING

AILMENT
I want to get the highest interest on my bank savings.

R℞ Interest paid on checking and passbook savings accounts is laughable. The only bank investments with potential are certificates of deposit (CDs). Because you agree to lock up your money for between six months and five years, banks pay higher interest on CDs than on other accounts. Don't get excited, though. With yields averaging around 4% for short-term certificates of deposit and just under 6% for the five-year variety, CDs barely beat inflation. Their appeal lies solely in being federally insured. Check newspaper ads and call savings and loans in your area to find the highest rates.

Even better, invest in out-of-state CDs and beat the averages by one-half to one percentage point. But before you do, be aware that shopping far from home has some minor drawbacks:

■ You may not get the quoted rate. Rates can change daily. When you mail a check, you get the rate in effect on the day your check arrives. You can do away with the delay with a same-day wire transfer of funds, but your bank may charge a $10 to $15 fee.

■ It is harder to check the pulse of a distant institution. But close monitoring of the bank's health is not needed. Just make sure the institution has federal deposit insurance and keep your deposit under $90,000 or so (so that the principal plus earnings does not exceed the $100,000 insurance limit).

How CD rates stack up. You have tracked down the CD with the best yield. But is it really? Sometimes even the analytical mind of Sherlock Holmes would falter in comparing CD yields. That is because they can be stated in so many ways. To make sure you are not comparing apples and oranges, ask an officer in each of your prospective banks—or your broker—exactly how much money you would take home when, say, a $1000 one-year certificate of deposit matures.

Saving strategies with CDs. Interest rates have been remarkably stable—and depressingly low—in the 1990s. If that condition changes and rates begin to fluctuate, some strategy will be needed to improve your yield. In times of flux, spread your cash among CDs with due dates six months apart. That way some of your money will soon be available to reinvest if rates rise, and some will be locked into what may prove to be superior yields if rates fall.

Use a different type of hedging if you decide on long-term CDs. Ask whether the bank will let you make partial withdrawals from one large CD. If not, put your money in several smaller ones. This strategy lets you avoid paying the early-withdrawal penalty on your entire investment if rates rise and you want to move part of the money to new, higher-rate CDs.

You can also let a broker shop for you if you are in the market for several CDs. You will forfeit a quarter point or so in fees, and you must have an account with the brokerage. You can often open an account simply by calling a broker and supplying a few basic facts over the phone. If not, request a mail-in application. Although there is no fee to sell you a certificate, brokers may charge for the account if you do not buy and sell securities with them regularly. Once you have opened a brokerage account, you can switch to higher-yielding CDs at other banks without having to open a new bank account each time. You will not have to pay early-withdrawal penalties either. Unlike banks, brokers maintain an active secondary market in CDs. You may not get face value if interest rates rise after you buy your certificate. But you usually will lose less on the sale than you would with an early-withdrawal penalty. And if interest rates have dropped, you can probably sell at a gain. Like bank CDs, brokered CDs are federally insured up to $100,000. Most brokers accept minimum deposits of $1000.

☐ Prevention

Investing with a bank or savings and loan is almost an oxymoron. Put your money almost anywhere else and you will earn more interest. (Stock yields are historically even higher on average than interest-bearing investments, but pose greater risk.)

Money market mutual funds. If the combination of yield, liquidity, and safety ranks high on your list, it is hard to top money market mutual funds. These funds invest solely in short-term debt securities, such as Treasury bills, commercial paper, and certificates of deposit. If you are in a high tax bracket, you may earn more, after taxes, with tax-free money funds that buy short-term tax-exempt municipal bonds.

The interest rate paid by a money fund depends on its portfolio and the cost of money, but it is usually higher than bank CDs. The minimum initial investment is usually $1000 to $5000. You can add to your account or withdraw money at any time without penalty or a charge. Most funds offer unlimited check-writing privileges, as long as each check is for $500 or more. There is no minimum balance requirement once the account is open, nor does your interest rate fall if your balance drops below a certain amount.

Money funds are *not* federally insured. However, funds can be trusted to go to great lengths (including covering any losses to protect investors) to keep public confidence in such funds high.

To invest, call a fund's toll-free number and ask for a prospectus and application form. You can also set up a money fund with a stockbroker.

Credit unions.   A credit union account is a lot like a bank checking account—but better. Credit unions usually exceed the rates paid by your local bank or savings and loan (S&L). Fees and minimum balance requirements tend to be lower, too. You do not belong to a group with a credit union? Ask friends and business colleagues if they are members of a credit union you could join. Your alumni association or church are other possibilities. Or write or call the National Credit Union Association (P.O. Box 431, Madison, WI 53701; 800-937-2644) for the address of your state credit union association, which can refer you to local credit unions you may be able to join. Be sure to pick one that is federally insured.

Finance companies.   Some finance companies, such as Beneficial Finance and Household Finance, are active in the savings market too. Beneficial, which markets CDs by mail and toll-free number (800-835-1015) from its insured Delaware banking subsidiary, recently was paying an 8.78% yield on a six-month CD and 9.05% on a one-year maturity CD.

☐ Resources

Top-yielding CDs are listed weekly in such newspapers as the *Wall Street Journal* and *Barron's*. Or you can subscribe to an interest-rate newsletter, such as *RateGram/RateFax* (single issues $10 and $25, respectively; 415-479-3815) or *100 Highest Yields* (eight weeks, $34; 800-327-7717), both of which include safety ratings.

AILMENT
I want to avoid being taken in by misleading bank advertisements.

Rx Many financial institutions use complicated and often misleading ads and gimmicks to puff up promised yields and downplay or even hide the true risks. To sidestep deceptive ads and invest in reliable CDs, watch out for these common ploys:

Teaser CDs. Some banks and savings and loans promote certificates of deposit that pay teaser rates—initial yields as high as 20% that expire within a few weeks. Your yield will usually be lower than with a fixed-rate CD. For example, a bank might offer a three-year CD with a 19.89% teaser rate that declines to 8.35% after three days. The combined rates return only $260.12 on a $1000 investment. Compare that with the $304.90 that you could earn on a three-year CD paying a fixed rate of 9.25%.

Other teaser CDs switch to variable rates after a short time, making their actual return impossible to predict. But the yield is likely to be lower than the initial rate's yield, and also lower than a fixed-rate CD with the same maturity. Instead of locking up money to earn a variable rate, buy six-month, fixed-rate CDs.

Tiered rates. Many institutions advertise high yields on CDs and savings accounts, but you have to deposit large sums to earn them. On so-called tiered-rate accounts, your money earns different rates depending on how much you have deposited with the bank. For example, a bank may offer to pay 6.8% on $2500 or more, but only 6.3% for deposits of $1000 to $2499.

Phantom yields. A number of institutions quote annual yields on three- and six-month CDs without mentioning that the yields are purely hypothetical. Reason: There is no guarantee you will be able to reinvest at an equally alluring rate when the CD matures.

Junk CDs. Beware of CDs promising yields two to four percentage points above the rest. They probably carry the highest risk. These are usually so-called junk CDs, offered by many consumer lending companies, banks, thrifts, and S&Ls. Junk CDs, also known as subordinated debentures or "sub debts," are nothing more than the bank's own IOUs and therefore are not federally insured. They are really long-term loans—and risky loans at that. In the event of bankruptcy, depositors, general creditors, and holders of "senior" debt get repaid first. Only then, if anything is left, are subordinate lenders repaid. You cannot sell your notes before they mature, because no secondary market exists. But the bank can call, or redeem, many of these subordinated notes the minute rates go down, cheating you out of the promised yield. Unless you have a "debt wish," junk CDs are a bad buy.

AILMENT

My checking account is too expensive.

R Comparing costs at dozens of banks and S&Ls is a tedious task that becomes even more laborious if you are thinking of moving your checking account from a bank to a credit union or a brokerage asset management account. Before you start dialing, write to the Consumer Federation of America (CFA) to see if this organization has surveyed checking account fees in your city. Contact the CFA at 1424 16th Street NW, Suite 604, Washington, DC 20036 (202-387-6121) and ask if there is a chapter near you. When you get the list, pick two or three of the best deals, then check the data to make sure it is not outdated. If there is no chapter in your area, pick up the phone and call half a dozen banking institutions with branches near your home or office and compare fees yourself.

There are two general rules when shopping for low-cost checking: S&Ls offer better deals than banks, and old-fashioned, non-interest-bearing accounts are cheaper than bank NOW (negotiable order of withdrawal) accounts, which pay interest and/or waive checking fees if you maintain a minimum balance of around $1000 to $2500 or more. Traditional bank accounts and S&L NOWs allow lower monthly balances to avoid checking fees than do bank NOW accounts—on average, it is $537 for S&Ls, $836 for non-interest-bearing accounts, and $1800 for bank NOWs.

You can avoid fees on most checking accounts by maintaining a minimum balance. Find out what it will cost to slip under the minimum. Monthly fees range from $1 to $10, while per-check charges range from 15 cents to 50 cents. At many banks with graduated fee scales, the lower your balance falls, the higher the fees you will pay. Be sure to ask how minimum balances are calculated. Some banks charge fees based on your lowest balance during the month. Look for a bank that bases its fees on your *average* daily balance.

Beware of double jeopardy. At some institutions, you are charged a flat monthly fee *plus* a fee for each check if you fall below the minimum balance.

Ask any bank you are considering for a list of all checking account fees. Don't overlook the cost of using ATMs. Most banks charge you 75 cents to $2 for making withdrawals from other bank ATMs. But about half also charge you 25 cents to $1 for using their own ATM. Then there is the price tag for bouncing a check—from $5 to $30 and averaging $13. Consumer activists cite a Federal Reserve Board report that the average cost to a bank for a returned check is just 36 cents. You do not have to be a deadbeat to have to worry about bouncing checks. All it takes is a check written against a deposit the bank has not yet credited to your account. You can also get zapped if you deposit a rubber check you received from someone else.

If you cannot or do not want to keep enough cash in your checking account to escape fees, consider no-frills accounts offered by some banks. You pay a flat monthly fee no matter what your balance. But there will be restrictions on the number of checks you can write each month or how often you can make deposits or withdrawals at a teller's window instead of an automatic teller machine. The bank will also keep your canceled checks instead of mailing them back to you.

If you are under age 19 or over age 55, you may be able to find a bank that will waive your checking account fees. About a third of all banks and S&Ls offer free NOW accounts to both senior citizens and minors.

AILMENT
My bank account was debited to pay an old parking ticket.

℞ Companies, municipalities, and the federal government have more rights than you may think to dip right into your bank account—without notifying you—when they think you owe them money. A local government (or a company) can garnish your checking account if it has obtained a judgment against you in court. Parking-violation judgments can be issued by a court automatically if you do not respond to a summons, so it is possible for a parking authority to obtain a judgment without your knowledge. (A marshal or sheriff carries out the court's order to withdraw the funds.)

If you want to dispute the debit, request a hearing with an administrative law judge. Call your municipal court to find out what paperwork is needed to get a hearing.

AILMENT
My bank account was debited to pay a credit card charge.

℞ You probably have just cause for complaint here. Unless you have committed fraud, a bank is *not* permitted to debit your checking account for credit card transactions that it cannot process. If your bank account is debited without your authorization (and no court judgment against you), you are entitled to a credit if you notify the bank promptly. Because banks process debits without checking for authorization, the bank will not know it is unauthorized until you bring it to some-one's attention.

AILMENT

I received an unsolicited ATM card from a financial institution.

R̸ If you want to keep the card, you must validate it before it can be used. Call the phone number supplied with the card. You will be asked to verify you are the person whose name is on the card before it is validated.

If you do not want the card, follow the instructions that came with the card explaining how to dispose of it.

AILMENT

I lost my ATM card (or credit card).

R̸ As usual, prompt reporting is the solution. Call the bank or credit card issuer as soon as you discover your loss. Make sure the lost card is canceled and a new card number is issued to you. Even if you call immediately, you will not get off scot-free if your card is used. But you can keep the cost of carelessness or bad luck to a minimum. For lost or stolen credit cards, your loss is limited to $50 per card. On an ATM or other card permitting electronic funds transfer (EFT), your liability for unauthorized use can vary:

- Your loss is limited to $50 *if* you notify the financial institution within two business days after learning of the loss or theft of your card.

- You could lose as much as $500 if you do *not* tell the card issuer within two business days after learning of the theft or loss.

- If you do not report an unauthorized transfer that appears on your statement within 60 days after the statement is mailed to you, you risk *unlimited* loss on transfers made after the 60-day period. That means you could lose all the money in your account plus your maximum overdraft line of credit.

Suppose, for example, your debit card and code were stolen on Wednesday. On Thursday, the thief withdrew $850, all the money in your account. Five days later, the thief withdrew another $500, triggering your overdraft line of credit. Even if you do not realize your card was stolen until you receive a statement from the bank, your liability will be held to $50 if you call the bank right away or to $500 if you call within 60 days. But what if you do not look at your statement or call the bank? If the thief withdraws another $1000, 70 days after the statement is mailed, you will be liable for the entire $1000 for transfers made after the 60-day period that began when the statement was mailed.

AILMENT

My electronic banking password (code) was stolen.

℞ Notify your bank in person or by telephone. If you act within 48 hours after your password is stolen, your liability for unauthorized charges is limited to $50. If more than 48 hours has passed, your liability is $500.

AILMENT

A lender wants me to pay back my loan using electronic funds transfer (EFT) from my bank account.

℞ The federal Electronic Funds Transfer Act forbids a creditor from requiring you to repay a loan or other credit by using EFT. The only exception is for overdraft checking plans. And, although your employer or a government agency can require you to receive your salary or a government benefit by electronic transfer, you have the right to choose the financial institution that will receive your funds.

So, if you do not want your loan repayment automatically withdrawn from your bank account electronically, simply throw away the authorization form. On the other hand, if you think the convenience of EFT outweighs the loss of control of your funds, complete and mail in the authorization.

AILMENT

I am worried about making preauthorized payments, because they will vary in amount from month to month.

℞ If money is tight, you do not want an unexpectedly large withdrawal to leave you strapped for funds or, worse, cause an overdraft. But there are several ways to avoid unwelcome surprises. You can ask to be notified of all varying payments at least 10 days in advance.

Or you may specify a range of dollar amounts and ask to be told only when a transfer falls outside that range. You may also choose to be told only when a transfer differs by a certain amount from the previous payment to the same company.

Note: You are not entitled to these protections if the automatic transfers are from your account to the bank that holds your account (or vice versa). For example, they do not apply to automatic payments made on a mortgage held by the institution where you have your EFT account. The EFT Act also does not apply to automatic transfers among accounts at the same financial institution.

AILMENT

I want to stop a preauthorized payment.

℞ You may stop any preauthorized payment by calling or writing the financial institution. Just make sure your order is received at least three business days before the payment date. You may be asked to follow up your telephone notice to stop payment with a written confirmation.

AILMENT

I use electronic bill paying and paid my mortgage company $10,000, instead of $1000, by mistake.

℞ Contact your electronic billing paying service immediately to stop payment. If payment has already been made, ask the service to request that your mortgage lender refund the excess.

AILMENT

I use electronic bill paying and need proof of payment to resolve a dispute with a merchant.

℞ Ask your bill paying service to investigate the dispute and to send you a written proof of payment.

R Today's checking accounts are much harder to untangle than those of two decades ago, because of new features such as debit cards, automatic teller machine withdrawals (which most of us fail to record), electronic deposits, and interest—however paltry—earned on our account balances.

Reconciling your bank statement with your checkbook need not be your life's work. Here is a speedy way to compare your checkbook with the bank's own tally:

1. Put a check mark beside canceled checks and deposits in your check register. If your bank returns your canceled checks, do not stop to put them in numerical order.

2. Begin reconciling from the balance you show for your last canceled check—do not add up checks that have not yet cleared the bank. For example, if check number 250 is the last one listed on your statement, do not skip down to your balance on the day you wrote check number 267.

3. Add deposits made, but not yet credited, and subtract outstanding checks written before the date of the last canceled check (in this case, check 250).

4. Add or subtract the *net* interest and service charges shown on the statement. For example, if the account earned $19 and you were charged $33 for checks, you would *subtract* $14 ($19 minus $33), but if you were charged only $10 for checks you would *add* $9 ($19 minus $10).

5. Compare the result with the ending balance shown on your statement.

Do not worry about discrepancies of $10 or less. Assume the bank is right, and enter the corrected total. If you are in a big hurry, just make sure your deposits, checks, and ATM withdrawals are correct on the bank statement.

☐ Prevention

Record all deposits and checks, including ATM transactions and electronic deposits. Keep running totals as you go. Create a buffer zone by never dipping below the minimum balance required to avoid service charges.

AILMENT

I have a complaint about my bank.

R First, try to resolve your problem directly with the bank by speaking with the manager or by going up the executive ladder to the president. Only if that fails should you initiate more formal complaint procedures.

Barring a resolution with the bank, here is how to file a complaint with the federal agencies responsible for carrying out consumer credit protection laws.

If your complaint involves any of the federal credit laws—or if you think any part of your business with a bank has been handled in an unfair or deceptive way—seek advice and help from the Federal Reserve Board. The practice you are complaining about does not have to be covered by federal law. Moreover, you do not have to be a customer of the bank to file a complaint.

Submit your complaint—in writing whenever possible—to the Division of Consumer and Community Affairs, Board of Governors of the Federal Reserve System, 20th and C Streets NW, Washington, DC 20551, or to the Federal Reserve bank nearest you (see addresses in Chapter 2). Describe the bank practice you are complaining about, and give the name and address of the bank involved.

The Federal Reserve will write back within 15 days—either with an answer or to tell you that more time is needed to handle your complaint. Additional time is required when the issues are complex or when the complaint will need to be investigated by a Federal Reserve bank. If that is the case, the Federal Reserve should keep you informed of its progress in resolving your complaint.

The Board supervises only state-chartered banks that are members of the Federal Reserve System. It will refer complaints about other institutions to the appropriate federal regulatory agency, and let you know where your complaint has been referred. Or you may use the addresses listed on the next page to write an agency directly.

The remedy of last resort is to go to court. If a financial institution has not followed the provisions of the Electronic Funds Transfer Act, you may sue for actual monetary damages. In certain cases when the institution fails to correct an error or recredit an account, you may sue for three times actual damages plus punitive damages of not less than $100 nor more than $1000. You are also entitled to court costs and attorney's fees if you win your lawsuit. Class action suits—where more than one plaintiff join together to sue—are permitted.

If an institution fails to make an electronic fund transfer, or to stop payment of a preauthorized transfer when you properly instructed it to do so, you may sue for all money damages that result from the failure.

National Banks

Compliance Management
Office of the Comptroller of the Currency
250 E Street SW
Mail Stop 3-9
Washington, DC 20219
202-874-5000
800-613-6743

State Member Banks of the Federal Reserve System

Division of Consumer and Community Affairs
Federal Reserve Board
20th Street and Constitution Avenue NW
Washington, DC 20551
202-452-3693

Nonmember Federally Insured State Banks

Compliance and Consumer Affairs
Federal Deposit Insurance Corporation
550 17th Street NW
Washington, DC 20429
800-934-FDIC
800-925-4618 (for the hearing impaired)
202-942-3100

Savings and Loan Associations

Division of Consumer and Civil Rights
Office of Community Investment
Office of Thrift Supervision
1700 G Street NW
Washington, DC 20552
800-842-6929
202-906-6237

Federal Credit Unions

Office of Public and Congressional Affairs
Office of Consumer Programs
National Credit Union Administration
1775 Duke Street
Alexandria, VA 22314-3428
800-755-1030
703-518-6330

Credit, Credit Cards, and Borrowing

The American Dream is still within reach—if you have enough borrowing power. The high cost of homes, cars, and a college education has many of us living on the installment plan. In fact, consumer debt in the United States now totals more than $3.2 trillion on car loans, mortgages, and credit cards. The average household owes about $35,000 and pays interest of about $3500 a year.

In fact, you probably could not pay entirely by cash even if you have it. If you have ever tried to make a hotel reservation or buy a plane ticket by phone, you know how essential credit cards have become. Hardly a day goes by without an unsolicited offer of unsecured credit arriving in the mail. At least one credit card is carried by 73% of Americans. The average person carries 5.2 cards, according to the Opinion Research Corporation. Even some children can use their parents' charge cards.

Credit is heady stuff. Dinner at La Grande Mignon, that power suit in the window, new brakes for the car—all made possible with a cavalier wave of a credit card. Charging is convenient, too, if you spy a must-have item when your wallet is sitting on empty. And, it's a lot safer than walking around with a wad of cash.

Of course, the American way of debt can easily lead to problems. Millions of consumers struggle to establish credit, get out from under too much debt, or unsnarl errors in credit reports and credit card bills.

In a turnabout of logic, how successful you are financially these days almost depends on how much debt you can rack up. You can face a very real crisis if you cannot establish credit. If you do not have a credit history or there is a black mark on your record, this chapter may be able to cure your ailment.

But having virtually unlimited access to credit can cause crises, too, unless you have developed smart credit management skills. Managing your borrowing power demands as much attention as handling your investments. In this chapter, therefore, we look at low-cost financing options, loan sources that save taxes, and such profitable moves as paying off old debts with cheaper new money. For example, if you use your next $1000 to pay down your credit-card balances, you will probably save about 18% a year before taxes—or three and a half times as much as you would earn by putting the same amount in a money market fund.

Some of our whopping consumer debt belongs to people who use credit wisely. But a sizable chunk is owed by men and women whose credit obligations have gotten wildly out of hand. For those who face mounting debts, this chapter will help you regain control of your credit by teaching you, for example, how to deal with credit reporting bureaus, how to dispute unfair items on your credit report, and how to reestablish credit.

Finally, we look at what to do when credit cards and credit inevitably trap you in the quagmire of computer errors and billing disputes.

■ BORROWING

AILMENT
I need to borrow money.

R̸ Good credit management calls for setting up borrowing reserves *before* you need money, so that you do not have to fall back on credit cards and other high-interest loans. But if you need or simply want a loan, there are four often used sources of money.

Home equity credit lines. Homeowners who expect to borrow repeatedly and can trust themselves to repay the money can make good use of home equity lines of credit.

The interest rate is variable and usually tied to the prime rate, currently 8.5% to 9.5%. But interest rates are not capped. If interest rates spurt up again—as they did back in 1980 when the prime rate went from 11% to 21.5% in three months—you may find yourself struggling to make the payments.

Generally, you can borrow up to 80% of the current appraised value of your house, less your mortgage balance. Expect to wait four to six weeks to qualify. You generally have between 7 and 20 years to repay what you borrow. Some lenders let you pay interest only, for up to 10 years.

However, borrowing this way, even at low rates, can be very costly. Up-front fees are high. Although most home-equity loans no longer charge points, most do require an application or origination fee ranging from $100 to $450. Up-front expenses also include a $200 to $350 appraisal fee, plus closing costs that can range from 1% to more than 5% of the amount you borrow, depending on your home state.

There are annual fees, too. And, you have to pay whether you draw down money or not. Many Western and Midwestern sources are charging $20 to $50 a year.

You can make up some of the costs in tax savings, though. The interest on the amount you borrow—up to the price of your house plus improvements—is fully deductible. Amounts above that are deductible only if the money is used for home improvements, medical expenses, or education costs. But you must add back that interest in figuring your alternative minimum tax liability.

Loans against securities. For fast money with little red tape or delay, you can use a brokerage house margin account for revolving credit. For example, Merrill Lynch has a nonrevolving margin loan called the Flexible Credit account. It lets you borrow against a high percentage of the value of such securities in your account as certificates of deposit, bonds, and mutual funds. You are limited to fixed-amount consumer and business loans, but you can tap the equity in your investments fast. Banks also accept securities as collateral for low-cost loans.

Interest rates on margin loans are variable and tied to the broker's call rate, currently 8% to 9.5%. Front-end costs are nominal or zero.

The amount you can borrow ranges from 50% (for stocks) to 92% (for Treasury bills) of the value of the security. The waiting time to qualify is usually no more than a week. After that, all it takes is a phone call to your broker to get a check. You can pay interest only.

On margin loans used to buy securities, interest is deductible up to the amount of your investment income. If the loan proceeds are not used for investment or business purposes, the interest is not deductible.

Unsecured credit lines. If your income or assets satisfy the bank, you can use these efficient loans to cover short-term needs or create a fast source of emergency cash at no initial cost. At some banks a $40,000 income or an equal amount of liquid assets qualifies you. So-called executive lines of $50,000 or more may be available to people making six-figure incomes.

Interest rates are variable and tied to the prime rate, currently 8.5% to 11.5%. Front-end costs are minimal or none. You can usually borrow $100,000 or more and the waiting time for good customers is only a few days. You may pay interest only. The interest on these loans is not deductible, unless you use the money to make taxable investments or for business expenses.

Life insurance loans. If you hold old policies with lots of cash value, you have substantial low-cost borrowing rights. There is no waiting time and no front-end costs. You can borrow all or most of the cash-surrender value of your policy for between 5% and 8% interest. As long as you pay the interest, you never need to repay the amount of the loan.

You will not get any tax savings from your interest expense, though, unless the funds are used to make taxable investments or for business expenses.

☐ Prevention

To avoid having to borrow, start now to build up your financial reserves. You will need enough rainy day funds to weather a recession, unemployment, or other financial setback.

Financial advisers say you should have accessible savings equal to three months of your gross income. That includes any assets that are readily converted into cash, such as money in savings accounts and mutual funds or widely traded stocks and bonds. If you do not have this three-month cushion, get serious about saving. Set a goal of saving at least 10% of your income. If you can, aim to save 15% to 20%.

There are several ways to save automatically. Enroll in a payroll savings plan at work that will put your money in U.S. savings bonds or in a credit union savings account. Get your bank to transfer money automatically from your checking account into your savings account. You can also invest in a mutual fund that will automatically draw a certain amount each month from your checking account. If you normally get a big income tax refund each year, reduce your withholding allowances to increase the take-home pay you have available for investment. Cut your spending by making a budget and sticking to it.

Make sure your emergency funds are in safe investments that can be quickly turned into cash. Such investments include federally insured short-term certificates of deposit, Treasury bills that mature in one year or less, and most money market mutual funds.

Be wary of tying up too much of your wealth in assets that are not easily convertible into cash. In a recession, it may be hard to sell certain hard assets, such as investment real estate or limited partnership shares. If you can sell without incurring a huge tax bill, consider disposing of some of your hard assets now to raise cash.

As a rule of thumb, your debt payments should not be more than 35% of your gross income if you have a mortgage, and not more than 10% if you do not.

If you currently exceed these levels, *do not* add to your debt. Start paying down your debt, only after you have saved three months' worth of income for your emergency fund.

Finally, diversify your retirement savings. If you were to go bankrupt or suffer serious losses, you would not want all of the money in your 401(k) company savings plan tied up in your employer's stock or bonds.

AILMENT

My wife and I are currently paying about $680 a month on outstanding student and auto loans. We don't know if we should pay off these debts or save for a down payment on a home.

℞ If you have enough income to qualify for a mortgage without paying off your debts, concentrate on saving for a house. Most lenders require that your debt obligations total no more than 36% of your monthly gross income. Total obligations include monthly payments for principal and interest on a mortgage, homeowner's insurance, property taxes, mortgage insurance, installment loans, revolving credit lasting more than 10 months, and payments on all other ongoing debt. If your current loan payments prevent you from qualifying for a mortgage, even with a down payment, then focus on paying off the loans.

AILMENT

I am having trouble getting credit.

℞ The first time you try to get credit, you may run up against an age-old frustration: It seems you need credit to get credit. Some creditors will look only at your salary and other financial information. But most also want a track record of wisely handling credit in the past. They rely on records kept by credit bureaus or credit reporting agencies, which collect and store information about borrowers. These records include the amount of credit you have received and how dutifully you have repaid it. If you do not exist in a credit bureau's files, you are an unknown quantity, and a creditor may automatically reject your application.

But there are easy ways to begin building up a favorable credit history. For example:

- Open a checking or savings account, or both. This does not create a credit file but it is proof that you have money and know how to manage it. Canceled checks can be used to show you pay rent or utility bills regularly, a sign of reliability.

- Apply for a department store credit card. About all you have to do to get one of these is walk up to a cash register. Then begin charging your store purchases, even if you carry cash. By repaying these credit card bills on time, you begin to establish a credit history.

- Ask your bank if you may deposit funds as collateral for a secured credit card. Some banks will issue a credit card with a credit limit usually no greater than the amount on deposit.

If your local bank will not issue a secured credit card, check with the following secured credit card companies:

Sterling Bank and Trust (800-892-BANK or 800-234-BANK).

First Consumer National Bank (800-876-3262).

Signet Bank (800-333-7116).

- If you just moved somewhere, write for a summary of any credit record kept by a credit bureau where you last lived. (Ask the bank or department store in your old hometown for the name of the agency it reports to.)

- Ask someone with good credit to co-sign your loan application.

- Find out why you were turned down. There may be a misunderstanding you can clear up.

Credit histories for women.   Under the federal Equal Credit Opportunity Act, reports to credit bureaus must be made in the names of both husband and wife, if both of them use the account or are responsible for repaying the debt. Divorced or widowed women might not have separate credit histories, because in the past, credit accounts were listed in the husband's name only. Still, under the Equal Credit Opportunity Act, creditors must consider the credit history of accounts that a woman held jointly with her husband. Creditors must also look at the record of any account held only in the husband's name, if a woman can show it also reflects her own creditworthiness. If an ex-husband was a bad credit risk, a woman can show that the record does not reflect her own reputation.

AILMENT

I took out a home equity loan and contracted for home repairs, but now I want to cancel the contract.

R̸ If you sign on impulse, you have precisely three business days to change your mind. There is another important limitation, too. The federal Truth in Lending Act gives you the right to vacillate on one kind of transaction only: when you use your home as security for a credit transaction. For example, you would have three business days to cancel a contract to remodel your kitchen or install a water softening system, if a lien can be put on your home for failure to pay off the installment contract.

The creditor must notify you in writing of your right to cancel at the time you sign the contract. And, if you decide to cancel, you must give the creditor written notice within the three-day period. The creditor must then return whatever up-front money you have paid and cancel the security interest in your home. No contractor may start work on your home, and no lender may pay you or the contractor until the three days are up. If you need a home equity loan immediately because of a financial crisis, you may relinquish your right to cancel by explaining your situation in writing.

The right to cancel (or right of rescission) is designed to protect you against decisions made in haste or under pressure that might put your home at risk. The law does *not* apply to a mortgage to finance the purchase of your home. If your home is used to secure an open-end credit line, a home-equity line, for example, you may cancel when you open the account or when your security interest or credit limit is increased. (In the case of an increase, only the increase would be canceled.)

Legal action.   If a creditor fails to disclose information about or does not comply with the rules concerning the right to cancel certain home-secured loans, you may sue for actual damages—any money loss you suffer. In addition, you can sue for twice the finance charge in the case of certain disclosures, or, if a lease is concerned, 25% of total monthly payments. In either case, the least a court may award you is $100, and the most is $1000. In any lawsuit that you win, you are entitled to reimbursement for court costs and attorney's fees.

Class action suits are also permitted.

Ailment

I defaulted on $5000 in student loans in 1992. Since then my income has been too low to pay off the loan. My credit rating is suffering, and I want to clear up this matter.

R℞ The U.S. Department of Education will be happy to welcome you back into the fold, but only on the government's terms. With nearly five million student loans worth a whopping $13 billion in default, Uncle Sam is understandably upset at the seeming abuse of its student loan program.

You will not be granted amnesty. You will have to repay your loan—plus interest. By now, your loan balance has probably ballooned to $9000, including interest. With penalties, you could be hit with a bill of as much as $12,000. The government could conceivably forgive the penalties and extra collection charges, but do not count on it.

To begin repaying your loan, first contact your lender or school to find out what process to follow. If you are uncertain who your lender is or if your school has no record of your loan, help is available from the Federal Student Financial Aid Information Center at 800-433-3243.

Depending on your circumstances, including your income, amount owed, and previous repayment efforts, you may be able to negotiate an extended loan repayment schedule, rather than face a huge lump-sum payoff. Further, by making 12 consecutive monthly payments at the agreed-upon rate, you will be considered "eligible for rehabilitation." Once you earn this status, the government will notify the credit-rating bureaus that you are trying to erase your loan default.

However, paying off your loan will not immediately clear your credit. That will take at least seven years from the time the default was entered on your report. Although under federal credit-reporting laws the default notice must be wiped off your credit report seven years after its entry even if you do not repay the loan, the Department of Education has probably gotten a court-ordered default judgment against you. Depending on your home state, the default judgments and renewals could stay on your credit rating for up to 20 years.

The Education Department has also started attaching the tax refunds of student loan defaulters.

☐ Prevention

Obviously, the best way to keep your credit in good standing is to repay your debts on time. But if complications arise, you should also learn how to correct mistakes and misunderstandings that can tangle up your credit report.

AILMENT

I think I have been denied credit as the result of discrimination.

℞ If you are indeed the victim of discrimination, you will have to put up a fight. But first, you need to make sure that you are not being denied credit for another, perfectly legal, reason. Let us take a look at what creditors can look for in granting credit.

Under the Equal Credit Opportunity Act, your application for credit must be considered on the basis of your actual qualifications for credit and not because of certain personal characteristics.

What creditors look for. Creditors want to make sure you are not only able to repay a debt, but also willing to do so. In some cases, they also want security to protect their loans. They speak of the three Cs of credit: capacity, character, and collateral.

To determine your ability to repay a debt, creditors can ask for employment information, your occupation, how long you have worked, and how much you earn. They also have a right to know your expenses, if you have dependents, whether you owe alimony or child support, and the amount of your other debts.

To check your character, creditors can look at your credit history, how much you owe, how often you borrow, whether you pay bills on time, and whether you live within your means. They also look for signs of stability, such as how long you have lived at your present address, whether you own or rent, and how long you have held your present job.

Collateral protects the creditor if you neglect to repay. Creditors may ask what you own that could be used to secure your loan, and what sources of income you have other than wages, such as savings, investments, or property.

No two creditors use exactly the same combination of facts to reach their decisions. Some set unusually high standards; others simply do not make certain kinds of loans. Some rely on their own instinct and experience. Others use a "credit-scoring" or statistical system to predict whether you are a good credit risk. While one creditor may find you an acceptable risk, another may deny you a loan, based on the same facts.

Information the creditor cannot use. The Equal Credit Opportunity Act does not guarantee that you will get credit. You must still pass the creditor's tests of creditworthiness. But these tests must be applied impartially and without discriminating against you on any of the following grounds: age, gender, marital status, race, color, religion, national origin, because you receive public income (such as veterans benefits, welfare, or social security), or because you have exercised your rights under federal credit laws (such as disputing an erroneous bill you received from another creditor). A creditor may not use any of those grounds as a reason to discourage you from applying for a loan, refuse you a loan if you qualify, or lend money to you on less favorable terms than it does to others with similar finances, credit history, and collateral.

Special rules

Age. The law is very specific about how a person's age may be used in credit decisions. A creditor may ask your age, but if you are old enough to sign a binding contract (usually 18 or 21, depending on your state law), a creditor may not:

- Turn you down or offer you less credit solely because of your age.
- Refuse to take retirement income into account.
- Close your credit account or make you reapply for it because you reach a certain age or retire.
- Deny you credit or close your account because you are too old to get credit life insurance or other credit-related insurance.

Creditors may "score" your age in a credit-scoring system, but if you are 62 or older, you must be given at least as many points for age as any person under 62.

Because your financial situation can change as you age, the law lets a creditor consider certain information related to age, such as whether you will retire soon or how long you will still be earning a salary.

Public assistance. You may not be denied credit just because you receive Social Security or public assistance (such as Aid to Families with Dependent Children). But some information related to this source of income could affect creditworthiness. So, a creditor may consider such things as:

■ How old your dependents are (because you may lose benefits when they reach a certain age).

■ Whether you will continue to meet the residency requirements for receiving benefits.

Housing loans. The Equal Credit Opportunity Act covers your application for a mortgage or home improvement loan. It bans discrimination because of race, color, gender, or because of the race or national origin of the people in the neighborhood where you live or want to buy your home. Nor may creditors use any property appraisal that considers the ethnic makeup of the neighborhood.

You are entitled to receive a copy of an appraisal report that you paid for in connection with an application for credit, if you make a written request for the report.

Discrimination against women. Both men and women are protected from discrimination based on gender or marital status. But many of the law's provisions were designed to stop particular abuses that generally made it difficult for women to get credit. Here are some of the protections:

■ Creditors usually may not ask your gender on an application form (one exception is on a loan to buy or build a home).

■ You do not have to use Miss, Ms., or Mrs. with your name on a credit application. But in some cases, a creditor may ask whether you are married, unmarried, or separated (unmarried includes single, divorced, or widowed).

■ Creditors may not ask about your birth control practices or whether you plan to have children, and they may not assume anything about those plans.

■ Creditors must count all of your income that you list, including alimony income and wages from part-time employment. But be prepared to show that this income can be counted on to continue.

■ Creditors may not consider whether you have a telephone listing in your name (many married women do not). But you may be asked if there is a telephone in your home.

Your own accounts.   You have a right to your own credit, based on your own credit records and earnings. If you are a woman, your own credit means a separate account or loan in your own name—not a joint account with your husband or a duplicate card on his account. You can choose to use your first name and maiden name (Mary Smith), your first name and husband's last name (Mary Jones); or a combined last name (Mary Smith-Jones).

If you are creditworthy, a creditor may not ask your husband to co-sign your account, with certain exceptions when property rights are involved. And creditors may not ask for information about your husband or ex-husband when you apply for your own credit based on your own income, unless that income is alimony, child support, or separate maintenance payments from your spouse or former spouse. However, this last rule does not apply if your husband is going to use your account or be responsible for paying your debts on the account, or if you live in a community property state.

Change in marital status.   Creditors may not make you reapply for credit just because you marry or become widowed or divorced. Nor may they close your account or change the terms of your account for these reasons. The exception would be if your creditworthiness has changed. For example, if you relied on your ex-husband's income to get credit in the first place, creditors may ask you to reapply.

If credit is denied.
Under the Equal Credit Opportunity Act, you must be notified within 30 days after you complete your application whether your loan has been approved. If you are turned down, you must receive this notice in writing, and it must cite the specific reasons for denial or tell you that you have a right to ask for an explanation. The same rights apply if one of your accounts is closed.

If you are denied credit, be sure to find out why. Perhaps the creditor thinks you have requested more money than you can repay on your income. Or maybe you have not been employed or lived long enough in the community. Discuss other loan or credit options with the creditor and ways you can improve your creditworthiness.

If discrimination occurs.
If it seems clear that you have been discriminated against, cite the law discussed above to the lender. If the lender still refuses you credit without a satisfactory explanation, contact a federal enforcement agency for assistance or bring a legal action. For violating the Equal Credit Opportunity Act, a lender may be sued for actual damages plus punitive damages—that is, damages for not obeying the law—of up to $10,000. If you win, the court will award you court costs and a reasonable amount for attorney's fees. Class action suits are also permitted.

■ CREDIT CARDS

AILMENT
I cannot decide which credit card is best for me.

℞ The first question you need to answer is, "How do I plan to use the card?" For example, if you will use your credit card to make lots of different purchases (food, clothing, cosmetics, etc.), stick with Visa or MasterCard, which are accepted pretty much everywhere. Examine the following features of each card you are considering to decide if it offers the mix that best suits your circumstances.

■ *Interest rate*. If you intend to regularly pay off the entire bill on time, the interest rate will not matter much. The most important factor is the annual fee. Shop around, and do not forget your own bank. A growing number of issuers offer no-fee credit cards for customers who maintain a minimum balance.

If you expect to run a tab on your card from month to month, then the interest rate becomes important. In general, the interest rate is not a significant factor in making a decision, unless your average outstanding balance exceeds $750 a month. If you maintain a credit-card balance, you will nearly always save more by choosing a low-rate card, even one with an annual fee, over a high-rate card with no fee. For example, on a $1200 average balance, your annual interest cost on a card charging 19.8% comes to $237.60. (Chances are you will pay an $18 to $20 annual fee, too.) By comparison, the yearly interest for the same balance on a card charging 13.9% would be just $166.80. Even when you add in an annual fee of $25, you still come out ahead with the lower rate. Some issuers charge a flat interest rate, others a variable one. The difference is not too important because banks can have few qualms about changing their "fixed" fees.

■ *Teaser rates*. Every new card offer tries to sell you on its low current rate. But this is usually a "teaser," aimed at bringing you into the fold. The low rate will be replaced with a much higher one in 3 to 12 months.

■ *Annual fee*. Many issuers charge no fee and make up the difference with higher interest rates on unpaid balances. Of course, you cannot go wrong with no-fee cards if you do not run a monthly balance.

■ *Other fees*. Pay attention to other fees as well, such as fees for exceeding your credit limit, fees for cash withdrawals, and even transaction fees. For example, the effective rate on small cash advances, including transaction fees, can sometimes be more than 100%. In addition, the interest rate clock starts ticking the moment you draw the money out of the machine, whereas you have a grace period of up to 30 days when you charge a purchase and pay the balance off by the due date.

■ *Balance used to compute interest.* Read the fine print. The Truth in Lending Act requires lenders to use a standard measure to express interest rates: the annual percentage rate (APR). But it does not define the amount outstanding on which this interest is charged. Depending on the math used to figure the balance on which interest is levied, you could pay two or three times as much interest on one card as on another, even though both charge the same APR. Some issuers charge interest using the "previous balance" method. That means the entire *previous* balance, rather than the *current* balance, is subject to interest charges. Other banks may charge interest on the average purchase balance, if any balance at all remains in the account. Both these methods can greatly increase the actual interest you pay.

■ *Grace period.* This is the amount of time, if any, before you are charged interest on a card purchase. To be eligible for an interest-free grace period on current charges, cardholders typically must have no outstanding balance from the previous month. The longer the grace period, the better. The industry standard is a 25-day grace period. But about 15% of issuers grant *no* grace period on any of your purchases. That means you will *always* pay interest charges on your purchases. Interest begins the moment you hand your card to a cashier or else from the day the bank enters that purchase on your account. If, for example, you charge a $1000 purchase early in the billing cycle, it might be a full month before you receive and pay the bill. Even at 14%, 30 days of interest on $1000 amounts to $11.50.

Credit standards. What are your chances of getting a particular card? If your credit history has been shaky, there is no point vying for an exclusive card, such as American Express. Instead, stick with more liberal issuers, such as department stores.

Frills. Once you have selected the right card, look at the enhancements. Credit cards can enable you to make phone calls, be towed when you are stranded, rack up frequent-flier miles, earn rebates, be reimbursed for lost or stolen purchases, and let you support a charity or sports team. While such enhancements are intriguing, financial terms are more important. The typical rebate or frequent-flier card interest rate is 5 points higher than that of an ordinary low-rate card.

Instead of frills, look for the three basics: a low rate, a full 25- to 30-day grace period, and a decent $15 annual fee. The rest is window dressing.

Doing the math. To find out which combination of fees and interest rates is best for you, do the following calculation: Estimate your average *outstanding* balance (the part on which you paid interest) over the past year. Multiply this amount by the percentage difference between the two cards. (For instance, if your average annual balance is $500 and the rate difference is 5%, you would save $25 with the less expensive card.) Then add in the annual fee. For example, an average outstanding balance of

$100 a year at 20%, with a $15 annual fee would cost you $35 a year. The same balance at 14% with a $35 fee would cost $49.

Because neither the interest rate nor the annual fee is tax-deductible, there is no need to calculate an after-tax cost based upon your tax bracket.

Where to shop. For the lowest rates or no-fee cards, you may have to go out of state. Each state has its own credit card rate regulations. Some set ceilings on interest rates, and some do not. Delaware has no rate ceilings. Michigan's ceiling is 30% a year, while Texas pegs its rates to the Treasury bill rate. While most merchants hesitate to take out-of-state checks, they do not really care if a credit card is issued by an out-of-state bank. A Visa card is a Visa card, whether it was issued by a large bank, a small bank, or even a brokerage firm.

Don't overlook your own bank. See if your banker offers any deals on credit cards, such as a break on fees and interest rates depending on how many banking services you use. Many credit unions, which are nonprofit cooperatives, also offer members no-fee, low-rate cards, as do some alumni, fraternal, and professional groups like the American Association of Retired Persons (AARP) and the National Education Association (NEA).

☐ Prevention

Here are several ways to beat the high cost of credit:

Number of cards. If you are paying annual fees for both MasterCard and Visa, cut your annual card fees in half by dropping one of the cards. Most shops and restaurants that accept one card will also take the other. And if you carry a travel and entertainment card, such as American Express, Carte Blanche, or Diners' Club, there is really no reason to hold both MasterCard and Visa.

Timing. Time purchases and payments carefully. Under nearly all credit-card agreements, an interest-free grace period applies only if you pay your balance in full; if you do not, interest will be assessed on new purchases almost immediately.

If you pay in full each month, you can get the most from the grace period by making big credit purchases just after your statement closing date and paying your bill right around the due date. By so doing, you will get interest-free use of the credit-card "loan" for some 50 days, a float that on, say, $3000 left in a money market fund yielding 6.5% would earn an additional $27.

If you maintain a credit balance, adopt the opposite tactic: Buy big-ticket items toward the end of the billing cycle. Then pay as much as you can each month the minute you get your bill. This slows the interest-rate meter and lowers your cost.

A note about using "convenience checks" to pay off balances on other cards or to make a purchase: These checks are charged to your credit card, and interest starts accruing immediately.

Pitches to avoid.   Avoid the "no annual fee" pitches. It sounds great, un-til you learn that the annual fee is waived for only the first 12 months. An-other variation: The card does not have an annual fee. What it does have is a $1.75 *monthly* fee for each month you use the card, meaning you will pay $21 a year if you use it regularly. You could hold your annual fee to zero if you never charge anything. Then there is the "skip payment" option where you do not have to make a payment every other month. But that does not stop finance charges from accruing during the months when you do not pay. The same is often true of deferred-payment offers where you do not have to pay for several months.

☐ Resources

For a list of either the lowest rate or no-fee cards nationwide ($4 each), and a list of the best secured cards and how to qualify for them ($4), write to Bankcard Holders of America, a nonprofit credit education and consumer awareness group at 524 Branch Drive, Salem, VA 24153 (540-389-5445).

CardTrack, RAM Research's newsletter on the best card deals, is avail-able for $5 by writing to P.O. Box 1700, College Estates, Frederick, MD 21702. The information is also available free on the company's Web site, http://www.cardtrak.com.

Finally, you can use the Credit Card Locator Kit from the Consumer Credit Card Rating Service (P.O. Box 5219, Ocean Park Station, Santa Mon-ica, CA 90405). The kit, which costs $14.95, offers advice on selecting a card and has details on more than a thousand cards nationwide.

AILMENT

I do not know how many credit cards to carry.

R︎ You can easily get by with just two cards: one no-annual-fee card that has a grace period for purchases you plan to pay off in full each month and another low-interest-rate card for purchases you want to finance. Ideally, this second card would also have no annual fee. If you run your own business, keep a third low-rate card for business use only. As a self-employed person, you are allowed a tax deduction for the interest you pay on financed business expenses. A business-use-only card will simplify your tax record keeping and substantiate deductible expenses if you are ever audited. For salaried employees, an American Express corpo-rate card—if your employer provides one—fills the third-card niche. Other-wise, stick with two cards.

Even if your extra cards are fee-free and you rarely charge a cent, lenders may count the total credit available to you as if you were poised for a spending binge. This could disqualify you from other borrowing, such as a car loan or even a mortgage. So notify your card issuers in writing that you want your unused cards canceled. Follow up with a note to the credit bureaus regarding your action; your credit-card issuer can tell you which bureaus to inform.

AILMENT

How can I use my credit card to save money?

R You can save money in the long run by using a new lower-interest credit card to pay off higher-interest credit-card debts. Here are three ways to pull this off:

- *Convenience check.* A check, with the account number of your new credit card on it, can be sent directly to the issuer of the old card to pay off the balance. The amount is then debited from your new lower-interest account as a cash advance.

- *Cash advance.* A cash advance on your new card can be used to pay off the balance on your old card. Be aware, though, that some card issuers charge a higher interest rate for cash advances and/or a cash advance transaction fee.

- *Balance transfer form.* The bank issuing your new card may let you fill out a form, giving account information about the credit card(s) you wish to pay off. After you submit this form, it usually takes about three weeks for the bank to complete the balance transfer(s). These transfers are typically treated as cash advances when you are billed by the new card.

AILMENT

I need a higher credit limit.

R Many card issuers will raise your credit limit automatically, particularly as your expiration date nears. If yours does not, call the issuer. The company will review your request and approve or deny it based on your current income, credit history, payment record, and other factors.

If you are turned down, you should receive a letter explaining why. Your next move would then be to apply for a credit card from another company and take advantage of this new credit line.

Consider whether you really need the added credit, however. Too much available credit can make you unattractive to future creditors.

AILMENT

I received an unsolicited credit card.

℞ It is illegal for card issuers to send you a credit card, unless you ask for or agree to receive one. However, a card issuer may send a new card to replace an expiring one, without your request.

If you do not want the card, simply cut it up and throw it away. You are under no obligation to mail it back to the issuer. If you are happy to add the new card to your collection, call the number shown on the back of the card to activate it.

AILMENT

My credit card issuer suddenly hiked my interest rate.

℞ It is something of a long shot, but you can call and threaten to cancel your card, if your lower rate is not extended for a few more months. If you have a good payment history, most credit issuers will keep extending that rate, rather than risk losing you. But you have to keep after them each time your extended rate is due to expire.

If that does not work, make good on your threat and cancel. In California and 19 other states, the law lets you cancel your card if a major change is made to the agreement and pay off the balance based on the old rules and rates. Because of a Supreme Court decision, this law does not apply to banks headquartered in certain states. As a result, many of the "bad apple" credit companies have their head offices in states where the rules are more lax.

If you can switch your balance to a lower-rate card, do so. To do this, write a convenience check against your new credit line or take out a cash advance, deposit the money, and then write a personal check to pay the old balance. But make sure you will not have to pay a higher cash-advance rate to do so.

Another caveat: Before you change banks, be aware that low rates are not always fixed. Some banks that offer MasterCard and Visa at lower-than-average rates do not point out that the interest rates are variable. For example, a 15.8% rate available now may fluctuate monthly or quarterly in line with Treasury bills, federal funds rates, or some other index. If rates were to rise sharply, you could pay more interest with the new card.

When you ask a bank about annual interest charges on credit cards, be sure to find out if the rate is fixed or variable. If it is variable, what index is used? How frequently is the rate adjusted? What is the maximum rate that the bank can impose?

If you cannot switch to another card and cannot pay off the balance, one alternative is to tap your equity in your home. You may be able to refinance the debt with a home-equity loan.

Finally, look for ways to reduce your expenses and start paying down your balance.

AILMENT

My credit card issuer wants to eliminate my grace period, because I pay off my balance in full each month.

℞ If you use your card frequently, but pay up every month, argue that your card usage generates significant interchange fees—that is, charges merchants pay to the issuer when they accept your plastic, generally 2% of your total purchase amounts. While you may not be paying the high finance charges the issuer prefers, you are still a profitable customer if you charge more than $3500 a year.

AILMENT

My credit card was lost or stolen.

℞ If your wallet is stolen, your greatest cost may be inconvenience, because your liability on lost or stolen credit cards is limited under the Truth in Lending Act.

It is imperative that you notify your credit card company as soon as you discover your loss. Call the telephone number for reporting a lost or stolen credit card shown on your monthly statement or on the back of a spare credit card right away. In most cases, you have 30 days after discovering the loss or theft to call the issuer, but any delay can be costly. Follow up with a letter, giving your card number, when the card was discovered missing, and when you called to report it. If you phone in before anyone uses the card, you are not liable for any fraudulent charges.

If someone uses the card before you report it, you may be held liable for the first $50 of charges per card.

If your actual card is not used, but someone gets one of your carbons or store credit-card receipts, you are not liable for any unauthorized charges. Stop using your card as soon as you notice one or more charges you did not make. Notify the issuer so your account can be closed and a new one opened that is untainted.

If your credit or charge card issuer does not comply with the above provisions of the federal Fair Credit Billing Act, refuse to pay the disputed charges. Write the issuer's compliance officer, whose job is to ensure that the law is properly administered. In your argument, cite where required procedures were not followed. The mere presence of a compliance officer in the process often prompts a more thorough investigation and raises the odds in your favor.

You can also call in your local consumer-affairs office or put out an SOS to local consumer reporters. Target only the one or two people or agencies you think can help. Agencies do not investigate as vigorously if they know other groups are also working on your case.

You can also bring your complaint to the attention of the Division of Consumer and Community Affairs, Board of Governors of the Federal Reserve System, 20th and C Streets NW, Washington, DC 20551. The agency follows up on every complaint and can force card issuers to adhere to the law.

When all else fails, you can hire a lawyer to write a letter to the issuer outlining your legal position. If the issuer is a bank that has dipped into your savings account, you can sue. If the matter goes to court, you can recover any damages you incurred, plus double any interest fees you were assessed, as well as attorney and court costs.

☐ Prevention

Offer your credit card for identification, but refuse to let merchants write your card number down on checks. Destroy carbons. Never give your card number over the phone, unless you placed the call to a company you know is reputable. If the call was unsolicited, refuse to give your credit card number—there is no way to be sure the caller is representing the company claimed. Finally, keep your card in sight when you give it to sales clerks to prevent them from making extra imprints.

Keep a list of your credit card numbers and notify card issuers immediately if your card is lost or stolen.

AILMENT
I do not understand my credit card statement.

 Here are some pointers to help you decipher your statement and perhaps save on fees and interest.

Transaction date/posting date. The transaction date is the day on which you charge a purchase or draw a cash advance. A record of the transaction is sent to your bank, which enters it in your account on the posting date. If you do not pay your balance on time, you will be charged interest on the average daily balance starting from the posting date.

Under rate/over rate change point. Some banks charge different interest rates, known as tiered rates, depending on the size of your balance. The initial rate, 16.7% on average, typically applies to charges of up to $2000. Above that amount, you may be assessed a point or two less in interest than the initial rate.

Annual percentage rate. After a typical grace period of 25 days, most issuers charge interest on your average daily balance if you do not pay off your account by the payment date. Rates for standard credit cards, which currently average about 18.1% a year, can be changed at any time by a bank, but it must give you advance notice—generally 15 to 30 days. A few banks charge variable rates, usually pegged 6 to 10 points above their prime lending rates.

Days in billing cycle. This is the time between monthly payment due dates. A cycle with extra days can result in a higher finance charge if you carry a balance, because the charge is computed for each day—and you have more time to use your card.

Payment due date. At the end of a billing cycle, you must pay a minimum amount if you do not pay your account in full. Pay nothing and some banks impose a monthly late-payment fee of about $10. *Note:* Banks cannot collect a late-payment fee if you live in California, New York, or Oklahoma. To find out whether your bank charges late-payment fees, read your cardholder agreement.

Minimum payment due. Most banks ask you to pay at least $20 on outstanding balances between $20 and $720. If your overdue balance exceeds $720, a bank will typically require you to pay a fraction—ranging from 2.5% to 5%—of your average daily balance, as well as any amounts that you have charged in excess of your credit line.

Do not be fooled into thinking you must either make the minimum payment or pay the whole thing off. You can pay any amount in between—and get out of debt sooner than with minimum payments.

If your company offers to let you skip one month's payment (usually January's), they will still charge interest on the entire balance.

Debit adjustments. If you write to your bank asking that a mistake be corrected, the bank must delete the charge from your account while it is being double-checked. If the charge turns out to be an error, it will stay off. But if there was no mistake—for example, if you simply forgot about a charge—the bank will rebill your account and add interest.

Finance charge. If you do not pay your entire balance within the grace period, your bank will assess a finance charge, usually your average daily balance, including old and new purchases, multiplied by one-twelfth of the bank's annual interest rate.

☐ **Prevention**

If you pay your account promptly to avoid finance charges, it is important that you receive your bill on time and receive credit for paying it on time. Check your statement to make sure your creditor follows these rules:

- *Prompt billing.* Check the postmark date. If no finance or other charge is added to your type of account before a certain due date, creditors must mail their statements at least 14 days before payment is due.

- *Prompt crediting.* Look at the payment date entered on the statement. Creditors must credit payments on the day they arrive, as long as you follow the payment instructions (e.g., by sending your payment to the correct address).

- *Credit balances.* If you have a credit balance (for instance, because you paid more than the amount you owe, or you returned merchandise), the creditor must send you a refund within seven business days after you request it in writing, or automatically if you still have a credit balance after six months.

AILMENT

There is a mistake on my billing statement.

℞ While you may be tempted to simply tear up your bill and send it back, there is a more effective way to straighten out the error. The Fair Credit Billing Act requires creditors to fix errors promptly and without damaging your credit.

Types of billing errors. Under the Fair Credit Billing Act, a billing error is any charge:

- For something you did not buy.

- For a purchase made by someone who was not authorized to use your account.

- For an item that is not properly identified, that is not for the actual purchase price, or that was entered on a different purchase date.

- For something you did not accept on delivery or that was not delivered.

Billing errors also include:

- Math errors.

- Failure to show a payment or other credit to your account.

- Failure to mail the bill to your current address, if you gave the creditor an address change 20 or more days before the end of the billing period.

- An item you do not understand or find questionable.

Correcting an error. If your bill is wrong or you want an explanation about an item on it, take these steps:

1. Notify the creditor *in writing* within 60 days after the first erroneous bill was mailed (see the postmarked date on the billing envelope). Write to the address the creditor lists for billing inquiries and include the following: your name and account number, the fact that the bill contains an error and *why* it is wrong, and the date and suspected amount of the error or the item you want explained.

You cannot be charged interest during this time if, in fact, the creditor made an error.

2. Pay all parts of the bill that are correct. While you are waiting for an answer, you do not have to pay the disputed amount or any minimum payments or finance charges that apply to it.

The creditor must answer your letter within 30 days, unless the problem is resolved before then. Within two billing periods—but no longer than 90 days—your account must be corrected, or the creditor must tell you why the bill was correct.

If the creditor admits an error, the creditor must correct your account and send you an explanation if there is an amount you still owe.

If no error is found, the creditor must explain the reasons for so finding and promptly send a statement of what you owe. This may include finance charges that accumulated and any minimum payments you missed while you were questioning the bill. You then have your usual time to pay any balance, but not less than 10 days.

3. If you still are not satisfied, notify the creditor in writing within the time allowed to pay your bill.

Maintaining your credit rating. A creditor may not threaten your credit rating while you are involved in a billing dispute. That means that once you have written about a possible error, the creditor cannot give out damaging information to other creditors or credit bureaus. And, until your complaint is answered, the creditor also may not take any action to collect the disputed amount.

All that changes after the creditor has explained why it believes you owe the disputed amount. Then, if you do not pay in the time allowed, you may be reported as delinquent, and the creditor may take action to collect. Even so, you can still disagree in writing. Then the creditor must report that you have challenged your bill and give you the name and address of each person who received unfavorable information about your account. When the matter is settled, the creditor again must report the outcome to each person who received information. Remember that you may also include your own side of the story in the credit report.

Filing a consumer complaint. If your efforts to resolve your problem with a creditor fail, consider filing a formal complaint. Here are the addresses of two federal agencies responsible for carrying out consumer credit protection laws:

Department of Justice
Civil Division
Office of Consumer Litigation
National Place Building,
   Suite 950 North
1331 Pennsylvania Avenue, NW
Washington, DC 20530
202-514-6786

*Lenders other than banks and
   credit unions*
Division of Credit Practices
Bureau of Consumer Protection
Federal Trade Commission
Washington, DC 20580
202-326-3233

For complaints about banking institutions, see Chapter 3.

Legal action. As a last resort, you may take the creditor to court. If you decide to bring a lawsuit, there are penalties for a creditor if you win. Under the Fair Credit Billing Act, a creditor who breaks the rules for correcting billing errors automatically loses the amount owed on the disputed item and any finance charges on it, up to a combined total of $50—even if the bill was correct. You may also sue for actual damages, plus twice the amount of any finance charges, but not less than $100 nor more than $1000. You are also entitled to court costs and attorney's fees if you win your lawsuit. Class action suits are also permitted. A class action suit is one filed on behalf of a group of people with similar claims.

☐ Prevention

As a preventive measure, keep credit card statements and receipts from credit purchases for a year. Without them, it may be your word against a merchant's or the card issuer's. If you have phone conversations with merchants or the card issuer, write follow-up letters that repeat what you discussed. If you get involved in a dispute, keep copies of all related correspondence, receipts, and telephone records, so you can prove you followed proper procedures.

One area in which you must be especially careful is charging overseas. Your card issuer can be held to the law, but overseas merchants cannot. Co-operation varies from country to country. If a merchant is unresponsive, the credit card issuer may not go to bat for you.

☐ Resources

Solving Your Credit Card Billing Questions, a brochure from Bankcard Holders of America, can help you formulate a response. Send $1 to Bankcard Holders of America (560 Herndon Parkway, Suite 120, Herndon, VA 22070). Another resource is *How to File a Consumer Credit Complaint*, available from Publications Services, Division of Support Services, Board of Governors of the Federal Reserve System, Washington, DC 20551.

AILMENT

My new love seat arrived with only three legs. I tried to return it, but the merchant would not take it back. He also refused to repair or replace it.

R̸ The Fair Credit Billing Act permits you to withhold payment on any damaged or poor-quality goods or services you buy with a credit card, as long as you make a bona fide attempt to solve the problem with the merchant.

Your legal rights may be limited, however, if the card was a bank or travel and entertainment card or a card *not issued* by the store where you made your purchase. In such cases, the sale:

- Must have been for more than $50, and

- Must have taken place in your home state or within 100 miles of your home address.

Wait until you receive your credit card statement showing the charge for the love seat. Then call the telephone number listed for billing errors or questions on the back of your statement. Explain that you received defective goods from the merchant and ask for the charge to be removed from your bill.

You must back up your telephone request in writing within 60 days after you were first sent the bill charging you for the love seat. Include in your letter your name and account number and the dollar amount of the bill, plus an explanation of why you are refusing to pay the bill.

If you did purchase the love seat using a credit card, consult an attorney about your legal rights. You may have to take the merchant to court to get your money back. If the love seat cost less than $5000, you can sue in small-claims court without hiring an attorney.

☐ Prevention

Do not use convenience checks to make major purchases. Savvy consumers use their credit card, not a bank check or debit card, whenever there is a chance they will want leverage against a merchant if a product does not work as promised or a service is not delivered as agreed.

You would expect the same rights to apply when you use a convenience check issued by your credit card company, because your charges are posted to the same account. But the law does not require card issuers to reverse the charge for a product or service you did not receive or were displeased with when you use convenience checks.

Instead, use convenience checks to transfer the balance from a card with a high interest rate to a less-expensive one. The checks are also a clever way to circumvent the IRS's refusal to charge tax payments to credit cards. The IRS *will* take a check drawn against your credit line.

AILMENT
I want to cancel my credit card.

 No problem. Simply write a letter and request cancellation. Include in your letter:

- Your account number.

- A request that the issuer inform its credit bureaus that you have closed the account.

- A request that the issuer send you verification of the cancellation in writing.

Send the letter by certified mail. Be aware that some cardholder agreements contain an acceleration clause that requires you to pay any balance in full when an account is closed.

The only way to ensure than an account has been closed is to request a copy of your credit bureau report (see next section for information on getting a copy of this report).

■ PROBLEMS WITH CREDIT

AILMENT
I want a copy of my credit report.

R If you have a charge account, a mortgage on your home, a life insurance policy, or if you have applied for a personal loan or a job, there is almost certainly a file or report, showing how swiftly you pay your bills, whether you have been sued or arrested, or if you ever filed for bankruptcy. Such a file may even include opinions about your character, reputation, or lifestyle. The companies that gather and sell such information to creditors, insurers, employers, and other businesses are called "consumer reporting agencies," and the legal term for the report is a "consumer report."

It is a good idea to request a copy of your credit record at least every other year from one or all of the big credit-reporting companies—Equifax, Trans Union, and Experian Corporation (formerly TRW). To find out what information a local consumer reporting agency has collected about you, either arrange for a personal interview at the agency's office, or call in advance for an interview by telephone. Most agencies want you to request your report in writing, including your name, Social Security number, current and past addresses, and some other form of identification. Many credit-reporting companies charge a fee.

The consumer reporting agencies in your area can be found in the Yellow Pages of your phone book, under such headings as "Credit" or "Credit Rating or Reporting Agencies." Or call your bank and speak to a loan officer, asking for the names, addresses, and phone numbers of the major credit bureaus in your area.

To contact the national credit-reporting companies, call or write:

Equifax Information Service Center
Attention: Consumer Department
P.O. Box 105873
Atlanta, GA 30348
800-685-1111

Trans Union Corporation
P.O. Box 390
Springfield, PA 19064-0390
800-916-8800; 216-779-2378

Experian Corporation
Consumer Assistance
P.O. Box 2104
Allen, TX 75013-2104
800-682-7654

Making three separate requests can be a hassle. First American Credco Inc. (800-637-2422), a San Diego, CA, credit-reporting company, sells a report with your combined credit history. At $24, plus handling, the merged report costs roughly the same as separate reports ordered directly from each of the big three. Equifax and Experian Corporation charge $8 and Trans Union charges $8 for an individual report ($16 for husband and wife)—except in states where those charges exceed a mandated limit: Colorado ($5), Connecticut ($5), and Maine ($2). Include your (and your spouse's) full name(s), current address, former addresses for the past five years, Social Security number(s), and birth date(s).

If you are married, request separate credit reports for husband and wife. You want to find out:

1. The gist of all the information in your file.

2. The name of each business (or other source) that supplied information on you to the reporting agency.

3. The names of everyone who received reports about you in the past six months (or the last two years, if the reports were for employment purposes).

AILMENT

I need to dig myself out of debt.

R Becoming debt-free will take self-discipline and personal sacrifice. If you can kick the debt habit, though, you will immensely improve your financial health. You will need all the support and help you can get. So here is some advice, if you are overwhelmed with debt.

■ *Do not avoid creditors.* Instead of skipping a payment, explain to creditors why you cannot pay, and stress that, in spite of your difficulties, you want to pay your debts. Produce a budget as evidence of your sincerity. If you make this effort before things get completely out of hand, creditors may temporarily waive or reduce your payments.

■ *Work out your own payment plan.* Secured creditors may not be too flexible, because you have pledged your assets to them as collateral. But unsecured creditors may be receptive to a revised payment plan. Figure out how much you can afford to pay toward all debts each month, and prorate payments based on how much you owe each creditor. Assure creditors that they are all being treated equally and that you will not borrow any more until their accounts are paid in full.

Also, ask creditors to "re-age" your accounts, that is, report your account to credit bureaus as current, so long as you make the new, lower payments on time.

■ *Seek credit counseling.* If you are plagued by calls from bill collectors, get in touch with a Consumer Credit Counseling Service (CCCS). (Call 800-388-2227 for a referral in your area.) These nonprofit agencies will counsel you for free or for only a nominal charge. Their counselors will help you draw up a budget and negotiate with your creditors. Since they usually have close ties with local lenders, the counselors can often arrange more lenient repayment terms than you could on your own. If the lenders accept the repayment schedule, you pay a single monthly check to the service, which then divvies up the money among your creditors.

If there are no nonprofit counselors in your area, you may think about turning to a commercial credit counselor. At best, they do the same thing a nonprofit counselor does—for a fee of as much as 15% of your debt. At worst, they take your money and do nothing to relieve your problem. Ask for references, and check the counselor's reputation with the Better Business Bureau.

■ *Avoid consolidation loans.* You may hope to stretch out payments for a longer time with a consolidation loan. But the finance companies offering these loans typically charge exorbitant interest rates. Using a home equity loan to pay off debt is not much better. It is true that interest rates are relatively low and interest on up to $100,000 is tax-deductible, but your home is the collateral. You could lose it if you fall behind in your payments. Many people who start again with zero balances on their credit cards quickly find themselves in debt again.

■ *Consider filing for bankruptcy.* If you have tried everything up to this point and nothing has worked, there is one last resort: bankruptcy. Petitioning for bankruptcy protects you from creditors and legal claims. When it is over, you can start over debt-free. For a complete discussion of bankruptcy, see page 63.

☐ Prevention

It does no good to break free of debt only to have a relapse later. To keep from going on another spending bender, here is a dose of common sense:

Make a budget and stick to it.   Drastic belt-tightening may be needed. Figure out how much you can afford to spend. List your income from wages and investments, and then subtract your regular minimum monthly expenses, such as rent or mortgage payments, food, car payments, insurance, and utility bills. Leave an allowance for large, infrequent costs such as annual insurance premiums and car and home maintenance.

To find out where your money goes, carry a pocket diary and write down how you spend every penny for a month. The shock of seeing how much dribbles away on "essentials" like video rentals and garage sale bargains could do you good. What is left is discretionary income you can spend—or better yet, invest.

Control impulse spending. Walk away and impose a three-day waiting period on yourself before buying. If you really need an item, you can buy it later. Shop for bargains, but do not go broke "saving" money.

Also try to reduce so-called fixed expenses. For example, cut utility bills by turning down the heat and lower insurance premiums by raising the deductibles on car and homeowner's policies.

Set a self-imposed repayment schedule—and stick to it. Start with the debts that carry the highest finance charges.

Watch for the warning signs of debt. You should not borrow *at all* if *any* of the following apply to you:

- You make late payments and receive collection notices from creditors.
- You take one cash advance after the other on your credit cards.
- You use credit cards to pay off debts on other cards.
- You take money out of savings to pay basic monthly bills such as rent or utilities.
- You do not have an emergency fund totaling at least three months of after-tax earnings.
- You spend more than 20% of your monthly take-home pay on non-mortgage installment debts, such as car payments and credit card bills.
- You have more debts than you could pay off in two years.

If any of these danger signals sounds uncomfortably familiar, it is time to cut back on your debts—not pile more on them.

Shave credit card costs. If you carry a balance on your credit cards, use bank-issued cards such as Visa or MasterCard instead of cards issued by retailers. The average interest rate on bank cards is about 16.7%, compared to 20% or higher for many retailer cards. And by shopping around, you can find bank cards with lower-than-average rates.

If you pay off your accounts in full each month, use cards that do not charge annual fees.

Pay by cash. Cut up your credit cards or lock them in a safe-deposit box.

The accompanying work sheet (Figure 2–1) will give you a quick picture of your credit obligations. Be sure to list all your *consumer* debts, noting the maturity dates for nonrevolving charges.

When you write down the interest rate of each loan, check to see if it is more than the after-tax return on your invested savings. If it is, you have a negative interest spread, and you should pay off that loan out of savings.

After you have totaled your monthly debt obligation, figure out the

FIGURE 2–1	Your Credit Picture at a Glance			
Creditor	Date of Maturity	Interest Rate	Monthly Payment	Balance Owed
			Total	$_____

percentage of your take-home pay it represents. If the figure is higher than 20%, you are in danger of credit overload.

☐ Resources

MasterCard and the National Foundation for Consumer Credit have teamed up to offer *In the Red: Learning to Manage Your Debt*. To get a free copy, call 800-633-1185.

If you would like help organizing your financial life, the Institute of Certified Financial Planners can help. The Denver-based group has published a 20-page booklet called *Taking a Fiscal Inventory: How to Put Your Financial House in Order*. For a free copy, along with a CFP referral list, call the CFP referral line at 800-282-PLAN.

AILMENT

I was turned down for credit because my credit report has an error and is also outdated.

R A study by Consumers Union indicates that nearly half of all consumer credit reports have errors. About 20% of these errors are serious enough to damage your ability to borrow or get a job, according to Consumers Union officials. Credit bureau errors can result if your Social Security number is reported incorrectly or if your name is similar to someone with bad debts. Paid-off loans and closed lines of credit may show up as current accounts, making you look overextended to creditors. Or there may simply be mistakes in reporting the amount you owe.

Dealing with the creditor.   If you know which creditor is supplying the wrong information, you can ask the creditor to make the correction. This can be effective, because the creditor usually wants to keep you as a customer and, of course, to recover any money you owe.

By law, creditors must keep account information for at least 25 months. Storage is expensive, and many companies purge information as soon as legally possible. For this reason, you may succeed by challenging the creditor to *prove it or remove it*, especially when the error has been persistent. To challenge the creditor, write a letter relating the particular prob-

---

SAMPLE LETTER

Requesting Copy of Credit Report

March 1, 1997

Veracity Worthy
2312 Reliable Lane
Honor, CO 81699

Experian Corporation	or	Trans Union	or	Equifax (CBI)
P.O. Box 2104		P.O. Box 390		P.O. Box 105873
Allen, TX 75013-2104		Springfield, PA 19064-0390		Atlanta, GA 30374-0241

Re: Copy of Credit Report

Dear Sir:

Please mail me a copy of my credit report. A check for $8 is enclosed.

My name is Veracity Worthy. I currently reside at 2312 Reliable Lane, Honor, CO 81699. I have lived at this address for four years. Before that, my address was 948 Dependable Avenue, Apartment #3, Candor, CO 80655. I lived there for seven years. My Social Security number is 987-65-4321. My date of birth is November 19, 1963.

Thank you for your prompt attention to this matter.

Yours truly,

Veracity Worthy

SAMPLE LETTER

Requesting Removal of Negative Information

April 10, 1997

Veracity Worthy
2312 Reliable Lane
Honor, CO 81699

Experian Corporation
Consumer Relations Department
P.O. Box 2104
Allen, TX 75013-2104

Dear Sir:

After examining a copy of my credit report, I discovered that incorrect information is being reported.

My account with The Millennia Company, Account #84334, was paid in full per my installment agreement and should be shown as a positive rating. Please remove this negative information.

I have never made a payment to the Paloma Products, Account #12828, 90 days late. Please correct this, as well.

I do not have an account with PricePlus, account #77551.

The Tax Lien Docket #93-6904 was paid in full on May 12, 1995. I do not owe this.

My name is Veracity Worthy. I currently reside at 2312 Reliable Lane, Honor, CO 81699. I have lived at this address for four years. Before that, my address was 948 Dependable Avenue, Apartment #3, Candor, CO 80655. I lived there for seven years. My Social Security number is 987-65-4321. My date of birth is November 19, 1963.

Thank you for your attention to this matter.

Yours truly,

Veracity Worthy

lem on your credit report. Unless the dispute is merely over an alleged late payment, ask for the following information:

- A copy of the original application you signed.
- A summary of the account showing all transactions.
- Proof of the debt, including all charge slips and other documents.
- If the above information cannot be produced, demand that the creditor cease sending the disputed information to the credit bureau.

For sample letters, see pages 50 through 57.

Dealing with credit bureaus. You can always bypass the creditor and appeal directly to the credit bureau for correction. If Experian Corporation's or Equifax's central complaint lines or Trans Union's local office do

---

SAMPLE LATE PAYMENT LETTER #1

March 1, 1997

Veracity Worthy
2312 Reliable Lane
Honor, CO 81699

Pay-Later Appliances
Attention: Credit Department
334 Pushbutton Street
Honor, CO 81699

Re: Account #5552

Dear Sir:

I have just examined a copy of my credit report, and discovered that you are reporting late payments on my account. I have checked my bank records and dispute the information you are reporting.

I am a long-standing customer and would like to remain so. Please send a correction to the credit bureaus you report to, stating that I am now and always have been current with my payments.

Yours truly,

Veracity Worthy

SAMPLE LATE PAYMENT LETTER #2

March 1, 1997

Veracity Worthy
2312 Reliable Lane
Honor, CO 81699

Pay-Later Appliances
Attention: Credit Department
334 Pushbutton Street
Honor, CO 81699

Re: Account #5552

Dear Sir:

I recently received a copy of my credit report from Experian Corporation. It shows that my account with your company was recorded as 90 days late. According to my records, my account was under dispute at that time because of returned merchandise. I had informed your credit department of this situation, and they assured me the problem would be taken care of.

This incorrect information can do serious damage to my credit rating. Please verify this information and notify me of the results by returning this letter and checking one of the following:

_____ Consumer is correct

_____ Consumer is incorrect

_____ Information not available

Verified by: _____   Date verified: _____

Thank you for your prompt attention to this matter.

Yours truly,

Veracity Worthy

---

not help, set your sights on senior management: at Equifax, the vice president of consumer affairs; at Trans Union, a consumer relations manager; and at Experian Corporation, the director of consumer affairs.

Your basic rights. You already have some weapons at your disposal. Under the federal Fair Credit Reporting Act:

SAMPLE LATE PAYMENT LETTER #3

March 1, 1997

Veracity Worthy
2312 Reliable Lane
Honor, CO 81699

Pay-Later Appliances
Attention: Credit Department
334 Pushbutton Street
Honor, CO 81699

Re: Account #5552

Dear Sir:

I have recently obtained a credit report from Experian Corporation. It shows that my account with your company was recorded as 90 days late. According to my bank records, my payment was sent on time, but your company failed to record my check until three weeks later.

This incorrect information can do serious damage to my credit rating. Please verify and remove the inaccurate information from my credit report at once. If your company does not act promptly, I intend to have my attorney bring a lawsuit against your company for violation of the Fair Credit Reporting Act.

Thank you for your immediate attention to this matter.

Yours truly,

Veracity Worthy

- You can see your report for free if you have been denied credit in the past 30 days. Otherwise, you pay about $8 to $16.

- You can ask the credit bureau to reinvestigate and correct or delete information found to be inaccurate, incomplete, or obsolete.

- If the creditor sticks by the information and you still believe the information is wrong, you can add a brief statement to your file, telling your side of the story.

SAMPLE NEGATIVE REPORT LETTER #1

March 1, 1997

Veracity Worthy
2312 Reliable Lane
Honor, CO 81699

Pay-Later Appliances
Attention: Credit Department
334 Pushbutton Street
Honor, CO 81699

Re: Account #5552

Dear Sir:

On January 26, 1997, I wrote your company and requested the following:

A copy of my original application showing terms of agreement.

A summary of the activity on my account, including all payments made, late charges, and interest.

Copies of all documents signed by me and all other items proving the amount of my credit obligation.

As of the date of this letter, I have received no response from you. You are still reporting negative information about my account to the credit bureau. This is to demand that your company either provide the requested information, or that you immediately cease reporting this negative information. [OPTIONAL WORDING: If I do not hear from you within the next 10 days, I will instruct my attorney to take legal action on this matter.]

Yours truly,

Veracity Worthy

Exercising these rights is not always easy. The creditor who turned down your credit application must tell you which credit bureau was used, but you are on your own in finding out which other bureaus are sending out the same erroneous information. If the creditor reconfirms an error, it is up to you to persuade the creditor to fix the mistake and report the correction to the bureau.

SAMPLE NEGATIVE REPORT LETTER #2

March 1, 1997

Veracity Worthy
2312 Reliable Lane
Honor, CO 81699

Pay-Later Appliances
Attention: Credit Department
334 Pushbutton Street
Honor, CO 81699

Re: Account #5552

Dear Sir:

Thank you for your cooperation in this matter. I have received a copy of my application and a summary of the debt. However, you did not include proof of the debt by sending all documents signed by me and other information necessary to prove the amount you claim I owe your company.

Your error in reporting this information to credit bureaus has caused me financial hardship.

If you cannot supply original documents proving my debt, please cease reporting negative information to the credit bureaus.

Thank you for your attention to this matter.

Yours truly,

Veracity Worthy

Action to take. Perseverance should pay off, however. Here is a step-by-step how-to:

■ Write, do not call, the credit bureau. Spell out the inaccuracy, and ask the bureau to verify and correct it. Request a corrected report by mail. The credit bureau must correct the mistake within 30 days of receiving your letter. It must then report the inaccurate or incomplete information to all national credit bureaus. Keep copies of all written communications with the credit bureau, and maintain a log of the dates, times, and gist of phone conversations. This documentation may be valuable later, if the bureau neglects to make legitimate corrections or if

SAMPLE CEO LETTER

Always include copies of previous letters and certified return receipts.

March 1, 1997

Veracity Worthy
2312 Reliable Lane
Honor, CO 81699

Bill Monger, President
Pay-Later Appliances
334 Pushbutton Street
Honor, CO 81699

Re: Account #5552

Dear Mr. Monger:

I need your help in resolving an important matter. I have written to your credit department several times, trying to clear up an apparent misunderstanding. Your credit department is reporting to the credit bureaus that I am a poor credit risk.

I have asked for documentation proving that I owe your company. To date, I have had no response. As a good customer, I feel I deserve more courtesy. That is why I am writing to you for assistance.

Unless your company can substantiate my failure to make timely payments, I respectfully request that your company cease reporting negative information about my account to credit bureaus. It is causing me financial damage by preventing me from obtaining additional credit.

I appreciate your cooperation in this matter.

Yours truly,

Veracity Worthy

---

inaccurate information pops up again on your credit record, as it often does. (See sample letters.)

Some sample wording:

"I do not recall having this account. It is not mine."

"I do not believe I was ever thirty (sixty, ninety, etc.) days late on this account."

"I paid this account in full as agreed."

"This is not my bankruptcy [insert date and amount]."

"I do not owe this judgment for $X amount."

"I do not owe this tax lien for $X amount."

"This account was the responsibility of a separated (or divorced) spouse."

"This lawsuit has been settled and I cannot be held liable for any additional damages (see legal documents attached)."

■ Call the creditor in question and find out what other bureaus it reports to. Then get your report from those bureaus, too. If you were denied credit, only the bureau listed on the denial letter must disclose the contents of your report without charge. Some bureaus will make you come in person to see your report.

■ The credit bureau will conduct an investigation, review all relevant documents, and ask the creditor whether the information you are challenging is true. The burden of proof is on the creditor. Unless the creditor can prove the information is true, the bureau must change your record, and notify the other national credit bureaus of the error or incomplete information. If the creditor satisfies the bureau that the data should not be removed from your file, you must next make your case in writing to the creditor, including copies of supporting documents. Ask that a correction be sent to all the credit bureaus the creditor reports to. Ask for a copy of the letter sent to the bureaus.

■ If you succeed with the creditor, write one more letter, asking the bureau, at no cost to you, to notify anyone who has received reports in the past six months (two years, if for employment purposes) that certain information was deleted. Include a copy of the creditor's letter. The bureaus will not send out the updated reports unless you ask.

■ Follow up to make sure that the corrected information was, in fact, sent out.

■ If the creditor will not concede an error, you have one final action left: You may add up to a 100-word statement to your credit file, essentially saying that you dispute the accuracy of the negative item and why. Do not be surprised if that does not end your credit woes. The credit-scoring systems used by lenders often ignore consumer statements.

Also, note that some credit bureaus will not permit statements explaining the reasons why you did not pay a bill you actually owe (e.g., because a mechanic botched a repair). Try to record the dispute anyway, emphasizing that you think the creditor is in error.

■ Request the bureau (if you are willing to pay a reasonable fee) to send your statement of the dispute to those who received reports containing the disputed information within the past six months (two years if received for employment purposes).

■ If you fail to get your credit record changed, warn lenders of the derogatory items in your file when you apply for credit and provide proof that all debts have been paid.

■ If a mistake you have corrected reappears on your credit report, go to the source. Demand that the creditor correct its records and what is sent to credit bureaus.

How long is information kept in your file? Files on open revolving accounts are kept indefinitely. But there is a limit to how long certain kinds of information may be kept in your file:

■ Bankruptcies must be taken off your credit history after 10 years.

■ Suits and judgments, tax liens, arrest records, and most other kinds of unfavorable information must be dropped after seven years.

Do not sweat the small stuff. Some mistakes are too trivial to bother about. For example, credit bureaus readily admit that income, employment, and other biographical information is often out of date. It is updated only when you apply for credit, and the creditor forwards the information as it requests your credit report. You can generally let those mistakes slide, since lenders usually rely on other sources to verify income, employment, and other personal data.

What if information about some of your accounts is missing? This could be important if your credit history is relatively sparse. In that case, it can make sense to bolster your creditworthiness by asking the credit bureau to add an active account you can verify.

Seeking outside help. You may be able to get assistance in resolving your credit bureau complaint from the following groups: local Public Interest Research Group offices (contact U.S. PIRG, 215 Pennsylvania Avenue SE, Washington, DC 20003), Bankcard Holders of America (560 Herndon Parkway, Suite 120, Herndon, VA 22070), and some state attorneys general. The Federal Trade Commission (Division of Credit Practices, FTC, Washington, DC 20580) collects complaints but does not resolve individual cases.

Where not to get help. Even if the error-correction process seems daunting, do not resort to a credit repair firm that advertises it will "fix" your credit report or erase a negative credit history. Some of these firms charge hundreds of dollars to take you through the aforementioned steps. Others try to remove accurate negative information by challenging every negative entry in a file on the off chance the bureau will not be able to verify everything. Credit bureaus know this and refuse to investigate when they suspect that a consumer has been advised by a credit repair firm.

Legal action. Under the Fair Credit Reporting Act, you may sue any credit reporting agency or creditor for breaking the rules about who may see your credit records or for not correcting errors in your file. You are entitled to actual damages, plus punitive damages if you can prove the violation was intentional. In any successful lawsuit, you will also be awarded court costs and attorney's fees.

A person who obtains a credit report without proper authorization or an employee of a credit reporting agency who gives a credit report to unauthorized persons may be fined up to $5000 or imprisoned for one year, or both. You may also bring a civil suit for up to $1000 in damages against the individual.

☐ Prevention

To keep closed accounts off your credit record, send a certified letter to the issuer of a credit card you cancel, asking it not only to cancel the card, but also to notify the appropriate credit bureaus that the card was canceled at your request. Then check your credit report in one or two months to make sure your request has been carried out.

☐ Resources

Bankcard Holders of America publishes the *Credit Check-Up Kit* ($2), which explains the credit reporting process and includes listing of local affiliates of Equifax, Trans Union, and Experian Corporation. The organization also assists members with stubborn credit disputes; membership costs $18 a year. The National Center for Financial Education (P.O. Box 34070, San Diego, CA 92103) puts out the *Do-It-Yourself Credit Repair and Improvement Guide* ($9.95), which includes sample letters for requesting credit reports, disputing errors, and adding consumer statements to your credit file.

You also can get pamphlets in the FTC's "Facts for Consumers" series on the following subjects: *Fair Debt Collection*, *Fair Credit Reporting*, *How to Dispute Credit Report Errors*, *Solving Credit Problems*, and *Women and Credit Histories*. Call the Bureau of Consumer Protection, Office of Consumer and Business Education, Federal Trade Commission, at 202-326-3650.

To get the free pamphlet *Consumer Handbook to Credit Protection Laws*, write to the Board of Governors of the Federal Reserve System, Washington, DC 20551.

AILMENT

A creditor has gotten a judgment against me.

R When there is a judgment against you, the creditor will naturally attempt to collect. If you do not pay up, you may be ordered to appear in court and list your assets. Most often the creditor will try to locate assets that can be attached, or seized to pay off your debt. Attachable assets include bank accounts, wages, vehicles, and real estate.

Hire an attorney. If you cannot afford one, the following checklist may help:

- Consult briefly with an attorney about what items are exempt from attachment in your state. Some lawyers recommend withdrawing funds from your bank accounts, but not closing them, because the creditor will keep searching for attachable assets.
- Use money orders to pay all bills until the problem is resolved.
- Homestead your house. This will protect part of your equity if your home is sold to pay the debt. You may need an attorney to help you with the paperwork.
- File with the court to exempt your current wages from being taken.
- If you own more than one vehicle, one can be taken if you have enough equity in it. Find out if there are any special exemptions in your state.
- Do you live in a community property state? If so, find out what assets are protected under your local community property law.

☐ Prevention

Before a judgment is entered against you, check the title to your vehicles. If any is jointly owned or leased, transfer the title to the other owner.

AILMENT

I am being harassed by a collection agency.

R   There are reputable and disreputable collection agencies. When your account is turned over to a collection agency, you will receive an official notice and demand letter that the agency is now legally in charge of your debt. Then the phone calls from the professional collector start. It sounds as if you are the victim of an overzealous collector who is trying to use fear and intimidation as a means of getting payment.

To defend yourself, you need to know your legal rights. Here are some of your key protections under the Fair Debt Collection Practices Act:

- Within five days after contacting you, the collector must send a written notice stating how much you owe, the name of the creditor, and what steps you can take if you do not owe the money.
- You have 30 days to send a certified letter to the collection agency stating that you do not owe the money. During that time, you may

ask for documentation of the debt and a record of any and all payments. Unless the agency sends this requested proof, it is barred from contacting you again.

- Even if you owe the money, the agency must stop contacting you if you write and tell it to do so. The agency may get in touch with you again only if a specific action is planned, such as filing a lawsuit.

- A collector may not call you at "unreasonable times or places," such as before 8 A.M. or after 9 P.M. If it is inconvenient to speak to a collector during usual hours, for example, because you work the night shift, you must notify the agency in writing. Specify when the collector may call.

- A collector cannot repeatedly phone to harass you.

- A collector may not call you at work if this will jeopardize your job. If a call is made that endangers your job, notify the agency of this fact in writing. Jot down when calls are made and what is said. A collector cannot tell anyone, other than your spouse, the nature of the business with you. The collector may identify name and company if asked, but not details of the debt or why the call is made.

- A collector can contact friends, family, and neighbors to find out where you are, but cannot divulge any information about you or the debt.

- A collector cannot threaten actions, such as filing a lawsuit, that the agency has no power to take. If the agency does not subscribe to a credit bureau, the collector cannot tell you it will report the collection to a bureau. Nor can the caller falsely imply being an attorney or a government employee or imply that you have committed a crime.

- You can tell the collector to speak only to your lawyer.

What can you do if your rights are violated? The Federal Trade Commission and state attorneys general usually do not handle individual cases, but will act if they see a pattern of abuse. Many states have their own debt-collection laws, which may be more specific than federal law or extend coverage to more kinds of companies. While federal law covers only third-party collectors, some state laws cover a creditor's in-house collectors.

You can sue, of course, but that is a costly option in a time of financial trouble. You can bring suit in state and federal court within a year of the violation. Under federal law, if you win, the court can award any actual damages you suffered, plus an extra amount of up to $1000. You can also be awarded court costs and attorney's fees.

☐ Resources

For a brochure about your rights, write to Public Reference Branch, Federal Trade Commission, Washington, DC 20580.

AILMENT
I am so heavily in debt, that I am thinking about filing for bankruptcy.

R/ Personal bankruptcies are a time-honored way for overextended debtors to wipe the slate clean and start their economic lives anew. But there is a substantial downside as well. Being declared a bankrupt will leave you under a cloud of financial disgrace and severely damage your credit rating. Perhaps other measures will work as well—simply ignoring your creditors, for example, if you have no property they can seize, or negotiating with them if you need just a little time to get back on your feet.

Types of bankruptcy. There are two kinds of personal bankruptcy, Chapter 7 and Chapter 13. The choice between them depends on the debts you have, the assets you own, and your earning power. If you have a lot of equity in your home, for example, you will probably lean toward Chapter 13, which lets you keep your property while you repay your debts. But you cannot qualify for Chapter 13 unless you earn enough to make those repayments.

In petitioning for Chapter 13, you work out a detailed plan for paying your creditors all or part of the money you owe them over time. If the court agrees to the plan, your creditors must discharge your debts after you have made all the scheduled payments. Your payments are made directly to a court-appointed trustee, who parcels the money among your creditors. Unlike Chapter 7, Chapter 13 lets you include in the plan for eventual discharge student loans and loans obtained by fraud. Because a Chapter 13 does not let you completely off the hook, it often carries less of a financial stigma. Chapter 13 petitioners generally find it easier to regain their credit after bankruptcy than Chapter 7 petitioners.

If you are self-employed or simply in too deep to fund an acceptable repayment plan, you may have no choice but to file the more drastic Chapter 7. The court then cancels all your debts and hands your estate over to a trustee to be liquidated and split among your creditors. You can keep some of your assets. The exact amount varies from state to state, but you usually would be allowed to keep $7500 of equity in your house ($15,000 for married couples), $1200 of equity in a car, $4000 in household goods, and about $500 worth of jewelry. If the equity in your home, for example, exceeds the protected amounts, the trustee will sell the property and then return to you an amount equal to your full protected equity.

Consequences of bankruptcy.   Personal bankruptcies have been growing at an exponential rate in recent years. Filing a Chapter 7 "discharge of debts" or a Chapter 13 "bankruptcy payment plan" may seem like salvation from seemingly crushing debt. But there are serious and lasting repercussions to filing bankruptcy.

If you do decide to file for personal bankruptcy, you should know that your credit record will be poisoned for 10 years, making it difficult, if not impossible, to borrow during that time. You could also wind up losing your house and property. Moreover, bankruptcy may not solve all your problems: Federal income tax owed, other overdue taxes, alimony, child support, debts not listed on your petition, student loans, and loans obtained by fraud (e.g., by lying about your income) cannot be discharged by declaring bankruptcy. (The latter two types of loans, however, can be discharged with Chapter 13.)

Bankruptcy can also have an adverse effect on your career. Your employer may be influenced by this admission of fiscal irresponsibility. You may lose out on promotions and the chance to prove you can handle greater responsibility.

Bankruptcy is not cheap, either. Filing fees alone exceed $100. And attorney's fees for the simplest bankruptcy run $150 to $300 at no-frills firms that do no more than help you with the paperwork. Firms that provide legal advice, attend creditors' meetings, and appear at court hearings charge more—often 10 times as much.

Should you file for bankruptcy?   Sometimes bankruptcy is the only answer. For example, if your house is about to be foreclosed upon and your car repossessed, a personal bankruptcy will, at least temporarily, hold creditors at bay and protect a limited number of your assets. Still, bankruptcy should be a final resort, used only when you are likely to lose everything—houses, cars, and personal belongings—because of insurmountable debts.

A good guideline: *Never file bankruptcy for a debt amount less than your combined assets plus one year's income.*

☐ Resources

The American Bankruptcy Institute, Metropolitan Life, and the U.S. Justice Department have released *Bankruptcy*, which explains the process and its repercussions. To get a free copy, write to Consumer Information Center, Department 608C, Pueblo, CO 81009.

One of the best discussions of bankruptcy is found in *How to File for Bankruptcy*, by Stephen Elias et al. (Nolo Press). This $24.95 book contains all the work sheets you need to assess whether you should file for bankruptcy and what type of bankruptcy best suits your financial situation.

AILMENT

I am trying to rebuild my credit after a bankruptcy.

R̸ If you are willing to work hard and exercise self-discipline, you may be able to rebuild your credit—as quickly as within two to three years after a bankruptcy—to a point where you will not be turned down for a major credit card or loan.

Most major creditors are swayed just as much by positive credit information as by negative. They look for steady employment and any sign that you can repay your debts. The first step, of course, is to create a budget that you can—and will—live within. Then you must open a passbook savings account at a local bank. As soon as you have $500 or $1000 saved, apply for a savings passbook loan. This is a loan secured by your bank savings.

Your goal is not to get a bank loan; it is to establish a positive credit history. Even if you want to, do not pay back the loan too quickly. It takes about six to nine months for your diligent payments to appear on your credit report. Ask your bank if it reports this type of loan to credit agencies; if it does not, go elsewhere.

Some banks automatically offer their savings account holders a secured credit card. The credit limit will be somewhat lower than the amount in your savings account. If you have your spending impulses under control, accept one of these cards. Interest rates on these cards are quite steep, so use the card sparingly and only if you can pay off the entire bill promptly.

Department stores and gasoline companies are also more liberal than major credit card companies about extending credit. Get one or two of these charge cards and charge some small purchases that you can easily repay.

Most major credit card and loan issuers will overlook a negative credit history, if you can show two or three years of consistent financial responsibility. Furthermore, most will ignore a personal bankruptcy filing after five years of good behavior.

☐ Resources

For more information about credit rebuilding and responsible spending and budgeting, contact Consumer Credit Counseling Service at 800-388-2227. Another source is *Money Troubles: Legal Strategies to Cope with Your Debts*, by Robin Leonard (Nolo Press, $18.95).

CHAPTER THREE	**Consumer Issues**

Your airline has folded its wings. The emerald once worn by Empress Carlotta turns out to be a garnet that graced one Mabel Tawdry. Your new, labor-saver dishwasher scrubs the pattern off your china, and leaves the dried egg yolk. All of these things, and worse, could happen to you. If they do, what recourse do you have? Can you get satisfaction—if not revenge—after the fact?

The answer, more often than not, is yes. Dealing with defective products, overcharges, misleading or fraudulent advertising, and commercial invasion of your privacy takes patience and persistence, but you can win. You simply need to learn the fine art of complaining, as outlined in this chapter. We are not talking about whining, throwing tantrums, or threatening a multimillion-dollar lawsuit. Not from the outset, anyway. If you know whom to call or write and what legal protections you have, you can usually remedy the complaint without resorting to drastic action.

As usual, prevention provides the best relief. Before making major purchases, carefully read the product descriptions so that you know exactly what features or options you're buying. Ask questions if the description is incomplete or vague. If you are buying on credit, read the finance contract from beginning to end before you sign it.

You can often forestall future problems with good recordkeeping, too. If you become embroiled with a seller over a disputed bill or unscrupulous behavior, you will need to establish a paper trail. Keep copies of all receipts, dates, and records of phone calls made as well as a summary of your complaints. Smart companies still believe the customer is always right—but you may have to prove it.

The advice that follows should help you find ways to resolve any type of consumer complaint, even if your specific ailment is not covered here.

AILMENT
I have a complaint about a product or service.

R When a problem arises, go to the product manufacturer or service provider first. If you do not receive immediate satisfaction there, keep going right to the top. Top executives want to know where the lines of communication with their customers have broken down, and you are likely to get prompt attention.

Another suggestion: When it comes to warranties, hope for the best, but expect the worst. Keep all guarantees and warranties in a safe place. You might need them later to prove you are entitled to free service. Get the salesperson's promises and guarantees in writing, and read everything before signing.

If you cannot get satisfaction from the source, consider taking your case to small-claims court. You can file suit for up to $5000 in damages in this court, where no lawyers are allowed. Call your local small-claims court for the necessary forms and instructions.

□ Prevention

Examine products carefully before buying. Read warranties and contracts carefully. Never hesitate to call government agencies for help.

□ Resources

Keep these key numbers handy:

U.S. Office of Consumer Affairs: 800-664-4435. This office assists consumers with complaints about government agencies or private businesses. Office hours are from 10 A.M. to 2 P.M., EST, Monday through Friday, for consumers from the 50 states, the District of Columbia, Guam, Puerto Rico, and the U.S. Virgin Islands.

Federal Information Center: 800-688-9889. An information specialist at this Maryland office can unravel the red tape of federal agencies. You will be told the function and location of the agency you need.

Federal Trade Commission: 202-326-2222. This agency protects consumers when merchandise has crossed state lines. Infractions of the Fair Credit Reporting Act are also investigated here (see Chapter 2). If you have uncovered telemarketing fraud or if you are a victim of deceptive advertising or marketing, call this office.

Food and Drug Administration: 888-332-4543. When you find, say, a fingernail in a can of food or something wrong with a drug, take your complaint here (that is, after you call your doctor if the food or drug has made you ill). This agency also handles complaints about cosmetics.

Disabled American Veterans: 606-441-7300. If you are having difficulties with the Veterans Administration, you can call on the DAV, even if you are not disabled or a DAV member.

State and local agencies. Do not overlook your state and local government agencies, either. You can always turn to your state or county Department of Consumer Affairs, your state's Attorney General and Department of Real Estate, and your City Attorney's office. See the government listings in the White Pages for telephone numbers.

AILMENT
I purchased tickets from an airline or tour operator that has since gone bankrupt.

R/ This problem is increasingly faced by travelers whose tour operators have closed up shop. You stand a good chance of getting your money back *if* you used a credit card to pay for the tickets or tour. If you charged your tickets to American Express, MasterCard, or Visa, they will refund your money even if the bill has been paid and the 60 days for disputing charges has passed. Visa requires you to notify them within 120 days of the scheduled date of the flight, rather than the usual 60 days from the date of the bill as required by the Fair Credit Billing Act. MasterCard extends the dispute period to 60 days after the date of your flight, and American Express allows up to a year and sometimes longer.

If you paid cash or if the deadlines set by the credit card companies have passed, find out from the Department of Transportation (DOT) whether the airline has an escrow account set aside to issue refunds. If it does, make copies of all original documents to send to the depository bank. And check with a travel agent. In rare cases, another airline will honor your ticket.

A lawsuit is your last option. You have to weigh the cost of legal fees, at least $5000, against the chance of recovering your money from a bankrupt company. If you were not the only one taken, you may be able to join a class action suit. You may also be able to sue your travel agent to get the commission it received.

☐ Prevention

Protecting your money from travel flops is not simple. There is little state and no federal regulation of travel agents or tour operators. And in a business with small profit margins, it is easy for start-up air carriers and tour businesses to fail.

Public charter companies must post a bond with the Department of Transportation (DOT) and deposit money in an escrow account. Before flying on a new low-fare airline, call DOT's Consumer Affairs Office (202-366-5957) to find out whether the carrier has a prospectus number. If so, ask whether there have been complaints. Write your check or money order to the bank where the money is kept in escrow (ask your charter operator where that is).

If you are planning a tour, make a few telephone calls before you pay. Find out if the tour operator is a member of U.S. Tour Operators Association (USTOA), a New York–based tour organization (342 Madison Avenue, New York, NY 10173; 212-750-7371), and make sure membership is current. USTOA requires a $1-million bond from its members, who must have been in business for at least three years under the same ownership or management. Another trade organization, the National Tour Association (546 East Main Street, Lexington, KY 40508; 800-682-8886), offers a more limited monetary protection, up to $250,000 if a member company goes bankrupt. Also call the Better Business Bureau. Both USTOA and the BBB can tell you whether there have been complaints and possibly whether the company has had financial difficulties.

Before you send your money, call a hotel or airline listed on the tour and confirm that past reservations have been honored and paid for.

You can also buy trip cancellation and interruption insurance from a third-party insurer—*not* the cancellation insurance offered by the tour operator itself, which is worthless if the company goes under. American Express Travel Protection Plan (800-234-0375), Access America (P.O. Box 90315, Richmond, VA 23286-4991; 800-284-8300), and Travel Guard Internationale (1145 Clark Street, Stevens Point, WI 54481; 800-826-1300) sell this type of insurance, which usually costs about 5% of the total price of the trip. Buy coverage that includes operator bankruptcy and default, because many companies merely shut their doors.

If you are flying, do not buy a multiple-trip pass, even if you are promised a free flight for doing so. Otherwise, prevention is not all that practical. For example, you can wait until just before you get on the plane to pay for your ticket. (Of course, you then take the risk that the flight you want will be fully booked.)

About your only reliable safeguard when making any large purchase is to use a credit card for everything, instead of paying by check or cash.

AILMENT

My wallet/purse containing my credit cards and checkbook was stolen.

 You cannot act too fast when checks and credit cards fall into the hands of thieves. To limit the damage, take the following steps:

1. Cancel your credit, department store, and ATM cards right away. The telephone number to call to report a lost or stolen credit card is usually printed on the back of your monthly statement.

2. Issue "stop payments" on stolen checks, but do not quit there. Cancel the account, too. Using computer software, thieves can replicate your checks and change their numbers.

3. File a police report. Banks, credit card issuers, and insurance companies may require such a report as proof of the crime.

4. Call the three credit bureaus to place a fraud alert on your credit records: Equifax, 800-525-6285; Trans Union, 800-916-8800; and Experian Corporation (formerly TRW), 800-682-7654.

5. Monitor your credit reports regularly even after your file appears to be clean. Sometimes thieves lie low for a while, then reemerge.

☐ Prevention

Either use a credit-card registry service, or, if you do not, keep a list or photocopies of all your cards with account numbers, expiration dates, and telephone numbers to call for each.

Keep your checkbook at home. If you need to write a check while you are out, put one blank check in your wallet. (Be sure to make a note of the check number, payee, and amount to enter in your check register when you get home.)

AILMENT

I was charged too much when I called a 900 number.

R To help protect consumers, a Federal Trade Commission (FTC) rule has set up procedures for resolving billing disputes. When your telephone bill arrives, check it for any 900 number (pay-per-call) charges. For each such charge, the bill should include the date, time, and—for services that have per-minute rates—the length of the call. These charges must appear separately from local and long distance charges on your telephone bill.

If you discover an error, follow the instructions on your bill. The bill will tell you whom to call or write. The bill *must* include a local or toll-free number that you can call with questions about your pay-per-call charges and to learn more about your rights. In most cases, this will be your local or long-distance phone company, but it could be the 900 number company or an independent firm that does the billing for that company. You can also call your phone company to get the name and address of the 900 number service provider.

When disputing a charge, include the following information: your name and telephone number, the date and amount of the disputed charge, and the reason you believe the charge is in error.

You must notify the company listed on your bill within 60 days after the first statement with the error was sent. The company must write back within 40 days, unless it resolves the dispute before then. Within two billing cycles, but no longer than 90 days, the company must either:

- Correct the billing error and notify you of the correction, or
- Investigate the matter and either correct the error or explain why it has not done so.

You cannot be charged a fee for investigating or responding to the billing dispute. And no one can try to collect the disputed charge from you—or report it to a credit bureau—until the company handling the dispute has either corrected the error or explained its reason for not doing so. Companies that do not comply with these rules lose the right to collect up to $50 of each disputed charge.

Under the FTC rule, the phone company cannot disconnect your regular local or long-distance telephone service because you do not pay a 900 number charge. But you could be blocked from making future calls to 900 numbers if you fail to pay legitimate pay-per-call charges.

If you have a problem with a 900 number service, you may want file a complaint with the FTC. Write: Correspondence Branch, Federal Trade Commission, Washington, DC 20580. This will not solve your problem (the FTC does not resolve individual disputes), but complaints about 900 number scams help the FTC enforce the law against such companies.

FTC Regional Offices

Suite 5M 35
Midrise Building
60 Forsyth Street SW
Atlanta, GA 30303
404-656-1399

101 Merrimac Street, Suite 810
Boston, MA 02114
617-424-5984

55 East Monroe Street, Suite 1860
Chicago, IL 60603
312-353-4423

1111 Superior Avenue, Suite 200
Cleveland, OH 44114
216-522-4207

1999 Bryan Street, Suite 2150
Dallas, TX 75201
214-979-0213

1961 Stout Street, Suite 1523
Denver, CO 80294
303-844-2271

11000 Wilshire Boulevard, Suite 13209
Los Angeles, CA 90024
310-235-4000

901 Market Street, Suite 570
San Francisco, CA 94103
415-356-5270

150 William Street, Suite 1300
New York, NY 10038
212-264-1207

915 Second Avenue
Seattle, WA 98174
206-220-6363

Note, however, than even if the 900 number charge is removed from your phone bill, the service provider might continue to pursue the charge by other means, such as referring the matter to a collection agency. If that happens, you have additional rights under the Fair Debt Collection Practices Act (see Chapter 2).

If a debt collector gets in touch with you, you have certain rights under federal law. For example, you can write to the collection agency telling it not to contact you again about the charge. Once the collection agency receives your letter, it cannot contact you again legally except to say there will be no further contact or that it intends to take some specific action.

Because an unresolved debt can remain on your credit record, you also are entitled to dispute the report. Even if you do not succeed in getting the disputed item removed by the credit bureau, you can include your version of the incident in your credit report.

☐ Prevention

The FTC rule is designed to help you avoid excessive 900 number charges and prevent misunderstandings about costs. Under the FTC rule, 900 number services must give you the following information:

The advertisement. Print, radio, and television advertisements for the 900 number service must state the total cost of the call if it is a flat fee. If the charge is by the minute, you must be told the per-minute rate and the initial cost of the call, as well as any minimum charge. If the length of the program is known in advance, the ad also must state the total cost of the complete program. If there are different rates for different options, the ad must state the range of fees. You must also be given the cost of any other 900 number to which your call may be transferred, plus any other fees the service charges.

This information cannot be hidden in small print. The cost of the 900 number call must be at least half the size of the telephone number.

The preamble. When you dial a 900 number that costs more than $2, the first thing you will hear is an introductory message, or preamble. The preamble must describe the service briefly and tell the name of the company providing the service and the cost of the call. It must also say that anyone under age 18 needs parental permission to complete the call. After you hear this information, *you must be given three seconds to hang up without being charged.*

Exceptions: The 900 number rule does not apply if you have signed a contract with the information service. Be careful about entering into such an arrangement. If you sign a contract, your calls to the service and resulting bills will not be subject to the rule's requirements.

The rule also excludes calls charged to a credit card. However, the bills for such calls would be covered by the dispute resolution procedures of the Fair Credit Billing Act (see Chapter 2).

Children, sweepstakes, and more. The FTC rule also covers other 900 number sales practices. These include services that encourage children to pick up the phone and, for instance, talk to a cartoon character. Under the FTC rule, companies cannot advertise to or target pay-per-call services at children under 12 unless the services are educational and dedicated to areas of school study. If the ad is directed to consumers under the age of 18, it must state that parental permission is required to make the call.

Sweepstakes promotions are also covered. Some services let you enter a prize sweepstakes simply by dialing a 900 number and, in some cases, entering some type of code. Ads for sweepstakes must state the odds of winning (or how odds will be calculated). Also, the ad or the preamble must tell you that there is another (free) way to enter the sweepstakes. You must be told how to enter free of charge or where to get that information. You do *not* have to call and incur a charge to enter. This does not apply to contests where you have to demonstrate a skill, such as answering a question correctly.

Some 900 numbers may provide information about federal programs, even though they are not affiliated with any government agency. This could mislead consumers. Under the rule, the ad and the preamble must state that such services are not authorized, endorsed, or approved by a federal agency.

Finally, the use of 800 numbers is regulated. The rule generally prohibits:

- Using 800 numbers for pay-per-call services.
- Connecting 800 number callers to 900 numbers.
- Placing collect return calls to 800 number callers.

Collect calls. Pay-per-call services *cannot* make collect calls to you if the charge would be more than, or in addition to, the regular long distance charge for the call. Services that do not impose this additional charge *could* call collect. However, you *cannot* be charged for the call unless you have clearly indicated that you accept the charge.

☐ An Extra Ounce of Prevention

Scams involving 900 numbers abound. In general, you can protect yourself if you observe some guidelines.

■ Deal only with reputable companies. Some companies or organizations sponsor 900 number services for opinion surveys, sports information, or other topics of interest to you. Before calling a 900 number, be sure you understand the cost of the call and exactly what information or service you will receive.

■ Think again before calling a 900 number for a "free" gift. Television ads, postcards, or telemarketers may urge you to call 900 numbers for "free" prizes. But you pay for those "free" gifts when you make the 900 number call.

■ Do not confuse 900 numbers with toll-free 800 numbers. You pay for the 900 number call. The company pays for the 800 number call.

■ Talk to your children. Tell them not to call 900 numbers without your permission. You can have the phone company block 900 number calls from your phone. Under a Federal Communications Commission rule, your local phone company may charge a "reasonable" fee for blocking. However, if you are a new subscriber, you can request free blocking within 60 days after service begins.

AILMENT

I am on too many mailing lists.

REven if you always paid cash, hoofed it instead of drove, made anonymous donations, and made calls only from pay phones, you would probably end up on a list of like-minded consumers. And most of us, even those who complain loudest about junk mail, cannot resist occasionally stimulating the flow by responding to mail offers.

But you can cut clutter in your mailbox and silence your phone by attacking on two fronts: escaping from the lists you are on and eluding new ones. To get off lists, contact:

■ *The Direct Marketing Association's Mail Preference Service and Telephone Preference Service.* National mailers who belong to the DMA are asked to remove names of folks who say, "Delete me." Most DMA members voluntarily comply. Write to DMA at P.O. Box 9008, Farmingdale, NY 11375 and ask to have your name added to its Mail Preference Service—a list of persons who do not want unsolicited mailings. You can also take yourself off only selected lists by notifying marketer Polk (800-635-5522 or http://www.polk.com). *Note:* This will probably also put a stop to catalogs, coupons, and other offers you might like.

■ *Experian Corporation and Trans Union.* Both will pull your name from their marketing files if you request it.

■ *Banks, credit card issuers, and the phone company.* Tell the consumer service departments you do not want your name sold or traded for any purpose.

You can also write to catalog companies, publications, charities, and other organizations to ask that your name be removed from any lists they sell or rent.

☐ Prevention

To stay off new lists, plan ahead: Many companies disclose that they will sell your name and give you a chance to opt out by checking a box or by writing to a certain address.

When there is no disclosure, but you think your name might be sold anyway, write on the order form, application, or questionnaire that you do not want your name sold or traded.

Too busy to fill out endless postcards? If a solicitor encloses a postage-paid reply mail envelope, stuff the unwanted material into it and mail it back.

AILMENT

I am concerned about protecting my privacy.

R̸ Keeping your name and personal data confidential is like trailing behind a circus parade with a whisk broom. Thanks to computers, for every file with personal snippets you wipe out, another three or four will probably sprout up. But if you have the energy and time for this crusade, here are some tips to control the puzzle pieces of your life being circulated.

■ Be protective of your Social Security number. Your credit reports, bank account, and other financial records are usually linked to it. Only your employer, bank, brokerage firm, or someone required to report your income to the IRS legally need your Social Security number. Do not give it out to anyone else. Do not have it printed on your checks or driver's license (most states let you choose a different operator's license number). It makes no sense to carry your Social Security card around with you either. Check with your bank to make sure it does not use all or part of your Social Security number as a password—if so, ask for a substitute number.

■ Tear up your credit card receipts. If a cashier offers to rip up the receipt for you, watch to make sure it is done.

■ Do not fill out a survey. Appliances, electronic equipment, and computer equipment usually come with a warranty card and a "product information questionnaire" asking about your hobbies, occupation, income (within ranges), family makeup, and so on. You do not have to return the questionnaire to get warranty coverage. All that is needed is your name and address. If you provide more, your answers will most likely go into the

National Demographics & Lifestyles (NDL) database and be sold to catalog companies, publishers, and other mailers.

■ Avoid entering sweepstakes and other contests to stay off mailing and telemarketing lists aimed at "opportunity seekers."

■ Think twice about joining a "buyer's club" or using a debit, credit, or check-cashing card when paying for groceries. Your name and address can be linked to the list of the items you are buying that is created when the price scanner "reads" your groceries. It will not be long before your taste in everything from toilet paper to tuna is known.

■ Find out what is in your credit report. If you cannot stamp out all of the information compiled about you, at least you can reduce the potential harm by making sure it is correct. Order your credit report at least every other year and check it for accuracy (see details in Chapter 2).

Digital defenses. To guard the bytes and pieces of your financial privacy when you go on-line:

■ Do not send your Social Security number, account numbers, password, or other confidential data via E-mail, unless it is encrypted (that is, scrambled so that it can be read only by someone who has the right decoder). And watch what you say, too: If you brag about a big financial score, do not be surprised if some IRS agent with a computer finds out about it.

■ If you buy or do business on the Internet, make sure the transaction is encrypted.

■ If you have monthly charges billed to your credit card, find out how your Internet service provider protects its database of customers' credit card numbers. If you do not like the answer, switch providers.

■ Be creative in choosing a password. Avoid obvious ones like your name, initials, or birth date. In fact, any dictionary word can be cracked by password-guessing software. Invent a mixture of upper- and lowercase letters, numbers, and symbols. Do not stick with the same password for too long, and do not write it down and tape it to your computer.

CHAPTER
FOUR

Home Ownership

If you long for a white picket fence and a porch swing to call your own, you are far from alone. More than 60 million Americans own their own homes, and nearly 90% of those who have yet to buy say home ownership tops their list of financial goals.

Writing mortgage checks and paying property taxes prove you are thrifty and responsible. These monthly liabilities can also save homeowners a bundle in taxes. And with luck, when you close the door for the last time, you will walk away with a profit.

But home ownership brings burdens as well as benefits. Your home's value will slump unless it is well maintained. You need a steady income to keep up steady mortgage payments. Your home could be damaged by natural disaster or depreciate in value.

Even before you buy, you face a raft of decisions and obstacles. Should you rent or buy? How can you scrape up enough cash to get in the front door? Will you qualify for a loan? Which neighborhood and house is right for you? How can you get the best deal in a rising or a falling market?

Once you make your bid, any number of ailments can befall you before the seller turns over the keys. Even after you have moved in, you may discover defects you were unaware of.

Homes are expensive and the problems you encounter as a current or future homeowner can be extremely costly, too. The bankruptcy courts are full of people who thought real estate was an easy route to riches, but instead met with misfortune, misrepresentation, or misunderstanding.

The advice in this chapter should protect you from economic downturns, stingy lenders, greedy sellers, and untrustworthy buyers, among others. It can save you money whether you already own your home, live for the day you see the last of your landlord, or are still a looking.

■ BEFORE YOU BUY

AILMENT

I do not know whether it is better to buy a house or to rent.

℞ Rev up your calculator. You have to do the math. You need to figure the cost of both renting and buying over a number of years. As a homeowner, you must take into account closing costs, maintenance expenses, the income tax savings you will receive by deducting mortgage interest and property taxes, and the projected rise in value of the property. As a renter, you must consider the rent you would pay on a comparable residence and your net return from putting your down payment into another investment.

To illustrate, compare what would happen to a couple with combined annual earnings of $50,000 who bought a $150,000 house. Assuming a 10% down payment and an 8.5% interest rate, the mortgage, property taxes, and insurance would cost about $1200 a month. If a similar home could be rented for $800, this couple would be paying $4800 more each year to buy.

Some of that difference can be recovered through tax breaks. Our couple would save roughly $2270 annually in federal taxes. And in most states, they would save on state taxes as well. Assuming that the combined tax breaks amount to $3000 annually, our couple would still be $1800 richer if they had continued to rent.

But if their home appreciated 5% a year for the next five years, home-buying might gain the edge. That is because they would earn 5% on the entire cost of the home, even though they had only invested $24,000. (That is the $15,000 down payment, plus five times their $1800 annual negative compared to renting.)

After accounting for a 6% realtor's fee when they sell, this couple would walk away with a $29,950 before-tax profit. To generate a similar profit in the stock market would require about a 20% annual return.

The problem is that no one knows whether a house is going to appreciate. If this same house did not gain any value over the five years, for example, this couple would have lost more than $18,000 on the deal—$9000 in brokerage commissions, plus the $9000 negative ($1800 times five), plus the use of their money, which could have generated a consistent annual return.

In general, it pays to be a renter when house values lag behind inflation and a high vacancy rate holds rents in check. Also, don't buy if you expect a job transfer because you will probably have to sell before the house appreciates enough to cover your purchase closing costs. *Note:* An alternative in this case is to lease a house for two or three years with an option to buy. Although you may pay slightly higher than market rent to get a lease-option, you will not incur the financing costs of getting a mortgage. When you are transferred, if the value of the home has appreciated, you can exercise your option and then sell the house. But if the home's value has not appreciated substantially, just walk away, and you will be no worse off than you would be as a renter.

You also do not want to buy if local economic conditions are poor—for example, if a small town's major employer has just shut down the brass ring factory.

AILMENT

I am a buyer in a seller's market.

 Success in a seller's market requires knowledge of the market and the confidence to act quickly when you see what you want. Here are steps you can take to develop these qualities:

■ *Define your needs.* Figure out your top price and monthly payments, then the size, location, and condition that are essential to you. Do not confuse what you want with what you need.

■ *Study the market.* Know which school systems are best, where public transportation is convenient, and which taxes are affordable. Then track the sales prices of houses in your preferred areas.

■ *Comparison shop.* Be open to various house styles and comparable communities. Look at houses in a variety of price ranges—from $50,000 below to $50,000 above your target price—to get a feel for the market. Keep notes: size, price, condition, and special features of homes you like.

■ *Use a broker.* That is the best way to see everything available. There is no reason you cannot establish relations with more than one broker, even within the same area. One agency may have exclusive rights to show certain homes. Even where a multiple listing service (MLS) exists, different brokers will show you different sets of homes.

■ *Do your own legwork.* In a tight market, don't leave it all up to a broker. You may be able to pick up a genuine bargain if you run across a house being sold directly by its owner. Look for such houses listed in real estate classified ads—you can spot them by such phrases as "principals only" or "no brokers." Or watch for them in employee or church newsletters. A private seller may be willing to drop the price a bit because of saving a broker's fee. But be cautious: Sometimes an owner cannot get a broker because the owner has overpriced the house.

You can also house hunt by taking your purchase offer door-to-door in the neighborhood that appeals to you. This long-shot tactic works best with condominiums that have a number of look-alike units. If you see one you like, contact all the owners of the other units, or ask the board of directors to alert members of your interest.

Watch for tax lien sales, where houses are auctioned off to pay back taxes. Or attend foreclosure sales held by banks or other lenders. You might also phone area lawyers, if you are interested in buying a house from an estate. All of these methods take time, but in a seller's market, it is worthwhile to pursue every avenue.

Finally, consider placing your own ad in the local papers. List the communities you would accept, the size of the house you want, and a general price range.

■ *Make house hunting a top priority.* Once you have zeroed in on an area, stand ready to drop everything to look at a new offering. If you cannot come at once, make an appointment to see the property as soon as possible, even if that means a late-night or crack-of-dawn visit.

■ *Line up sources of financing in advance.* Find out who is offering the lowest mortgages and who approves loans the fastest. Consider alternate, temporary financing, if need be, to seal your deal quickly.

■ *Act decisively.* When you spot what you want, offer your second-best price at once. If it is rejected, come up with your top price fast. Let the seller know you are flexible on closing dates (if you are). If possible, do not make your bid contingent on getting a mortgage.

As a buyer in a seller's market, your object is to close negotiations quickly and get a signed contract from the seller. The reason? In this kind of market, bidding wars for houses are commonplace, and sellers often get offers higher than their original asking price. So try to sew up a deal fast.

AILMENT

We want to take advantage of rising real estate prices in buying our new house.

 Here are a few of the ways you can capitalize on a healthy real estate market:

- Buy as much land as you can, even if it comes with a smaller house than you want. You can always expand the house when you have more cash, but the increasingly more valuable land may eventually be beyond your financial reach.

- Get the longest-term mortgage available if you need to hold down monthly payments in order to buy in an area where prices are booming.

- Shop in November and December, when the weather keeps all but the hardiest buyers indoors. There will be fewer competing buyers to drive up prices.

- Settle for a longer commute if it helps you get more house for your money.

- Make a serious offer on an unfinished house—or take on a fixer-upper.

AILMENT

How can I protect myself from costly mistakes when I make an offer on a home?

 Even in a buyer's market, caution is needed to sidestep serious mistakes. But following a few simple rules can make your home-buying experience an enjoyable and profitable adventure.

Know what price you can afford. Your first stop, before beginning your search for the perfect home, should be the office of one or more mortgage lenders. Start money shopping with your bank or savings and loan (S&L) and then check out a mortgage broker, too. Once you fill out a loan application, the lender can prequalify you for a mortgage. Add this amount to what you have saved for a down payment, and you will know the top dollar you can pay for a home. You do not have to accept the mortgage for which you prequalify, but you can be reassured to know you can get a loan. This fact will make your offer a lot more attractive to sellers, too.

Not all lenders are equal. Some lenders sell all their loans in the secondary mortgage markets to tough lenders, such as Fannie Mae and Freddie Mac. If you fit their loan rules, you will usually get the best interest rate and terms, especially if you want a fixed-rate mortgage.

Portfolio lenders who keep their loans are usually more flexible. For example, Fannie Mae and Freddie Mac do not want the borrower to spend more than 28% of gross family income on mortgage payments. But many portfolio lenders will approve home loan payments of up to 33% or even 40% of household income if there are few other installment debts.

Inspect at least 10 neighborhood homes. Once you select the ideal neighborhood, do not rush to buy. Before making a purchase offer, view at least 10 houses in the area to compare floor plans, lot sizes, and prices. Ask lots of questions about each home. The quickest way to take in a slew of homes is to attend Sunday afternoon open houses. Soon you will be able to spot bargains and avoid overpriced homes.

Ask each agent why the seller is selling. You may be able to successfully bid lower, for example, if you know that a seller is taking an out-of-state job and has to move quickly.

Do not assume the realtor is on your side.   Many home buyers think the real estate agent represents them in negotiating with the seller. This is usually not true. The listing agent always represents the seller. Another agent at an open house who works for the same broker also represents the seller. Although these agents have a fiduciary duty to be honest with buyers, their primary loyalty is to the seller.

Be careful what you say to the seller's agents. For example, if you make an offer, but hint that you might go higher, the agent might encourage the seller to counter with a higher offer.

Of course, as a buyer, you can hire an agent to represent you exclusively. But the agent would have to work for a different broker than the listing agent. When the sale closes, the listing and selling agents split the sales commission, so having a buyer's agent will cost you nothing extra.

Ask the realty agent and seller to disclose all defects in writing. You cannot make an intelligent purchase offer until you know what drawbacks the home may have. Some states, such as California, require written disclosure of all known problems with the home from both the seller and the realty agent.

Then, to be sure nothing was overlooked, include a clause in your written offer worded to this effect: "Seller and realty agent have disclosed in writing all known defects in this property." The seller and/or agent will then be liable for the costs of repairs if they knew of any undisclosed defect that later becomes apparent, such as corroded plumbing.

Obtain a comparative market analysis.   Before making your purchase offer, have the realty agent prepare a written "comparative market analysis" form. This is the same form that was given to the seller when the home was listed for sale. It shows recent sales prices of similar neighborhood homes, as well as asking prices of comparable nearby residences now listed for sale. You can then add or subtract dollar amounts for the pluses and minuses of the home you want to buy in computing your offering price.

Be ready to negotiate.   Offering 5% to 10% less than the asking price will not insult the seller. And do not hesitate to go even lower if it is justified by the comparative market analysis form. You can always raise your bid, but once your offer is accepted, you cannot lower it.

Insert inspection contingencies and a mortgage finance contingency clause.   Although you have already prequalified for a mortgage, include a mortgage finance contingency clause in your written purchase offer.

Such a clause might read, "This purchase offer is contingent upon the buyer and property qualifying for a new first mortgage of at least $125,000 at not more than 8% fixed interest for a term of 30 years with a monthly payment not exceeding $925, with a loan fee not more than two points."

In addition, make your purchase contingent on the home passing a termite inspection and a professional home inspection.

AILMENT

I want to own a home, but I do not think I have enough money to afford one.

R̷ More and more Americans are being priced out of the housing market—not only middle-class buyers, but also wealthier buyers who simply cannot scrape up the huge sums needed for a down payment. Rising home prices coupled with stagnant incomes have kept more and more people from realizing the American Dream. If you are in danger of being squeezed out of the housing market, here are a few tips:

- Shop in a lower-priced neighborhood that you think will turn around.
- Beat other buyers to the door, and make a low, early offer on a house.
- Offer a seller about 10% below recent sales prices for similar houses and bargain hard and persistently from there.
- Try to overlook a home's cosmetic problems.
- Look to banks and other mortgage holders as sources of bargains. Foreclosed property can often be picked up for less than its market value.
- Ask your agent to phone corporate relocation specialists to find sellers seeking a quick sale. Many transferees would rather take a low offer than leave a vacant house behind.
- Put up with a longer commute to a less expensive house.
- Ask your state housing agency if it offers cut-rate mortgages.
- Get an adjustable-rate mortgage (these offer an initial interest rate and monthly payments below those of a fixed-rate loan).
- Buy an unfinished house (unless you are all thumbs).
- Buy a factory-built house.

- Buy with relatives or friends.

- Try to buy when:

  Classified ads are touting price reductions.

  The average selling time has lengthened to at least six months.

  Sellers are anxious enough to pay some of your closing costs.

  The local commercial vacancy rate is rising.

Finally, make your cash go farther by keeping your down payment as low as possible. A 10% down payment is excellent; you shouldn't put down more than 20% unless you get a big price reduction in return. By making a small down payment, you maximize your income tax deductions and minimize your risk in case home prices decline.

AILMENT

I do not have enough money for a down payment.

℞ First, find out from a lender the lowest amount you can put down and still buy the home you want. Developers of large housing tracts sometimes offer downs of around 5% to 7% in order to attract buyers.

If you are still having a problem scraping up the necessary buy-in, here are some possible sources of cash for a down payment:

- Gift or shared-equity loan from parents or relatives.

- Finding a cosigner for loan.

- Loan secured by personal assets or securities.

- Personal, unsecured loan from a lender.

- Computerized loan networks to find the best terms.

- Renting with an option to buy.

- Sale of personal assets or securities.

- Borrowing from your 401(k) plan.

- Withdrawal from your retirement plan (subject to 10% penalty before age $59\frac{1}{2}$).

- Cash value of life insurance.

- Second mortgage from seller or other lender.

- Lowering withholding allowances to increase take-home pay (but not so low that you owe big tax dollars next April).

- Low down payment FHA or VA loan.

- Doing repairs in exchange for lower down payment or sale price.

- Asking real estate agent to take a note or IOU for commission instead of cash.

- Using income tax refund as part of down payment.

- Special loan assistance offered by employer or union.

- Consolidation loan to reduce monthly payments on other debts.

- Obtaining a business loan to use for down payment.

- Paying yourself extra rent each month (for example, if your actual rent is $750, budget $900 and deposit the extra $150 in a money market account).

- Taking a temporary second job.

- Refinancing your automobile.

- Accumulating more funds during escrow period.

- Buying private mortgage insurance to repay the lender if you default on your low down payment loan (you pay a monthly premium based on the size and type of your loan).

- Accepting a higher mortgage rate in exchange for lower points up front.

- State financial aid for first-time buyers.

■ BUYING AND SELLING A HOME

AILMENT

I want to buy a house that is being sold by an estate "as is," but the executor refuses to make any repairs.

R Probate properties are commonly sold "as is." That means the seller makes no warranties or representations and refuses to pay for repairs. This is logical for an estate, because the executor probably is not familiar with the house.

Before you make a purchase offer, ask the realty agent to prepare a written comparative market analysis form. This form shows recent sales prices of comparable nearby homes. By adding and subtracting for the pros and cons of the "as is" home and comparing it to nearby houses sold recently, you can arrive at an intelligent offer price. In your offer, make your purchase contingent on your being able to obtain a satisfactory complete professional home inspection report.

An "as is" property can be an excellent bargain. "As is" sellers are at a severe disadvantage, because most buyers want to purchase homes in tip-top condition. When "as is" sellers refuse to pay for repairs, buyers have to lower their offer price to compensate. The sales price is usually reduced far more than the repairs will cost.

AILMENT

We plan to put our home up for sale next month. The only real estate agent we know is the one who sold us the house. This agent wants us to sign an "exclusive listing," so it can be worked on only by the salespeople within that company.

R̪ Do not sign it. Most real estate agents belong to their local multiple listing service (MLS), which distributes the listings of members to all other members. This gives your home the widest possible market exposure and the best chance to bring top dollar.

Your agent wants to keep your listing out of the MLS because the agent does not want to split the sales commission with a salesperson from another firm. This is good for the agent, but it is bad for you as the seller, because your home is then available only for sale by the salespeople in the listing agent's firm.

AILMENT

I am being transferred and have to buy a home in my new city. I am worried that I will be taken advantage of as an out-of-towner.

R̪ Take your time before buying. Your best bet is to lease a home with an option to buy. Then you can try out a home, lock in the option purchase price, have all or part of your rent credited toward the down payment, and later decide if the home and its location are right for you.

If you want to purchase a home right away, ask a realty agent to prepare a written comparative market analysis form, showing recent sales prices of homes in the neighborhood you prefer, as well as the current asking prices of comparable neighborhood homes.

AILMENT

We finally found the ideal home for our family. We made a full-price, all-cash offer through the real estate agent with no contingencies. But the seller refused our offer.

R/ I am sorry, but you will have to keep searching for the perfect home. The homeowner cannot be forced to sell, even at the full asking price for cash with no contingencies. The reason you cannot force the seller to accept your offer is because the listing contract was between the seller and the listing agent. You were not a party to that agreement. The seller has breached that contract by turning down your offer. That means the listing agent is entitled to the full commission, even though no sale takes place. If that does not sway the seller into accepting your offer, probably nothing will.

AILMENT

We signed a contract with a builder to buy a new home, which is not yet completed. We put $10,000 down. Since then, I have become disabled and will be off work indefinitely. Making the mortgage payments will be difficult without my paycheck.

R/ Legally, you have a firm contract to purchase the new house, and the builder does not have to cancel it because of your illness. Of course, the decent thing for the builder to do is cancel the sale and quickly refund your $10,000. He is in a no-win situation, because you probably will not be able to finance the purchase.

If the builder refuses to refund your $10,000, notify the mortgage lender that you are out of work. The lender will likely cancel the mortgage approval, thus more or less forcing the builder to rescind the sale.

If the builder still refuses to refund your $10,000, retain an attorney and bring a lawsuit for rescission of the sale, due to your inability to qualify for a mortgage. Just receiving a letter from an attorney, notifying the builder of your planned rescission lawsuit, may be enough to persuade the builder to give your $10,000 back.

AILMENT

Our offer on a home was accepted by the seller about five weeks ago. We obtained our mortgage and were ready to close the sale, when the seller decided not to sell.

R/ When home seller's remorse strikes, your realty agent needs to sit down with the seller and emphasize the advantages of going through with the sale.

If that does not work, your only practical remedy is to hire a real estate attorney to file a specific performance lawsuit. This will force the seller to deliver the deed as agreed. To prevent the seller from selling to another buyer or refinancing the property, your attorney will record a *lis pendens* against the property title, which gives constructive notice of the pending litigation.

The seller's only defenses against the sale are fraud, duress, mistake, or inadequate consideration. For your purchase offer to be deemed inadequate by the court, it must be far below market value. It is to your advantage to have an expert appraiser ready to testify as to recent sales prices of comparable neighborhood homes if that becomes necessary. Your attorney can advise on the best tactics.

When you win the specific performance lawsuit, the court will order the seller to perform that side of the contract and deliver the deed to you. Because each property is unique, monetary damages cannot compensate you for your loss.

Another choice is to sue the seller for breach of contract damages. But proving damages in your situation would be very difficult.

AILMENT

Through our realtor, we made a fair offer to buy a house listed for sale with another realtor. Our offer was turned down and the seller did not make a counteroffer. Now, six weeks later, the listing agent has called to say the sellers have decided to accept our offer after all. But we have been looking at other properties.

R After your original offer was rejected by the seller, it could not later be accepted. Even if the seller had countered your purchase bid, that would have been a rejection of your offer, and the offer could not be later accepted. You have no legal obligation to buy the house, unless you decide to make a new offer that the seller accepts.

AILMENT

We want to make sure the house we buy is not a lemon.

R The solution to your problem is to include a home inspection contingency clause in your written offer. Such a clause might read: "This purchase offer is contingent upon buyer obtaining a satisfactory professional home inspection report at buyer's expense within five business days. If such report is not approved by buyer, this sale shall be canceled, and buyer's earnest money deposit promptly refunded in full." Of course, wait until your offer is accepted by the seller before hiring a home inspector.

Be sure to accompany the inspector to learn if any discovered defects are serious. If the inspector uncovers a major defect, you can either renegotiate the purchase price or cancel the sale and get your earnest money deposit refunded.

AILMENT

I do not know how to find a good home inspector.

℞ A home inspection, which typically costs between $250 and $350, is money well spent. Look for an inspector who carries "errors and omissions" insurance and is a member of the American Society of Home Inspectors (ASHI), which certifies inspectors. ASHI accreditation requires candidates to pass two written tests and to have performed at least 250 inspections.

Ask prospects for samples of inspection reports and compare prices and services. Ask how much time they will spend on the property. For a detached house, they should spend at least one and a half hours. Make sure you will be allowed to go along when the inspection is made.

Although all home inspectors should spot signs of structural problems, if you have particular concerns, consider hiring a home inspector who is also a licensed engineer. Their fees are comparable.

Be wary of inspectors referred by the agent or broker, and do not hire anyone who also does home repairs. This is a clear conflict of interest.

Problems that show up often in home inspections include water damage, poor attic ventilation, and faulty roof construction. Some things— such as a snow-covered roof or air-conditioning in the winter—cannot be adequately checked. Have the seller put money in escrow until these items can be tested.

☐ Resources

ASHI can suggest members in your area. Call 800-743-2744 to have a membership list mailed or faxed to you. For a copy of ASHI's standards, send $4 to ASHI, 3299 K Street NW, 7th Floor, Washington, DC 20007.

AILMENT

I am having a new home built, and I want to buy a home warranty policy.

℞ You cannot buy one yourself. New home warranty policies are sold only to home builders; they are not available to the general public. Ask your builder about providing such a policy. If your builder is not aware of such a policy, you may have reason to worry. Your builder may not be able to qualify.

The best home builders purchase 10-year home warranties for their buyers from reliable warranty companies. If any home defects occur, the builder is responsible. But, if something happens to the builder, such as bankruptcy, the warranty company takes over and pays to repair any defects.

☐ Prevention

Do not sign a building contract until the builder makes a new home warranty policy available.

AILMENT

Our home sale contract said the sale was to close within 30 days and that "Time is of the essence." But the buyers could not get a mortgage, so we verbally extended the time by 15 days. After waiting a month beyond the scheduled closing date, we sold our home to other buyers. Now the first buyers are suing us.

R̞ Hire a real estate attorney to answer the complaint. Your problem is an example of why everything, especially the extended closing date, should be in writing. The written time extension would have stated that the buyer was being given only an additional 15 days. Your giving them an extra month to close the sale was more than reasonable. After you win the case, you may want to consider suing their attorney for malicious prosecution.

AILMENT

About three months ago we signed a six-month listing for the sale of our home. Now we think that was far too long. The housing market is slow in our area, so we would rather try to sell later. But our real estate agent says we will owe her the full sales commission if we take our house off the market, because the listing has not expired.

R̞ Read the terms of your listing. Most listings state that if the seller takes the property off the market without cause the full sales commission is owed to the broker.

That is not really unreasonable. Your agent has spent time and money marketing your home. If she refuses to let you off the hook for the commission, just let your listing expire. Cooperate with the agent and let her continue showing the house to prospective buyers. If she gets a full-price all-cash offer that exactly meets your listing terms, you can accept it.

As a matter of public relations, most realty agents will let sellers take their house off the market if they promise in writing to list the home with that same broker in the future.

☐ Prevention

Do not sign a listing that lasts more than 90 days.

■ FINANCING

AILMENT
I need the best financing deal.

R̸ Get ready to wend your way through a maze of choices: how much to borrow, the best type of loan for you, and the duration and terms. With a little research and some speedy calculations, though, you can get a winning mortgage.

Sources of funds. First, do your homework and discover which banks in your area are offering the lowest mortgages and those that will commit funds quickly. When you check out the lending institutions that offer the lowest rates, be certain you can lock in the quoted rate for a couple of months—until your purchase closes. Some lenders fail to mention that the advertised rate is for the current week only. When you discover that fact at closing time, it is too late to get another mortgage, and you may have already paid the lender several hundred dollars in nonrefundable application fees. Or the rates jump between the time you apply and the date the lender finally commits the funds—often four to six weeks later.

Another good source is your company's credit union. These lenders charge low application and closing fees, their rates are often competitive with banks', and they charge no "points" to borrow. (A point equals 1% of the loan; most lenders charge from one to four points at closing.)

Mortgage choices. The type of mortgage you pick depends on how long you intend to be in the home, how much you can currently afford, and whether you think interest rates are headed up or down.

You can choose a conventional fixed-rate, fixed-term loan that typically runs from 15 to 30 years. Or an adjustable-rate mortgage (ARM), which generally offers a lower initial interest rate than a conventional loan. An ARM's rate can rise or fall every 6 to 12 months, however, depending on the underlying index—usually a combination of Treasury security rates. Then there are various balloon mortgages, where mainly interest is paid over a fixed period and at a fixed rate. At the end of a fairly short time (usually about five years), the entire loan comes due, often requiring hasty refinancing—and more loan fees.

The prime difference between fixed- and adjustable-rate mortgages is who is at risk. In fixed mortgages, the lender assumes all the risk, profiting if interest rates go down—or suffering if rates rise. After losing enormous sums during the inflationary 1970s, bankers devised ARMs (also known as variable-rate mortgages). With an ARM, the borrower, not the lender, is at the mercy of fluctuating interest rates. If rates go up, mortgage payments do, too. If they fall, the borrower pays less each month. To compensate for the extra risk, the borrower gets a bonus: The *initial* interest rate will likely be a couple of percentage points below the rate for conventional mortgages. But the annual rate in future years could be higher or lower.

That low initial rate can be alluring. And variable-rate mortgages are a good deal if you think interest rates will drop and stay down over the term of your mortgage. But you might be wrong. So hedge your bet with a cap. Your rate should rise no more than 2% in any one year, and it should have a lifetime cap of, say, 15%. Make sure this is written into the loan agreement. The lower the cap on your ARM, the higher the interest rate will be. You must decide how much risk you want to bear. Bear in mind that effective interest rates on 30-year mortgages reached 18.23% as recently as 1981.

The type of mortgage you choose should reflect your financial strategy. If, for example, you intend to retire within the next 10 to 15 years, consider a shorter-term conventional mortgage. But if you are on a steady rise up the corporate ladder, you may not mind the risk of a variable-rate mortgage or a larger fixed-rate loan that would squeeze you a bit financially right now. Or if you are planning to resell the house in four or five years, you may choose a balloon mortgage. Your carrying charges would be lower while you live in the house, and you will be out before it is time to refinance.

The cost of money. Renting money—which is all a mortgage lets you do—costs money, and the longer you rent it, the more you pay. But some lenders rent it for less than others, so it definitely pays to shop around. Even a fraction of a percentage point more on a loan means a lot more dollars that have to be paid. For example, a 30-year mortgage for $100,000 at 9.75% costs $859 a month; at 10%, monthly payments grow to $878. A mere $19 difference, but multiply the $19 by 12 (months per year) and then by 30 years, and the difference comes to $6840—the extra amount you will pay for the same $100,000 you borrowed.

You can slash the cost of money by borrowing it for a shorter period of time. It will not seem cheaper, because your monthly payments are higher if you shorten the loan. But over time, you will be making many fewer monthly payments with a shorter-term mortgage. And you will generally pay a *lower* interest rate with a shorter-term loan. That is because you reduce the lender's risk of inflation when you pay off faster, so a lower rate can be charged.

Generally, the rate on a 15-year loan is .25% to .5% less than on a 30-year mortgage. On our same hypothetical $100,000 mortgage, the spread works out to monthly payments of $859 each for our 30-year loan vs. $1044 monthly for a 15-year mortgage. By repaying the loan at 21% more a month, though, the cost of the money plunges almost 40%: $100,000 for 30 years at 9.75% costs $309,240; for 15 years at 9.5%, it costs only $187,920. You save $121,320 in interest!

Mortgage size.   How much mortgage can you afford? Obviously, that depends on your income, your monthly payments on other debts, and your lifestyle. Then there are the dependents who rely on you, your health and the health of your dependents, and your chances of increasing your income or net worth over the next 15 to 30 years.

Bankers use a standard formula to decide how much credit to extend to you, and are seldom swayed from this restrictive view. There are two parts to this formula. The first is called the 28% rule. The monthly principal and interest costs of the mortgage you want are added to the monthly charges for real estate taxes and insurance. Combined, they should not exceed 28% of your current monthly gross income.

Part two of the formula says that all of the above costs plus the monthly payments on your other debts—car loans, credit card balances, tuition loans, and such—should not total more than 34% to 36% of your monthly gross income.

Other options.   Mortgages are the most popular way of financing a home, but there are other fountains of funds. If you have just sold a home, you could roll the proceeds over into your next home. By reinvesting the cash you get out of your old home, you may need only a small mortgage or none at all. Sinking all of the proceeds into a new house is equivalent to putting it into an investment paying the current mortgage rate. If you can invest for a higher return, you are better off leveraging your home purchase with a small down payment and a mortgage. Take into account the tax savings you will get by deducting mortgage interest on your income tax return in computing where you will get the better yield.

Other short-term sources of funds are your brokerage account, life insurance policies, other real estate, your retirement plan (subject to a penalty if you are under age 59½), or any tangible asset you own. Or you can get an unsecured loan from a relative or friend. If this person has a large sum of money in a bank, you can return the favor by offering to pay a higher rate of interest than the bank.

AILMENT

We found a five-bedroom "fixer-upper" that my carpenter husband can improve at minimal expense. Even though we were preapproved for a loan, we cannot find a mortgage lender for a 75% loan for this house. We have tried three lenders, and they all have taken a look at the house and turned us down.

℞ Go back to the lender who preapproved you for a home loan. Ask to see their appraisal of the property. Was it for as much as you offered to buy the house? If so, the lender must honor its loan approval commitment to you. If not, find out why. Maybe your offer was too high.

There is a chance the lender asked for a low appraisal to get out of making your loan. Ask to have the appraisal reviewed or the house reappraised by a second appraiser. Explain your plans for improving the house, and why the loan will be safe. To intimidate the lender, ask for the name and address of the lender's federal and state regulatory agency.

If that does not work, your seller is about your only remaining source of financing. Ask the seller to carry your mortgage for 5 or 10 years. If the house is in bad condition, the seller may agree to finance your purchase.

AILMENT

Although we were preapproved for a loan and have excellent income and credit, the lender rejected us after the home we want to buy was appraised. We suspect the real reason is because of the ethnic makeup of the neighborhood.

℞ If your suspicions are right, you are victims of illegal redlining by your lender. Give the loan officer 24 hours to reconsider, and suggest that the loan officer consult with the president of the firm about the legal consequences of redlining. Also, send a registered letter to the lender's president to confirm your conversation.

If that does not work, phone the nearest office of the U.S. Department of Housing and Urban Development for assistance. Also, notify the lender's state or federal government regulators.

Meanwhile, contact other mortgage lenders in your city. Ask if they make loans in your chosen neighborhood. If any lender doing business in your city says "no," that is illegal redlining.

AILMENT

I am a war veteran and have not used my Veterans Administration home loan entitlement. Am I still eligible for a VA mortgage? Where can I get VA mortgage information?

The best source of accurate, up-to-the-minute VA home loan qualification rules is a local VA-approved mortgage lender. Most banks, S&Ls, mortgage brokers, and mortgage bankers can answer your questions about qualification rules for no-down-payment VA mortgages.

AILMENT

We sold our home and carried back a second mortgage. The buyer took over payments on our VA mortgage. Last week, I received a notice from the VA lender that payments are four months in arrears. However, the buyer is current on our second mortgage payments. At this time, I do not have the money to pay the missing first mortgage payments.

Because the buyer did not assume the mortgage and the VA mortgage is still in your name, a default on it will reflect adversely on your credit.

The best solution, if possible, is for you to pay to reinstate the VA mortgage and then foreclose on your second mortgage. In most states you can begin foreclosure on your second mortgage if the first mortgage is in default. Please consult a real estate attorney for details.

☐ Prevention

Have the buyer assume your old mortgage to release you from further liability on it.

■ AFTER ESCROW CLOSES

AILMENT
My developer went bankrupt.

R When a developer goes under midway through a project, it can take years and cost homeowners thousands of dollars to straighten out the mess. Worse yet, developers brought in after a bankruptcy may fail, too, causing additional hardship.

Be prepared for a long wait. If your home is still unfinished, a bankruptcy filing does not void your contract. The court tries to give the builder a chance to reorganize the business, so home buyers and other creditors have to wait to see if the company can deliver. If delay follows delay, however, you may petition the bankruptcy court to get out of your deal.

Your situation is better, though still an ordeal, if the developer went broke after building your home. There is a good chance you will have to settle for less. Covenants that dictated how your subdivision would look or the quality and size of the homes may be thrown out or changed by a bankruptcy judge or lender trying to find a workable solution. So instead of single-family homes, you may find townhouses—or much-lower-priced homes that are cheaper to finish—surrounding you. The promised pool may never be built. Houses may sit half-finished down the street for years or be auctioned off for a fraction of what you paid, depressing your home's long-term resale value.

While the situation is daunting, buyers are not powerless.

■ *Know what you bought.* Reread the documents that came with the purchase and the closing to find out what the developer intended. Know which phase or section of the project you are in and what was planned for that section.

■ *Check for warranties.* See if any homeowners' warranties came with your purchase. Some 40% of all new homes include such insurance policies. Most pay to fix anything in your house that goes wrong in the first year. Major structural flaws will be repaired for up to 10 years. With the builder gone, you may need to tap that policy for repairs.

■ *Organize your neighbors.* United, you can become an effective force. Developers and lenders know the value of word-of-mouth sales.

■ *Hire a lawyer to review your documents.* Ask what legal steps you can take.

■ *Find out where your developer keeps its funds.* Deposits on unfinished homes or association dues already collected by the developer should be banked separately from the developer's accounts. If you act fast, you or your lawyer may be able to prevent the developer from making off with such funds.

■ *Meet with the new developer.* Someone—a lender, a government agency, or another builder—will step in to finish the project eventually. Identify and meet with this successor as soon as possible to protect your interest. Check the sales materials you received from the bankrupt developer for the lender's name. Or look up the mortgage loan documents in the land records office to find out what company holds the developer's mortgage.

■ *Involve local government.* If your developer had a performance bond, ask the city to "pull" the bond and use the proceeds to complete roads, street lights, and other public improvements.

Once a lender or government agency has taken over the project, you and your homeowners' group will be bargaining over what kind of homes will be built and how much of the project will be completed. Be realistic. Some niceties may have to go, and cheaper homes may be inevitable if the project is ever to be finished. Try to convince the lender that the more improvements made to existing properties, the easier it will be to sell the rest of the lots.

☐ Prevention

An ounce of prevention can save you the headaches of dealing with a failed developer. Before buying:

■ *Know the developer.* A company with a 20-year track record has a better chance of surviving a downturn than a recent start-up. Visit other projects the developer has completed. Ask homeowners about the quality of their homes, how any complaints were dealt with, and whether the builder delivered on all its promises. Reputable builders will repair most defects at no charge for the first year or so.

■ *Read the disclosure papers and sales documents.* Have an attorney review legal documents, especially those dealing with your deposit. The deposit should be kept in a separate escrow account. If it is not, make that a contingency of your purchase. The name and address of the escrow agent should be identified.

■ *Find out the developer's plans for your phase of construction.* For example, pools and tennis courts may not be scheduled until a certain number of units are sold. Determine whether any covenants dictating the size and style of housing apply to a single phase or to the whole project. Sometimes developers write in escape clauses that, for example, let them switch to a cheaper model house if there is a downturn in the market. Ask for evidence of a performance bond or other guarantee to cover the completion of roads and other public services.

■ *Purchase title insurance.* Rules vary from state to state, but title insurance will generally protect you from having to pay off any liens subcontractors might attach to a project if the developer fails to pay. Buy an endorsement that covers liens.

AILMENT

The purchase of our new home closed last month. The seller promised to move out "in a few days," but is still living in the house and claims to have nowhere to go.

R̸ Your holdover home seller is legally a tenant at sufferance. Although the individual is a trespasser in your home, the police wisely will not want to get involved in the dispute. So there is little point asking them to throw the seller out.

Unfortunately, your holdover seller must be evicted like a nonpaying tenant, even though you never intended for the seller to become your tenant. Hire the best eviction lawyer you can find, because the seller will probably delay being evicted as long as possible.

☐ Prevention

Do not close your home purchase until the seller has moved out and the property can be reinspected shortly before the deed is recorded.

AILMENT

I bought a two-bedroom cottage that was rented to a tenant who promised to move out when the sale closed. Last week my deed was recorded, but it turns out the tenant has a lease that does not expire until next year. The tenant now wants $5000 to move out.

R̸ A point of law called the statute of frauds requires all real estate agreements to be in writing to be legally enforceable. If you take the tenant to court without having the promise to move out in writing, it is doubtful a judge will terminate the tenant's lease.

Given the high cost of hiring an attorney, it is better to see if the tenant will move out for less than $5000. Whatever agreement you reach, be sure to put it in writing.

☐ Prevention

Any person buying a tenant-occupied property should insist upon receiving a copy of the lease or month-to-month rental agreement before making a purchase offer.

AILMENT

We recently bought a newly built home. The builder promised to arrange for upgraded carpets, landscaping, and top-of-the-line kitchen appliances at no extra charge. But we are disappointed with the carpets, minimal landscaping, and off-brand appliances.

R Under the statute of frauds, real estate agreements that are not in writing are unenforceable. The reason is to prevent misunderstandings like yours. If the builder's promises are not in writing, you do not have much legal recourse. You can take the builder to small-claims court without an attorney, but do not expect significant results. For further details, consult a real estate attorney.

☐ Prevention

Always get any representation regarding real estate in writing. Without written proof of the seller's promises to you, you have nothing. It is your word against that of the home builder.

AILMENT

About six months ago, we bought our home directly from the seller without using a realty agent. Last month we applied for a building permit to add a bathroom. When checking our plans, the building inspector discovered the patio was constructed without a permit. Other improvements were built improperly and must now be corrected at an additional cost to us.

R You need to seek recourse from the seller for the extra cost. The seller should have disclosed to you that the patio was put on without a building permit. Illegal construction reduces the value of the property you bought and also could be dangerous. If you cannot work out a fair settlement with the seller, consult a real estate attorney.

AILMENT

When we bought our new home, the mortgage company insisted that we buy our homeowner's insurance from its affiliated insurance company, which we did. But after we moved in, I found out we are paying about $295 more a year than another insurer charges for the same coverage.

R If your mortgage lender is federally regulated, as banks and S&Ls are, you cannot be forced to use a specific insurer or insurance agent. Many states have similar laws. In that case, you can change insurers at any time. But if you cancel your homeowner's policy now, you probably will not get a full prorated refund. Instead, wait to change insurers until your annual policy expires and then switch to the insurer you prefer.

What if your lender is not federally regulated? There seems to be no law prohibiting a private mortgage lender or an individual lender from naming the insurer, although most do not. Check again with your lender to determine if this applies to your situation. If so, you are probably stuck paying the higher premium, at least for a fixed period of time.

Finally, any lender can require that you insure through a company that has at least a minimum rating.

■ PROBLEMS DURING HOME OWNERSHIP

AILMENT

Our home loan was sold to another company. We are not happy about the way this company is handling our impound account and would like to pay our own taxes and insurance. How do we go about doing this?

R/ Impound accounts, which collect funds from mortgagors each month to pay for property taxes and home insurance when they come due, have been the subject of repeated consumer complaints over the years. (In some areas, these accounts are also referred to as escrow accounts, not to be confused with the escrow process used when a home is purchased.)

The principal complaint? The mortgage lender has the use of the borrower's money for the entire year, but pays only minimal interest. A close second: The lender requires borrowers to contribute more to the account than is necessary to pay for taxes and insurance.

(These gripes are in addition to the problem of fraudulent or incompetent loan companies that either abscond with account funds or "forget" to pay tax or insurance bills.)

However, aside from cases of fraud or incompetence, you may have no choice but to put up with the arrangement. Why? Under many state laws, if a home mortgage is for 80% or more of the home's value, a lender can require the borrower to maintain an impound account. Impound accounts are required on Veterans Administration (VA) or Federal Housing Administration (FHA) loans, too. And lenders often require impound accounts on homes the owner will not be living in or for borrowers with a record of erratic mortgage payments.

The best way to get rid of an impound account is to change the circumstances that created one, but this could be time-consuming and expensive. For example, if your home has appreciated, you need to convince the lender that your loan-to-value ratio has fallen below 80%. This could mean paying for a new appraisal of your home. Before hiring an appraiser, ask the lender for names of their approved appraisers in your area. When the appraiser visits your home, have proof of recent comparable neighborhood home sales ready to justify your home's market value.

You could refinance, but the high cost argues against it. You might also simply tell your lender that you want the account dropped. It probably will not work, but it will not cost anything to try.

If you have evidence of poor service or more serious transgressions, you could take your complaints to the agency licensing your lender.

If the lender is a mortgage broker, you can complain to your state's Department of Real Estate. If it is a bank, complain to the Federal Deposit Insurance Corporation (FDIC) by calling its consumer line at 800-934-3342.

AILMENT

Last month we received notice that our home would be sold for unpaid property taxes and penalties. We thought our mortgage company was paying the taxes out of our escrow (impound) account. But the tax collector was still sending our property tax bills to the previous owners. Our mortgage company has enough money in our escrow (impound) account to pay the taxes. But they say we must pay the penalties.

℞ Since your mortgage company undertook the obligation to pay the property taxes, it is responsible for paying them, plus any interest and penalties for late payment. Phone your loan servicer to find out who owns your mortgage. If it is Fannie Mae or Freddie Mac, the nation's largest lenders, contact them to report the loan servicer's negligence. Consult an attorney if your loan servicer continues to hold you liable for penalties.

☐ Prevention

Although your mortgage company was supposed to pay the property taxes, it is your responsibility to make certain they are paid. You should have insisted on getting a copy of the annual property tax bills for your records and income tax deductions.

AILMENT

A hurricane seriously damaged my house.

℞ Settling a major claim can be difficult, even if your insurance company acts in good faith. You will be faced with making critical judgments based on subjective information at a difficult personal time. The first suggestion you are likely to hear is that you should hire an independent adjuster (IA) to help negotiate with your insurance company. But consider the pros and cons carefully. Once an IA is involved, insurance companies sometimes get defensive, even adversarial. Claims can take longer to settle and are more likely to end up in arbitration or in court. Another point to consider: IAs typically collect 10% of the total settlement. And you may need every cent to restore your property.

Instead of hiring an IA, you will probably be better off finding an engineer to certify the condition of the house before and after its reconstruction. A certification will become a must when you sell the house—to prove to prospective buyers that the house is structurally sound again.

If possible, get your insurance company adjuster to let you hire an engineer at the company's expense, even if your policy does not expressly allow it. Argue that you need this expert advice to determine the extent of the damage to the foundation and other load-bearing structures. Find a qualified engineer who is also experienced in arbitrating insurance claims. The engineer can become a useful negotiator on your behalf in the debate with the insurance company over the extent of the structural damage and the need for certain repairs or replacements.

Your insurance company may have a program of hiring its own "preferred contractors." Although your insurance adjuster will probably insist that the preferred contractor will be working for you, there is bound to be some conflict of interest. If you feel strongly about having a say in whether the house is salvageable, for example, you should reject the insurance company's preferred contractor, and hire one of your own choosing.

Ask your engineer to recommend a contractor or get referrals from relatives or friends. Talk to the contractor's recent clients and visit several completed jobs. Before work begins, the contractor must agree with the insurance company about the "scope of work." This is the stage at which you need to haggle over every detail, or your house may not be restored exactly as it was originally.

Ask—persistently if need be—for copies of all documents. You will need them to negotiate the settlement, and later, for taxes. The most valuable document will be the detailed estimate. In it, your contractor should itemize the cost of every repair, including material costs, overhead, and profit. Your insurance company will also probably get its own estimate. Obtain a complete copy of each revision of the cost estimate, including calculations of the contractor's overhead and profit. You may need them all for negotiating purposes, especially if you decide to make substantial changes to the house.

You have reached settlement once the contractor and the insurer finally agree on the scope of work and the cost. Be sure to insist that you be allowed to approve the settlement.

Even with the settlement check in hand, you may still have a problem. The check may be made out in more than one name—yours, the mortgage company's, and the contractor's.

Because the mortgage company has an interest in your property, it has the right to be sure you replaced it using a qualified contractor. However, as long as you are paying your mortgage and insurance premiums, the insurance money is yours to spend as you think best. The contractor cannot legally refuse to sign the check either.

Some states have laws that require mortgage companies to deposit insurance settlements in interest-bearing accounts. If your state lacks such a law, insist on depositing the check in a local interest-bearing account in your name.

If you decide to remodel at the same time at your expense, you will need separate estimates and permits. Furthermore, you will have to negotiate a separate scope of work with the contractor for the new layout.

AILMENT

I am hiring a contractor to work on my house, and I want to make sure no mechanics' lien is filed after the work is done.

℞ You should get an unconditional lien waiver and release signed by the contractor and each material supplier, subcontractor, and laborer. This cuts off the right of any of these parties to record a lien on the residence.

You may also want to check once every year or two for any documents recorded with the county recorder that may not belong in the record. If a lien is recorded against your property, pay any amount you legitimately owe. If a lien is incorrect, you should challenge it immediately. First try to get the lien removed by writing to the contractor. If that fails, consult a real estate attorney about filing suit.

☐ Prevention

When it comes time to pay the contractor, write the following on the back of your check, just above the endorsement line:

"Depositing or cashing this check is acceptance of payment in full and constitutes an agreement not to file a mechanics' lien."

AILMENT

What should I do if someone is injured on my property?

℞ First, do all you can to help physically, such as making the victim as comfortable as possible and calling for medical assistance. Do not, however, say anything to suggest or admit guilt or negligence. No matter how sorry you feel for the injured person or how guilty, do not increase your potential liability by laying blame on yourself.

Instead, let the law decide who is responsible. Notify your insurer in writing (and speak to your attorney as soon as possible). Do not talk with the injured party or his attorney about liability until you have done this.

Note that 99% of such lawsuits do not go to trial. Sometimes a suit is threatened but never filed, or is dropped before trial. In many cases, the parties agree to an out-of-court settlement.

If you carry insurance, the insurance company will generally handle any claims against you. It is only when your insurer believes the claim has no merit that you are likely to wind up in court. Even then, the insurer will provide an attorney and pay any damages awarded (up to the limit of the policy), along with court costs. *Warning:* If your insurer will *not* pay punitive damages, consider hiring your own attorney to fight this issue if your actions may have made you liable for punitive damages.

☐ Prevention

Given the potential liability, it is foolhardy not to carry adequate liability insurance. Without it, it takes only one person seriously injured by your negligence to ruin you financially.

The liability portion of your homeowner's policy will cover injuries on the premises and damage to other people's property caused by your negligence. It will not pay for injuries you inflict on purpose.

A typical homeowner's policy includes $100,000 of liability insurance. This will not go far if someone is severely injured. For a slightly higher premium, you can raise your coverage to $300,000 or $500,000; some companies offer $1 million or more. This covers harm caused by your children and pets, too, except intentional harm by a child over 13.

Standard homeowners' policies will not cover:

- Employees and clients of your home-based business, including the children in your home-based day care, if you take in more than three children.

- Claims by one member of your household against another.

- Any disease you pass on to someone.

If you see clients or customers in your home, obtain a separate business rider. And if you have a swimming pool or other special hazard, check the policy to make sure you are covered.

If you have domestic employees—even part-time ones—you may be required to carry workers' compensation insurance, which costs a little over $100 a year. (There may be civil and criminal penalties under your state law if you do not carry it.) Contractors working on your house should already have workers' compensation for their employees. Before you hire a contractor, ask to see proof that they are adequately covered.

What if someone is so badly hurt on your property that your home-owners' policy does not cover all of the costs? That is when you need an umbrella liability, or "personal excess liability," policy. This fairly inexpensive policy would protect you from a big judgment that would eat up your regular policy coverage.

Your premium for the umbrella policy is determined by the number of houses, rental units, and vehicles you own. If you have one house and two cars, a typical premium costs $100 to $150 for $1 million in coverage. You will get $2 million in coverage for only about $50 to $100 more in premium costs.

An umbrella policy is most critical if you have a lot of assets to protect. The wealthier you are, the more you have to lose if someone is injured on your property. Consult your insurance agent for help in deciding what type and amount of coverage is best for you.

AILMENT

The interest I pay on my mortgage over the next 30 years will be almost three times more than the price of my house. How much interest can I save by adding $200 to my monthly mortgage payment?

R Without more details about your mortgage, it is impossible to answer your question. By using a pocket financial calculator, in a few seconds you can calculate your savings.

For example, suppose you have a new $100,000, 30-year mortgage at 8% interest with a $733.76 monthly payment. Increasing your monthly payment by $200 to $933.76 will pay off the mortgage in a little over 15 years. The interest savings will be about $88,000 and the loan will be paid off almost 15 years sooner.

AILMENT

My spouse and I are retired and living on a fixed income. We want to get the equity out of our home without having to sell or move out.

R A home equity loan or line of credit is one option, but only if your retirement income is sufficient to repay the loan. Another solution is to take out a reverse mortgage. Reverse mortgages let elderly homeowners borrow against their home equity with the guarantee that the money does not have to be paid back until after they die or move out of the house.

A reverse mortgage (also know as a reverse annuity mortgage), or RAM, is the opposite of a conventional mortgage loan. The loan is paid to the homeowner in monthly installments. The amount you receive depends on the amount of home equity you borrow against, the interest rate, and the length of the loan.

The maximum amount you can borrow depends on your home's value. Because of the cost to the lender and the risk that the home may decline in value, reverse loans are not made for the full amount for which the house might be sold. Usually, the loan amount is between 60% to 80% of the appraised value of the property.

The following illustrates how the RAM works: A reverse mortgage loan of $120,000, at a fixed rate of 14% for a 10-year term, plus a 1% loan origination fee and other charges, would give you a monthly income of $463. If $5000 were paid out right away to pay off an existing mortgage or make repairs, the monthly income would be $386. After 10 years, the loan must be repaid or renegotiated.

Reverse mortgage loans can be used for a variety of needs—for instance, to supplement a small income, to meet medical expenses, or to pay for in-home nursing care for a spouse.

You repay the loan at a scheduled time or, under some arrangements, whenever you choose—usually by selling the home. Some older borrowers take out a loan expecting that the term will match or exceed their life expectancy.

Other ways to unlock home equity. There are several other choices for senior homeowners who want to convert their home equity to cash, either as a monthly payment or as a lump sum. Besides the reverse mortgage, you could opt for either a sale/leaseback arrangement or a deferred payment loan.

Sale/leaseback. The sale/leaseback arrangement is one of the oldest ways to convert equity. All such arrangements involve an investor who buys the senior's home and grants the seller a life tenancy (that is, the right to live in the home until death) or a more limited tenancy. The seller then pays a specified amount of rent. Investors profit from tax savings created by taking depreciation on the property.

Under a sale/leaseback, you may receive payment in a lump sum, in equal monthly payments based upon an annuity purchased by the investor, or in monthly mortgage payments from which the monthly rent is deducted. Which method is used will depend on your income needs and your and the investor's tax situation. The sale agreement should clearly spell out your right to continued occupancy, the rent schedule, rent increases, and who is responsible for the future maintenance and care of the property. If the arrangement involves monthly mortgage payments, the agreement should state who receives the balance of the sales proceeds if you die before all payments are received.

One advantage of sale/leasebacks is that the transaction is completed at the beginning, so that you can predict your future income and expenses. You are also protected against buyer default by the mortgage and the annuity purchased at the time of sale.

The following example shows how a sale/leaseback might work: A 90-year-old widow sells her house, appraised at $80,000, to an investor for $63,000, a 21% discount. She receives a down payment of $6320 (10%) and a 12-year promissory note for the $56,880 balance. She receives a monthly payment of $679 from the investor, including interest at 10% per year, from which she pays rent of $285 back to the investor, leaving $394 as net income. The buyer purchases an annuity which will continue the $679 monthly payment after the note is paid off.

Deferred payment loan (DPL). These loans let homeowners postpone payment of all principal and interest either for a specified term or until the house is sold. Deferred payment loans help seniors raise the funds to make improvements or repairs that make the home more salable or increase its value—or just make it more comfortable to live in. If your income is too small to qualify for a conventional loan, you could use a deferred payment loan to create an income-producing unit in your home, which would provide greater monthly income and could be used to repay the loan at term.

Is home equity conversion for you?

Equity conversion is not practical unless you own a home which is almost or completely paid off. Homes worth $100,000 or more, owned by single individuals over age 75, in neighborhoods with a good chance of appreciating in value, are considered the best risks for equity conversion by lenders and investors.

The lower the value of the home, the less equity income you can draw from it. If you have a home of lower value, consider whether it will provide monthly payments large enough, when averaged over a term of 10 or more years, to be worth the cost of the loan. Of course, if you are in a financial bind, an extra $50 or more per month may be welcome. The equity in even a modest home ($40,000) may be enough to provide funds for home repairs or to meet medical or home care expenses.

Homeowners interested in lifetime income arrangements should compare several different plans. Also, they should weigh the added costs of annuities against the risks of term loans or other arrangements.

Costs. Depending upon the method of equity conversion, costs could be in the form of interest and various fees or commissions. You may receive less for the property than its full market value and miss out on the benefit of future appreciation in the property's value.

Reverse mortgages carry big up-front costs and are very expensive if you keep them for only a few years. It is not until you have received more money and the up-front costs have been spread over more years that the total annual loan cost rate goes down. A slightly less costly alternative if you know you will remain in your home for only a few more years is a fixed-term reverse mortgage. Fixed-term plans must be repaid within 5 to 12 years, or when the homeowner dies or moves out of the house, whichever is earlier. Fixed-term plans are available in only six states: Arizona, California, Maine, Massachusetts, Minnesota, and parts of New York State.

Risks. With a reverse mortgage, the main risk is that you will live longer than the term of the loan and will have to sell your home to repay it. Also, there is some risk that the home will depreciate in value over the term of the loan. In that case, the sales proceeds might not repay the entire loan.

In sale/leaseback arrangements, there is a danger that the investor may default on the monthly payments you depend upon for income. With all fixed-income payment equity plans, there is the risk that inflation will erode the spending power of the payment and you will not have enough income to meet basic needs.

It has taken you a lifetime to achieve the debt-free ownership of your home. Think twice about whether you want to assume any new mortgage debt or relinquish complete ownership of your home. Consider, too, that you will also be "spending" all or part of your children's inheritance by encumbering the property.

☐ Resources

For more information on specific plans and home equity conversion in general, write to the American Bar Association, Commission on Legal Problems of the Elderly, 1800 M Street NW, Washington, DC 20036.

Or call your local Department of Housing and Urban Development office (see the listing in your White Pages under United States Government). To speak with a HUD representative in Washington, DC, call 800-697-6967.

☐ Prevention

In considering your options, obtain the following information about each plan: initial cash payment; net monthly payment you will receive; schedule of payments, if interest or payments are variable; whether the payments are taxable or tax-free; how long monthly payments last; how much equity you will still have at term or after a specified period of time; amount and terms of any annuity; in the case of variable interest rates, the effect of a specific rate change (e.g., from 8% to 10%) on payments and loan balance; any prepayment penalties or penalties for revoking the agreement; and the disposal of the property at the end of term.

For reverse mortgages and deferred payment loans, the following should be disclosed: loan to value ratio, the right of the lender to escalate payments or change the term of the loan, what happens if you die before term, and your rights if the loan is sold to the secondary market or another investor.

Any loan plan including an annuity should compare the annuity's rate of interest with the mortgage interest rate to make certain the annuity will yield a monthly payment large enough to cover future rents and provide living expenses.

Because home equity conversion plans are so different from conventional loan arrangements, seek legal and financial advice before adopting a plan. This counseling should involve your heirs, so that they understand the effect of the arrangement on their inheritance.

AILMENT

Because of declining property values, my house is worth less than the mortgage on it.

℞ Many homeowners are tempted to walk away from their house (and their mortgage) when the dwelling's market value drops below the loan amount. Letting the bank take over the house seems easy. But it is not wise. In some states, if the bank loses money selling the house after the foreclosure, it can sue the borrower for the difference between the sale proceeds and the higher mortgage amount. Also, the IRS counts the difference as taxable income to the borrower. Finally, your credit is ruined.

So what are your options? To be honest, there is no perfect way out, especially if you are facing foreclosure. No matter which decision you make, you will probably face financial hardship. But to help you minimize the damage, we will discuss some escape routes and weigh their pros and cons. Before making a move, however, you should sit down with a tax professional to determine whether the option you prefer has adverse tax effects and, if so, the potential tax bill.

■ *Refinance your home.* This is more of a pipe dream than an actual solution. If you have no equity in your home, you will not be able to refinance to get a lower interest rate unless you throw more good money after bad to buy down the loan balance on a refinanced mortgage. I do not recommend you do this.

■ *Negotiate for better terms.* If you are unable to pay your home mortgage, try to work with your mortgage lender to arrange lower monthly payments or to stretch your payments over a longer period of time, so that your monthly cost is more manageable. That way you get to stay in your home, and because you have changed only the terms of your loan agreement (and not the loan amount), there is generally no tax due.

■ *Rent out your home.* If you have a compelling reason to move out of the neighborhood, such as job relocation, rising crime, or failing schools, do so. If the home is unsalable or you would take too big a loss on the sale, rent it to help make the mortgage payments.

If the amount of rent you can charge will leave you with a negative cash flow you cannot handle, write a letter to your mortgage lender's president, explain the facts, and ask for a mortgage interest rate reduction to avoid foreclosure.

You may face a stumbling block, though, unless you have a VA or FHA home loan. That is because there is probably a PMI (private mortgage insurance) company involved if you have more than an 80% mortgage. Your lender may refuse to reduce your interest rate because the PMI company objects. If foreclosure occurs, the PMI company will wind up paying most of the lender's loss.

■ *Sell your home.* You may try to sell your home, even though you will not get enough money out of the sale to pay off the amount of your mortgage. In that case, turning over the sale proceeds, plus the amount you still owe on the loan, will leave you with a loss. On the positive side, you probably would have no tax bill.

Or, you can try to get your lender to accept a short sale. Short sales generally work when the market price for the home is close to the mortgage amount, but after paying commissions and sales fees, the proceeds would be insufficient to pay off the bank loan. In that case, the bank might agree to accept the proceeds of the sale as full payment of the mortgage.

Although a short sale would solve your mortgage problems, it can create tax troubles instead. If your bank agrees to accept less than the contracted mortgage amount, you could have "discharge of indebtedness" income. In the topsy-turvy world of taxes, you could suffer a huge loss on the sale of your home, receive no cash when escrow closes, and still have a "gain" on which you must pay tax.

For example, suppose you paid $190,000 for a home, on which you carry a $150,000 mortgage. If you sell the home for $130,000 and your lender agrees to forgive the other $20,000 still owed on the loan, you will have to pay taxes for the $20,000 in debt forgiveness. In the 28% tax bracket, that is a tax bill of $5600.

You might think there would be some tax relief when you take a loss on your home. But there is not. A capital loss on residential real estate is not deductible, because your home is owned for personal, not business or investment, purposes.

■ *Persuade your lender to reduce your loan amount.* Your lender may agree to a lower loan amount (or "short-pay") if you can show—by producing detailed financial statements—that you cannot pay the loan you have now, but could and would pay if the loan amount were reduced to a level commensurate with your income.

As with short sales, a short-pay can result in tax liability. Even though a short-pay means your home's value has fallen dramatically and you are in financial trouble, the IRS generally considers the forgiven debt to be taxable income to you.

■ *Give your lender the deed.* If you have little or no equity in the house, one means of walking away is to quitclaim the deed to your home to the lender. Before you do, though, make sure the lender promises not to declare anything adverse on your credit report.

Another out, if the lender will not accept a quitclaim deed (or a deed in lieu of foreclosure), is to record a deed to the lender, paying the transfer fees. Then mail it to the lender. The lender will probably keep the deed, rather than deal with the paperwork of returning the title to you and foreclosing. Then you can truthfully say you never were foreclosured on or defaulted on your mortgage.

You should consult a real estate attorney for more details.

■ *Let the lender foreclose.* Allowing your home to be taken and sold by the lender is obviously a last resort. Not only will you lose your home and good credit, but you will probably owe the IRS. In the first place, the lender is going to turn around and sell your house at a rock-bottom price. If the lender accepts that amount without pursuing you for the balance due on the loan, you will have debt forgiveness income.

In rare cases, your tax problems grow even worse, especially if you have postponed tax on the gain from the sale of a previous home by trading up to the home you just lost in foreclosure. Why? The IRS considers a foreclosure to be a sale. The "sales price" is the loan amount at the time of the foreclosure. Up to $250,000 in gain is tax-free ($500,000 for married couples). But you will owe tax on any gain in excess of this amount.

Let us illustrate by taking a hypothetical taxpayer, Dick Poorhouse, who bought his first home 25 years ago for $50,000. Twenty years later, he sold it for $400,000 and used the proceeds to buy a $600,000 home, which has a $550,000 refinanced mortgage. Because of the rolled over gain, his tax basis in the property is just $250,000—the $600,000 purchase price minus the $350,000 in deferred gain.

Now the bank forecloses on the home. The IRS considers the foreclosure a sale at the $550,000 loan amount. So Poorhouse has a $50,000 taxable gain—$550,000 minus tax basis of $250,000 minus $250,000 exclusion of gain. His tax liability comes to roughly $14,000.

Taxes and insolvency.   You may be able to delay paying tax on this type of income if you are insolvent—that is, your liabilities are greater than your assets—or are involved in Chapter 11 bankruptcy. Consult your tax adviser to see if this relief applies to you.

If you cannot avoid liability and the tax due seems insurmountable, try to negotiate an "offer in compromise" with the IRS. These are deals that allow hard-up taxpayers to pay the government less than they owe because they simply do not have the money or prospects to pay more (see Chapter 8).

■ WHEN YOU DECIDE TO SELL OR RENT OUT YOUR HOME

AILMENT

We want to sell our house, but the market is soft right now.

Rx The best advice in a down market is not to sell. If you are forced into a job-related move, consider renting out your house and waiting for a better time to unload it.

If your home will not rent at a profit and you cannot afford a negative cash flow, be prepared for a lot of hard work before the For Sale sign goes up. To make a speedy sale, you must make your house attractive to buyers before it goes on the market.

Among the steps you might take:

■ List your house with a knowledgeable and aggressive broker. A soft market is no time to try to save the customary 6% broker's commission by selling your home yourself. Interview four or five brokers, especially about their marketing strategies, before signing a listing. Make sure the broker you choose will advertise your house through a multiple listing service, which alerts every agent in the area that it is for sale.

■ Do not haggle over the broker's commission. That is the broker's only incentive to work hard for you. In fact, if housing sales are particularly slow in your area and you are in a hurry, consider offering a higher-than-average commission. A 7% commission on a $120,000 house, for example, would cost you $8400, or $1200 more than a 6% commission. But the lure of extra money might stimulate the broker to show your house to more prospective buyers. The result: a faster sale at a better price.

■ Set a reasonable price. Price is even more important than location in a soft market. Use recent selling prices of comparable homes in your area as a guide. Do not pad the asking price by 5% to 10%—it could keep potential buyers away.

■ Make cosmetic repairs and improvements. That leaky roof, peeling paint, and dripping faucet are not going to attract buyers. Eliminate messy clutter, too. Do not undertake major remodeling, though. Unless a project adds substantially to a home's value, you will not recoup your cost with a higher sales price.

■ Consider creative financing. Offering financial incentives to prospective buyers may help clinch a sale. Instead of lowering your asking price, offer the buyer a "decorator's allowance" of $1000 to $5000. Cash in pocket helps buyers furnish their new home.

Paying some of the buyer's costs—for example, the points charged by the mortgage lender—can also lead to a deal. You can also carry back a second mortgage yourself, but because of the risk of default, you should do this only as a last resort.

AILMENT

Ten years ago, a friend and I bought a duplex. We lived together in one apartment and rented the other to tenants. After a year, my friend moved away. I would now like to sell this duplex, but I have no idea where the co-owner is living.

You need a real estate attorney, who will probably recommend a quiet title lawsuit for court approval of the sale.

First, you will need to try to find your co-owner—for instance, by publishing a legal notice in the appropriate local newspaper. If your friend cannot be found, the court can order the property sold with your co-owner's sales proceeds held in trust. A quiet title lawsuit is an effective way to solve many title problems. But it often takes a long time. If you have a prospective buyer you do not want to lose, offer to lease-option the duplex until the quiet title lawsuit can be resolved.

AILMENT

About five months ago, my wife and I were divorced. The final decree says we are to sell our house and split the profits equally. The realty agent found a buyer, but my ex-wife refuses to either sign the sales contract or sign a quitclaim deed.

Your attorney may have to go back to court to get a court order requiring your ex-wife to comply with the divorce decree. She can be held in contempt of court if she will not cooperate.

AILMENT

I intend to rent out my home, but I do not know how much rent to charge.

R First, check your newspaper's classified ads to see if there are similar properties for rent and at what amount. If there are no comparable homes, use this rule of thumb: Charge a monthly rent equal to around three-fourths of 1% of the home's market value. For example, if the home is worth $150,000, a monthly rent of $1125 would be about right.

<table>
<tr><td>**CHAPTER**
FIVE</td><td># Insurance</td></tr>
</table>

" It is hard to exaggerate just how much of our money goes, one way or another, to insurance," writes Andrew Tobias in *The Invisible Bankers* (Simon & Schuster, 1982), his study of the insurance industry. We put our money directly into health, life, auto, and property insurance. We help to fund Social Security, a publicly funded insurance program. Our taxes pay for police and fire protection. And the price of every product and service we buy includes a pass-along of insurance premiums. Tobias estimates that this "Gross National Premium" totals around five hundred billion dollars.

Of course, the cost of not having insurance can be even higher, if the dreaded happens. You buy insurance, no matter which type, to protect your family from financial catastrophe. So, you do not need a policy that in itself turns out to be a disaster.

To begin with, you should take defensive measures by avoiding three common mistakes. First, pick the coverage that is best for you *before* you choose the insurance company. Second, do not use life insurance as your only form of savings or investment. That is not its primary purpose, and in fact, life insurance has historically paid low rates of return compared to most other investments. Finally, do not buy insurance for its potential tax savings; you will probably wind up with insurance that does not do its true duty, which is to reimburse you or your loved ones for loss.

Even though you can buy insurance against every imaginable risk, only a few types of coverage have real value. In an industry where deceptive sales practices and false promises are common, you often can avert a crisis by simply reading each and every policy, new or renewal, before you sign it.

In the natural world, catastrophe can come in the form of wind, fire, flood, or accident. When you buy insurance—or even when you already own it—potential disaster takes other forms. In this chapter, we look at cures for costly insurance premiums, choosing the wrong coverage, placing

115

your bet with the wrong insurer, rejected claims, loss of coverage, and being denied coverage, among others.

Insurance is nothing more than a gamble. What you get for your premium is the promise that the house will pay you whenever you lose. With the help of this chapter, you may be able to win now and then, too.

■ GENERAL INSURANCE ISSUES

AILMENT
I am confused by all the insurance products available.

R℘ The only insurance you may have a real need for are life, disability, health, auto, and home. The National Insurance Consumer Organization (NICO), a consumer advocacy group, calls limited policies that protect against a single disease or event "junk insurance." Your insurance purchases should be aimed at protecting you from certain catastrophic losses. In other words, you need *comprehensive* coverage for a broad range of misfortunes, not a small dose of disaster, and *catastrophic* protection against economic ruin, not temporary belt-tightening.

Insurance against being mugged, fired, crushed by a falling satellite, swindled, audited by the IRS, or ambushed by extraterrestrials are only some of the more unusual policies available. Here are a few of the more popular specialty policies that you can easily do without if you have regular comprehensive coverage.

Hospital indemnity insurance. The tab for this coverage, which provides extra cash for hospital patients, is not much—a few hundred dollars a year—but you do not get a lot, either. Many policies pay around $100 for every day you are in the hospital, compared to the $1160 a day a hospital stay typically costs. And such policies often have a waiting period of a year for people with preexisting conditions. You certainly do not want to substitute hospital indemnity insurance for comprehensive health insurance, because indemnity policies provide minimal protection.

Dread-disease insurance. Insurers play on your fears—or family history—to sell you peace of mind in case you contract cancer and other specific illnesses. For example, if you are under age 65, you might pay around $6 a month to help with the cost of cancer treatment. If you wind up in the hospital, you are paid $80 a day, which will barely buy hospital aspirin. The benefit rises to $200 a day only after 90 days in the hospital.

Student accident insurance. Accident insurance offered through your child's elementary or secondary school is cheap, typically less than $25 a year for school-time coverage and $40 to $150 for round-the-clock coverage. But, the reimbursement is usually limited in amount and duration, and many policies have a maximum benefit of $25,000, not enough to cover the cost of some athletic injuries, for example. Many student policies kick in only after your family plan pays for the claim, although you could recoup some of your deductible or co-payments. Even with primary coverage, which pays regardless of other insurance coverage, payment you get under other health coverage will probably be reduced, so your combined benefits will not exceed your actual expenses.

Life insurance for kids. Loss of a child rarely means a loss of family income. But insurance sellers push this insurance, which may cost only $100 a year for a $5000 term policy, stressing that either your kids may not be insurable later or by starting young you can lock in a lifetime of relatively low premiums or a policy is a good way to save for college. Insurance should protect against financial catastrophe. Do not buy it until you actually need it; your money can be working harder for you in other investment vehicles.

Credit life insurance. Credit life has been called "the nation's worst insurance rip-off" by the Consumer Federation of America and "disgracefully overpriced" by NICO. You should only buy it as a last resort if you cannot meet the health requirements for other insurance policies or if, at your age, other policies cost even more than credit life.

The purpose of credit life is to pay off your mortgage or car loan balance if you die. It is expensive and the hefty sales commission built into the price of credit insurance tends to pump up costs even more. Also, your loan is paid off even when that may not be the best financial solution for your heirs.

Rental-car insurance. Collision-damage waivers, with daily rates in the $10 to $15 range, can add 50% to the cost of a car rental. Most likely this coverage is unnecessary, because you're probably covered under your own auto insurance policy. Even if you are not, some credit cards, such as Visa Gold, Gold MasterCard, and most American Express cards, automatically offer rental-car protection in most cases. If your auto insurance policy does not provide this coverage, add a rental-car rider; the cost should be no more than $25 to $30 a year.

Flight insurance. If you have life insurance anyway, why buy more for plane crashes? This insurance is still sold in vending machines and at counters at the airport, but these days credit card companies often pitch it, too.

AILMENT

I need a good insurance agent.

℞ There are two types of agents: those that represent just one company, called captive agents or direct writers, and independent agents who work for different insurers, usually five or more.

An independent agent can give you more choices. If a product offer by one company does not fit your finances, an independent agent has an array of other products to offer. A captive agent can sell only his or her company's product, even if it is not right for you. Still, a captive agent may offer the best rates or service in certain areas.

In the long run, your choice should be based on price and your sense of the agent's honesty and competence.

Here are some questions to ask:

- *How long have you been an agent?* The agent you choose should have a minimum of five years of experience. Why five? Because most doubtful agents will have left the business by their fourth year; a five-year veteran is committed to the field and will likely be around to give you continuing guidance.

- *What are your professional credentials?* Look for an agent who is either a chartered life underwriter (CLU) or chartered financial consultant (CFC). Best of all, the agent should also be a Certified Financial Planner (CFP).

- *How do you keep up to date on the latest insurance legislation, tax law changes, and products?* Although there is no continuing education requirement, the agent should attend courses and seminars on his or her own initiative.

- *Are you a full-time agent?* This will screen out part-timers, who do not keep up with new developments.

- *What is the quality of the companies you represent?* Most or all of them should be rated A+ in *Best's Insurance Reports.*

- *Do you carry malpractice insurance?*

- *How does the policy you suggest fit my needs?*

- *How much are the premiums on the amount and type of coverage I need?* Explain your financial situation to the agent during the interview or consult your financial planner about your insurance needs before the interview.

- *How often will you be in touch with me to review your coverage?* Your agent should check back with you at least once a year.

Other factors to consider:

- Be sure the agent's explanations of price, amount of coverage, and policy benefits are clear and specific.

- The agent should be willing to make three or four visits to sell you a policy, rather than demanding an immediate decision.

- Ask for recommendations from well-to-do friends—physicians, lawyers, accountants. An agent with prosperous clients usually sells large policies, gets high commissions, and thus can limit the number of clients, so will probably have the time to return your phone calls and keep on top of your needs.

- Be wary of an agent who sells life, health, and disability insurance along with property/casualty (homeowner's) and auto. Few people can master the complexities of all fields.

- If the agent offers products that seem too good to be true, you know better, right?

To do a background check, contact your state insurance commission for a record of any license suspension or revocation.

AILMENT

I am looking for a financially sound insurance company.

R Before you buy an insurance policy or annuity, give the prospective insurer a financial stress test. Look at its capital, defined in insurance jargon as "surplus," or net worth, plus the "mandatory securities valuation reserve," which is set aside to bail out bad investments. The rule of thumb is that capital should be at least 5% of assets. Another measure is return on assets as reported by Standard & Poor's. For 1985 through 1989, S&P rated companies above-average if they earned at least 4% on assets. The best advice: Buy from large companies licensed nationwide, especially in New York, where the insurance industry is tightly regulated. Stay away from any policy offering above-market yields: That is a sure sign of high risk.

The major rating agencies can do a lot of your spadework. A. M. Best Company has been rating insurance companies the longest. Over the past several years, S&P, Moody's Investors Service Inc., Duff & Phelps, Weiss Research, and a few others have expanded their coverage of the industry. Not that the rating agencies are infallible—most neglected to post warnings when Executive Life and Mutual Benefit Life began to fail.

FIGURE 5-1 Insurance Company Ratings				
Description	A. M. Best	S&P/D&P	Moody's	Weiss
Superior, negligible risk	A++ A+	AAA	Aaa	A+
Excellent, small, slightly variable risk	A A–	AA+ AA AA–	Aa1 Aa2 Aa3	A A– B+
Good, high claim-paying ability now	B++ B+	A+ A A–	A1 A2 A3	B B– C+
Adequate, but less protection against risk	B B–	BBB+ BBB BBB–	Baa1 Baa2 Baa3	C C– D+
Below-average quality, higher- than-average risk	C++ C+	BB+ BB BB–	Ba1 Ba2 Ba3	D D– E+
Financially weak, high risk factor	C C–	B+ B B–	B1 B2 B3	E E–
Nonviable, or about to be	D E F	CCC CC D	Caa Ca C	F

Ask your insurance agent to dig up a company's latest ratings for you. You can also trek to your local library to look up a company's rating, but the data there may be outdated. Better yet, call the rating agencies directly. Standard & Poor's will rate an insurer for free over the phone (212-208-1527), but it will not provide backup details. Others are more comprehensive, but you pay for the information. A. M. Best, for example, has a telephone number that charges you $2.50 per minute (900-420-0400). Weiss reports on a company for $15 over the phone (800-289-9222; in Florida, 561-627-3300). For a fee, the raters will also mail you written analyses. For instance, Weiss sends out one-page company summaries for $25 each or 18-page reports for $45. One-page summaries of three companies will cost you $55 ($95 for three in-depth summaries). Write to Weiss Research at 4176 Burns Road, Palm Beach Gardens, FL 33410.

☐ Prevention

Obtaining an insurance company's rating is the first step. But what does it mean? Figure 5–1 is a chart of the different agencies' ratings and how they translate into performance.

AILMENT
I am worried about the financial health of my insurance company.

℞ With several major insurance companies, including Mutual Benefit Life and Executive Life, winding up in the hands of regulators in the early 1990s, it is only prudent to take your insurer's pulse from time to time. Sometimes, tracking your insurer is simply a matter of keeping up with the news. The wonder is not that some 1100 of Executive Life's policyholders bailed out in the six weeks before the state takeover, it is that the rest did not. The company's woes had been well publicized.

Besides watching the media for bad news about your insurance company's performance, here are three other ways to protect yourself:

1. Compare the ratings your company has received from the major rating agencies. Look for high grades and close agreement by the different agencies. In general, a company is in good health if it receives a rating of B+ or better from Best, a C or above from Weiss, or one of the top three or four grades from Standard & Poor's, Moody's, or Duff & Phelps. Review your company's ratings every six months or so to make sure it has not been downgraded.

2. Check with your state insurance department to find out if there have been any warning signs of impending financial problems.

3. If you have money in a guaranteed investment contract (GIC) in your employer-sponsored retirement plan, ask your employee-benefits office who is the GIC's insurer. Make sure your employer spreads the risk by investing with several different insurers. Diversify your other investments among stocks, money-market funds, and bond funds, to ensure that you do not have too much of your savings tied up in insurance.

If your research indicates that your insurer is headed for intensive care, consult with a financial planner or insurance agent to help you decide whether switching your annuity or policy to another company is worth the surrender charges, new commissions, and taxes you may owe. One alternative to transferring: Borrow against your current policy. That way, you will have already taken out your full cash value if the insurance company goes under. This money does not have to be paid back—any unpaid balance will be subtracted from the proceeds your beneficiaries get when you die. If the company repairs its financial health, you can repay the loan.

☐ Prevention

One way to avoid concern that your insurer will fail, taking your cash value with it, is to buy term life insurance. With term insurance none of your contribution goes to savings. You are buying only payment of a death benefit when you die. Even large insurers seized by state regulators still pay death benefits, although the payout may be delayed briefly.

AILMENT
I was denied insurance.

R̸ Maybe you do not win any Brownie points with insurance companies because you are what they consider a bad risk. Perhaps your job requires dealing with hazardous materials or working in dangerous areas, increasing the chances you will get hurt or sick at work. Or maybe your auto gets no more respect than a bumper car, or your house is a magnet for burglars. If so, many insurance agents will refuse to grant you coverage at any cost. What is your recourse when you want or need insurance and you are between "the rock and a hard place"?

Get another opinion.   Do not blindly accept your insurance agent's assessment. Make sure you really are as risky as the insurance agent thinks. Many health insurers and doctors supply the Medical Information Bureau, a recordkeeping organization, with files on their policyholders and patients. Check the accuracy of your file for free by writing to the bureau at P.O. Box 105, Essex Station, Boston, MA 02112.

Look close to home.   If you are indeed a high-risk insurance candidate, check with your employer first to see whether you can get life, disability, or health insurance coverage at work. Your employer might permit you to purchase supplemental coverage. Or you may be able to buy insurance through a professional association that qualifies for a group insurance discount.

Second best.   The truth is, you can usually get *some* coverage—for a price. There are always some companies that will insure risky people by selling what are called substandard policies. The coverage usually costs more or is less comprehensive than the norm. For example, someone with a dangerous job or a medical problem could pay three times as much for disability insurance as the typical policyholder. To locate a substandard policy, find an insurance agent who specializes in high-risk individuals.

Health insurance.   If you're repeatedly turned down for coverage because of your health, contact your state insurance commissioner. Ask whether the Blue Cross/Blue Shield insurer in your area is required to open enrollment to all applicants at any time during the year.

The insurance office can also tell you whether your state is among the 25 or so that guarantee health coverage for high-risk people through what are called assigned risk pools. About 100,000 people are currently covered by these pools. Premiums in these pools are generally 125% to 150% of the state average charged to healthier people, and can be as much as 300% higher. Policies may cap lifetime benefits at as little as $25,000 or set no ceiling on out-of-pocket expenses, such as co-payments. All of them exact waiting periods, usually at least six months, before covering preexisting conditions. Some states will waive the wait if you pay a surcharge or have been dropped from another plan. To qualify for a high-risk pool, you must be a state resident (although residency requirements vary) and have been turned down by at least one insurer or have a policy whose premiums are higher.

If a divorce cut off the health insurance coverage you received from your ex-spouse, check with your state insurance commissioner. Most states have laws allowing people who lose health insurance through divorce to buy individual policies from their former carriers.

If you are over age 55 and have Medicare, you automatically qualify for group coverage arranged by the American Association of Retired Persons (AARP, 601 E Street NW, Washington, DC 20049). AARP's arrangement to provide coverage is through Prudential (800-523-5800). Coverage is for Medicare supplemental and hospitalization only.

COBRA. If you lose your job or retire, you can usually extend your employer health coverage for another 18 months under the Consolidated Omnibus Budget Reconciliation Act (COBRA). You qualify for COBRA if:

- You lose or leave your job for reasons other than "gross misconduct";

- You lose health benefits because your hours were cut; or

- You retire.

Your employer must have a health plan and employ 20 or more workers for at least half of the calendar year. Federal employees receive COBRA-like protection under "Temporary Continuation of Coverage" rules. You do not qualify if you work for a church or the government of a U.S. territory or the District of Columbia. Also, you cannot continue group coverage if your employer stops offering health insurance altogether.

Your family members can qualify for up to 36 months of COBRA coverage if:

- They are covered under your employee plan at the time you die, become eligible for Medicare, or divorce.

- They have group coverage as part of your retirement package and your employer files for Chapter 11 bankruptcy.

- Your child loses coverage by dropping out of school or growing up.

Once you qualify for COBRA, the system works just like your old employee health plan. But you must pay the entire cost of insurance, plus 2% in administrative fees. The result: COBRA premiums average about $140 a month for single coverage and $360 a month for family coverage.

Your employer must notify you within 14 days of a qualifying event regarding your eligibility for COBRA and the cost. You would be wise to shop around for a cheaper policy during the 60 days you have to decide whether you want it. Then if you find a better deal that has a waiting period for preexisting conditions, you can sign up for the new insurance and start the clock running while you keep your coverage under COBRA.

Once you opt for COBRA, you get another 45 days to send your first payment. That payment must be large enough to cover the previous three months, however. After that, you must make payments by the last day of each month or your coverage will be canceled.

Life insurance.   Relatively few people are turned down by life insurance companies or charged a high-risk premium. Probably fewer than 10% of applicants must pay higher than usual premiums and fewer than 5% get turned down. This includes applicants of all ages, including the older years when people are more likely to have health problems.

If you are denied life insurance, first make sure you need it. If you have a working spouse and no minor children, you have only a minimal need for life insurance. If your family needs the security of insurance, however, look to mail-order life insurance companies to fill the void. Some plans are sold without any medical requirements; you are guaranteed acceptance if you pay the premium. To avoid being swamped by deathbed or other high-risk applicants, the insurers may employ several safeguards:

- The full face value is not paid for deaths occurring during the first two years the policy is in force, and sometimes longer.

- The premium may be set considerably above rates for medically screened plans sold through agents.

- The policy may be offered only during limited enrollment periods.

- Only a modest amount of insurance may be available for purchase.

Mail-order insurance companies set premium rates on the basis of sales costs as well as actuarial considerations. Only 1% to 2% of the people solicited by mail actually buy the insurance. Therefore, the rates have to take into account the costs of mailing to the other 99% or 98% who fail to respond to the solicitation. Association plans may produce a higher response because of the sponsor's endorsement, but the insurer has to figure in fees to brokers and others involved in the deal. The same sort of situation applies to policies marketed on television: TV time is expensive, and the company may be sharing part of the revenue from each order with the TV stations on which it advertises.

Home insurance. Having qualified to buy a home, it seems only right you should be able to insure it. But if you live in one of the many disaster-struck parts of our nation, home insurance can no longer be taken for granted. In Southern California after the Northridge earthquake, for example, many homeowners felt the ground shifting under them again when several major insurers, including State Farm and Allstate, announced no new home insurance policies would be issued and in some cases, existing policies would not be renewed. In the wake of Hurricane Andrew, many Florida homeowners have been forced by their insurers' flight from risk to turn to the newly created Property & Casualty Joint Underwriting Association (JUA). JUA is the insurer of last resort and, by law, costs 25% above what homeowners pay on the ordinary market.

But you could be turned down for coverage or face nonrenewal of your years-old policy for a variety of reasons. You could easily face trouble if you live in an area prone to brush fires, burglaries, or floods. Some companies even reject applicants because of a rocky credit report.

Where should you turn? First, look to the company that already sells you car or life insurance. Then try an independent agent who works with smaller companies that may be more willing to take on new customers (expect to pay more). Shop around. Get quotes from six to eight companies. Ask agents for a premium quote in writing. Your state department of insurance may be able to help you with comparison shopping.

When insurers reject applicants, especially those with low property value or bad credit reports or those who live in high-crime areas, the result is often insurance redlining. If you suspect discrimination—illegally denied coverage on the basis of race or national origin—call your state's insurance commissioner's office, which has information on state-approved insurance rates, claims-paying ability, and consumer complaints. Put your complaint to regulators in writing (see sample letter on page 126) and send a copy to the insurance companies involved.

If you suspect you are being treated differently because of your race or national origin, look up the nearest fair-housing group, which can investigate whether federal civil rights laws are being violated. You can also call

---

SAMPLE LETTER TO STATE INSURANCE REGULATOR

July 14, 1997

State Insurance Commissioner
Nevada State Division of Insurance
1665 Hot Springs Road, Suite 152
Carson City, NV 89710

Dear Sir:

Recently, I was denied homeowner's insurance by United Mutual Insurance. I believe this denial was made on the basis of the neighborhood I live in and was not based on any genuine risk involved in insuring my residence.

I would appreciate an investigation by your office into this seeming discrimination. Please let me know if there is any additional information or documentation I can provide to assist you in your inquiries.

Thank you.

Sincerely,

Robert C. Dwelling

cc: United Mutual Insurance

---

the National Fair Housing Alliance at 202-898-1661, or the U.S. Department of Housing and Urban Development's housing discrimination hot line, 800-669-9777.

Self-insurance.   If all else fails and you are financially able, try self-insurance. This means setting aside enough assets to produce an income equal to the amount of your desired life or other insurance needs. As a guideline, save an amount equal to the insurance premium you would have been making if you had not been turned down for insurance.

☐ Prevention

When buying a health, term life, or disability insurance policy, whether through an agent or a group, get one that guarantees renewal or that renews on a statewide, not individual, basis. That way, as long as you pay your premiums on time, the insurer cannot cancel your coverage or raise your premiums, no matter how often you file for claims.

Telephone numbers of state insurance commissioners. The phone numbers of all the state insurance commissioners' offices are shown below.

Alabama
334-269-3550

Alaska
907-465-2515

Arizona
602-912-8400

Arkansas
501-371-2600

California
800-927-4357
213-897-8921
(Los Angeles)
916-322-3555
(Sacramento)

Colorado
303-894-7499

Connecticut
860-297-3800

Delaware
302-739-4251

**District of
  Columbia**
202-727-7424

Florida
904-922-3100

Georgia
404-656-2056

Hawaii
808-586-2790

Idaho
208-334-2250

Illinois
312-814-2420
(Chicago)
217-782-4515
(Springfield)

Indiana
317-232-2385

Iowa
515-281-5705

Kansas
913-296-7801

Kentucky
502-564-3630

Louisiana
504-342-5900

Maine
207-624-8475

Maryland
410-333-6300

Massachusetts
617-521-7794

Michigan
517-373-9273

Minnesota
612-296-6848

Mississippi
601-359-3569

Missouri
314-340-6830

Montana
406-444-2040

Nebraska
402-471-2201

Nevada
702-486-4009

New Hampshire
603-271-2261

New Jersey
609-292-5363

New Mexico
505-827-4500

New York
518-474-6600
(Albany)
212-602-0429
(New York City)

North Carolina
919-733-7349

North Dakota
701-328-2440

Ohio
614-644-2658

Oklahoma
405-521-2828

Oregon
503-378-4271

Pennsylvania
717-787-5173

Rhode Island
401-277-2246

South Carolina
803-737-6160

South Dakota
605-773-3563

Tennessee
615-741-2241

Texas
512-463-6464

Utah
801-538-3800

Vermont
802-828-3301

Virginia
804-371-9694

Washington
360-753-7300

West Virginia
304-558-3394

Wisconsin
608-266-0102

Wyoming
307-777-7401

■ AUTOMOBILE INSURANCE

AILMENT
My auto insurance premiums are too high.

℞ The auto insurance rates you pay can vary wildly depending on the insurance company, agent, or broker you choose, the types of coverage you request, and the kind of car you drive. That means you have a lot of leeway to lower your insurance costs. Here are a number of steps you can take to reduce your premiums.

Comparison shop.   Prices for the same coverage can differ by hundreds of dollars, so it pays to shop around. Ask your friends, check the Yellow Pages, or call your state insurance department (see telephone numbers on page 127). You can also check consumer guides, insurance agents, or insurance companies. This will give you an idea of price ranges and tell you which companies or agents have the lowest prices. But do not shop price alone.

The insurer you select should offer both fair prices and excellent service. Quality personal service may cost a bit more, but is well worth it when your car is being towed away from a major fender bender. So talk to a number of insurers to get a feel for the quality of their service. Ask them what they would do to lower your costs. Check the financial ratings of the companies, too (see page 119). Then, when you have narrowed the choice down to three insurers, get price quotes.

Are you a loner or do you belong to a group? Although most car insurance is sold to individuals, a few employers, trade associations, labor unions, credit unions, and other groups now offer auto insurance structured like group health plans. If you are eligible for this type of group coverage, you may be able to save up to 40% off the cost of individual policies.

Ask for higher deductibles.   Deductibles are the base amount of money you must put out before the insurance company begins to reimburse you. To reduce your premium costs, take large deductibles on provisions covering damage to your own car—specifically, collision and comprehensive coverage (for fire, theft, or vandalism). Increasing the collision deductible from $100 to $1000 slashes the premium as much as 65%.

Do not cut back on your policy's liability limits, though. By far your severest risk as a car owner is that you will be sued for your last dime by some alleged victim, who claims to have been injured by you or that you wrecked the individual's car, house, or other valuable property. Insurance advisers say your policy's liability limits should be at least $100,000 for one injury, $300,000 for all injuries in an accident, and $50,000 for property damage—in an agent's shorthand: 100/300/50.

Drop some coverage on older cars. If your car is worth less than a thousand dollars, it may not be cost-effective to have collision or comprehensive coverage. Even if you total the car, your insurer will pay no more than its market value and that may not substantially exceed the annual premiums and deductible amounts. Consult used-car price guides or ask an auto dealer or your bank to tell you how much your car is worth.

Avoid duplicate coverage. *Medical payments* coverage (for injuries to people in your car) regardless of liability might overlap your own health care coverage. In that case, a relatively minor $5000 to $10,000 worth of coverage might be enough.

Turn down unnecessary add-ons. The department of motor vehicles in your state can tell you whether you are required by law to buy protection against uninsured motorists—which pays for injuries to you and your passengers caused by hit-and-run, uninsured, or underinsured drivers. You might also reject uninsured motorist protection if your health and collision coverage already covers you or if you live in a strong no-fault state, such as Michigan. If your state requires it, consider $15,000 per injured individual and $30,000 total per accident.

Be skeptical of other add-on policy features such as life insurance, disability pay, or reimbursement for towing charges.

Buy a low-profile car. Before you buy a new or used car, check the insurance cost. Cars that are expensive to repair or favorite targets for thieves have much higher insurance costs. You can obtain and refer to the Highway Loss Data Chart by writing to the Insurance Institute for Highway Safety, 1005 North Glebe Road, Arlington, VA 22201.

Take advantage of low-mileage discounts. Some companies offer discounts to motorists who drive fewer than a certain number of miles a year.

Consider insurance cost when moving. Costs obviously tend to be lowest out in the country and highest in the center of cities, where there is more traffic.

Ask for automatic seat belt or air bag discounts. You may be able to profit from discounts on some types of coverage, if you have automatic seat belts and/or air bags.

Ask about antilock brakes. Some states, including Florida, New Jersey, and New York, require insurers to give discounts for cars equipped with antilock brakes, and some insurers have a nationwide discount in place.

Inquire about other discounts. Discounts can save hundreds of dollars on your auto insurance bill. While cuts for good drivers are now universal, nearly every other type of discount varies company to company.

Some insurers offer discounts for more than one car, no accidents in three years, drivers over 50 years of age, driver training courses, antitheft devices, students with good grades, children away at college without a car, renewing your policy, and others. At least one insurer, Farmers, gives breaks to nonsmokers, for example, while another does not care if you smoke, but will give you a rate cut if you are a scientist. Some companies apply discounts automatically, while others need to be reminded. When you shop around, therefore, you need to ask each insurer what discounts it offers.

☐ Prevention

Getting some discounts requires planning ahead. For example, the biggest discount today is given to good drivers. So it makes more sense than ever to drive carefully, and if you do get a traffic ticket, to attend traffic school, which negates the ticket's impact on your insurance. And if you have more than one moving violation on your driving record, your insurance rates are guaranteed to skyrocket. Besides bestowing rate cuts on good drivers, insurers now apply huge surcharges to bad drivers.

Think about insurance, too, when buying a car. Check with your insurer before buying to find out whether that killer sports car is loaded with an equally murderous premium rate. Ask, too, what options, such as antilock brakes, will bring a discount.

■ Homeowner's Insurance

AILMENT
My homeowner's insurance costs too much.

Ҏ Your house can just as easily be overinsured as underinsured. How much home insurance is too much? You need enough insurance to let you rebuild and refurnish your home in case of a major fire or other disaster. To do that, you need to insure for at least 80% of the *replacement* value of your house (i.e., your property, *minus* the value of the land and the foundation). If you do not insure your house for at least 80% of its full replacement value, you will not receive full reimbursement for the costs of repairs or rebuilding.

With help from your insurance agent or a professional appraiser, determine whether your policy covers 80% of the cost of building a house like yours today.

An agent may suggest that you cover your house for 100% of its replacement value. Be skeptical. Total losses are rare, and a $100,000 policy may cost about 20% more than an $80,000 policy, even though the insurer is taking little additional risk.

You will want to insure your belongings against disaster and theft, too. Most policies cover the contents of the house for 50% to 75% of the amount the house is insured for. So if your house is insured for $100,000, the contents are insured for $50,000 to $75,000. Spend a bit extra, though, to insure the replacement value of your possessions. The standard homeowner's policy covers the contents' actual cash value. That means replacement cost minus depreciation: Those three-year-old Armani suits that cost you $1000 apiece might be valued at less than a quarter of their cost by an insurance adjuster. Opt for a replacement cost endorsement. It will boost your premium by 10% to 15%—about $40 on a $100,000 policy—but your insurance will pay the entire cost of repair or replacement.

In addition, you need personal liability coverage of at least $100,000. This protects you up to that amount from a judgment for damages if someone is hurt on your property or you or your family members damage someone else's property. You can raise the coverage to $300,000 for only a few dollars more. If you have a lot of assets to protect, get an inexpensive umbrella liability policy for broader coverage, including such things as libel and slander. With an umbrella liability policy, you can boost coverage to $1 million for an additional $130 to $150 a year.

Get your insurance agent to help you estimate the amount of insurance you need. A real estate agent or an appraiser can provide a second, independent opinion.

Once you know the replacement value and depth of coverage you want, you must choose from among several types of policies. Homeowner's insurance generally comes in three grades. The most basic, HO-1, is naturally the cheapest; HO-3 is the most comprehensive and expensive. (Other HO policies cover condominium and co-op owners and renters.) The HO-3 is the standard, one-size-fits-all homeowner's policy and typically covers your home for risks other than floods, wars, earthquakes, and a few other specifically excluded catastrophes.

When you go beyond the basic coverage of the HO-3 policy and its add-ons, you enter the world of the package deal. You can pick and choose to some extent, but often you cannot choose one thing without taking another, whether you want it or not.

In sizing up competing policies, decide which extras you really want, and ask whether you could save money by simply adding them to the basic plan. That may not always be the case. If you really want most of the extras, a package deal is often your best buy.

Once you settle on a policy, you can whittle down the cost by agreeing to absorb small financial losses yourself. Taking a $500 deductible instead of $100 can trim 20% to 25% off your homeowner's premium; with a $1000 deductible, savings run as high as 35%.

Discounts for smoke detectors, dead bolt locks, fire extinguishers, and other devices that make your home safer will also pare your premium costs under different policies. Credits may range from 2% for having a smoke detector to 10% for having your car insurance with the same company. Premiums range widely, so again, it pays to shop around.

AILMENT

I work out of my home, and my homeowner's policy does not reimburse me for losses resulting from the business use of my property.

℞ It is important to review your coverage with an insurance agent, if you work from a home office or are setting up one. You may be able to buy a rider to extend your basic homeowner's or apartment-dweller's insurance to cover certain business risks, including liability coverage for anyone (such as a client or delivery person) who is injured on a business call to your home.

AILMENT

I telecommute and my employer provides all my office equipment. Do I need business insurance?

℞ Probably not. If you do not regularly meet customers at home or have business documents delivered your exposure to liability is minimal. In addition, your office equipment is probably covered under your company's business policy. However, you should ask your employer, to make sure you would not be responsible for replacing the equipment if it is stolen or destroyed. If the equipment you use at home is not covered, ask your employer to add it to the company's policy. Your own homeowner's insurance will not cover any loss, because the equipment belongs to your employer, not you.

■ DISABILITY INSURANCE

AILMENT

I want adequate disability insurance at the lowest cost.

℞ The biggest financial catastrophe of all is a serious long-term disability. The disability coverage you do have is probably not deep enough. Workers' compensation coverage is often limited to short-term, work-related accidents. If you're in a car accident while on vacation, you will not be covered. In fact, most accidents and illnesses are not job-related, and workers' compensation usually limits benefits and how long you can receive them.

Social Security disability benefits will not do the trick, either. To collect, you must be so severely ill or disabled that you cannot do any kind of work. Furthermore, the payments may not be enough to live on comfortably.

You may have employer-paid disability insurance, but many of those plans are also insufficient and pay far less than your usual income, halting benefits after a few months or carrying so many restrictions that it is hard to qualify.

The result: You may need disability coverage that either stands on its own or supplements your group plan at work.

How much coverage?   You do not want to pay for more coverage than you need. How much of your income should you insure for? If you are paying for the policy yourself, aim to replace 60% to 70% of your current before-tax earnings for as long as you are off work. Only one in five workers gets this much coverage as a fringe benefit. You do not need to replace 100% of your earnings because the benefits you receive from a policy you pay for yourself are tax-exempt. If your combined federal and state tax brackets total 35%, a policy that pays 65% of wages tax-free replaces your after-tax salary. (Actually, you could come out ahead because disability insurance payments also escape Social Security tax.)

To further cut the cost, carefully calculate the least amount of income you would need to make your mortgage payments and to buy groceries and other necessities. Then insure yourself for just enough to scrape by. If your spouse works or you have other sources of income, you may not need much, if any, disability insurance.

As you tally up all of the income you could count on if your paychecks stopped, do not overlook the following:

■ *Paid sick leave.* How much have you accumulated and how much more will you add to it in the future?

■ *Company insurance.* If your employer provides disability coverage, nail down how much income you would receive and for how long. Almost all employers in Hawaii, New Jersey, New York, Rhode Island, and Puerto Rico pay benefits for up to 26 weeks of nonoccupational disability; in California, benefits can run for up to 52 weeks. Elsewhere, nearly 90% of medium-size and large firms offer some form of salary continuation for incapacitated workers, but benefits are often limited or short-lived. And employer-paid benefits are taxable, unlike benefits from a policy you pay for.

■ *Social Security.* You must meet strict eligibility requirements to collect benefits. For example, you cannot collect Social Security disability if you will be sidelined for less than a year, or if you can do certain kinds of work, even if they are not your normal occupation. And even if you do qualify, there is a five-month waiting period before you can collect benefits. For details, get a copy of the pamphlet *Disability* from any Social Security office.

The amount of benefits you would receive depends on your age, earnings before being disabled, and eligibility of family members.

■ *Other government programs.* These include disability benefits paid by the Veterans Administration, armed forces, civil service, state vocational rehabilitation programs, Medicaid, and others.

■ *Workers' compensation.* Under state programs, benefits are paid for work-related injuries and occupational diseases. Although the amount varies by state, benefits usually replace two-thirds of your income and are tax-free. Most workers are covered.

■ *Savings and investments.* Calculate how long your assets would last if you had to dip into them.

■ *Retirement plans.* Do you have an individual retirement account? The normal 10% penalty for early withdrawals is waived if you cannot perform "any substantial gainful activity" because of a condition that is expected to last continuously for at least 12 months or that may result in death. If you have a company pension plan, find out whether it provides any income for disability.

The difference between what you would need and what you can count on is the gap that disability insurance must fill.

Keeping costs down. Disability insurance premiums can vary widely according to your age, occupation, waiting and benefit period, and whether your coverage is group or individual.

The older you are, the higher your premium. Premiums also are higher if you work in a high-risk occupation, or if you have an existing medical problem, work part-time, are self-employed, or unemployed. Premiums also range widely among companies. Talk to different agents, and shop around.

The best way to keep adequate disability insurance within financial reach is to select the most economical mix of features:

■ *Defining disability.* A policy insuring your ability to work at your normal occupation may cost more than one covering you only if you cannot work at any job at all. Many professionals consider own-occupation coverage an essential feature, but its usefulness depends on your field. Some policies will cover your own occupation for two or three years, before changing to cover any occupation.

■ *Length of coverage.* The benefit period—the time during which benefits will be paid—can run from one year to life. The shorter the period, the cheaper the policy. The best bet is coverage that will carry you all the way to the age of 65, when Social Security, Medicare, and company retirement benefits can take over. You can save a lot of premiums by settling for shorter-term coverage, up to five years, for instance, but this may not be prudent.

■ *Renewing the policy.* Guaranteed-renewable policies cannot be canceled, and your premiums cannot be raised unless they go up for all policies in that class. With noncancelable policies, the company guarantees fixed benefits, at a fixed premium. Opt for a policy that is noncancelable to age 65.

■ *Elimination period.* Long-term policies require waiting, or elimination, periods of 30 to 365 days or more and do not pay until 30 days after that. The longer the waiting period, the lower the premiums. If you have large savings, employee benefits, or other resources, you can save by extending the elimination period. A 90-day wait is typically the best compromise for most workers; that is about how long sick leave and other resources can be expected to last. You will save even more if you can afford to go to 180 days or longer.

Features to skip. Disability policies can come with a long list of riders. But most of them simply are not worth the cost. Here are some of the most common ones to turn down:

■ *Cost-of-living adjustment (COLA).* You can add a provision to make sure your benefit keeps up with inflation. It sounds appealing, but this option can add 15% or more to the premium. With a low rate of inflation expected for several years, it seems safe to forgo the option now, reserving the right to add it later.

■ *Additional coverage clause.* This would enable you to purchase additional coverage without a medical exam, at guaranteed standard rates, if your income goes up.

■ *Waiver of premium.* With this, you would not have to pay premiums while you are disabled. If you are worried about that, find out whether it would be cheaper to increase the disability benefits by the amount of the premium.

■ *Recurrent disability clause.* If you recover from a disability, but are disabled again from the same cause within six months of returning to work, there will be no elimination period—benefits would start again immediately.

Strategies for saving. If you are young, buy *rising-premium policies*, which start out low and increase each year as your chances of becoming disabled increase. Level-premium policies have fixed premiums each year, but you do not get a cash payout when you give up the policy. Buying rising-premium policies makes sense because most people end up changing policies anyway. Rising-premium policies (also called step-rate policies) can be converted to level-premium if you choose without reapplying. Rising-premium policies can be as much as 75% cheaper than level-premium for young people; but you usually cannot buy them after age 45 or 50.

However, if you plan to hold onto a policy for a long period, say 30 years or more, it would probably be more economical to buy level-rate insurance or to switch to it as soon as you can afford to.

Other cost-effective strategies:

■ *Check out a low-load policy.* Low-load products are sold directly to the customer or through a marketer for a flat fee, eliminating agent commissions. Any low-load should save you 15% to 20%.

■ *Shop around.* Because policies from different companies vary so much in cost, coverage, and features, you should compare at least a dozen. If you know a competent agent, ask for advice. When you talk to agents or to companies directly, ask whether they offer any special discounts, other than the reduced rate for nonsmokers.

If you are a woman, look for a policy that charges the same rate for both sexes, since policies that take gender into account charge women more. Similarly, companies that rate premiums according to area would give you a better deal if you live in the Southeast or Midwest, where premiums are low, than if you are in California or Florida.

Some companies charge less for paying annually instead of monthly.

■ *Insure early.* The longer you wait to buy a policy, the more expensive it will be. Insurance companies increase premiums about 4% a year until about age 50, when premiums can jump 7% to 10%. So it pays to buy young. If you purchase a policy at age 35, for example, when premiums are less expensive, you can lock in that lower price.

Where to buy. First, find out how much, if any, group coverage you have through your employer. If you do not think your company's coverage is adequate, you may be able to save money by purchasing supplemental coverage through your company plan. The cost is probably 50% less than buying it on the outside. If your employer does not offer supplemental coverage, a professional association may. You might also try for coverage through your company retirement plan or a disability coverage option on your health or life insurance plan.

One drawback to employer group policies: You cannot take them with you if you leave your company. As a partial safeguard, or just as a supplement to a group policy, consider an individual disability policy. While far more expensive than group coverage, individual policies can pay up to $25,000 a month. And they have more liberal terms. Most cannot be canceled as long as you pay your premiums, regardless of your health.

A policy you buy on your own may also have a partial, or "residual," disability provision built in or available at extra cost. If you return to work partially disabled and cannot work every day, or have to take a lower-paying job, the policy will fund the shortfall, usually if your drop in income is 20% or more. That can be important for small business owners, who cannot go hunting for new business. One snag: You must qualify for this coverage, and if you have a preexisting condition, you may run into problems.

☐ Resources

For more information, write the Health Insurance Association of America, P.O. Box 41455, Washington, DC 20018, for a free booklet, *The Consumer's Guide to Disability Insurance*.

AILMENT

I am self-employed and need disability insurance.

R You can have a tough time buying disability insurance when you work for yourself, especially if you run your business out of your home. Why? Insurance companies are wary of issuing home workers disability insurance, because it is so hard to tell if you are actually disabled. With employees who leave the house at eight each morning to go to the office, disability is much more easily established.

But some self-employed individuals with long work records who spend at least a part of their time meeting with customers outside their homes can buy insurance in the private market. Doctors, dentists, and salespersons who regularly meet with customers can usually get coverage.

In addition, some trade groups catering to the growing ranks of independent contractors and consultants have begun to offer insurance products, too. The National Association for the Self-Employed, for example, offers both disability and health insurance to members. The rates vary based on the amount of coverage and the type of business. To apply, you must be a member of the group. The association's membership fee is $72 a year.

A few states, including California, also have disability insurance pools. Self-employed individuals can buy in by paying a premium to the state.

If you are a new business owner, however, you may not be able to find an adequate safety net. The reason is that disability insurance benefits are based on the amount of your earnings. When you are starting a new business, profits can fluctuate wildly in the first several years. In most cases, insurers will not promise a fixed benefit, unless you have a record of steady earnings for at least three years.

The bottom line: You may have to create your own safety net during the early years of your business. That means saving a substantial amount of money before you get started, relying on relatives, or securing a personal line of credit that can be tapped if you are unable to work for a long period.

AILMENT

I want to protect my business, which has high overhead expenses, in case of disability.

℞ You probably need more than one disability policy: one to cover your own lost income and a second to cover overhead expenses so that your company can meet the payroll, if you are out of commission. Overhead insurance pays all the costs of keeping a business going if the top or other key person is out for an extended period. Make sure the policy you choose pays benefits long enough for you to find and train a replacement or until the business can be sold if necessary. If you have partners, you may also want buyout insurance, which will give other owners enough cash to buy the business. And there is key-person insurance to protect against loss of income if an essential employee cannot work.

If you are a professional who bills by the hour, you might need "residual" disability benefits. These will make up for part of your lost earnings if from the beginning your disability lets you do some of your work, but not all. Similarly, if you are self-employed, you can buy "recovery" benefits, which supplement your income after you are back on the job, but before your earnings are returned to their former level.

■ LIFE INSURANCE

AILMENT

I need to cut the cost of life insurance.

℞ Most people need more life insurance than they have and can pay less than they do now to get it. The first question, of course, is whether you need life insurance at all. The person who needs the most life insurance is young, with few assets, earning a salary that other people depend on. As your children grow, get an education, and leave home, and as your assets grow, you can cut back on your coverage. You do not have to drop your policies. Just ask your insurance company what the premium would be for less coverage—$150,000 instead of $200,000—and start paying for *that*.

Once your estate is large enough for your spouse to retire on, you may not need any life insurance at all. What your spouse would need will be about two-thirds of what *both* of you would need to retire on. Also ask yourself if you can afford to retire. If so, you might not need the income re-placement that life insurance provides.

Do you need insurance for other purposes. Maybe your assets are illiq-uid: They might include a business or lots of real estate that you would not want to be sold after your death just to pay estate and inheritance taxes. One solution is more life insurance.

Amount of coverage needed. If you need insurance, the next question is, How much? The amount will depend on your age, financial resources, family status, debts, and the number and ages of your dependents. Those with no dependents may not need life insurance, while those with large families could need a lot. The National Insurance Consumer Organization (NICO), a consumer advocacy group, suggests this rough rule: In a one-income family with two children, the working parent should carry policies large enough to replace five times that individual's present annual salary. Add a year's salary for each additional child. Then tack on enough to cover emergencies and large upcoming expenses, such as a lump-sum balloon mortgage payment. Two-earner couples should take both salaries into ac-count, and each should have appropriate life insurance policies.

Say your gross pay is $60,000 and your employee benefits include a $50,000 term life policy. In addition, you have a $40,000 second-mortgage final payment due in four years, and you estimate you will need $75,000 for your kids' college costs. The suggested death benefit is $375,000: $300,000 (five times $60,000 wages), plus $75,000 for college, $40,000 for the balloon-mortgage payment, and $10,000 for emergencies, but minus the $50,000 of insurance from your employer.

A more exact way to compute the amount would be to figure how much money your dependents will need for at least 10 years and to buy enough coverage to meet those needs. A financial planner can help you with this calculation. But be wary of commission-based planners. Some are insurance agents who stand to profit highly from selling you a lot of life in-surance.

If you want to go it alone, or at least get started on the math before see-ing a planner, here are some things to consider:

■ *Your budget.* How much do you earn and how much do you spend each year? Spending would probably be a little more modest if one spouse dies, but not much. If you regularly use credit to spend more than you make, use the amount you spend rather than your income in your calcula-tions.

■ *Age.* How old and independent are you and your spouse? If one of you died, could the surviving spouse handle most of the current monthly payments on that person's wages alone?

■ *Your wages.* A one-earner couple must consider how much insurance would be required to replace the income earner's wages and provide for the family, possibly for the nonworking spouse's lifetime.

If the reason one spouse is not working is to take care of young children, figure how long that spouse will need to stay at home before the children are in school or more self-sufficient. Then consider how much this spouse is likely to earn when working and whether extra income will be needed to keep up a certain standard of living. Could the surviving spouse handle the cost of day care and housekeeping, for example, on wages alone?

Two-income couples should factor day care expenses into the family budget, and estimate whether there would be enough to cover it if one wage earner died.

■ *Your spouse.* If you died, would your spouse remarry—and have another income coming in? If you do not want your spouse to feel forced to work, or pressured to remarry, opt for lots of insurance.

■ *Children.* How many do you have and how old are they? Generally speaking, the younger the children, the greater your immediate insurance needs. Your life insurance needs will probably diminish as they get older.

■ *Goals.* What financial goals would you have if one of you were to die? Would you remain in the same house even if on a slightly lower budget? Or would you want an identical standard of living? Do you want your children to work their way through public colleges, or attend expensive private schools with the option of not working?

■ *Other sources of income.* Add in how much the surviving spouse would get annually from Social Security, company pensions, and any company-paid life insurance before figuring how much insurance to buy. (You can get an estimate of survivor's Social Security benefits by completing a form SSA-7004 and sending it to the Social Security Administration.)

After looking at all these variables, consider whether your survivor's income will fall short of expenses for each year considered. The shortfall is the life insurance you need. Remember to allow for inflation by increasing the needed amount by a small percentage—say, 4%—each year. Also make sure you leave yourself some latitude for onetime and unexpected costs, including medical and burial expenses.

Do you want your survivors to live off only the income produced by the amount you leave them or invade the principal? What sum—before taxes—would provide a sufficient return (at 7% to 9% a year)? If you plan for your spouse to invade principal, figure on your spouse living 150% of the normal life expectancy.

The best kind. In addition to the amount of life insurance you need, another vexing question is: What kind? Life insurance comes in two basic formats: term and cash-value. With *term* insurance, your annual premium buys only a death benefit. *Cash-value* insurance, such as whole-, universal-, or variable-life, combines a death benefit with a savings or investing plan, and is commonly used to ensure a sizable death benefit for your heirs, to pay estate taxes, or to save for a long-range goal, such as college or retirement.

Term premiums are structured in two main ways. Annual (yearly) renewable term (ART or YRT) policies increase in cost each year; guaranteed-level-premium policies lock in a rate for a set period—say, 5 or 20 years. So an ART premium for a 45-year-old might go from $260 to $1300 a year over 10 years, while a level premium stays at $512. Long-term, level-premium policies are generally less expensive than ART policies.

Term insurance comes with a lower price tag than whole-life. If your calculations indicate you need $250,000 or more of protection, annual renewable term insurance can make the cost manageable. Premiums will rise each year, but as your children grow up, you probably will need less insurance. For a man aged 35, a $250,000 policy from Metropolitan Life costs about $282 the first year; for a woman that age, $267. Compare that with whole-life. The whole-life premium never goes up, but at age 35, $250,000 of whole-life protection from Metropolitan costs a man $3352 and a woman $2925. Why the price difference? Only a part of the whole-life premium you pay goes to the death benefit. A large chunk also goes into a tax-deferred investment fund.

If you buy term insurance, invest your cost savings. If you worry that you will buy term and *spend* the difference or that your investments will fizzle, consider cash-value insurance instead. Although it is more costly, cash-value life at least assures that your family will have enough if you die.

Do not let your insurance agent try to discourage you from buying term insurance. Many agents have an unsurprising motive—commissions. Given the same face amount, the agents will make 5 to 10 times as much selling whole-life or universal-life as opposed to term.

If you decide on a cash-value policy, universal-life is a big improvement over traditional whole-life: The returns are "interest-sensitive" (closer to current rates), sales commissions are lower, and you can adjust your premium payments. (Although some whole-life policies are interest-sensitive, premium payments are not nearly as flexible.)

Variable-life policies can be superb investments if you want to invest in mutual funds and have confidence in the stock market. But if you want *guaranteed* life insurance, buy term or fixed universal.

Joint policies for two-earner couples. "First-to-die" coverage may be a less costly option than buying separate policies each naming the other spouse as beneficiary. One policy covers both; if either dies, the other collects.

The idea works best when each spouse's income is equally vital to maintain the family's lifestyle. First-to-die insurance generally saves 10% to 25% of the cost of separate policies, because premiums are based on a hypothetical "joint equal age."

A typical case: One insurer charges a 55-year-old husband nearly $18,000 a year for his own $1-million whole-life contract. A similar policy for his wife, also 55, costs roughly $11,000. But one first-to-die policy runs about $24,000, a 17% savings. Another insurer will sell two 35-year-olds a $200,000 policy for $255 monthly, versus $341 for separate policies.

Joint coverage is not for everyone. An older husband might prefer his own whole-life policy, while his younger spouse buys low-cost term coverage. But you can find plans to suit different needs. For example, Nationwide sells "joint decreasing term" coverage that lets the surviving spouse pay off any remaining mortgage balance.

First-to-die policies also enable the survivor to do some estate planning (see Chapter 10).

Other considerations. Ask about discounts. Discounts for so-called preferred risks can save you a bundle. Nonsmokers frequently pay 10% to 40% less than smokers, according to the American Council on Life Insurance. If you are physically fit and a nonsmoker from a family free of chronic diseases, ask about discounts that run 15% to 20%. Women have longer life expectancies than men, and thus pay premiums that usually are 5% to 35% lower.

Be sure your policy is renewable regardless of changes in your health. But a guaranteed insurability rider that lets you buy more coverage at specified times of your life without a physical may not be a good buy. Most such riders cancel the guarantee if you skip one increase.

You also may want to pass on an accidental death benefit that doubles your coverage if you are killed in an accident. Accidental deaths do not increase your insurance needs, and the gamble rarely pays off. Only 3% of all deaths occur in accidents.

If your insurance company reserves the right to raise rates under certain circumstances, be sure you know in advance the maximum rate you can be charged.

Reexamine your insurance coverage whenever there is a major change in your economic status—a higher-paying job, a new home purchase, the birth of a child, retirement, or divorce.

A life insurance policy is a legal document. Before signing, read every word of the contract, and if necessary ask your agent for a point-by-point explanation of the language.

After purchasing new life insurance, you usually have a 10-day "free look" period in which to change your mind. If you do so, the company will return your premium without penalty.

Which insurer?   Once you zero in on how much and what kind of insurance you need, it is time to go comparison shopping. You can save hundreds or thousands of dollars over the years by insuring with a low-cost company, but first make sure it is financially secure. A cut-rate policy is no bargain, if the company behind it is shaky. So avoid any insurer with a rating of less than B+ from A. M. Best (see discussion of insurance ratings on page 121).

Which policy makes the final cut will depend on cost, a task that sounds simpler than it is. You must sift through a host of variables: how much the premiums rise in a term policy, how fast the cash value will grow in whole-life, what—if any—dividends the company will pay, and how much of your premium will be swallowed up by commissions and expenses. Given the endless permutations, you cannot simply compare premiums or accept agents' price illustrations at face value. Most companies write a dozen or more basic policies, with various riders that may be added, to boot. The number of combinations is mind-boggling.

NICO will estimate for you the rate of return on a whole-life policy by comparing it to an annual renewable term policy that provides the same death benefit. You have to furnish a printout from your insurance agent, illustrating the costs of the policy year by year. NICO's fee for an estimate is $40 for one policy and $30 for each additional one that you send in the same envelope.

To help you comparison shop, NICO has adopted two cost indexes. Most states require insurance agents to calculate these indexes for you. The indexes tell you which of two policies is cheaper, but the shortcoming is that they do not help you determine whether both are overpriced. You need a yardstick for judging if a policy provides you the insurance you need at a competitive price. NICO recommends getting premiums and cost indexes for the size policy you need and for a person your age from USAA Life Insurance Company (9800 Frederickburg, San Antonio, TX 78288; 800-531-8000). Use those figures for comparison. You can also get a list of the maximum rates NICO recommends for annual renewable term policies by writing for the booklet *Taking the Bite out of Insurance* (P.O. Box 15492, Alexandria, VA 20239).

The interest-adjusted net payment cost index measures the present value of all the premiums you will pay for the next 10 or 20 years, assuming you could earn interest on the money. The index number represents the cost of insurance for each $1000 of death benefit. The lower the number, the cheaper the policy. This index can be used to compare either term or whole-life policies. The second index—the surrender cost index—measures the present cost of cash-value policies if you canceled them and took your cash in 10 or 20 years.

In using the indexes, remember the following:

1. The indexes work only for similar policies. You cannot compare term and whole-life policies, for example, but you can weigh policies that pay dividends against those that do not.

2. A low index for a policy of a given amount issued to a person of a given age does not necessarily mean the same policy is a good buy in other amounts or for other ages. Some companies give preferential rates for, say, 45-year-olds or for purchasers of larger coverage.

3. The more variables you add, such as the fluctuating premium of universal-life policies, the less exact the two indexes become.

4. Small differences in index numbers may be offset by other policy features or better service from the company or agent.

5. Do not base your decision solely on a low index number. Make sure the policy meets your needs, you can afford the premiums, and you understand its features.

6. Apply the cost index only to new policies. Do not use it to determine whether your current policy should be replaced by a new one.

One way to make price checking easier is to pay someone to do it for you. A firm called Insurance Information Inc. (800-472-5800) will send you the names, prices, and A. M. Best ratings of the five cheapest term policies it can find for a person of your age, sex, place of residence, and smoking habits. Be sure to specify the size of the policy you want. The fee is $50. A good insurance agent can also give you this type of information (see page 118 for a discussion on finding a good agent).

☐ Resources

You can get helpful work sheets by writing for a copy of "A Consumer's Guide to Life Insurance" from the American Council of Life Insurance, Dept. C346, 1001 Pennsylvania Avenue NW, Washington, DC 20004.

AILMENT
My cash-value policy does not provide enough coverage.

R Your most economical move is to keep the policy and supplement it with term insurance that gives you the additional coverage you need. But first, double-check any assumptions you may be making about your cash-value policy.

Don't automatically accept an agent's word that your coverage is inadequate. When pushing you to replace your insurance, some agents assume that a cash-value policy earns only the minimum guaranteed rate (usually around 4%). That assumption can significantly understate the value of a permanent policy held long-term. In fact, about 90% of the time, replacement is not justified.

If you do decide to bail out and buy a new policy, timing is important. The surrender charges on some universal-life policies take a huge drop between the ninth and tenth years. Similarly, a lot of universal-life policies have surrender charges that drop from 100% to zero in years 5 through 10, producing high marginal rates of return in those years. Think twice about switching your policy just when it finally begins to pay off.

NICO will analyze the rate of return you would have to earn if you invested the difference in premiums in order to beat the rate on an existing or proposed policy (P.O. Box 15492, Alexandria, VA 20239).

Consider, too, whether you will be eligible for new coverage. "Evidence of insurability" probably will be required. Because of adverse changes in your health, occupation, or finances, you may now be "uninsurable" or only eligible for coverage at a higher premium rate. Discuss your present insurability with your insurance agent before you walk away from your old policy.

AILMENT

My life insurance agent suggested I trade in my low-cost term insurance policy for cash-value coverage with premiums that cost five times as much.

R The decision to switch depends mainly on your age. While term insurance is the best buy for young people, the premiums on annual renewable term policies increase as you grow older. By the time you reach age 50, cash-value insurance, such as whole-life, universal-life, and variable-life, can cost you less over the rest of your lifetime. With a cash-value policy, your annual premium will not go up as long as you make payments. Moreover, part of the premium is invested in a tax-deferred account you can borrow against; term policies have no such cash buildup.

One incentive for conversion: You will not have to pass a medical exam as you typically would if you were buying another company's cash-value policy. In that case, if you had a serious illness, such as cancer or diabetes, you might be refused coverage.

No matter what your age or health, do not convert unless you are sure you will keep the new policy for at least 10 years. You need that much time for the cash-value account, which might yield about 8.5% a year, to exceed the policy's front-end expenses.

Conversion does not involve any additional charges, and many insurers offer financial incentives to soften the impact of the new, higher premiums. For example, you might get 52% off the new policy's minimum premium in the first year, or you might be allowed to add the premium savings to the policy's cash value.

Of course, there are big payoffs for your insurer and agent if you convert. Insurers prefer cash-value policies to term because they receive more cash flow. Agents' commissions, usually half of the first-year premiums, are often four or five times higher on cash-value policies than on term. So you can expect a hard sell from your agent. Ask yourself: Do I really need this type of insurance and would I buy this policy anyway?

AILMENT

An insurance salesperson has suggested that I exchange my current cash-value policy/annuity for a "better" one.

℞ Because some newer policies are potentially more lucrative for you than older ones, it is natural to wonder whether you should make a change, even if you are not approached by a salesperson. But remember, any agent has a financial interest in moving you to a new policy, whether it is in your best interest or not.

Deciding whether to make a switch boils down to analyzing the costs and the benefits. Before you leap, here are guidelines and pitfalls to watch for:

■ Is there a surrender charge or are there other costs if you give up the old policy? These charges usually apply for the first five to seven years of a policy or annuity, but can remain in effect for as long as 15 years. If you cancel the policy early, a substantial surrender charge will be deducted from your cash value to reimburse the insurer for agent's commission, the underwriting costs, medical examination, and other administrative expenses in setting up the policy. You could forfeit most or all of your investment.

This penalty gradually declines to zero after quite a few years. So a 20-year-old policy, for example, can almost always be surrendered for the full policy value, free of any charges. But surrendering a $400,000 policy bought just three or four years earlier incurs a penalty that can amount to $2000 or more.

Even while surrender charges are in effect, however, you may be able to cash in or roll over 10% of the present value of an annuity each year without paying a fee.

■ If you move to a new company, your annual cash buildup and even the money you moved from your old company will be subject to a surrender charge for quite a few years, if you later decide to give up the *new* policy.

■ What will the new insurance cost? On many life policies, part of your premium buys insurance for death benefits, and the rest is used to build up a cash value. The cost of that death benefit is greatly affected by your age and health. If it has been some time since you bought the first policy, your new premiums may be considerably higher, if you are still insurable.

■ If you die within two years of taking out a new policy, the insurer can investigate to see whether you misrepresented medical information when applying. Your beneficiaries could wind up with nothing.

■ If the cash accumulation projected by the salesperson seems higher than what your old policy is earning, ask yourself whether it is realistic or just so much smoke. Anybody can "project" anything. The number to focus on is the amount that is guaranteed under the worst-case scenario.

The worst-case scenario is usually based on about a 4% compounded return. But the much higher "projection"—allegedly based on current performance—is the one emphasized to convince you to switch. You may even be promised an extra .5% or 1% of yield sometime in the future. Discount such airy suggestions; current performance is all you can base your decision on. And keep in mind that even the high current rate that is so tempting may be due to the company's investing clients' money in volatile, high-risk securities.

Ask the agent to show you a sheet from the *A. M. Best Insurance Report (Life & Health)* giving facts about the company. Examine how its funds are invested, compared to those of your present company.

■ Check the loan provisions in the new policy against those in your present policy. Can you borrow cheaply on the policy if you have a financial emergency or a hot stock tip? Make sure the new policy's loan terms are clearly explained to you and compare them to your present policy's loan terms.

■ Will you owe taxes on the cash gains your old policy has made over the years? Gains built up within a tax-deferred annuity that is cashed before you reach age 59½ are considered income on which you must pay taxes and are subject to a 10% penalty. You can continue deferring taxes by rolling the annuity into a policy from another insurer—a tactic known as a 1035 rollover. The easiest way to do that is to have the new insurer notify the old insurer of the cancellation and request a transfer of funds. Even then, you may have taxable income if you had a loan against the policy and the loan is paid off by the exchange.

Benefits of an exchange.   In some cases, you can earn a higher rate of interest with a new insurer. That, over time, might turn out to be a good deal even after all the expenses of the exchange are considered.

If you are thinking about switching out of concern for the safety of your policy, it is harder to weigh the financial benefits. Why? When you buy insurance, you are buying a long-term contract. The insurer's long-term health is germane to the long-term viability of your investment. That means you must not only determine how healthy an insurer is today, but also try to predict how healthy it will be 10 years from now. Even experts have a tough time doing that.

Regardless of cost, consider canceling a policy and moving to another company if your current insurer is rated B– or lower by Best's or if the rating has been lowered twice since you bought the policy, especially if your state has no guarantee fund or your policy represents a sizable fraction of your net worth—say, 25% or more.

The bottom line: An exchange might make sense, but you need to sit down with pad and pencil and run through the numbers before you decide. Often, the best answer is to stay put.

AILMENT

I do not know if my cash-value whole-life (or universal-life) insurance policy is doing as well as the salesman predicted or "illustrated."

℞ To find out exactly where you stand, ask your agent to reillustrate your policy, based on the latest actual dividends or interest. Also request a table showing what would happen to your earnings if yields fall; if you are in a whole-life policy and your dividend is based on the company earning 9%, ask the agent to illustrate yields of 6%, 7%, and 8%.

These projections are worthwhile if you are saving for something specific. For example, if you are counting on $300,000 in 20 years, you need to know, for planning purposes, if you may reach only $250,000. That way, you can redirect your other investment and spending decisions.

When you get a revised illustration of your policy based on current rates, things may still look sunny. But there can be a lag of months or years before insurance companies pass along reduced earnings. There are all sorts of ways for an insurer to cut payouts, too, while keeping interest rates or dividends high for marketing purposes. Watch out for these:

- Higher monthly charges for expenses or mortality (the cost of death) protection on a universal-life policy. That means a smaller portion of your payments filters through to build cash value.

- Cutting dividends or interest paid on assets, if you borrow against the policy.

- Basing illustrations on a rate paid only as a bonus if you hold onto the policy for 10 or 20 years. But some companies can pay the bonus only if enough other policyholders have quit and paid surrender charges into the pot.

And what if the newest illustration clearly shows you have a loser—say, you are earning little more than the low guaranteed rate, or the company's earnings are falling like a rock, or the company has been downgraded to less than a good rating. In that case, you may want to consider moving to a new insurer. The drawbacks are new commissions, reopening your health status, and a lack of certainty. The second company may be doing well now, but you have no guarantee it will continue to do so.

What about cashing in your policy, and searching for a better investment? One catch is that if you pull the plug on insurance, you will be taxed on the amount by which your cash value exceeds the premiums you have paid. Another is that bailing out means forfeiting your stake in the cash-value contract—the commissions you have already paid—and the benefit of paying a level premium in later years. You also face the prospect of reinvesting the money while yields are low.

If you decide to switch to term insurance and try to beat a good whole-life policy by investing the difference, you will need to earn double-digit returns on your investments to match the tax-deferred returns inside the policy. If double-digit investment returns become easily attainable again, insurance companies will make the same moves and dividends will recover. So, unless your insurance company has become a disaster, your best bet is to ride out disappointing times.

☐ Prevention

You can dodge disappointing yields by choosing your insurance product wisely. The key is not to place too much faith in the agent's answers to your questions about the best insurance investment. Only about half the information insurance salespeople give their clients is accurate. The main problem arises when agents try to compare the relative values of different life products. Many agents cannot perform a sound analysis, because they are not trained to do so (see page 118 for a discussion on selecting a good agent). Moreover, many salespeople do not do their own research; they simply accept the data supplied by the insurance company's marketing department, if it makes the product look good.

Be skeptical of all claims, especially guarantees of return, and ask how the salesperson got the information. The more questions you ask, the better sense you will get of whether the agent is knowledgeable.

Among other things, check:

■ *Mortality expenses.* Are cost projections realistic? Some companies base illustrations on assumed future reductions in mortality expenses, but new diseases, such as AIDS, could dramatically increase death payouts.

■ *Interest rates.* Are they competitive with rates paid on other policies? Are they guaranteed for a certain period? On similar policies offered by the same company, what happened to rates after the guarantee expired?

■ *Policy charges.* Do they reflect all the expenses incurred by the company?

■ *Track record.* With variable policies and variable annuity contracts, the portion of your contribution that does not pay for insurance costs is invested in mutual funds. Ask what types of funds are available; how they have performed, especially during bear markets; and what is the expertise of the portfolio managers. Also, find out how often you can switch among funds and at what cost, if any.

■ *Insurance rating.* On policies and annuities paying fixed interest rates, usually adjusted annually, the company's financial strength is of prime importance. Find out how A. M. Best rates the insurer. Stick with firms carrying Best's B+ or better. Also, ask what the net return will be after deducting all charges and expenses. Does this return compare favorably to that of similar investments?

■ *Liquidity.* Are there any back-end surrender charges? How much money can you withdraw from the policy or annuity, and do you need to pay it back? Are there any "bailout clauses," which let you walk away from a fixed-rate product without paying a surrender fee, for example, if the insurer decreases the return upon renewal? Do you get a "free look" period that lets you get out without charge if the policy interest rate falls a point or two below the initial rate or the rate of the company's new offerings?

☐ Resources

If you want to keep tabs on your present insurer, each year the September/October issue of Insurance Forum lists the financial-strength ratings of about 1000 insurers from A. M. Best, Duff & Phelps, Moody's, and Standard & Poor's. There is also a watch list of insurers and a list of companies whose ratings changed over the past year. Cost: $10 from Insurance Forum, P.O. Box 245-K, Ellettsville, IN 47429.

AILMENT

I am terminally ill and need extra money so that I can live comfortably for the rest of my life. I have heard I can cash out my life insurance policy to see me through my final days.

R An entire industry has sprung up around these so-called viatical settlements. Before you decide this is the right move for you, however, you should know how they work.

All types of life insurance policies are eligible for such sales—term, whole-life, universal-life, and even group life from an employer. Selling an insurance policy usually takes from six to eight weeks.

Usually, the amount paid in advance on life insurance policies is between 50% and 80% of the policy's face value. Small policies pay out the lowest percentage. Another factor is your life expectancy; the longer it is, the less you can expect to get for the policy.

In general, viatical settlement companies that buy these policies are looking for people with less than two years to live. They also want policies that are at least two years old. Attempts to sell a policy during its first two years could cause the insurer to investigate whether medical information was falsified on the original application. The result could be loss of coverage.

If you decide to sell your policy, get at least three bids for a net cash-out value (after all expenses) and do not accept partial or installment payments.

Before selling your policy, ask your insurance company whether it offers an accelerated benefits program or will make you a loan against your policy. Many companies will advance you some of the proceeds during your lifetime, with the remainder to be paid to your beneficiary upon death.

With most policies, a physician must certify that your death is anticipated within six months or a year or, for long-term care benefits, that you cannot perform certain daily activities or that you need permanent care in a nursing home. Less common are policies that pay for a specific disease, such as cancer, regardless of how long you are expected to live.

Depending on the policy, you can get 25% to 100% of the death payment, distributed either in monthly installments or as a lump sum. Insurers add the cost of the accelerated benefits rider to the premiums or exact a percentage of the face amount plus an administrative fee, or both.

You should collect accelerated benefits only as a last resort and not as a substitute for savings or other insurance. Unlike death benefits, accelerated benefits can make you ineligible for some government programs, such as Medicaid. Further, collecting accelerated benefits defeats the goal of the life insurance policy, which is to provide for your family.

If you sell your life insurance policy, the proceeds are federally tax-free. If you receive accelerated death benefits, they are also tax-exempt if you are terminally ill, that is, if you are expected to die within two years. Chronically ill persons may exclude up to $175 a day in accelerated death benefits.

Even if you expect to live longer than two years, you may be able to borrow against the face value of your policy. You could also name a friend or relative as the beneficiary of your life insurance policy in exchange for a loan. Proceeds you receive through those methods are not taxed.

☐ **Resources**

The National Association of People with AIDS (202-898-0414) distributes a list of viatical settlement companies it considers to be reputable.

AILMENT

My spouse died, and I do not know how to collect his life insurance.

R̸ You don't have to go through the legal process of probate—which can tie up an estate for at least six months—to collect the death benefit. If you are the beneficiary of the policy, you only have to mail it, along with a certified copy of the death certificate, to the insurance company's claims department. Within a month, a check will arrive for the face value of the policy.

AILMENT

I invested $15,000 in a single-premium annuity. The cash value today is more than double my initial investment. I want to withdraw the money to buy a higher-paying annuity without being taxed on the gain.

R̸ Just have your new insurance company send a tax-free exchange form to your old insurance company to effect the transfer. One word of warning: Most companies charge a surrender fee of 1% to 6% if an annuity is cashed in or transferred before a specified date, generally five to eight years after it was bought.

AILMENT

I traded in my old annuity for a new one by making a tax-free 1035 exchange. Now I am preparing my federal income tax return.

R̸ You should have received a Form 1099 from your old insurance company, showing how much interest the former policy earned. You must report that gain on your income tax return for the year of the exchange. But then you deduct it to show the net gain as a zero.

Attach a separate page—essentially a note to the IRS—explaining that you made a tax-free 1035 exchange. Include the numbers of both policies as part of your explanation.

AILMENT

I cannot pay my whole-life insurance premium.

R℞ Most companies give you a 31-day grace period in which to make an overdue payment. They assume you want to keep the policy in force. If it is impossible for you to continue making payments for an indefinite period, there are several things you can do with a whole-life contract:

■ Borrow from the cash value built up in your whole-life contract to pay the premiums.

■ Let the full amount of the policy remain in force as "extended term insurance" for a limited time. What you are doing is using the policy's cash value to buy term insurance for a certain period. How long you may keep the contract in force under "extended term" without paying further premiums depends on your age and the number of premiums actually paid. Of course, this tactic works only if enough cash value has accumulated in the contract. Some life contracts provide an optional "automatic premium loan" feature.

■ Arrange for the cash value of the contract to be applied toward a paid-up lifetime contract—for an amount less than the original contract.

■ Surrender the contract and collect its cash value. This, of course, cancels your protection.

■ HEALTH INSURANCE

AILMENT

My health insurance costs are eating me alive.

R℞ Affordable health insurance is hard to come by. The problem, of course, is that being without a minimum amount of health coverage can ruin you financially for life, if you or your loved ones suffer serious injury or disease. That means you really cannot reduce your costs below a certain amount. At a minimum, you need a major medical policy that pays 80% of most doctor and hospital bills in excess of your deductible. Ideally, your total yearly share of the bill should not exceed $2500. The policy should have no exclusions for costly diseases, such as cancer, and if it pays a maximum lifetime benefit, it should be no less than $250,000—preferably much higher.

If you are employed with group coverage. When you have job-related health insurance, your price-cutting options are few. Still, more and more employers are offering health care choices—health maintenance organizations (HMOs) versus traditional fee-for-service care, for example.

If you are weighing which fee-for-service plan to choose, data from a 1991 Bureau of Labor Statistics survey of employers indicates the following to be better-than-average coverage for traditional care: doctor visits, both in and out of hospital, 80% covered; semiprivate hospital room, 100% for 120-plus days; surgical fees, 100%; lab fees and X rays, 80%; home health care, 80%; mental health and substance abuse treatment, 100% of inpatient services up to 30 days and limited outpatient therapy; dental injuries, 80%; miscellaneous dental care, 50% to 100%, with a $1000 annual limit.

Prepaid plans, such as HMOs, typically charge $5 to $10 per office visit or prescription. Most other medical services are fully covered, although mental health care is usually limited to 30 to 60 inpatient days and 20 to 30 days of outpatient therapy at $20 per visit.

Do not sacrifice a longstanding relationship with a physician to gain a small monthly price advantage. But if your company lets you choose annually between two comparable health plans, determine which best meets your needs for the coming year. For example, if you know your child will need braces and one plan offers substantially better dental benefits, it may be worthwhile to switch for a year.

With group plans, employers pick up most of the tab. In 1993, single employees, according to the Department of Labor, paid an average of $31.48 a month for fee-for-service and $31.77 for HMO coverage. For families, fee-for-service plans cost $102.48 and HMOs cost $121.84.

If you lose your job, federal law requires companies with group health plans to offer continuation of coverage for 18 months at modest costs. Divorced, separated, or widowed spouses, as well as children no longer young enough to qualify for company coverage, can remain insured for 36 months. The temporary coverage is usually more comprehensive and less expensive than what you can buy on your own.

If you are an employee without group coverage. If you are not covered by a group plan, the search for low-cost health insurance starts with professional associations or other societies you belong to or could join.

If that fails, consider signing on with an HMO; for a fixed annual premium, an HMO provides almost all of the medical services you may need. You pay no significant deductibles to an HMO. The yearly premium for single people is around $1000; for couples with children, more than $2500.

Individual major-medical policies cost about the same as HMOs, but reimbursement tops out at no more than 80% of your medical costs. Each year, you also pay an amount equal to your deductible before your expenses are covered. Nonprofit Blue Cross and Blue Shield are often your best choices, but any policy you buy should be guaranteed renewable. That way the insurer cannot cut off your coverage, no matter how many claims you file.

Of course, when you do not get health insurance from your employer, costs are much higher. Premiums for a nongroup policy for a family of four from Blue Cross and Blue Shield that covers 80% of hospitalization, surgical costs, office visits, and major medical expenses range from $200 to $600 a month, depending on deductibles, specific types of coverage, and location.

In most cases, the only way to significantly decrease your premiums is to raise your deductible to $5000 or even $10,000. When you do this, you are, in effect, buying a policy that covers catastrophic illnesses only.

If you are a senior citizen. Consider so-called *medigap* insurance, which pays medical expenses—such as long-term nursing care—not covered by Medicare. Free help analyzing this often complex coverage is available through the American Association of Retired Persons (AARP), as well as through many state commissions on insurance or aging.

If you are self-employed. Compare group and nongroup rates. There is no guarantee that group rates are a better buy than getting insurance on your own—especially if you are young and healthy. Beware of trade groups that aggressively market their insurance; such sales tactics are often used to conceal uncompetitive rates.

You might save more by joining a health maintenance organization, because HMOs have neither significant deductibles nor high co-payments. Typically, you pay a nominal amount or nothing for each office visit.

Check small-business pools. Some states have passed legislation requiring health plans for small businesses to be available to individuals. Many plans offered by small-business groups are already open to individuals.

Local groups are more likely to have HMO options than a nationwide professional association, and sometimes it is worth joining your local chamber of commerce to get access to a small-business health plan that also accepts self-employed individuals. There are also some regional health insurance pools.

AILMENT

I have a preexisting medical condition.

R̸ Medical conditions as serious as a heart ailment or as minor as a headache can haunt you when you sign up for a new policy, even with group coverage. Insurers routinely restrict payment for conditions that predate your enrollment.

Restrictions are toughest on individual polices and in group plans with fewer than 25 people. If you have a serious medical condition, a carrier may refuse to cover you at all. If your ailment is less serious, the company may take you on but refuse to cover that condition for a year or two—and then promise only to review the situation.

Most states require insurance companies to enroll you if you are a member of a group of about 50 or more. But you will probably still have to wait at least six months before you are covered for a preexisting condition.

About half the states impose so-called no-gain, no-loss protections, which means that if an employer switches group policies, the new carrier has to cover all employees from day one. (For information on the laws where you live, contact your state insurance department.)

However, no-gain, no-loss laws do not protect new employees. Even large groups will make you wait—six months is typical—before they will pay on claims related to a condition you have been treated for during the past year.

If that is your predicament, you can simply sweat out the wait, paying any expenses out of your own pocket. Or postpone elective treatment until the waiting period has passed. If you must switch jobs and you anticipate major expenses soon, take advantage of your right under federal COBRA legislation to extend insurance from your previous job for up to 18 months at your own expense.

AILMENT

I own a small business, and one of my employees has developed diabetes. Now my insurer is trying to cut out coverage for diabetes treatment.

R Your insurer's action may be unlawful. Under the 1990 Americans with Disabilities Act, which covers companies employing 15 or more people, insurers usually cannot drop or reduce coverage for a disabling illness or condition on an individual basis. They *can* reduce coverage for all employees or for a category of treatment—say, mental health care. Self-insured companies are included under the law, and some states have similar laws for companies with fewer employees. If you believe your coverage has been threatened because of your employee's disability, contact your state insurance commission.

AILMENT

I work for a company with fewer than five employees, and our group health coverage may be reduced or eliminated.

R Insurers often cancel small group policies if claims under them increase sharply. Some of the policies are conditionally renewable, which means the insurer can cancel them if it drops all similar policies in the state. Others are optionally renewable, letting the insurer cancel coverage at will when it is time to renew. More often, employers drop the insurance because of skyrocketing premiums. Each year, about 30% of companies with fewer than 30 employees let their coverage lapse or buy cheaper replacement policies with more limited coverage.

Ask your employee-benefits officer whether your company's insurer can cancel your policy. Most Blue Cross and Blue Shield insurers and health maintenance organizations (HMOs) cannot do so. They must automatically renew policies as long as the premiums are paid.

About 30 states require private insurers who cancel group policies to offer individual coverage to the group's members, regardless of their health. But all of these conversion policies are expensive and most provide extremely limited protection.

A better option might be to purchase a policy from Blue Cross/Blue Shield. In about a dozen states, the Blues open enrollment to all comers for three months or longer at least once a year. Call your local Blue Cross/Blue Shield office for the date of the next open-enrollment period.

Check, too, with your professional associations, which often sell lower-priced coverage to members. Finally, if you have serious medical problems, phone your state insurance commissioner to find out whether your state has a high-risk pool for persons who do not qualify for regular health insurance policies.

AILMENT

My health insurer refuses to pay for my treatment, as they judge it to be an experimental treatment.

R Some of the fiercest controversies involve treatments that an insurer deems experimental and, therefore, not covered by insurance. Often there are gray areas: A bone marrow transplant, for example, might be considered conventional for Hodgkin's disease (cancer of the lymphatic system), but experimental for breast cancer.

If you are at odds with the insurance company, file an appeal either by phone or in writing. A third party will usually be brought in to decide the matter. As a last resort, take your case to court. Research by Susan Stewart, a bone marrow transplant recipient, shows that patients were reimbursed in 85% to 90% of the bone marrow transplant cases litigated in 1990.

AILMENT

My health insurance claim was not paid in full.

R Your first step, of course, is to figure out what went wrong. There could be a valid reason why your claim was denied or scaled down—or there could be an error. Before venting your outrage, make sure the rejected claim was not for treatment that was recently excluded from coverage. More and more employers are trimming coverage, with psychiatric and obstetric bills undergoing the most surgery. Check, too, that you have already met your deductible or were not responsible for co-payments.

If you still believe your claim should have been paid in full, try these tactics:

■ *Involve your insurer's sales representative.* The person who sold your employer's company the policy has a stake in keeping you satisfied. Calls from a subscriber can sometimes be more effective than those from a doctor's office.

■ *Call your doctor's office.* The person in charge of billing can tell you whether a simple coding mistake on the claim form caused the problem or whether more information is needed.

The doctor or a member of the office staff may be willing to write an appeal on your behalf. In smaller practices, you may be charged for this— usually from $50 to $150. Or save money by having the doctor co-sign a letter you write yourself. Explain the error or misunderstanding in detail.

■ *Write, write again.* There is always a chance you can wear the insurer down if you make a big enough nuisance of yourself. To provoke action, warn that you will write to your state's insurance commissioner. If that does not work, actually write to the commissioner.

Do your own claims audit.   To err is normal these days as complex computer-coded medical insurance claims forms make insurance companies—and doctors' offices—more error-prone. As you check your rejected claim for accuracy, here are some common slipups to look for:

Wrong procedure codes.   Each procedure billed by your doctor has a five-digit code number, which insurance companies and Medicare use to compare what the doctor billed with procedures covered by your policy. If an insurance clerk enters the wrong code into the computer, you will be re-imbursed the wrong amount or denied coverage altogether.

Your remedy: There is an insurance company error if the insurer's code does not match the doctor's code on your bill. If your insurer does not in-clude procedure codes with its benefit statements, call and ask for the codes. Bringing the error to the insurer's attention should promptly correct such a problem.

If the codes match, but your insurer says you are not covered, confirm that your policy does indeed cover the doctor's treatment. If so, ask the doctor's office to review its billing code. Different insurers may use differ-ent codes for the same procedure.

Downcoding.   Your insurance company may believe that a procedure is less involved than the doctor's bill suggests. If so, the claims processor might change the doctor's code to one for a lower-cost service. Your insurer could also downcode if a new technology has not yet been entered into its computer database.

Your remedy: Have your doctor document the usual charge and send this documentation with a letter appealing the change to your insurer.

Combined codes. If you consult more than one doctor on the same day or the same procedure is performed more than once (for example, you have broken bones set) you may be paid for only one procedure. Or if you have, say, a valve replacement done at the same time as coronary bypass surgery, your insurance company will probably pay less than the full cost— often half the cost of the less-expensive procedure.

Your remedy: Do a thorough match between your doctor's bills and the insurance payment to see if your insurer considered all the charges.

Deductible miscalculated. If you have a plan covering your family, there may be a separate deductible for each family member, which is supposed to be waived when the family deductible is met.

If you belong to a health maintenance organization (HMO) or a preferred provider organization (PPO), there may be a higher deductible for using doctors outside the network than for using the network's own physicians.

Formulas for calculating deductibles are complex, and insurers do not always keep careful track of deductibles.

Your remedy: Keep tabs on your medical bills so you know exactly when you have reached your deductibles.

Missed coverage. A claims processor may simply fail to notice or realize that a particular service is covered. This can happen, for example, when an insurer decides to pay for a procedure it did not cover before.

Your remedy: Know what benefits your policy covers and be suspicious if a claim for a treatment that was previously covered is rejected.

■ UNHEALTHY INSURANCE COMPANIES

AILMENT
The company that sold me an extended warranty has filed for bankruptcy.

 If you are stuck with a useless warranty, there are places you can turn to for help:

■ If you bought your warranty from the out-of-business store that sold you the product, call the insurer backing the plan. If it was an independent warranty company that failed, complain first to the store. If that brings no results, find out whether an insurer was involved. If so, go to the insurer.

■ If neither the store nor the insurer will honor your claim, call the manufacturer and ask for free repairs. Most manufacturers will accommodate such requests, especially if you are forceful, in the interests of customer relations. In most cases, you will be sent to an authorized dealer near you. If the dealer cannot fix the product, ask for a replacement.

■ If you are still dissatisfied, report the problem to your state insurance commissioner or consumer affairs division. If there are enough similar complaints, your state may bring suit against the store or insurer. Or you can act as your own lawyer and sue in small-claims court.

AILMENT

My insurance company has been seized by state insurance regulators.

R When regulators take over an insurer, they usually freeze assets to prevent a run, which means you cannot borrow from your policy or cash it in. The yield on the policy or annuity may be reduced to the minimum guaranteed amount. Death benefits and annuity payments normally continue, although you may get only a percentage of the regular amount.

Note: If your money is in a variable annuity or variable policy, you are in luck. Your money is held in segregated accounts and unless it has been invested in one of the insurer's products, your money is not tied to the insurer's fate. But your account could be frozen for a short time if the insurer goes into conservatorship.

Unless you can prove hardship, there is nothing to do but sit tight. As frustrated as you may be, most experts recommend that you keep making your premium payments. Many policies include a provision that automatically "borrows" the premium money against your policy's cash value if payments are skipped. Before long, there is nothing left to borrow against, and the policy will no longer be in force.

☐ Prevention

The easiest way around the question of solvency is to buy term insurance. That is pure life insurance, and it is usually sold for one-year periods, so long-term stability is not an important consideration. Term insurance is cheap, and although it grows more expensive as you grow older, by that time your family may not be as dependent upon you for future income.

But term insurance may not be what you seek; maybe you want an annuity or the tax-sheltered savings and investment that whole- or universal-life offer. If so, buy through an experienced, trained agent. Seek out a chartered life underwriter, who has completed courses and examinations in such subjects as life insurance law and financial planning and has at least three years' experience in the field.

Ask your agent for the ratings issued by Moody's, Standard & Poor's, and *Best's Review* for your insurance company. You want companies rated B+ or better by *Best's*, Baa or better by Moody's, BBB or better by S&P, and C or better by Weiss.

CHAPTER SIX

Investments

The ultimate goal of investors is to get rich and stay that way. In the best of all possible worlds, you would unerringly pick investments primed to take off, and you would protect your newfound wealth by bailing out at historic highs. Since the beginning of the 1990s, investors have come close to doing just that as the Dow has soared ever upward. So far, crises have been minor and temporary. But investing in the stock market is a lot like gambling, and no one wins on the roll of the dice every time.

The world of investments encompasses more than Wall Street, of course. In fact, there is more competition for your money than ever before. Banks, credit unions, insurance companies, mutual funds, and brokerages all want to sell you products that may or may not be the right choices to meet your particular goals.

This is a case where you cannot avoid all financial risks. The greatest risk—losing to inflation—comes from not investing at all. The trick is to avoid financial setbacks or worse catastrophes.

You may not control the economy, but when it comes to personal finance, the choices are yours. If you are an informed investor, you can profit substantially. Most experts agree that the keys to success are research, timing, and prudence. To sidestep disaster and enjoy gains, you must do your homework before committing your money. Diversify by spreading your capital over a number of well-researched choices, and always keep some money in safer, more conservative investments. Finally, you must pay attention to your investments and learn when to cut your losses.

This chapter will help educate you about mutual funds and teach you how to read the financial pages. It will help you save money on purchases of securities, benefit from respected investment strategies, and stanch sudden losses. You will also learn how to judge the value of stocks, get money quickly out of your mutual fund, and save taxes when you cash out. The chapter also discusses what you can do if you have a complaint about your broker. For information about investments in residential property, insurance, and pension plans, see Chapters 4, 5, and 9.

■ STOCKS

AILMENT
I do not know how to read a stock table.

℞ Stock tables in your daily paper can help you track the performance of stock you own and investigate the ups and downs of companies you would like to invest in. Figure 6–1 is an excerpt from a newspa-

FIGURE 6–1 Sample Stock Table

52-Week High	52-Week Low	Stock	Div	Yld %	P/E	Sales 100s	High	Low	Last	Chg
12 3/4	8	MorrKnud	...	...	dd	1085	12 1/2	12 1/4	12 1/2	...
7 1/2	3 1/2	MorrKn wt	...	...	...	4	6 5/8	6 5/8	6 5/8	...
32 1/8	23 7/8	MortnInt n	...	...	...	4404	30 1/8	29 7/8	30	− 1/8
19	14	MortnRst	...	...	44	77	15 1/4	15	15 1/8	..
50 1/8	5 7/8	Mossimo	..	..	8	645	6 1/4	6	6 1/8	− 1/8
69 3/4	44 1/8	Motorola	.48	0.8	32	24561	58 5/8	57	57	− 1/8
45 3/4	31 3/8	MuellerInd	...	...	12	1343	38 1/2	37 1/4	38 1/4	+ 3/4
22 3/8	17 1/4	Multicre s	...	...	18	849	18 7/8	18 5/8	18 7/8	+ 1/4
12 7/8	12 1/8	Muniast	.86	6.7	q	124	12 3/4	12 5/8	12 3/4	...
12 3/8	11	MunAdv	80	6.6	q	23	12 1/8	12 1/8	12 1/8	..
9 1/2	8 1/2	MunHi	62	6.7	q	573	9 3/8	9 1/4	9 1/4	..
9 1/8	8	MIOT	.60	6.9	q	368	8 3/4	8 5/8	8 3/4	+ 1/8
9	8 1/4	MIOT2	.60	7.0	q	135	8 3/4	8 5/8	8 5/8	− 1/8
10 1/8	9	MIOT3	.72	7.3	q	192	9 7/8	9 3/4	9 7/8	..
9 1/2	8 5/8	MuIT	.57 a	6.2	q	475	9 1/4	9 1/8	9 1/4	+ 1/8
10	8 7/8	MuIT2	.57	6.2	q	231	9 3/8	9 1/8	9 1/4	+ 1/8
9 7/8	8 3/4	MuIT3	.57 a	6.2	q	94	9 1/4	9 1/8	9 1/4	+ 1/16
12 1/2	11	MunPrt	.80	6.6	q	31	12 1/8	12	12 1/8	+ 1/4
11 7/8	10 3/8	MunPrt2	.75	6.5	q	7	11 1/2	11 1/2	11 1/2	+ 1/8
9 1/2	8 3/4	MuPIT	.60 a	6.5	q	520	9 1/4	9 1/8	9 1/4	+ 1/8
11 3/8	10 3/8	MuniFd	.73 a	6.7	q	950	11	10 3/4	10 7/8	...
13 1/2	11 5/8	MFLFd	80	6.3	q	214	12 5/8	12 1/2	12 5/8	+ 1/8
13 1/2	11 7/8	Muniv2	90	6.8	q	383	13 3/8	13 1/8	13 1/4	+ 1/8
12 7/8	11 5/8	MuvMIln	.83	6.5	q	11	12 3/4	12 5/8	12 3/4	+ 1/8
13 1/4	11 5/8	MuvNJFd	.80	6.4	q	12	12 5/8	12 1/2	12 1/2	...
12 1/4	11	MuPAIns	.73	6.3	q	18	11 3/4	11 5/8	11 5/8	..
15 1/8	13 7/8	MunCA	.94	6.3	q	246	14 7/8	14 3/4	14 7/8	+ 1/8
14 1/2	12 7/8	MuCAIns	.88	6.3	q	328	14	13 3/4	14	+ 1/4
14 5/8	13 3/8	MuCA2	.90 a	6.3	q	342	14 1/4	14 1/8	14 1/4	+ 1/8
15 3/8	13 7/8	MunFL	.94 a	6.3	q	68	14 7/8	14 3/4	14 7/8	+ 1/4
15	13 1/2	MuFLIn	.88 a	6.1	q	166	14 3/8	14 1/4	14 3/8	+ 1/4
15 1/4	14 1/4	Muniyld	1.02 a	6.8	q	243	15 1/8	15	15	..
14 3/8	13 3/8	▲MunIns	.96 a	6.6	q	1948	14 1/2	14 3/8	14 1/2	+ 1/8
15 1/4	13 5/8	MunMI	.92	6.5	q	81	14 1/4	14 1/8	14 1/4	...
14 5/8	13	MunMIln	87	6.4	q	60	13 5/8	13 5/8	13 5/8	...
15 3/8	13 5/8	MunNJ	.94	6.3	q	73	14 7/8	14 3/4	14 7/8	+ 1/8
15 1/4	14	MuNJIn	93	6.3	q	66	14 7/8	14 5/8	14 7/8	+ 1/4
15 3/8	13 7/8	MunNY	.92 a	6.1	q	203	15 1/8	14 7/8	15 1/8	+ 1/4
13 3/4	12 1/2	MuNY2	90	6.6	q	687	13 3/4	13 1/2	13 5/8	...
14 7/8	13 3/4	MunPA	.91 a	6.3	q	286	14 3/8	14 1/8	14 3/8	+ 1/8
13 7/8	12 1/4	MunQlty	.92	6.8	q	770	13 1/2	13 3/8	13 1/2	+ 1/8
14 1/8	12 1/2	MunQl2	.93 a	6.8	q	420	13 3/4	13 5/8	13 5/8	− 1/8
54 1/4	37 1/2	MurpO	1.30	3.0	16	728	43 5/8	43	43 1/2	...
5 1/8	11/16	MusicLd	...	...	dd	163	1 1/4	1 1/8	1 1/8	...
40	26 7/8	MutRisk s	.36	1.0	19	320	37	36 3/4	37	+ 1/4
20 3/8	11 1/2	Mylan	.16	1.3	18	9832	12 1/2	12	12 1/8	+ 1/8

per's alphabetical stock table. For example, assume you are interested in buying shares of Motorola.

52-Week High/Low—the highest ($69.75) and the lowest ($44.125) closing daily prices during the preceding 52-week period.

Stock—company name (Motorola) and the type of stock (common stock in this case; "pf" means preferred stock).

Div—the annual dividend paid for each share of stock during the preceding 52-week period ($.48).

Yld—the percentage yield or return per share of stock, calculated by dividing the annual dividend per share by the current market price ($.48 divided by $57 = .8%).

P/E—the price-earnings ratio lets you compute the company's latest 12-month earnings per share by dividing current market price by the figure given ($57 divided by 32 = $1.78).

Sales—trading volume, or sales, is shown in 100-share increments (in our example, 2,456,100 shares were traded during the day).

High/Low—the trading price range on that day ($58.625 high, $57 low).

Last—the closing price on that day ($57).

Chg—the net change, or dollar amount by which the closing price per share advanced or declined from the previous trading day (in this case, a loss of $.125).

AILMENT

I want to buy stock directly from a company, not through a broker.

℞ Buying stock through direct-purchase plans and dividend reinvestment plans (DRIPs) is like buying from a factory outlet. You go straight to the firm that sells the product—in this case, company shares—and buy wholesale. There is more time and effort involved, but in the long run you can save thousands of dollars by cutting out the middleman (broker).

There are about a thousand companies, predominantly banks and utilities, offering direct-purchase plans. Although that is only a fraction of the companies listed on major U.S. exchanges, the participating firms include many household names, such as Kellogg Company, Kmart, McDonald's, J. P. Morgan, Honeywell, and Philip Morris. A few foreign companies with American depositary receipts (ADRs), which represent shares of foreign companies traded in the U.S., also offer DRIPs, including SmithKline Beecham and British Petroleum.

Investors usually have to own at least one share of stock to enroll in a DRIP. But if you agree to reinvest your dividends, some companies, such as Bank of New York, Minnesota Power & Light, and Texaco, will sell you your first shares directly, up to a set dollar amount. In addition, there are now over 130 companies that do not limit their offering to existing shareholders. You can jump in at any time.

Pros and cons.   The key advantage to direct purchase is the price. You can invest under a dividend reinvestment plan (DRIP) without paying any brokerage fees. Your savings: between $25 and $150 per trade once you have your account set up. Around 170 companies also let you buy additional shares directly from the company at a 3% to 5% discount on the market price. In many cases, you can buy stocks directly from the company without waiting for dividends to accrue. Most companies accept monthly contributions as small as $10 to $50, for little or no transaction fee.

Another advantage: By regularly reinvesting your dividends in a DRIP, you benefit from dollar cost averaging (see page 182). If your directly purchased company suddenly falls out of favor, you can view that as a buying opportunity and stock up.

What is the downside? You will not get any professional advice, so you must be able to research and evaluate whether a company's shares are a bargain or a bust. And buying direct is not as easy as making a phone call to your broker. In almost all cases, the shares must be held in your name, not your broker's.

Also, some companies do charge trading fees when an investor sells stock. But these fees are extremely modest, typically topping out at $3 or $4 per sale.

There are some tax handicaps, too. Any fees and commissions the DRIP company pays on your behalf must be reported as taxable income on your tax return. (It will show up on your Form 1099-DIV.) The flip side of this same rule reduces your capital gain by the amount of the commission paid when the shares are sold. Still, the up-front tax liability is a consideration, especially if reducing taxes is one of your top financial priorities.

Another drawback is that some companies buy shares at less-than-ideal times—for example, at the end of the month or when deposits exceed a certain dollar amount. As a result, you could send in cash to buy when shares are one price, only to have your money sit in the company's trust account until a later date when the price is higher.

☐ Resources

There are several directories of DRIP companies. One of the most comprehensive is the *Directory of Companies Offering Reinvestment Plans*. You may be able to find it at your public library, or you can order it from Evergreen Enterprises, P.O. Box 763, Laurel, MD 20725-0763; 301-953-1861. The price is $29.95, plus $2.50 for delivery.

Another source is *Moneypaper* (1010 Mamaroneck Avenue, Mamaroneck, NY 10543; 914-381-5400; sample issue at no charge; $81 per year to subscribe).

Other directories are available from: Direct-Purchase/Dividend-Reinvestment News, P.O. Box 388, Etiwanda, CA 91739 ($149); and DRIP Investor, 7412 Calumet Avenue, Suite 200, Hammond, IN 46324 (free sample; $59 for 12 issues and starter kit); or visit the Securities Transfer Association Web page at http://www.netstockdirect.com.

Finally, for more information on direct-purchase plans, contact the National Association of Investors Corporation (NAIC) at P.O. Box 220, Royal Oak, MI 48068; 248-583-6242.

AILMENT

I do not know whether to let my broker hold my shares in street name (that is, in the brokerage firm's name).

R℞ Now that proceeds from stock transactions must change hands within three working days (down from five days), you could be in a bind if you want to sell but cannot get your shares to the broker that quickly. Certainly, the brokerage industry has steadily pushed its clients into holding their stocks in street name. In fact, many, if not all, brokerages by now charge clients at least $15 for stock certificates.

Still, there are advantages to keeping stock in street name. Assuming you are dealing with a financially sound and reputable brokerage, allowing your broker to hold your stock in street name is at least as safe, and arguably even safer, than holding onto your own certificates. It is certainly far more convenient, especially with the advent of "T plus 3" settlement rules, since you will not face the hassle of making sure than you get your certificate to your broker within three days of a sale. If you currently receive dividend checks, you can instruct your broker to mail them to you or deposit them in your cash account at the brokerage.

Brokerages generally carry insurance from the Securities Investor Protection Corporation, which insures each trading account held in the brokerage's name for up to $500,000. Many brokerages carry additional insurance on their own, too. For example, Charles Schwab, the nation's largest discount brokerage, insures each account for an additional $99.5 million, bringing the total amount of available insurance to $100 million per account. (But be advised: Your account value is insured only in the event a brokerage fails; you are not covered for buying a series of stock losers or price nosedives when the markets crash.)

Keeping stocks in street name is also a recordkeeping godsend. The brokerage firm will send you a consolidated statement that shows all your dividends, interest, capital gains, sales, purchases, and current market value. This is especially helpful at tax time.

The drawbacks: With your stocks in street name, you will not be able to participate in dividend reinvestment programs (DRIPs), or if you can, you may have to pay a commission.

If you decide to convert your portfolio to street name, simply take your certificates to your broker and enroll.

AILMENT

I inherited an old stock certificate from my father. I do not know how to find out if the certificate has any value today.

R℞ This is actually a common dilemma. In fact, even if the issuing company is no longer listed on one of the exchanges, it may still have value. Some old companies have merely changed names and locations, so besides price appreciation, you may be owed past dividends. Other companies may have liquidated, but there may be money held in trust for you somewhere. And other, dormant, companies may own assets, so they have potential value.

Even if the company is long gone and bankrupt or the stock certificate has been canceled your shares could have collector's value. A canceled share of Standard Oil Company, signed by John D. Rockefeller, for example, sold at auction for $12,500 in January 1993.

One way to determine if your old stock is valuable is to do a little research on your own. Or you can hire a search firm to do it for you. But if you have numerous shares in different companies, paying research fees can be prohibitively high. You should do a little preliminary work on your own.

The first step, in either case, is to talk to a stockbroker about whether the company is still listed and trading on a major stock exchange. If the shares are not too old, the broker may know the company's history, even if it is not trading. You should have little difficulty catching up with firms that have changed names, merged, or filed for bankruptcy in recent years.

☐ Resources

There are several search companies that could help you, but the best bargain is Prudential-American Securities Inc., 921 East Green Street, Pasadena, CA 91106 (818-795-5831). It charges $40 for each company researched. Send duplicate copies of your stock certificates or other investment materials to Prudential-American, along with a check for the appropriate amount.

Other companies that will research whether your shares have intrinsic or collector's value are R. M. Smythe (800-622-1880) and Stock Search International (800-537-4523). Smythe charges $75 per stock; Stock Search, $85.

AILMENT

I bought 200 shares of a networking company three years ago. Now the company is being acquired and I have gotten a letter saying that all outstanding shares will be purchased by the acquiring company. I do not want to sell.

R/ What happens if you choose not to tender your shares at the time of acquisition depends on the terms of the deal between the two companies. In some cases, shareholders are allowed to exchange their stock for a commensurate amount of shares in the acquiring company. This would keep you from having to report a taxable gain this year on your appreciated shares.

It is also possible that the acquiring company will let uncooperative shareholders hold onto their old stock. But you would have no market for your shares, and any dividends the shares generated would end. Sooner or later, you will have to give in and take the new stock.

The bottom line: You will have to accept whatever deal the majority of shareholders approves, if you want to preserve your investment in the stock.

AILMENT

I bought 100 shares of General Electric stock through a company payroll savings plan in the 1960s. I have no record of what these shares cost. Since then, the stock split three times and those initial shares grew to a total of 800. In addition, I purchased 200 more shares through GE's dividend reinvestment program. I have no record of what these shares cost. I sold the 1000 shares a few months ago and received $54,000. I do not know how to figure my taxable gain.

R/ First, check with your company's payroll office for any records of your stock purchases. If the records exist, you will then have to research the stock splits. This history can be found in records kept by brokerage firms, and, of course, General Electric. (Any correspondence with General Electric should be sent to its investor relations department.)

If your company has no record of your stock purchases, you will need to estimate when you bought the stock and look up the per-share price at that time, using research materials at your brokerage or through General Electric.

This work must be done. Your broker will report the sale of your 1000 shares to the IRS, and the IRS will expect to see the $54,000 proceeds reported on your tax return. If you cannot reconstruct your original cost, the IRS can make you pay taxes on the entire $54,000.

If your broker cannot or will not help you, you can retain a stock research firm. These companies offer a variety of research services involving public companies and their stock. For example, they can give you the stock split dates and the market value of your stock on any given day in history. Of course, there is a fee.

There are several stock research companies, but Prudential-American Securities Inc. (921 East Green Street, Pasadena, CA 91106) charges reasonable fees.

AILMENT

I cannot afford to lose a lot of money in the stock market.

R℞ One way to safeguard your stock investment from a sudden downfall is to use stop (or stop-loss) orders. If you know how to use them properly, stop orders can reliably protect your profits or cut your losses.

To place a stop order, simply tell your broker to sell your shares automatically if they drop to a certain price. Both discount and full-service brokers accept stop orders, but only on New York or American Stock Exchange stocks. Investors typically set the sell price at 10% to 15% below the stock's current level. Your order will cost you nothing. Your broker will send it to the specialist for your stock on the floor of the exchange. This specialist will then sell your shares if they drop to your specified price. In the jargon of Wall Street, you will be "stopped out" of your stock. Your broker will get the regular commission, and you will pocket your profit.

A stop order can last for a day or indefinitely. You can cancel it at any time. If your stock's price advances, you should obviously keep raising your targeted selling price to protect your extra profit.

Stop orders have their limitations, though. For one thing, there is no guarantee you will receive the exact price you specified. When a stock falls to your price, the specialist sells your shares on the next trade. Say your stock drops to 75, turning your stop order into a sell order. If the next bid for that issue is 74$\frac{7}{8}$, that is the price you will receive. But the next bid could be for 70. The specialist may try to minimize the spread by buying the stock for his or her own account at a price in between. But the specialist is a businessperson, not a philanthropist, and in this case the price you receive is likely to be closer to 70 than 75.

Even when the stop order works as intended, the results may be unwelcome. Suppose, for example, you are stopped out just before the stock rallies to an all-time high. Professional traders often add to this volatility for their own profit. They may dump thousands of shares to force a stock's price down and trigger stop orders. This pushes the price still lower, at which time they start buying at bargain prices.

To lower your risk of being victimized by this kind of maneuver, you can place your stop orders lower than most investors—say, 16% to 20% below the current price. In any event, set your stops at least 20% lower for any stock that experiences wide price swings.

AILMENT

According to the "T plus 3" rules for settlement of stock and bond transactions, I have to pay my broker within three days of purchase. But when I sell securities, the check is mailed to me and arrives five to eight days after the settlement date. I want to get my money faster.

℞ There is only one way to get your sales proceeds almost as quickly as you must pay for purchases. Go directly to your broker's branch office and pick up your check. The check will not be cut until the end of business on the third day following the sales transaction. If you wait to get the check in the mail, it will spend at least another day or two in the postal system before you get it.

AILMENT

My stock has lost value and become virtually worthless.

℞ No one picks winners every time. When the price of your stock declines, you need to ask yourself, "Does it have a chance of improvement?" Of course if the company is bankrupt, there is no question. Your only consideration is how to take your tax loss (see page 172). But if the company has simply lost value, you must decide whether to hold or sell. If you do not know whether the stock is worthless, you need to find out and assess the company's chance of recovery.

Decline in value.   Now is the time to be calm and objective. Remember, stocks should be bought with every intention of holding them awhile. You should sell out in a hurry only if the stock price has tumbled and you see no chance for a rise in value or you need immediate cash.

Remember, a stock's price at any time reflects supply and demand. If the stock is closely held, if its "floating supply" (the amount available in the market) is limited, the price can be depressed for a long time if some large holder is selling a sizable block not necessarily because the stock is less desirable, but because the seller needs the cash.

How can you tell the difference between a temporarily depressed stock and a genuine loser? Start with the company's annual report. Only a trained analyst can *really* read between the lines of a corporate report, but there are a few points every investor can easily check for danger flags. For example, a dividend cut is less important than a drop in earnings. If the latter happens, you have a right to know why. Often there are legitimate reasons—for example, new product development or plant expansion. There are also economic reasons. A bad earnings record in itself is no reason to switch if other companies in the same sector are also suffering.

The price-to-earnings (p-e) ratio of a stock, which can always be computed from the reported figures, is actually a more reliable measure of investment values than straight earnings per share, for it tends to reflect how other investors regard the stock. Suppose the ratio drops from 15 to 10 in one year. That indicates a serious loss of investor confidence in your company, unless stocks in general were under heavy selling pressure and p-e ratios dropped all along the line.

A decline in the p-e ratio is a danger signal meriting an intensive study of other figures in the annual report. Look at the income statement, and see how net sales have fared. And what about operating costs? Have they risen substantially? How does the margin of profit compare with the figures for earlier years? How does it compare with other companies in the same industry?

Now to the balance sheet, especially current assets and current liabilities. Has there been any big drop in the company's cash position or its holdings of government bonds? An undue increase in accounts receivable or in inventories? Any big increase in inventories of finished goods can prove risky if prices drop sharply. Or it might suggest a lot of unsalable merchandise on hand. But an increase in inventory of raw materials could be hopeful.

The most important current liability figure is accounts payable—that is, how much cash the company must lay out in the near future.

Even more important than current assets and liabilities is the relationship between the two. As a general rule, most securities analysts believe current assets should be twice as large as current liabilities.

Finally, has stockholders' equity or net worth (usually on a per share basis) grown over time?

Compare all of these figures with the same numbers for earlier years and for other companies in the same field.

In evaluating company reports, you have a right to look for help and advice from your broker.

Worthless stock.   You have no hold or sell decision to make with worthless stock—you *cannot* sell it. You can console yourself with a tax write-off, however, equal to the amount of your investment. If you sold the stock to your broker for a nominal sum, such as $1, your loss is equal to your investment minus $1.

The only real question with worthless stock losses is *when* to claim your deduction. You do not have to wait until a company goes through bankruptcy or even closes its doors. The courts have given you the right to claim an "early loss deduction." In one case, the court ruled, "A taxpayer is often in a very difficult position determining in what year to claim a loss. The safe practice is to claim a loss in the earliest year possible."

Claim the deduction on your Form 1040, Schedule D, Capital Gains and Losses, if you think it became worthless in the current tax year, or use Form 1040X, Amended U.S. Individual Income Tax Return, if you are claiming the stock became worthless in a previous year. Your net capital loss deduction is limited to $3000 a year. You may carry over any losses that are not deductible to the next year. If the company eventually turns around and the stock regains some value, you must then declare any money you receive from the eventual sale as taxable gain on Schedule D.

You have seven years from the date of your return, instead of the normal three years, to claim refunds based on a deduction for a stock, bond, or other security that becomes worthless. For example, if you think an investment became worthless in 1991, and it is now 1997, you can still go back and claim the refund. You cannot deduct a loss for stock you think is partially worthless or a publicly traded stock that has simply decreased in value until you sell it at a loss. For tax purposes, worthless stock is treated as if it became worthless on the last day of the year.

☐ Prevention

You can eliminate some problems *before* they happen by:

■ Not investing emergency funds or money you will soon need for predictable expenses. You may be forced into selling stocks during a period of low prices when you must take a loss.

■ Knowing your investment objectives. Set a point at which you will sell and stick to it.

■ Limiting your risk of losing a bundle by placing a stop-loss order with your broker when you buy the stock initially. This safety device is an order given in advance, transmitted by the commission broker to the specialist who handles the particular stock, to sell out when the stock falls to a predetermined price. A stop-loss order requires your broker to sell your shares if their price falls below an amount you have designated. For example, you might buy 100 shares of stock at $50 a share and place a 10% stop-loss order of $45. That way, the most you can lose is $500, or 10% of your investment.

■ Staying objective. Don't become so sentimental about a stock or an industry that you hold onto a company long after the potential for growth and profit has passed. A stock that is selling at 25 is a $25 stock, no matter what you originally paid for it. Remember, a decision to *retain* a losing stock is the same as a decision to *buy* a loser.

Another mistake is to fail to sell a stock because you hate to admit you were wrong to buy it in the first place.

■ Taking an realistic look at your holdings at least once a year. Ask, "If I had the money, would I buy this stock at today's prices?" If the answer is no, consider selling, even if you have to take a loss. If you don't want to make the decision yourself, ask your broker for an opinion.

■ MUTUAL FUNDS

AILMENT

I want to invest in mutual funds, but I do not know where to begin.

R Before you begin looking for a mutual fund, consider three factors: what you want the investment to do (your "investment objective"), how much risk you are willing to take, and how many years you have to meet your goal. The answers to these questions will determine which type of mutual fund you invest in. Certain funds do well over time, but are volatile in the short run. If you have a short time in which to invest, you will want to avoid aggressive stock funds, for example, because you will not have time to recoup any losses. However, if you are investing for retirement and you are still in your 30s or 40s, it would be foolish to invest solely in low-yielding money market funds.

Of course, you probably have more than one financial goal. You might be investing to buy a new home, send your child to Stanford, and build a nest egg for retirement. While the college fund may be needed in five years, the retirement money could be sitting for another 20. And you might want to make the down payment on a home at any time.

Fortunately, mutual funds will let you juggle all these goals—but only if you spread your investments among several funds. It is wise to diversify even if you are investing for just one purpose. Diversification reduces your risks, and because many mutual funds have minimum investment requirements as low as $100, you can buy into several funds with only a small amount to invest.

Choosing the right fund. Once you know your investment goals, you can begin to review mutual funds with similar aims. The Investment Company Institute, a Washington trade group for the mutual fund industry, divides fund objectives into 22 broad categories, each offering different risks and rewards. These categories include aggressive growth, balanced funds, corporate bond funds, flexible portfolio, growth and income, income and equity, money market, global equity, and global bond funds. The trade group provides short explanations of each type in its annual *Directory of Mutual Funds*.

This directory is helpful if you need basic information about fund objectives, investment restrictions, and fees. It can be ordered from the Investment Company Institute, P.O. Box 27850, Washington, DC 20038 ($5).

Do not begin and end your investigation with this one directory, though. You should also look through more comprehensive mutual fund reports. Some of the best are published by Morningstar Inc. of Chicago. Because they cost roughly $400, borrow your financial adviser's or visit your public library. The Morningstar reports describe a fund's investment history, large holdings, and management, among other things. The company also ranks funds by performance and degree of risk.

Using these directories, you can narrow your search to a handful of funds. Now it is time to contact each fund company you are interested in and ask for a prospectus and an annual or quarterly report. The prospectus will describe the fund's background, investments, history, fees, and philosophy. It will also explain how you can buy and redeem shares, and inform you of various extra services, such as check writing and special withdrawal plans. Prospectuses also often contain graphs, charting the fund's performance over the past decade or however long it has been in business.

Most funds have a nationwide toll-free 800 number. If there is none, try reversing the charges. Many funds will accept collect calls from potential investors.

Reading the prospectus. Armed with the latest prospectus, you are ready to determine if this is the fund for you. Here is what to look out for:

■ *How will the fund help you meet your goals?* Mutual funds can give you two types of return on your investment: income and growth. "Income" means dividends or interest earned by the stocks or bonds in the fund; it is passed on to you at regular intervals. Income funds are good vehicles for retired persons, who need a steady cash flow to meet living expenses and who cannot afford to risk their principal. "Growth" is the increase in value (or price) of the fund's investments; this is reflected in a change in the mutual fund's share price. Growth funds work best with a long-term investment horizon—for example, when you are saving for college or retirement.

■ *How will the fund achieve its goal?* The investment policies section of the prospectus tells what the fund intends to invest in—bonds, stocks, precious metals, or foreign stocks, for example. It also describes what quality to expect from those investments. In addition, you will find out how much the fund may invest in any one industry, or what percentage of the fund will be held as cash, for example. If you see words like *high-yield*, *options*, or *hedging*, you are looking at a highly volatile fund. Spot the phrases *inverse floating rate obligations*, *interest only obligations*, or *principal only obligations*, and you are buying stock derivatives. Derivatives are highly volatile financial instruments that can create considerable risk in a mutual fund when they are used to speculate on the movement of the stock market.

■ *How risky is the fund's strategy?* Here is where you can evaluate the likelihood things will go wrong with the fund's plans. If you buy into a fund that scoops up new issues, for example, you stand to make big gains, but you also risk large losses. By studying the fund's track record, you can see how well it has avoided downfalls in the past.

International investors should check in the policies and risk section to see if the fund has limits on how much of its portfolio can be invested in one country or region. Check there, too, to see if the fund manager tends to hedge currency positions. That can make the fund more stable, but ultimately cost some return.

■ *How much will it cost to invest in the fund?* Fee tables will tell you whether the fund imposes a "load," a charge when you buy, reinvest, or redeem shares. Funds sold through brokers and financial planners carry loads of up to 8.5%, though you will generally pay less if you invest $10,000 or more. No-load funds and so-called low-load funds, which impose loads of between 1% and 3%, are sold by phone or mail by the fund sponsor. There is no evidence that load funds do better than no-loads.

Do not look only at initial sales charges or loads. High, ongoing operating expenses—12(b)1 fees for marketing the funds—can end up costing more on a long-term investment. It is especially hard to make up high expenses on an income-oriented fund. The average stock fund has an expense ratio of about 90 cents to each $100 in fund assets (.9%). That means that for each $10,000 in fund assets, the fund has about $90 in annual overhead costs that are paid out of shareholders' pooled assets. The average expense ratio for bond funds is about 80 cents (.8%). Expenses above 1.5% are too high.

Some funds also levy back-end loads or exit fees when you redeem your shares. Back-end loads generally start at around 5% and decrease gradually until they disappear after you have owned your shares for seven years. Exit fees remain at a fixed 1% or 2%.

Both sales charges and fund operating expenses can take deep bites out of your returns. Unless you want the benefit of a particular fund manager's expertise, stick with no-loads and funds that have low expenses.

■ *How well has the fund done?* A performance table shows how well you would have fared if you had owned shares in the fund over the previous 10 years. Per-share dividends, capital gains distributions, and the share price at the beginning and end of each year are included. The portfolio turnover rate is also listed. Generally, the higher the rate, the greater the fund's expenses. A rate exceeding 100% is considered high.

The performance section lists yield and total return figures. Total return includes both income and any change—up or down—in share price during a specified period. It assumes that distributions are reinvested in additional shares.

■ *Are there hidden tax burdens?* Unless you are putting the fund in a tax-deferred retirement account, you want to know what kind of tax bite you are buying. "Unrealized appreciation" means capital gains waiting to be taxed; capital loss carryforwards could cut your tax burden this year. A fund that buys and sells a lot during the year can be expected to generate significant capital gains income every year, too.

If you are looking for a tax-free investment, check the prospectus's table of tax equivalent yields. It will tell you how much return you need from a taxable fund to beat the fund's tax-free return.

■ *What special features are offered?* As funds grow in number, the services they offer become more important and competitive. Do you want telephone transactions, check writing, automatic investing?

One thing you will not find in the prospectus is a listing of what securities the fund owns. You can get that information, though, in the fund's Statement of Additional Information. Ask for a copy when you request the prospectus.

Buying mutual fund shares. Every fund's prospectus contains a section with instructions on how to invest in that fund. You can buy shares in mutual funds directly from the mutual fund company, or through a third party—a broker, a financial planner, an insurance company, or a bank. Some mutual fund companies have local offices where you can ask questions and purchase shares.

Check the minimum purchase and minimum redemption amounts. Most funds require an initial investment of at least $500, and many will not accept new accounts of less than $1000. Funds often set a lower IRA minimum initial investment, though. If you plan to use a money market fund as a checking account, make sure the fund does not have a $1000 minimum check amount.

What you pay for shares. When you buy into a mutual fund, the price you pay is called the "offering price." Every day, each mutual fund computes its offering price, using the following figures:

- The value of all assets in the fund that day.

- One day's percentage of the annual cost of running the fund ("fund expenses").

- The number of shares owned by investors that day.

The fund expenses are subtracted from the assets. The resulting "net asset" figure is then divided by the number of shares owned. This produces the net asset value (NAV) of a share.

For example, if GetRich Fund has assets of $100 million, after expenses, and the fund has sold 10 million shares, the NAV of each share is $10. If the assets of the fund increase in value tomorrow by $200,000 (after expenses) and the number of shares stays the same, the NAV will rise to $10.02.

With no-load funds, the offering price is the same as the NAV, because you do not pay a sales charge, or load. With load funds, the offering price is higher than the NAV. The sales charge is a percentage of the amount you invest—anywhere from 1% to 8.5%, the maximum allowed.

Sales charges of 1% to 3% are called "low loads" and are used to offset the fund operator's marketing and service expenses. Higher loads are usually charged by funds that use commissioned sales representatives.

All funds, whether no-load or load, carry a management fee that is paid by the fund to the fund's adviser. This fee is explained in the prospectus. It ranges from under .5% to over 1% of the fund's assets, on a daily basis. Because the amount taken out each day is minuscule, it does not affect the share price.

You can track the net asset value of your fund by checking the financial pages of any major newspaper or by calling the mutual fund company.

Keeping tabs.   Do not stop researching a fund after you buy it. Read new quarterly and annual reports to check the fund's progress and spot changes in direction. Mutual funds change, and so does the economy. Successful investing depends on staying alert to new situations.

AILMENT

I want to buy shares in a mutual fund, but I have heard that the end of the year is a bad time to buy.

R You do have to be careful when you buy mutual funds at the end of the year, because that is when most funds distribute their interest, dividends, and capital gains. While buying shares in November and getting a full year's worth of distributions in December may sound like a coup, it can be a costly mistake. When a fund makes a distribution, the price of your shares declines by the amount of the payout, so the value of your investment stays the same. But the distribution is fully *taxable*—even if the money is automatically reinvested. If you just bought into the fund, the distribution is, in effect, an instant return of part of your principal, except that now you owe taxes on it. For example, suppose you are in the 31% tax bracket and bought 100 shares of Payout Pronto at $49 two weeks before it declared a $4 per share dividend on December 23. You would get back $400 of your original $4900 investment. Your tax bill: $124.

To limit the tax bite, do not invest in a capital-gains-laden fund *until after* its ex-dividend date. Anyone who owns shares on the ex-dividend date is entitled to a distribution—and will owe tax on it. Generally, this is near the end of December, although funds on a fiscal year have two ex-dividend dates. (The distribution may actually be made a few days after the ex-dividend date.) To find out the ex-dividend date, check the prospectus or ask your broker or the fund's phone representative.

For an estimate of the size of a distribution, check the prospectus for the amount of past payouts. Some fund companies, such as T. Rowe Price, will send you an estimate of the coming payout. But the actual distribution may be larger if the fund proceeds to rake in substantial gains before the ex-dividend date.

☐ Prevention

Investors who want to buy more stock (perhaps to cash in on any run-up in market prices that typically occurs in January) without taking a hit from a fund distribution should bide their time in an index fund. Because index funds mimic the holdings of various market indexes, they have less turnover than most mutual funds and as a result, fewer capital gains.

AILMENT

I sent in a check and application to purchase exactly 100 shares of a fund. I expected the fund to refund any amount I had included that was above the purchase price. Instead, the entire amount I sent was used to buy 109.804 shares.

℞ With most funds, it is standard practice to make investments in dollar amounts rather than in shares. On the other hand, with redemptions, you can request either shares or dollar amounts. If you really want only 100 shares of the fund, simply redeem the extra shares purchased for your account. It will cost you nothing.

AILMENT

I do not know how to keep track of my mutual fund investment.

By law, every fund shareholder must receive a report of the fund's operation at least twice a year. These reports usually include a financial statement, a list of all securities within the fund's portfolio, and a summary of important investment developments.

Once a year, mutual funds also provide a Form 1099 to shareowners showing the total amount of dividends, interest, and capital gains realized during the year. Shareowners also get a new prospectus about once a year.

To find out how you stand on any given day, check the financial pages of your newspaper for the share prices of your fund. A sample of such a listing is shown in Figure 6–2; here is an explanation of how to read each column:

FIGURE 6–2   Sample Mutual Fund Table

Mutual Funds

For: Tuesday, May 6, 1997

Approximately 3,300 funds are listed daily, generally the largest by asset size. Performance data—and more funds—are published in Sunday's Business section. Some funds marketed outside California, institutional fund families and funds that do not wish to be tracked, are removed.

Net asset value (NAV) quotations are supplied by the funds. If prices are delivered late to NASD, no price appears here. NAV adjusted after dividends paid or capital gains distributed **Footnotes: n** means "no load", meaning no sales commission, **x** is ex-dividend, **e**—ex-distribution of gains, **s**—stock split or dividend, **r**—redemption charge may apply, **t**—redemption charge may apply and charges an annual fee, **p**—charges an annual fee to cover expenses not included in the sales fee, **f**—previous day's quotation. **Single-fund families (orphan funds) all in bold.**

Fund	NAV	Chg.	Fund	NAV	Chg.	Fund	NAV	Chg.	Fund	NAV	Chg.
AAL Mutual A:			**Amer Century 20th:**			**BT Index Funds:**			GrIIB p	18.39	−0.08
Bond	9.65	+0.01	Gift n	20.47	−0.05	InstEqIx n	18.66	−0.05	MunB	13.68	
CaGr	22.35	−0.11	Growth n	23.93	−0.18	InvEqIx n	18.47	−0.04	**Composite Group:**		
Intl	11.57	+0.11	Heritage n	12.66	−0.04	**BT Investment Fds:**			BdStkA p	14.87	−0.04
MidCSt	13.40	−0.03	IntDisc n	7.96	+0.05	CapApp n	12.77	−0.09	GrIncA p	18.48	−0.08
MuBd	10.95	+0.01	IntlGro n	8.79	+0.08	InstAstM n	12.83	−0.04	InFdA p	9.05	...
Util	11.69	+0.02	New Opp n	4.31	+0.01	InvEqAp n	12.86	−0.08	NWFdA p	21.52	−0.15
AARP Invst:			Select n	43.12	−0.09	InvIntEq n	19.12	+0.27	TxExA p	7.74	...
BalS&B n	19.15	−0.01	Ultra n	30.33	−0.16	InvLGvt n	9.79	...	USGvA p	10.35	...
CaGr n	47.68	−0.23	Vista n	12.34	−0.06	InvSmC n	15.88	−0.09	**Comstock Partners:**		
GiniM n	14.93	...	**Amer Century Benh:**			LcylRg n	12.73	−0.04	CapVIA	8.48	+0.06
GlblGr n	17.24	+0.15	AdjGov n	9.54	...	LcyMRg n	11.33	−0.03	CapVB t	8.32	+0.06
GthInc n	49.55	−0.02	Bond n	9.41	...	**Babson Group:**			PStgA p	7.81	+0.02
HQ Bd n	15.79	...	CaHYMu n	9.43	...	Bond L	1.51	...	PStgO t	7.82	+0.02
TxFBd n	17.82	+0.01	CaInsTF n	10.08	...	Enterp2	21.43	−0.05	**Concert Series A:**		
AHA Funds:			CaIntTF n	11.04	...	Enterp	17.13	+0.04	GrthA	12.30	...
Balan n	13.89	−0.03	CaLgTF n	11.20	...	Gwtfr	17.11	−0.09	HiGroA	12.18	...
DivrEq n	18.95	−0.07	CaLtdTF n	10.18	+0.01	Intl	18.38	+0.28	BalncdA p	12.27	+0.02
Full n	9.70	...	EurBd n	10.89	+0.10	Value	40.21	−0.01	SocAwA p	19.78	−0.03
Lim n	10.12	−0.01	GNMA n	10.45	+0.01	**BailardBiehl&Kaiser:**			**Concert Series B&C:**		

1. The first column shows the fund's name, abbreviated. Several names under one heading indicate a fund family.

2. The second column is the NAV (net asset value) of a share at the close of the preceding business day. The NAV column may also be called "sell" or "bid." This is the price you would have received (less any back-end load fee or redemption charge) if you had sold your shares on that day. Compute the most recent value of your holdings by multiplying the NAV by the number of shares you own.

3. In some financial listings, there is a third column for the offering price, also called "buy" or "asked." It is the price you would have paid to buy shares at the close of the preceding business day. An "n" in this column means the fund is no-load, and its offering price is the same as the NAV.

4. The final column shows whether the NAV rose, fell, or stayed the same, in cents, during the preceding trading day.

AILMENT

I want to compare the returns on two of my mutual funds for the year, but I do not know how their yields are calculated.

℞ Yields are just a part of total return—which is what you really want to compare. Here is how to calculate a fund's total return, assuming that you reinvested your capital gains and income distributions: Multiply the number of shares you now own by the current price per share. Subtract your original investment from the result. Then divide that figure by your original investment, and multiply by 100. What if you did not reinvest your distributions? After you multiply the number of shares you own times the price, add in the distributions.

Let us say your 200 shares, at a current price per share of $35, are now worth $7000. Your investment was $4000. You will divide $3000 by $4000 (getting .75), and multiply that by 100 to arrive at your percentage increase: 75%. For no-load funds, use the net asset value (NAV) per share as the current price; for front-end load funds, use the offering price (see page 179 for an explanation of how to read mutual fund listings).

That simple calculation assumes your funds were idle during the year. Active investors must endure more math. Cash infusions and withdrawals—and when you made them—affect your overall rate of return. For example, if a huge tax bill caused you to cash out shares or an inheritance revived your interest in investing, you should use the work sheet (Figure 6–3) to compute your personal total return. The work sheet calculation is fairly precise if you made regular additions and withdrawals. If your invest-

FIGURE 6–3 Mutual Fund Performance Work Sheet

1. Number of months for which performance is being measured (not more than two years). _____

2. Your investment at the beginning of the period (from your statement if it shows your first investment in the fund; otherwise, multiply the number of shares you owned by their price per share). _____

3. Current value of your investment (multiply the number of shares now owned by the net asset value per share). _____

4. Unreinvested income, if any (total dividends and capital-gains distributions received in cash during the period). _____

5. Net redemptions or net investments during the period (do not include reinvested dividends). _____

6. Computation of gain or loss:

   Step A: Add line 2 to one-half of the total on line 5. _____

   Step B: Add lines 3 and 4, then subtract half the total on line 5. _____

   Step C: Divide Step B sum by Step A sum. _____

   Step D: Subtract 1 from Step C result, then multiply times 100. _____

7. Computation of annualized return (divide line 1 into 12); multiply the result by Step D percentage. _____

ments were more erratic, compute your total return at the end of each quarter (or even each month). Then add the quarterly (or monthly) returns together to get the annual total return.

The work sheet uses one mutual fund, but you can repeat the same steps to compute the total return on a portfolio of funds. Start by figuring the beginning and ending values for each fund, then add them together to get beginning and ending values for the portfolio.

To find out how your fund rated this year, gather your account statements—or year-end cumulative statement—and turn on your calculator. For starters, enter the number of shares you held on January 1, their net asset value per share, and their total value. Record the same information for December 31. Reinvested distributions are reflected in those year-end totals, but cash distributions are not. So add up any income you did not reinvest and enter the total on line 4.

Finally, subtract the total proceeds from shares you sold from the total of all new money invested in the fund. If you withdrew more cash than you invested during the year, you will have a negative number on line 5. To account for front-end sales fees, investments in the fund should include the actual amount you spent to buy the shares, not their value when you bought them. Similarly, enter the cash you pocketed as the amount of any withdrawal.

If you only want to know how your fund's performance stacked up against others—or against the Dow Jones Industrial Average or Standard & Poor's 500 stock index—you can skip the math. Simply look up the year-end total return in a mid-February issue of *Barron's* and compare it against the same figure for similar funds.

☐ Resources

A computer software program called PFROI can do the mathematical gymnastics for you. PFROI (CAPTOOLS, 800-826-8082) delivers a more precise total return than the work sheet because the effect of account activity is computed to the day. The program, which runs on IBM-compatible PCs, is not all that user-friendly. But after you master the manual, PFROI will calculate the before- and after-tax return on virtually any investment, or all your investments as a group.

AILMENT

I want to smooth out the stock market's ups and downs.

R The most effective strategy for nervous types is a simple process called dollar cost averaging. All it means is investing a fixed amount at regular intervals, maybe every month or quarter, so that you end up buying shares at various prices—fewer shares when prices are high and more when they are low.

With dollar cost averaging, you don't try to time the market, and you don't have to worry that you will be investing all your money just when the market hits an all-time high. By using dollar cost averaging, you are diversifying over time.

Dollar cost averaging works with many types of assets, from gold coins to stocks. But the strategy works particularly well with mutual funds, which accept small periodic investments and will credit you with a fractional purchase of shares. For best results, pick a stock equity fund rather than a bond fund, because there are wider price swings in the stock market.

Most mutual fund companies require initial investments ranging from $25 to around $3000, with subsequent purchases of at least $50 to $250.

You can buy mutual fund shares with regular, automatic withdrawals from your paycheck or bank account. There is usually no charge for this service, other than the normal front-end sales fee if you invest in a load fund. Another option is to transfer cash gradually into a stock or bond fund from a money market portfolio in the same family.

You do not have to set up an automatic dollar cost averaging program. You may simply write a check each time you want to invest. Remember, though, that to succeed with dollar cost averaging, you must keep investing through at least one full market cycle. Do not give up if the market turns into a bear. That is when prices are lowest. With dollar cost averaging, it is more important to keep adding to your stake than to worry about whether the time is right to buy.

Of course, dollar cost averaging assumes that equity funds will rise over time. That is a fairly solid bet; the stock market has declined in just 19 of the 71 years going back to 1926.

When not to dollar cost average. Dollar cost averaging works just fine with a payroll-deduction plan. But it may not be the best investment method if you suddenly get a large chunk of cash—from a pension withdrawal or inheritance, for example.

Suppose, for example, you want to buy growth mutual funds with a distribution from a retirement plan. To dollar cost average, you would stash the money in a money market account, then start buying the funds in bite-size pieces, once a month. It might take you a year to fully invest your distribution. You would have avoided a serious loss if the market had dropped. But would you have come out ahead? Not necessarily. Stocks usually produce better returns than bank deposits or money market funds. And the market goes up more often than it goes down. That is why lump-sum investing almost always wins in years the market rises. So if you want to be in stocks, you stand a better chance of earning higher returns by investing as fast as possible.

On the other hand, dollar cost averaging lowers risk. In addition, in markets that rise only slightly, dollar cost averaging may close in on a lump-sum return.

A rule of thumb for cautious investors: Take no more than one year to invest a lump sum in stock mutual funds. For medium-term bond funds, take no more than five months.

℞ The interest earned by federal, state, and local bonds is exempt from certain kinds of taxes. Because federal and state bonds can be expensive to buy, many investors who want to save taxes choose mutual funds made up of tax-exempt bonds or money market instruments.

There are a wealth of mutual funds available that produce tax-exempt interest. These include funds that invest in U.S. government securities and state and local bonds.

U.S. Treasury securities.   Interest income from Treasury bills, notes, or bonds is exempt from state and local taxes. (The earnings are taxable on your federal return, though.) To take advantage of this tax break, choose a mutual fund that holds only U.S. government issues. After taxes, these funds pay nearly one percent more in high-tax states.

Be careful in choosing your fund, though. You need the right fund for your state's tax code. Pick the wrong one and live in the wrong state, and you could get an unwelcome surprise at tax time.

Here are a few of the traps: A lot of so-called government bond funds do not invest in direct government debt, but rather in paper that is merely guaranteed by the federal government. For example, the portfolio of the Value Line U.S. Government Securities Fund is 86% invested in Ginnie Maes, fully taxable by the states. Indeed, a lot of Ginnie Mae funds masquerade as "government" funds.

Some federal agency debt is tax-free; others are not. Tennessee Valley Authority bonds are considered a direct U.S. obligation and are exempt. So are bonds from the various agencies bailing out banks and thrifts. But Fannie Mae and Freddie Mac bond interest is taxable.

States that do recognize payouts from U.S. Treasury funds as exempt generally require that at least 50% to 80% of the earnings come from Treasury interest, or none of it is exempt.

Finally, six states play rough and tax in full any dividend from any incorporated fund, regardless of its source. Their argument is that these are dividends from fund companies, not interest from government bonds. These six states are Connecticut, Delaware, Mississippi, North Dakota, Pennsylvania, and Tennessee. If you live in one of these states, buy bonds directly from your state or municipality instead of investing in a bond fund.

Unfortunately, it is almost impossible to get clear information from a fund about the tax status of its investments. What you need to know is the percentage of income derived from direct U.S. government obligations. But the service representatives usually claim they do not know or cannot tell you.

Instead, ask if the fund sends out a statement showing the percentage at tax time. If not, request the portfolio (usually a semiannual financial statement, not in the prospectus) and compare it with a list of acceptable bonds. Generally, mortgage-backed federal issues are taxable by the states and nonmortgage issues are not.

State bond funds.   For people in states with high income taxes, there is a special type of fund called a "single state fund." These are mutual funds that invest primarily in bonds or money market investments issued by a particular state or the cities and towns in that state. Resident investors usually pay no federal or state taxes on income paid by these funds.

If you are a resident of a lightly-taxed state, you do not need to stick close to home. You can roam the country for higher yields from funds investing in other states.

Computing the true yield of tax-exempt funds.   The prospect of the tax bonanza awaiting municipal bond fund investors excites even the lowest earners. And that can be a problem, because muni bond funds are not for everyone.

The reason: Tax-exempt bonds usually pay less than taxable investments. That means you need enough tax savings to make up the difference in yield. Before you commit your money, use this simple formula to decide whether a tax-exempt fund will net a better return than a taxable stock or bond fund: Subtract your top tax bracket from 100%, and divide the tax-exempt interest rate by the result. For example, if your combined federal and state bracket is 31%, a tax-free yield of 5% is equivalent to a taxable yield of 7.25% (5% divided by 69% [100% – 31%]).

Investors in high-tax states, such as California and Massachusetts, can boost tax savings by sticking with home-grown bonds, which are exempt from state and local, as well as federal taxes.

Some final points: Income from some muni bond funds, including sewer, mass transit, and airport bonds, is taxed to the few taxpayers hit by alternative minimum tax. If you are a senior citizen, municipal bond interest counts in figuring the amount of Social Security benefits taxed.

AILMENT

My mutual fund account was closed out fraudulently by someone posing as me on the phone.

R̸ Unfortunately, fraud involving mutual funds exists in part because calls to investment companies' 800 numbers can be made anonymously. Add in the ability of sophisticated crooks to gain personal information and access to investment accounts, and the result is a growing problem of identity fraud, in which one person impersonates another to gain access to the other's money. Such frauds are usually committed by someone you know, such as an estranged spouse or a disgruntled employee. But fraud by strangers is the fastest-growing type.

Fortunately, you do not have to fear for your savings. It is unlikely you will suffer a permanent financial loss. Mutual fund companies are insured against theft and generally will reimburse an investor who has been victimized. Notify your mutual fund of the fraud, if you have not already done so, and it will probably restore your positions in full. Expect to be inconvenienced by long interviews with the fund's detectives and executives about your financial life and the individuals with whom you do business, though.

You should also take other steps immediately:

■ Call the major credit-reporting bureaus. They will send you a copy of your credit report and place a fraud alert on your account. Their names and numbers are Equifax, 800-685-1111; Trans Union, 800-680-7289; and Experian Corporation (formerly TRW), 800-301-7195.

■ If a check or statement is lost in the mail or if you have received no mail for several days, call the U.S. Postal Service at 800-ASK-USPS. Someone pretending to be you may have put a vacation hold on your mail (intending to go to the post office and pick your mail up) or have given the Postal Service a change of address to redirect your mail to another location.

■ If it appears that a thief has your Social Security number, contact the Social Security Administration at 800-772-1213 for information.

☐ Prevention

Here are six ways to protect your accounts from fraud:

1. *Consider using a full-service broker.* A broker who knows you personally and recognizes your voice may prevent fraudulent transactions and notice odd activity in your account. Of course, a broker is no solution if the trouble is with checks or a credit card linked to your brokerage account. And, using a full-service broker will cost more. It could even lead to other problems: The greatest number of fraud complaints to the Securities and Exchange Commission (SEC) are about brokers misrepresenting their products or churning accounts.

2. *Cancel phone privileges.* Many brokerage firms will let you require that withdrawals be made only in writing or even only in person. The security may outweigh the lack of convenience.

3. *Watch your mailbox and what you put in the trash.* Statements and other documents are prime sources of information for criminals. If a mutual fund statement fails to come in the mail, be concerned. You can buy an inexpensive paper shredder for financial documents.

4. *Read your financial statements.* If you do not spot a fraud or error within a certain time frame, you lose some of your rights to recover the funds.

5. *Use optional safety features.* Some companies will let you create a password that is necessary to do business. You could also request that any transaction be confirmed with an immediate call back to your home number.

6. *Stay informed about fraud.* You can get tips from the SEC by calling 800-SEC-0330, or on the Internet at http://www.sec.gov. Information on avoiding fraud, suggestions for choosing brokers, and links to tips and warnings from several government agencies can also be found on the Internet at http://www.investorprotection.org.

AILMENT

I do not know whether I should sell my mutual fund shares.

℞ The decision to sell your shares requires as much careful thought as evaluating a fund before you buy it. In some ways, deciding to call it quits is harder.

To spot the right time to sell, you need to compare your funds with others that have similar objectives and stack them up against your personal financial goals. As long as your fund is giving you what you want, hold onto it. But if you believe another fund can do a better job, sell.

You should also consider selling your fund shares in the following circumstances:

■ *When your finances change.* As you near your goals, your needs and your tolerance for risk should change.
■ *When the fund changes.* If the fund no longer meets the criteria that led you to invest in it, consider a replacement.

You might also decide to sell if a successful manager retires or quits. Fund groups like to keep such losses quiet. But if you notice a change in performance, volatility, or the fund's investment style, ask the fund if the manager has left.

Should you sell just because there has been a change in command? Stay loose. It takes at least six months for a new manager to have much impact. Take that time to investigate two important questions:

First, does the fund depend on creative, ongoing investment decisions and tend to have a high portfolio turnover? The turnover rate indicates how often securities are bought and sold. This number can be found in fund financial statements. An annual rate of 200% means two complete changes in the composition of assets and suggests that the manager's role is quite active. A turnover of 20% or less indicates that the manager plays little role in the fund's success. Instead, investment decisions may be made by committee, computer, or in line with a rigid investment philosophy.

Second, Is there something unique about the outgoing portfolio manager that will be missed?

If the answers are no, wait and see what happens. If yes, the manager is a factor. Reevaluate the fund—heavily discounting past performance and emphasizing the incoming manager's credentials—to decide whether to continue with that fund.

■ *When performance lags behind similar funds.* If your fund is a mediocre performer in a swaggering bull market, you will naturally want to pull the plug. But don't be too hasty. In a volatile market, today's big winner could be tomorrow's also-ran. To prevent a premature sell-off, give your fund at least a year to prove itself. With a conservative growth and income fund, it could even take two years for a fund to distinguish itself. Do not sell a fund just because it is not in the Top 10. But if it is not ranked among the top 10% of funds in its category for four to six quarters in a row, it is time to shop for a more successful fund.

■ *When the market turns against you.* Most diversified funds, whether invested in stocks or in bonds, tend to rise and fall with the general markets. So, you can improve your return by switching into a money market fund during a bear market, then easing back into stocks and bond funds when there is an upturn.

Of course, timing the market is easier said than done. Another response to a market slide is to hang onto your fund shares and even grab a few more. A diversified mutual fund is almost sure to rebound when the market recovers. If riding a roller-coaster market is too harrowing, pick a fund that has weathered all types of markets, and stick with it.

■ *When you can cut your taxes.* If your fund drops, for example, you can sell your shares and deduct your loss against any capital gains and up to $3000 of other income. If you think the fund has promise, you can buy it back after 30 days without losing your tax deduction.

AILMENT

I want to redeem my mutual fund shares for the lowest possible tax liability.

R To keep your gain and taxes at a minimum, sell your highest-price shares first. The key is to tell your broker or mutual fund the exact shares you want to sell. If you do not identify which shares you are selling, a first in, first out (FIFO) rule applies. It assumes the shares you have owned the longest are the first ones to be sold. Because these are often the shares with the lowest tax basis, selling them could result in a big tax bill. (*Note:* You may want to redeem shares with the lowest basis if you have a net *loss* on all of your transactions for the year, as the gain would be offset by your losses on other deals.)

You can compute the cost of your redeemed shares three different ways:

1. *Specific identification.* If you have not yet sold your shares, you can steer clear of the FIFO rule by telling your broker which shares you want sold, by either their purchase date or their cost, or both. Then make sure the broker confirms the sale in writing within a reasonable time.

Suppose, for example, that you have accumulated shares in the BigCap Fund over five years at prices ranging from $9 to $28. The current net asset value is $22. Because the current price is $22, you earmark for sale the shares you bought at $28. This gives you a loss of $6 per share when you redeem.

On the other hand, suppose that you have already taken a capital loss on another investment. In this case, you should specify that you want to sell the shares with the lowest cost basis—those in the $9 range. This increases your capital gain to absorb some of the earlier loss.

For each block of shares you own, keep the following information: date of purchase and reinvestment, cost per share and total cost, date of redemption, number of shares, per-share price, sale proceeds, and shares remaining. In a confirmation letter to the fund, you should specify the shares sold so that you can later back up your tax treatment.

If you have already sold your mutual fund shares, you can use one of the other methods to pay the least tax or take the greatest loss. These methods can also contain the damage if the transfer agent for your no-load mutual fund will not take the trouble to isolate the shares you want to sell by their purchase date, as is often the case.

2. *Average cost.* Single-category method: To compute your average cost, divide the total you have invested, including reinvestments, by the total number of shares. The average-cost method keeps you from having to tediously reconstruct your cost when shares have been bought in small lots over many years—for instance, with a dividend reinvestment plan. If you use the average cost method, you must keep on using it for that particular mutual fund, unless you get written permission to switch from the IRS. By contrast, you do not have to stick with the first in, first out or share identification methods in later years.

Your mutual fund may send you a year-end statement showing the average basis of your shares and your profit (or loss) on redemptions for the year based on that basis and the redemption price. This useful information cannot always be transferred directly to your tax return without adjustment, however.

For one thing, if you have identified specific shares to be redeemed in the past, the average basis shown on the statement could be out of whack. The mutual fund statement assumes that all shares sold got the average-basis treatment. The average basis will be wrong, too, if you were given or inherited some of the shares.

To ensure accurate average-basis figures in the future, advise your mutual fund that you previously redeemed specific shares.

With the average cost triple-category method, you divide your shares into three groups: those held longer than 18 months (long-term shares), those held between 12 and 18 months (mid-term shares), and those held for 12 months or less (short-term shares). Then, figure the average cost per share for each group. You must notify the mutual fund which group the shares you are selling come from, or the IRS will assume they were long-term. This approach gives you more flexibility than the single-category method, but is not recommended unless you truly enjoy bookkeeping.

To use the short-term average basis, you must get written confirmation that you advised the fund at the time of the trade that you were redeeming shares from the short-term group. Otherwise, you must use the long-term average basis.

3. *FIFO actual cost.* If you do not specify either of the previous methods on your tax return, the first in, first out (FIFO) rule applies. For example, if you owned 2000 shares and sold 400 of them, your cost basis would be the actual cost of the first 400 shares you bought.

If your fund shares have been declining in value over the period you have been accumulating them, the first in, first out method will produce the biggest deductible loss.

Mutual fund exchanges.   If you switch assets from one fund to another, the transaction is considered a sale and a purchase for tax purposes. The gain or loss on the shares sold must be reported on your tax return (except for exchanges in an IRA or other tax-sheltered account). Before you make your exchange, minimize the tax effect by specifying the shares you want to switch to a new fund.

☐ Prevention

As you accumulate shares over the years, by direct purchase and reinvestment of dividends and distributions, it is important to keep complete records. Doing so will make it easier to avoid paying tax twice on reinvestments, and you will have the figures you need to compute your gain or loss using the most advantageous method.

I asked my mutual fund to transfer my IRA money to another mutual fund company, but they are dragging their feet about it.

℞ The company that is losing your IRA business probably does not consider the transfer a top priority. If your transaction has not been completed within two weeks, pick up the phone or have your broker do so, if you are working with one. Check on the status of the transfer with the company losing the account. If the paperwork has been received and it is in order, the money is legally required to be out of the fund within seven days.

Contact the firm to which you are making the transfer, too. They should be more sympathetic to your problem.

☐ Prevention

It is usually faster to make an IRA rollover than a transfer. With the former, you actually receive a check for the proceeds in your account, then mail it to the new trustee of your choice. Transfers go directly from one institution to another. The drawback with rollovers is that you may make only one a year or risk an IRS penalty. There is no limit on how many direct transfers you can make. And if you take the cash yourself in a rollover, the company will withhold 20% of your IRA proceeds for income tax. But you must still roll over the entire amount within 60 days to avoid income tax and an early withdrawal penalty.

I want to get my money out of my mutual fund.

℞ One of the most attractive features of a mutual fund is its liquidity. It is usually as easy—if not always as speedy—to take your money out of a fund as it is to put it in.

A mutual fund will buy back, or redeem, your shares at any time. Most redemptions can be processed within a few days, especially if you know the rules about selling shares and have made advance arrangements. Even if the market crashes, a fund must redeem your shares before 4 P.M. Eastern time on the first trading day after it receives proper notification. The fund can use its cash reserves or a line of credit to pay you, without actually selling your shares.

Here are some of the ways you can cash out:

■ If you have not set up telephone exchange or redemption privileges, you must send in a redemption letter requesting that some or all of your shares be sold and the proceeds returned to you. It will probably be several weeks before you receive your money.

Most funds require a signature guaranteed by a commercial bank or a major brokerage firm for redemptions above a certain amount. (Signature guarantees are always needed if you are redeeming shares from an IRA or pension account.) Signature guarantees are meant to prevent fraud, because mutual fund managers do not get to know their customers personally, the way banks and brokers do.

■ In a money market fund with check writing privileges, you can also redeem some or all of your shares simply by writing yourself a check.

■ In a family of mutual funds, you can exchange one mutual fund for another, usually by telephone. In fact, you can switch from one fund into your money market fund, and write yourself a check. That is one of the easiest and quickest ways to convert your investment into cash.

What price will you get for your shares? They will be redeemed at the net asset value determined at the end of the business day your request is received. Some funds charge a fee on redemption, and that will also be included in figuring the net asset value of your shares.

AILMENT

I wrote a redemption letter in time to get a short-term loss and sent a copy of the original application along with my letter. The fund said I needed to send a signature guarantee, and the delay cost me a bundle in taxes.

R$\!\!\!/$ Written requests for redemption (see sample letter on page 195) usually must be signed by each shareholder, exactly as the account is registered, with signatures guaranteed by a commercial bank, trust company, or brokerage firm (attestation by a notary public is not accepted). If the shares are registered to a trust, corporation, executor, administrator, or other fiduciary, additional paperwork is required, and this can differ with each fund.

But according to Rule 22 of the federal Investment Company Act of 1940, which governs all mutual funds, redemptions must be made at the closing price as of the end of the business day on which your properly documented request is received. Redemption proceeds must be mailed within seven calendar days, although many funds are speedier. Only the Securities and Exchange Commission can authorize exceptions to these rules. (Of course, if you sell fund shares you recently purchased by check, the redemption check will not be mailed until your purchase check clears.)

SAMPLE REDEMPTION LETTER

Dear Sirs:

Please redeem (Number of Shares) of my holdings in (Name of Fund). [Or: Please close out my position in (Name of Fund).]

Sell the shares that I purchased on (Date).

My account number is _____ .

Please send the proceeds to (Your Name and Address).

Sincerely,

(Your Signature* Exactly as Your Name Appears on Your Mailings)
(*In case of a joint account, both owners must sign.)

If your redemption request was in proper form, and there was still a delay that caused you to suffer a loss, contact the fund and demand restitution. If the fund is at fault and will not pay, contact the Securities and Exchange Commission, Office of Consumer Affairs, Investor Services, 450 Fifth Street, NW, Washington, DC 20549; 202-942-7040.

☐ Prevention

Read fund prospectuses carefully and refer to them when making redemptions. If you have questions, call the fund for clarification of requirements. Write down that person's name and the date of your contact, so you can refer to a specific individual in case a problem develops. Also, note the date and name of any person you communicate with at the SEC.

☐ Resources

The Consumer Information Center, Pueblo, CO 81009, provides a free catalog of federal consumer publications. Among the government publications are a number of free and low-cost booklets on money management.

The American Association of Individual Investors, 625 North Michigan Avenue, Suite 1900, Chicago, IL 60611, is geared to helping investors better manage their assets. It publishes *AAII Journal* and the annual *Individual Investor's Guide to No-Load Mutual Funds*. AAII has local chapters throughout the country, produces a home-study curriculum, and provides a series of one-day investment seminars.

The Investment Company Institute, 1401 H Street NW, Washington, DC 20005, publishes an annual *Mutual Fund Fact Book* with statistics on specific funds, background on trends in the mutual fund industry, and brief mutual fund definitions (available for $25). The Institute also produces a variety of free brochures on personal finance.

The National Association of Investment Clubs, 711 West Thirteen Mile Road, Madison Heights, MI 48071, publishes a teach-yourself *Starting and Running a Profitable Investment Club* and *Better Investing* magazine (available by subscription).

The No-Load Mutual Fund Association, P.O. Box 2004, JAF Station, New York, NY 10116, publishes an annual *Investor's Directory* of funds with other explanatory material (available for $2). Also offers a "No-Load Mutual Fund Resource List"—a bibliography of newsletters, magazines, books, other publications, and organizations, including advisory services (free with self-addressed stamped envelope).

Magazines

Barron's, published every Monday by Dow Jones & Company, Inc.
Kiplinger's Personal Finance Magazine, published monthly by The Kiplinger Organization.
Money, published monthly by Time Warner, Inc.

■ Stock Brokerages

AILMENT

My brokerage firm just went broke.

Large-scale brokerage troubles are rare, and investors do have protection. The Securities Investor Protection Corporation, or SIPC, steps in when a brokerage fails. All brokers and dealers registered with the Securities and Exchange Commission and with the major stock exchanges are required by law to become SIPC customers. The agency insures customer assets at failed brokerages up to $500,000 per customer, including a maximum of $100,000 coverage for each customer's cash account.

Meanwhile, your account has probably been frozen while a court-appointed receiver sorts through the firm's books to figure out who is owed what. Once the receiver identifies customer claims against the brokerage firm, the SIPC can begin to reimburse accounts.

First, the receiver will try to locate and return the actual securities in customers' accounts at the time the brokerage failed. If securities are missing—in other words, if the account has been a victim of fraud—the receiver will use SIPC funds to purchase the same securities and return them to the account. If, for some reason, the securities cannot be returned, the receiver will reimburse the customer for the market value of the missing securities as of the day the SEC filed court papers to liquidate the firm.

What the SIPC does *not* protect against is any market-related losses while accounts are frozen or being liquidated or transferred to another brokerage. And of course there is no compensation for the emotional wringer you are put through while your money is in limbo.

AILMENT

I have a complaint against my stockbroker.

R If you have lost respect for your stockbroker, you are not alone. The number of dishonest brokers is probably no more than in any other line of work, but the pressure to produce commissions does lead to abuses. Customers never *really* know whether brokers are telling them to buy or sell because it is right for them or because the broker wants to earn a commission.

What forms do stockbroker abuses take? You name it. For example, when the SEC brought charges against PaineWebber in Beverly Hills and four other offices, abuses included theft of customer funds, trading in the accounts of customers known to be dead, making trades customers never wanted, excessively trading accounts simply to generate commissions, lying to customers about the value of their accounts, fraudulently filling out customer account documents, and selling unregistered stock. Industry-wide, an SEC inquiry in 1994 found evidence of serious rule violations at 25% of brokerage branch offices inspected.

Another more subtle practice is deliberately putting customers into securities that are not appropriate for their risk or income limits. Courts have held that even discount brokers can be liable if they fail to protect clients—even sophisticated ones—from committing financial suicide.

Making your complaint. Luckily, most complaints against brokers can be settled with a letter or a phone call to the brokerage firm itself. Serious complaints—churning of your account, high-pressure tactics that lead you to choose an unsuitable investment—might require a more serious step if the brokerage refuses your demand for reimbursement. In most cases, that will be arbitration. Any member of a securities exchange or of the National Association of Securities Dealers, Inc. (NASD), is subject to a uniform binding arbitration procedure, whether the squabble is over a few hundred dollars or several thousand, or even if the dispute is not over money at all but over a matter of procedures or ethics.

The NASD, the Municipal Securities Rulemaking Board, and each of the stock exchanges are self-regulatory organizations (SROs). The SEC does not arbitrate disputes but refers them to the arbitration program run by the SRO involved in the dispute.

Before it comes to that, the SEC, the NASD, and most of the SROs will try to mediate. They will send your complaint to the brokerage firm, ask for a written explanation, and try to get both sides to agree to a settlement. If that does not work, it is up to you to decide whether to go to court or seek arbitration.

If a deal offered to you through the mail turns sour, the procedure is different: Send full details to the Chief Postal Inspector, U.S. Postal Service, 475 L'Enfant Plaza West SW, Washington, DC 20260. If the case seems urgent, call the USPS at 202-268-4267.

Arbitration. Most disputes are subject to arbitration, in accordance with the agreement you generally sign when you open a new account. These agreements are not always in your best interest, but you usually cannot avoid signing them, because most firms will not open an account unless you do. (Older broker-investor agreements may not contain the arbitration clause.) In most cases, customers must arbitrate through industry-subsidized groups, such as the National Association of Securities Dealers (NASD), instead of a more objective forum, such as the American Arbitration Association (AAA). If your agreement does not have an arbitration clause, you are not much better off, because a circuit court has ruled that AAA hearings must take place in New York City, where the association has its headquarters—even though the AAA has 38 offices nationwide.

If you do not have an arbitration clause and prefer AAA to suing, determine whether the cost of a two-day hearing in New York is worthwhile. Figure on paying from $300 to $2000 to file your complaint, $150 to $300 per arbitrator, and at least $125 an hour to your lawyer. Otherwise, you will generally have to arbitrate before the NASD or the NYSE. Both charge $15 and up to hear a complaint.

Actually, compared to civil-court proceedings, arbitration is fast and inexpensive. SEC figures show nearly half of claims for less than $5000 are completed within four months. Fees vary depending on the amount of damages you claim. For damages of $5000 to $10,000, for example, you will pay around $200. Investors win their arbitration hearings about half of the time, according to NASD statistics.

But arbitration is far from perfect. Generally, your case will be heard by a three- or five-member panel. (If you are claiming damages of less than $2500, only one arbitrator will hear your case.) Panelists typically include a brokerage-industry employee, a businessperson such as a banker, and a lawyer. Panels are usually impartial. But the hearings are held in private, and arbitrators do not have to explain their rulings or make them public. Decisions can be very arbitrary; given similar situations, two panels can arrive at wildly different outcomes. What is more, unfavorable arbitration rulings are practically impossible to appeal.

If you want to file for arbitration, you should first collect all account statements and other documents relating to the case. Then contact a securities attorney to see if you have a solid case. If you do, request an arbitration form in writing from the Director of Arbitration of the AAA (140 West 51st Street, New York, NY 10020; 212-484-4000), the NASD (33 Whitehall Street, New York, NY 10004), the New York Stock Exchange (11 Wall Street, New York, NY 10005), the American Stock Exchange (86 Trinity Place, New York, NY 10006), or any other exchange. (See sample letter below.) Ask for a copy of the Uniform Code of Arbitration, which all panels adhere to, as well. Almost any exchange could have jurisdiction because most securities firms are members of all major exchanges, some or all of the regional boards, and the NASD.

Your initial cost for filing a claim ranges from $15 for claims of $1000 or less to a maximum of $1500 for disagreements in excess of $5,000,000. Fees may be returned to you at the discretion of the arbitrators, and you can get all but $25 back if you settle the dispute before arbitration begins.

Along with your claim form, include documentation of your charges,

SAMPLE LETTER REQUESTING ARBITRATION FORM

July 13, 1997

Director of Arbitration
New York Stock Exchange
11 Wall Street
New York, NY 10005

Dear Sir:

Please send me the form(s) necessary to make a complaint against a securities dealer and to request or institute arbitration. I would appreciate any written information or instructions about the arbitration process as well, including the Uniform Code of Arbitration.

Thank you.

Sincerely,

John Q. Investor

the amount of damages you suffered, and whether you will be represented by an attorney.

You do not need a lawyer at the arbitration hearing. If your case is relatively small—$10,000 or less—you might handle it yourself and save on legal fees, which may run $5000 to $10,000. But it might be worth paying that much if the disputed amount comes to $100,000 or more. With or without a lawyer, you forfeit the right to sue later if the arbitrators rule to your dissatisfaction.

A brokerage cannot refuse to cooperate, but it can file a counterclaim if it believes your contentions are frivolous. You will not get anywhere, for example, if you merely lost money on a recommended stock, unless you can show the broker promised you its price would not fall or held back negative information.

If your case involves less than $5000, the exchange will put it through a simplified arbitration procedure. The one arbitrator will usually rule based on the documents you submit without calling a hearing.

The procedure becomes more like a trial if your claim is for more than $5000. The exchange will schedule a hearing in a nearby city at a convenient date, and appoint a panel of arbitrators. You and your attorney, as well as the broker, can call witnesses. The arbitrators and either side's counsel can subpoena persons and documents. The proceeding is under oath and all documents are kept confidential.

The arbitrators will not rule on the spot but will mail their decision to you and the brokerage firm, normally within 30 days. You may or may not get an explanation with the ruling, which can include a monetary award. The decision is final.

You probably will not recover your full loss. Rarely will you get punitive damages, although this is changing, especially where evidence shows wrongdoing or negligence by supervisors and the firms themselves. Arbitrators awarded unprecedented punitive damages to brokerage customers between 1991 and October 1995—$41.9 million, according to figures supplied by the *Securities Arbitration Commentator*, a Maplewood, NJ, publication. Punitive damages can be appealed by the brokerage firm.

☐ Prevention

The best way to avoid conflicts with your broker is to assume more responsibility for your money. Start by choosing a stockbroker you can trust. Before deciding, check the broker's record by calling the NASD toll-free hot line at 800-289-9999. This hot line discloses information about criminal indictments, arbitration decisions, court judgments in civil lawsuits, and pending disciplinary action by the NASD, SEC, NYSE, or other stock exchanges. It *will not* tell you about pending customer complaints or arbitrations and civil cases in which there was a settlement, rather than a final ruling by an arbitration panel or court. Obviously, multiple customer complaints and numerous settlements are strong indicators a broker may not be trustworthy.

Another source of information is your state securities commission (you can get the number by calling the North American Securities Administrators Association hot line at 800-942-9022). The NASD Public Disclosure Program (P.O. Box 9403, Gaithersburg, MD 20898) will provide a report on an individual or firm for $30. Finally, you can write to the SEC's Freedom of Information Branch (450 Fifth Street NW, Mall Stop 2-6, Washington, DC 20549) for any federal records of complaints.

Try to find a brokerage firm that does not require an arbitration clause. Your best bet will be smaller, regional houses like Buell Securities (1310 Silas Deane Highway, Wethersfield, CT 06109; 860-258-2300). If the firm you pick requires an arbitration clause, try to have it amended. If the agreement states you must use NASD or NYSE panels, scratch out that clause and write in that you can choose the American Arbitration Association, your local chamber of commerce, or your Better Business Bureau. If the agreement states your potential dispute must be governed by New York law, cross that out and write in "federal." (New York law prohibits arbitrators from awarding punitive damages, no matter how flagrant or abusive the broker's practices.) With luck, the brokerage will accept the changes. If not, try another firm.

When you open your account, read every word your broker gives you to sign. Do not sign anything unless you understand what it means. Be sure every piece of information and every number you give the broker is accurate. Often, a broker or an office manager will urge you to give slightly inflated figures on income, assets, and net worth—all in order to get your account approved. This can come back to haunt you if trouble arises. You signed it, so you will be in the wrong.

Open only the kind of account you need. For instance, do not sign a margin agreement if you do not intend to ever borrow from your broker to buy securities. Give your broker a written explanation of your investment objectives. Go into as much detail as possible. For example, if you are interested only in high-quality bonds, specify that you wish to invest in corporate or municipal securities rated A or higher by Standard & Poor's. That way, a broker who involves you in unsuitable stocks or bonds cannot claim a communications breakdown. Keep a copy of your letter.

Ask about questionable commissions, preferably before the deal is completed. In fact, if you think your broker is pushing a particular product without good reason, ask whether the broker stands to gain any extra incentive provided by the brokerage house or the investment's backers.

Read every piece of paper the brokerage firm sends you, such as confirmations of trades. If you find trades you never made, insist on instant corrections. If you meet resistance, go over the head of your broker to the office manager or, if need be, to the director of compliance. Any delay will be used to prove that your negligence contributed to the problem.

Be equally careful with each monthly statement. If it is not 100% accurate, insist on having it fixed right away. (See sample letter below.)

Finally, if you find yourself doing something totally new at the broker's suggestion, be skeptical. For example, you may have been doing about 10 stock trades a year. Suddenly, the broker's suggestion that you trade stock options has you making 20 trades a month. It may be a sound technique, but before you even start, be sure you understand it thoroughly and can handle it.

☐ Resources

For more information about arbitration, write for: *Securities Arbitration Rules*, American Arbitration Association, 140 West 51st Street, New York, NY 10020.

SAMPLE LETTER TO CORRECT MONTHLY STATEMENT

July 14, 1997

Director of Compliance
Pacific Rim Securities, Inc.
6000 Avenue of the Stars
Los Angeles, CA 90067

Re: John Q. Investor
    Account Number 106-55-4328

Dear Sir:

In examining my June 30, 1997, statement for the above-numbered account, I discovered the purchase of 400 shares of a company named Durapaint on June 12, 1997, for $4250. I never authorized this purchase.

I therefore request that this transaction be reversed and my account be credited in the amount of $4250, plus interest from June 12, 1997, to the date of the credit.

Thank you.

Sincerely,

John Q. Investor

■ BONDS

AILMENT

I do not know how to read a bond table.

℞ The information found in bond tables can come in handy. The bond tables in your daily paper tell you a bond's current market value and help explain how bonds are traded. For illustration, we are going to look at Figure 6–4—an excerpt from an alphabetical bond table. Let us assume you are interested in the BellSouth $7\frac{1}{2}$% bond, maturity in 2033.

Corporate bonds are sold in $1000 denominations that represent the

FIGURE 6–4 Sample Bond Table

NYSE BONDS

Company	Cur. Yld	Vol	Price	Chg
ADT Op zr10	...	5	79 3/4	+ 1/4
AMR 9s16	8.3	75	109	+ 7/8
ATT 4 3/4 98	4.8	18	98 1/4	− 3/8
ATT 6s00	6.1	25	98	+ 3/8
ATT 5 1/8 01	5.4	10	94 3/8	− 5/8
ATT 7 1/8 02	7.0	69	101 1/2	+ 1/8
ATT 7s05	7.0	50	99 3/4	− 1/8
ATT 7 1/2 06	7.3	13	102 3/4	...
ATT 8 1/8 22	8.0	231	101 7/8	+ 3/8
ATT 8 1/8 24	8.0	165	102	+ 1/8
ATT 8 5/8 31	8.2	22	105 1/2	+ 5/8
AirbF 6 3/4 01	cv	145	110	+ 3/4
AlaBn 6.1s99t	6.2	5	98 7/8	...
AlskAr 6 1/2 05	cv	10	122	...
AlskAr 6 7/8 14	cv	16	98 3/4	− 1
AlldC zr99	...	5	85 3/4	− 1 1/2
AlldC zr2000	...	1	80 1/4	+ 1/4
AlldC zr05	...	20	55	+ 1/4
AlldC zr09	...	65	40 3/8	+ 1/8
AldSig 9 7/8 02	8.9	5	111	− 2 1/2
Alza 5s06	cv	31	100	− 1/2
AMedia 11 5/8 04	11.0	10	106 1/4	− 1 3/4
Ametek 9 3/4 04	9.2	2	106 1/8	+ 1/4
Amoco 8 5/8 16	8.3	37	104 3/8	+ 1
Amresco 8 3/4 99	8.8	25	99	− 1
Amresco 10s03	10.1	3	99	− 7/8
Amresco 10s04	10.0	25	100 1/2	+ 1/2
Anhr 8 5/8 16	8.5	1	102	− 1 7/8
AnnTaylr 8 3/4 00	8.8	56	99 3/4	...
Apache 9 1/4 02	8.6	5	107	− 3
Argosy 12s01	cv	24	71 5/8	+ 1 1/8
Argosy 13 1/4 04	14.3	196	93	+ 1/8
Arml 11 3/8 99	10.9	10	104 5/8	+ 1 5/8
ArmWld 9 3/4 08	8.9	8	109 5/8	− 2 1/4
AutDt zr12	...	11	62	+ 2 1/2
BBN 6s12	cv	220	97	− 1/2
BkrHgh zr08	...	17	77	+ 1 3/4
BarBks 10 7/8 03	9.4	45	116 1/8	+ 1 3/4
Barnet 8 1/2 07	8.0	5	106 3/8	...
BellPa 7 1/8 12	7.4	29	96 1/8	+ 1/4
BellsoT 6 3/8 04	6.5	10	97 3/8	+ 1 1/8
BellsoT 7s05	7.0	50	100 1/2	...
BellsoT 5 7/8 09	6.5	50	90 3/8	+ 1 1/4
BellsoT 7 7/8 32	7.8	18	101 1/4	...
BellsoT 7 1/2 33	7.7	51	97 3/8	+ 1 5/8

face, or par value, of the bond. In bond quotations, the last digit is dropped, and a $1000 corporate bond appears as $100. Each point change, therefore, represents a $10 change in value; each fractional increase represents a percentage of that ($10) point ($97^3/_8 = 973.75).

For example, note what information the bond table provides about a specific BellSouth bond.

> Company—the company name (BellSouth), its coupon rate (fixed dollar return as a percent of par value, $75 divided by $1000 = 7^1/_2$%, and date of maturity (2033).
>
> Current Yield—the bond's current yield is 7.7%. If the current price is below par (below $1000), the bond is selling at a *discount*; you will receive the same fixed return but, because you pay less for the bond, you realize a higher return. (If you had bought on the date of the illustration, you would have gotten your BellSouth $7^1/_2$33 at a discount, because it is trading below $1000.) Another benefit to buying a bond at a discount is that, if you hold it to maturity, the full face value of the bond will be paid to you. (You will receive $1000 for your BellSouth $7^1/_2$33, but because you paid only $973.75 for it, you have a $26.25 capital gain in addition to the interest you will receive.) If the price is above par, the bond is selling at a *premium*; you will pay a higher price for the same fixed return and realize a lower return on your investment.
>
> Volume—the total number of bonds sold on that date (51).
>
> Price—the bond's closing price on that day ($973.75).
>
> Net Change—the increase or decrease in the price per bond as a percentage of 100 on that day (in this case, $1^5/_8$ point, a gain of $16.25 per $1000 bond).

Not included in the bond table, but a very important factor, is a bond's *yield to maturity*. This is the total rate of return you can expect to receive, and it involves a mathematical formula that accounts for the term (length of time) the bond will be held, whether the bond was bought at a discount or a premium, and the amount of interest to be paid.

AILMENT

My bank does not have the denomination of U.S. savings bond I want.

R Ask your bank to order the denomination you want from their Federal Reserve bank, by forwarding your application with the appropriate issue price. This will take longer than buying the bond over the counter. However, the issue date on the bond will reflect the date of your application, not the actual date of issue, so you will not lose any interest. The Federal Reserve bank will either mail the bond directly to you or send it to your bank to pass along to you.

AILMENT

I want to give someone a U.S. savings bond, but I do not know the person's Social Security number.

℞ No problem. The issuing agent will use a special gift inscription designed for such cases. Your Social Security number is placed on the bond, along with the recipient's name and address.

AILMENT

I want to use U.S. savings bonds to build college funds for my child.

℞ There are two ways you can use savings bonds for college:

Child as owner. First, you can register the bonds in your child's name, either alone or with yourself as beneficiary (*not* as co-owners). Although the interest U.S. savings bonds earn is taxable on your federal return, it is exempt from state and city taxes.

Since you do not collect regular interest payments on your bonds, the interest does not have to be reported until you cash in the bonds. However, you may elect to report the interest, showing the increase in the bond's redemption value each year. Once you have elected to report the annual increase, you must continue to do so unless you request permission from the IRS to change. Both reporting methods have tax advantages, depending on your child's age when the bonds are purchased, your child's total annual income, the number of bonds held in your child's name, and your tax bracket. Consult with your tax adviser before choosing one reporting method over the other.

The election to report savings bond interest each year must be made on a timely filed return. An election made on an amended or late-filed return will not be accepted. To make the election, attach the statement in Figure 6–5 to your return for the first year you report the income.

Parent as owner. The interest Series EE U.S. savings bonds earn will permanently escape federal taxation if they are used to pay for higher education. To qualify, the EE bonds must be purchased after 1989. You must be age 24 or older when you buy the bonds and buy the bonds in your own or

FIGURE 6–5   Election Statement

Election to Recognize Current Income
on Noninterest-bearing Discount Bonds
under Code Section 454

John Q. Taxpayer
SSN: 987-65-4321
Form 1040, Calendar Year 199X

Taxpayer hereby elects, under Regulation section 1.454-1(a)(1), to include in current income the annual increase in the redemption price of all noninteresting-bearing discount obligations he now owns or may hereafter own.

your spouse's name. Converting old E or EE bonds to new bonds after 1989 will not qualify.

The interest exclusion is available only for college tuition and fees paid in the same tax year you redeem the bond. Tuition and fees must be reduced by nontaxable scholarships and fellowships and employer-provided educational assistance. Tuition for nursing schools and some vocational schools qualifies, but not the cost of any education involving sports, games, or hobbies unless it is part of a degree program.

The tax break begins to phase out if your adjusted gross income goes over $76,250 for married couples and $50,850 for singles (indexed for inflation). The exclusion disappears entirely when your income reaches $106,250 married and $65,850 single. These limits apply when the bonds are cashed, not when they are purchased.

Use Form 8815 to compute your tax-exempt savings bond interest.

AILMENT

I want to change the beneficiary name on my U.S. savings bonds.

℞ Complete Form PD 4000, available from your local bank or the nearest Federal Reserve bank or branch. If a living beneficiary is being removed, the beneficiary's signature is needed for Series E bonds; the consent of the beneficiary is not necessary for Series EE bonds.

AILMENT

I do not know which interest rate applies to my U.S. savings bonds.

R You can get charts showing the minimum guaranteed rates applying to all outstanding bonds, and the market-based averages, by writing the Office of Public Affairs, U.S. Savings Bonds Division, Department of the Treasury, Washington, DC 20226.

For current rate information, call toll-free: 800-US-BONDS.

AILMENT

I have a number of U.S. savings bonds bought in different years, and I do not know how to find out how much they are worth.

R Free copies of simplified redemption tables for $25 Series E and $50 Series EE bonds (PD 3600) and detailed redemption tables for Savings Notes (Freedom Shares) can be obtained from the Bureau of Public Debt, P.O. Box 1328, Parkersburg, WV 26106-1328.

You can buy the Series E and EE bond redemption booklets, which contain values for all denominations. Each book, containing six months of values, costs $3.25 for Series E or $1.75 for Series EE, from the Superintendent of Documents, U.S. Government Printing Office, Washington, DC 20402. The price is subject to change.

AILMENT

My U.S. savings bond has been lost, stolen, or destroyed.

R You need to file an application proving your loss. If your bond was lost or stolen, you need Form PD 1048. For mutilated or partially destroyed bonds you also fill out Form PD 1048. You can usually get these forms from your local bank, the nearest Federal Reserve bank or branch, or the Bureau of Public Debt. It helps if you have kept a record of the bonds, with their issue dates and serial numbers, in a safe place separate from the bonds. Send the completed form detailing your loss, along with partially destroyed bonds if burned or mutilated, to the Bureau of Public Debt, P.O. Box 1328, Parkersburg, WV 26106-1328. Once these documents are received, the bond will be replaced at no cost. Reissued bonds bear the original issue date.

For more information on lost, stolen, or destroyed bonds, contact the Bond Consultant Branch, Bureau of Public Debt, Parkersburg, WV 26106-1328; 304-480-6112.

CHAPTER SEVEN

Divorce

One of the most complicated and painful life events is divorce. Besides the emotional turmoil, you must deal with financial upsets and uncertainties that can change your standard of living or leave you feeling impoverished.

There is no way around it. Divorce is bound to cost you money, not just in out-of-pocket legal fees, but also in the expense of supporting two households. Most American families spend as much as they make, or more, thanks to ready credit. So, finding yourself with the same expenses but only half the income—or less—is not easy. It should be obvious that you will have to tighten your belt, at least for a while.

The financial complexities of a divorce are as numerous and hard-hitting as the emotional ones. In this chapter we will look at the financial ailments that follow in the wake of divorce. These cover such aspects of a breakup as alimony, child support, legal costs, property settlements, and possible income taxes. Read the suggested remedies carefully: What you don't know about divorce can be expensive. Don't assume that you will automatically get half of everything, or that you will wind up with the house, maintenance, child support, and a share of your former spouse's retirement benefit.

Divorce is simply a reality. More than one million U.S. couples divorce every year; 50% of all first marriages end in divorce and 60% of second marriages do, too. You may be represented by these statistics, but there is no reason for you to suffer financial hardship as well.

AILMENT

My marriage is ending, and I do not know what needs to be done.

Elizabeth Taylor may know the drill, but if you have made only one trip to the altar, bewilderment about how to proceed when a marriage sputters can add to the pain of divorce. The following checklist can ease your transition to a single life.

When divorce is in the talking stage. Begin stashing your savings in a bank account of your own. That way you will have cash to pay the household bills if your spouse unexpectedly stops paying a share.

You need your own credit, too. If you have been relying on your spouse's credit, apply for credit cards in your own name. Or have a friend or relative co-sign a small bank loan. (See Chapter 2 for advice on establishing credit.)

List all separately and jointly owned assets, including investments, cars, jewelry, artwork, and furnishings. This inventory, along with a reckoning of outstanding debts, will be necessary when the time comes to divide up your property. Visit your joint safe-deposit box, and have your bank witness and verify its contents.

When you decide to call it quits. Notify banks and brokerages where you have joint accounts that you intend to divorce. Make it clear that brokerage transactions now require the written approval of both spouses.

Close out joint charge accounts. If you want to keep these accounts open, tell creditors in writing that you will no longer be responsible for what your spouse buys.

Ideally, you and your spouse will be able to agree on how such standard issues as how to divide assets, who will have custody of the children, and the amount of child support and alimony. If the two of you cannot agree on child support or alimony, itemize your monthly and yearly expenses as backup when your case goes to court.

Hire the best attorney you can afford. Get the names of experienced divorce lawyers from friends, the state or county bar association, or other attorneys. Or call the local chapter of the American Academy of Matrimonial Lawyers. Interview at least two candidates. Make sure you get an estimate of the total fee.

Let your attorney do his or her job. Do not try to negotiate directly with your spouse. That makes it too easy to ask for too little or give away too much. Cooperate with your lawyer by providing complete information about your finances.

Set your priorities. You cannot walk away from your divorce with everything. You must decide how much and what you can afford to give up. If you insist on keeping a particular investment, tell your lawyer at the start.

Review the tax regulations regarding divorce. Learn about court cases that could prove useful to you. Visit your local law library or ask your friends and coworkers for information. For example, if you live in New York State, you should know about the Boden Rule. In this case, the court ruled that once child support is agreed to, a custodial parent who later says, "I want more child support" must show that the increase in the child's needs was *unforeseen*. Mrs. Boden wanted her husband to pay for college, but the court said she should have foreseen that this need would arise.

Once the divorce becomes final.   Rewrite your will to name your children or someone other than your spouse as your heir. Review your life, health, and disability insurance coverage, and replace any protection you have lost. Change the beneficiaries on policies you kept in the divorce, unless your settlement requires you to continue to protect your ex.

AILMENT

My husband moved out a couple of weeks ago, with promises to pay the bills and send me spending money. Surprise, surprise—I have not seen a nickel.

R̸ For what it is worth, the law is on your side. No matter which state you call home, a spouse has a financial obligation to his or her family. Moving out of the house does not end this responsibility. You can start a support proceeding in court to enforce your spouse's obligations without filing for a divorce.

Although the procedure differs from state to state, most courts let you initiate the support proceeding yourself without hiring an attorney. First, you need to determine which court handles support proceedings. Some states and cities have separate family courts; in other states, family court is a division of a particular civil or county court. Of course, if you want and can afford an attorney, you are entitled to one.

☐ Prevention

Prenuptial (or before-marriage) agreements can help keep separate property out of your spouse's hands in the event of divorce. No matter how smitten you may be, asking for a prenuptial agreement makes you seem more like Scrooge than Romeo. Many brides- (and grooms-) to-be will even refuse to sign one.

Luckily, there's a more agreeable way to safeguard your separate property. You can set up a revocable living trust. These instruments are more commonly used in estate planning as an effective way to transfer wealth to spouses and other beneficiaries at death. (For a complete discussion of revocable living trusts, see Chapter 10, on estate planning.)

Instead of using a formal prenuptial agreement, you can put your separate assets in a revocable living trust. If you name yourself as trustee, you keep control of your assets as long as you are alive. If you name your spouse as beneficiary, your spouse will receive the property if you die while still married. Because the trust is revocable, you can change the way the assets are invested or name a new beneficiary at any time.

You will need an attorney to set up the trust. Revocable living trusts generally cost from $500 to $1500 or more to set up, but this may be a small price compared to what could be lost in a divorce.

AILMENT

I do not have enough money to hire a lawyer to represent me in a divorce.

R It's possible to avoid lawyers entirely by using one of the do-it-yourself divorce kits found at many bookstores. They usually provide sample settlement agreements and tell you how to file petitions and other documents. However, generally such kits should be used only by couples who have been married less than five years, have no children, and have less than $50,000 in assets.

If you do not fit these criteria, you should hire a lawyer to draft your settlement agreement, which sets forth the division of property, custody, and support. This agreement must be approved by the court to make sure it is fair to both parties and conforms to state law. A good attorney will know what you can expect to get in your state, and with the aid of an accountant may be able to structure a settlement that will save taxes. (For the **RX** to taxes in a divorce, see page 219.) For the name of a marital law specialist, contact the American Academy of Matrimonial Lawyers, 150 North Michigan Avenue, Suite 2040, Chicago, IL 60601 (312-263-6477).

If you do need a lawyer, you and your soon-to-be ex can keep legal fees down by avoiding disputes. Time your lawyer spends bickering on your behalf will be paid for out of your pocketbook. And if no agreement is reached, you must wage an expensive court battle. Be civilized and try to settle as many issues as possible on your own before embroiling your legal army. You can slash legal bills still further by trying divorce mediation. In mediation, a neutral party will help you work out an agreement that can be taken to your respective attorneys for review. Trained mediators charge between $50 and $500 an hour for six to eight one- or two-hour sessions. A referral costs $125 plus fees. In California and some other states, judges will refer you to court mediators for help in resolving custody and visitation disputes. There is usually no charge for mediation in these cases. To find a qualified mediator, get in touch with the American Arbitration Association, which has offices in 38 cities.

No matter whether you hire an attorney or choose a do-it-yourself divorce, there are always some court costs that must be paid. Usually, the person bringing the action is expected to pay. But if the judge is persuaded that your spouse is broke, you may wind up paying, even if you did not initiate the action. For example, there is a filing fee for submitting your petition and a summons fee to serve your spouse with the divorce papers.

The court reporter must be paid by the hour, and in some states, a magistrate or commissioner will bill you for making a preliminary report to the judge. The judge may also charge you for general court costs. You will want a certified copy of the final decree. And if you appeal to a higher court (in a custody case, for example), a transcript of the trial will set you back hundreds of dollars. Of course, the costs start all over again at the appellate level.

Attorneys' fees vary widely. You can pay a flat fee or an hourly rate. With a flat fee, you pay an agreed-upon amount for the entire process: drawing up divorce papers, taking depositions, court appearances, and so on. On a hourly basis, you pay anywhere from $100 in rural areas to $325 and up for Park Avenue lawyers. With a flat fee, you know the exact price in advance. If you pay by the hour you are billed only for the actual amount of time your lawyer spends on your divorce. In either case, the terms of your agreement should be in writing. You do not want an argument later over what the lawyer should have done or how much you owe.

If you are destitute, free legal help may be available from your local Legal Aid office. Call your county or state bar association for information about free legal services that may be available in your area. You will have to fill out a financial statement to show that you qualify before a lawyer will be assigned to handle your case.

AILMENT

I want to get as many assets and as much income as possible out of my divorce.

R/ Your financial fate in a divorce depends on a number of factors, including where you live, the kind of assets you own and how they were acquired, your temperaments, your lawyers, and whether the divorce is settled amicably or goes to court. You can significantly affect the outcome, however, depending on which of several legal options you choose.

You can, for example, simply split everything 50-50 and walk away. This strategy may be a good idea if (a) the two of you acquired your assets as an equal team, (b) you can easily identify and value the assets, and (c) the assets are subject to fairly straightforward tax treatment.

The more valuable or complex the asset, however, the more difficult it is to value. Some examples: nonmonetary contributions to the marriage, such as homemaking services; closely held businesses; limited partnership interests; and the future earning power of a professional degree or license. In such cases, you should probably resign yourself to working out a settlement agreement.

More than 90% of divorce actions are settled out of court. The key is knowing when to settle and for how much. With a lawyer's help, try to figure out how a judge might divide the assets. Then aim for a settlement that is at least equally attractive. Put emotions aside and treat your divorce like a business deal. There will be a point at which taking a few dollars less makes good business sense, especially if the settlement lets you keep assets that are important to you.

State law.   Do not worry too much about complying with the letter of your state's divorce laws. In most cases, the laws are so ambiguous and the judges have so much latitude that you can hammer out any settlement that is mutually agreeable. In fact, without a settlement, you run the risk of a judge imposing a compromise that you object to completely.

In a divorce, it seldom matters whether you consider an item "yours," "mine," or "ours." Only one state (Mississippi) divides property according to title; if it is in your name, you generally get to keep it. In three of the nine community-property states (California, Louisiana, and New Mexico), property acquired during marriage (community property)—along with all community debts—is divided equally between the spouses. In no state must you divvy up wealth you had before marriage.

In most of the so-called separate-property states, only assets you acquired during the marriage by gift or inheritance are treated as yours to keep. The rest is "marital"—in theory, property acquired through both of your efforts. This marital property is subject to some kind of division. Thus, when you are negotiating, you should try to have as many assets as possible designated as separate property—or, if not that, then at least as marital, so you will have a shot at keeping part of them.

Note: You will want a rough idea of the current divorce law in your state—and in the states where you formerly lived. Property you acquired while living in one state normally comes under that state's rules, even if you have moved to another by the time you divorce.

Claiming an asset as marital property is surprisingly easy, because life is seldom tidy. For example, suppose your spouse brought a portfolio of stocks into the marriage and later added shares bought using funds from your joint bank account. The dividends were spent for the family's benefit, and shares were traded. Even if the account is held separately, you may be able to claim the source of the portfolio has become mixed and is now at least partly marital property.

A closely held business poses a similar puzzle. Let's say the business was purchased with borrowed money that was later repaid from a joint bank account. One of you worked in the business full-time, while the other helped out occasionally. In a case like this, your theory of how the asset should be classified is as good as your spouse's.

Most separate-property states and six community-property states (Arizona, Idaho, Nevada, Texas, Washington, and Wisconsin), use an "equitable distribution" formula to split assets. In such states, each of you must get your fair—but not necessarily equal—share of marital property. Fairness depends on a number of factors including how long you were married, how much each of you contributed financially, your ages, and your earning ability. Also considered are whether one of you will lose pension and inheritance rights at divorce, your probable finances in the future, the liquidity of your property, and how hard it is to value.

Unfortunately, equitable distribution laws are far from fair for full-time homemakers who cannot show they contributed hard currency to make half the down payment and pay the mortgage on the house. To correct this injustice, many states put some value on the labor of running a household and raising children. In some states, women have also successfully claimed a cut of such career assets as a spouse's business, retirement plan, or professional degree.

Alimony. Depending on where you live, a settlement may have to provide for alimony payments and child support. In negotiating, keep certain things in mind: Depending on age, earning potential, and length of marriage, the wife should aim for alimony or spousal support. But if you can get $1 million in assets, you will not need monthly income. In that case, do not wait for a check every month—go for the assets. Of course, if the earning capacities are reversed, a husband should ask for the same type and amount of support as a wife, if your state allows men to get alimony. Typical situations in which men are granted alimony are when the man is not well enough to work, when he is going back to school temporarily to get a better job, or when he was married to a wealthy woman and did not work or was unemployable.

Unfortunately from the wives' point of view, courts have become stingy in granting alimony. These days, alimony seldom lasts longer than five years, and young, healthy wives who were not married for at least five years usually do not get alimony at all. Some states do allow rehabilitative alimony, which lasts until the nonworking spouse gets specific training or finds a job.

If you do get traditional-style alimony, ask your lawyer to include an escalation clause, so that as your ex-husband's salary goes up, so does your income. The settlement agreement should also protect alimony income by requiring the paying spouse to take out life and disability insurance. You should try to get life insurance, with a clause authorizing you to obtain information about your ex-spouse's health periodically from the insurance company. You also want health insurance for yourself—forever, if possible—and for the children "until emancipation," that is, until they marry or reach the age of majority. If you really want to be aggressive, you can ask for non-insured medical and dental expenses (including orthodontia), psychiatric care, summer camps for the kids, college—even cosmetic surgery for them.

Child support.   Generally, both parents are expected to share in the support of children, in proportion to their means. Each state, though, has its own complex formula for determining who pays what. As a rule, child support stops when a child reaches age 18 (21 in some states). But if both parents are college graduates, a court may require the wealthier parent to underwrite the expense of the kids' higher education.

The amount of child support is based on the children's needs and the ability of *both* parents to pay. Health and age are factors: Teenagers are more expensive to clothe and feed than toddlers, for example. Other than that, there are no hard-and-fast rules for setting child support. As always, it is best to negotiate with your spouse to determine what you can afford, then present the agreement to the judge. Most judges will accept the parents' decision, unless the judge feels the children have been shortchanged.

The settlement agreement should address which parent pays for medical and dental insurance, and who will pay for all ordinary medical costs, such as regular checkups, and extraordinary medical and dental expenses, such as a major operation or orthodontia. Child support may also include payments for private schooling, summer camp, dance lessons, scout equipment, travel between the two parents, and other extras.

The family home.   When there is enough other property to compensate the husband for his share of the house, the family home usually goes to the wife as outright owner. This is because she is generally the custodian of the minor children. Be careful what you ask for though: You may find you cannot afford to maintain the house once you get it.

Even with too few assets to compensate the husband for losing the house, the wife is often allowed to live there until the children are grown. Then the house is sold, and the proceeds divided. But that could wind up being a trap for the husband. He may have to pay tax on his share of any capital gain because the house will no longer be his principal residence.

If the home is jointly owned, you may choose to sell the house and split the money. If you want to sell and divide the proceeds, but you have children, you can agree to delay the sale—for example, until the youngest child leaves for college.

Other property settlements.   Before the Great Divide, you will both have to take stock of your assets. Most states require both parties to make full financial disclosure to each other. Trying to hide assets is shortsighted: If you do not make full disclosure, the agreement can be overturned at a later date, by an irate judge. You also risk a perjury or fraud conviction.

Start with the obvious assets: cash in the bank, securities, a house or condo, cars, furniture, art, jewelry, and other valuable objects. You probably owe money on some of these, so you should note this fact in your itemization.

Do not forget pension and profit-sharing plans (vested or not) and un-exercised stock options. Your business, interests in limited partnerships, and the value of a professional license or practice may also be on the "split list."

Valuing your assets.   Once you have determined what you have and where it came from, you need to assign a value to it. That includes separate property, too, because its value can affect how much alimony or child support must be paid. In some cases, it may also help the judge decide how much marital property to parcel out to each party. If your separate property seems much less valuable than your spouse's, you are likely to get a larger share of the remaining marital property.

For purposes of divorce, an asset's value is what it is worth on the day you sign a separation agreement or the day your divorce action is started. Infrequently, the day used is the date trial begins. It can pay to bargain for a cutoff date when the value of your separate assets compared to the value of your spouse's will be lowest. The right timing can also be a big factor if you own assets, such as high-tech stocks, whose value fluctuates widely.

It is not hard to come up with market values for such things as houses, cars, and listed securities. More difficult are pension interests, closely held businesses, and limited partnership interests. For example, a pension to be paid out over a period of years, starting at some date in the future, is not simply worth the total of those future payments. Because the payments will be made years from now, the money is not available for investment. For this reason, a pension that will be distributed in the near future is worth more than one that will not be paid out for 20 years. The future value is also affected by whether the pension is taken in installments or in a lump sum.

Closely held businesses, particularly professional practices, raise problems, too. A medical or dental practice may sell for more than the value of its equipment because of its large patient list and good location. But it may be tough to put a dollar value on it, short of actually putting it on the market.

Limited partnership interests should be valued by taking into account such factors as the purchase price, the value of past and future tax benefits, potential earnings and gain on sale, and taxes to be paid.

Do not overlook taxes in fixing values. For example, if you own a stock with a market value of $100, purchased two years ago for $50, it might be valued at $80 to adjust for the capital gains tax that must be paid if it is sold. Treating it as a $100 asset in making the division will shortchange the party who takes it. Furthermore, if you and your spouse will be in different tax brackets, the stock will be worth more to the spouse who pays less income tax.

Who gets what?   Even if you agree on a simple 50-50 split, there may be some assets that just cannot be carved up. Thus, a wife might keep her marriage counseling practice while her husband keeps a rental property of equal value. If the building is worth less than the business, the husband should get cash or other assets to balance out the values. If not enough cash is currently available, the wife could pay it in installments.

If one asset is more valuable to one spouse than to the other, you should divide it accordingly. For example, your higher-income spouse who needs tax shelter might take the low-income housing partnership interest, while you take an equal value in cash.

Asking for some assets, such as stock options, involves risk. The value of options lies in their *potential* if the underlying stock takes off. Suppose your spouse has an option to buy stock at $10 a share. The option is worth nothing when the stock is selling at $8, and $2 if it is selling at $12. If you believe the stock will rise, you should ask for your share of the options. If they are nontransferable, the agreement can provide that your spouse will exercise your share of the options on your behalf at your request. If they do become valuable, you will put up the option price, get your stock, and take your profit. Of course, the stock could fall and then you would get nothing.

In dividing property, be practical. If there is not enough cash to fully compensate one spouse, arrange for the cash to be paid in installments. A pension can be shared either by giving one spouse a lump sum, or else by paying over a portion of the benefits as they are received.

☐ Prevention

If you agree to sell the house and divide the proceeds, be sure to have it appraised by two or more qualified appraisers to prevent fraud.

There are other options. If you have children, you as the husband could let your wife live in the house until all your offspring are grown. If you have a big family and a small mortgage payment, this might be cheaper than having to pay extra support to put them up in another house. Or you could agree to let your wife stay in the house until she remarries. In either case, you will have to spell out some kind of arrangement as to which of you will make the mortgage payments and which will be responsible for maintenance.

No matter what you do with the house, you should use its disposition as a lever to get equity in the settlement. If you give her the house, then she should give you something in return like the summer cottage and the newer car, or the stocks and bonds, or the outright ownership of the family business. You should keep all your personal property and everything you brought to the marriage, and so should she. Everything else is negotiable.

If there are outstanding debts, someone has to pay them, and the decision on these matters should be incorporated into the property division. If you pick up $3000 in *her* dental bills, there should be some reciprocation from her side.

AILMENT

I do not have my own health insurance. I have always been covered under my spouse's group plan.

℞ You are in no immediate danger of losing your health insurance coverage. Under a federal law called COBRA, you are entitled to continued coverage under your former spouse's group plan for three years, at a cost of no more than 102% of the regular premium. But this law does not apply if you are covered by another group plan, however inadequate. If you are already covered under COBRA for some reason apart from the divorce, the total coverage time is still 36 months. During that period, you have the same right as active employees to change options when the plan holds open enrollment or even add your new spouse if you remarry. *Note:* Companies with fewer than 20 employees and church workers are excluded from COBRA.

Other options. Unless you have a health problem, a better way to ensure continued coverage is to get your own health insurance through your employer or an individual policy. If your new coverage has a waiting period for preexisting conditions, double up by paying for COBRA coverage, too, until the waiting period is satisfied.

AILMENT

I want my share of my former spouse's retirement benefits.

℞ In many marriages, the working spouse's pension is second only to the family home as the couple's most valuable asset. If you were the spouse who stayed at home and raised the children, divorce can threaten your financial future. Even if you worked outside the home, you may not have accumulated sufficient retirement benefits—if any—to lift you out of poverty in old age. Moreover, because pensions are based on earnings, women's pensions are almost invariably smaller than men's. If you are in this predicament, you are wise to explore your pension rights thoroughly. If you depended on your spouse's earnings during marriage, you will depend on them during retirement.

Whether your last years are golden depends on where you live. Only two states—Mississippi and West Virginia—do not divide pensions, as a rule. Courts in the nine community-property states generally view pensions as community property, acquired during the marriage and belonging to both spouses equally. (Arizona, California, Idaho, Louisiana, Nevada, New Mexico, Texas, Washington, and Wisconsin are community-property states.)

The remaining separate-property states and the District of Columbia divide marital assets equitably, regardless of whose name is on the title. In at least half of these states, company or union pensions, IRAs, and Keogh plans that were built up during marriage are divisible in divorce, usually 50-50, with no negative tax consequences. Once the pension is divided, your share cannot be taken away—unlike alimony and child support, which can end when you remarry, for example, or your children reach age 18.

Just because a state divides pensions does not mean the court will do so in your case. For example, if your spouse is not yet vested (guaranteed benefits) in the company's pension plan, there is less of a chance you will share in it. Or a court may refuse to divide pensions if you are young and both of you work.

Even if you win a share of the pension, you may be given the option of accepting marital property of equal value instead. If you want to sever all ties or if your former spouse is in poor health or decades away from retirement, this can be a sensible choice. In fact, waiting can be risky, because with some plans, the nonparticipating spouse gets nothing if the plan participant dies before reaching retirement age. *Note:* Because accepting other property can have tax consequences, a lawyer or accountant should review your decision before it is made final.

AILMENT

My former husband is a retired Army colonel, and I want a share of his military pension.

℞ Your rights depend on when you split up. If your divorce was final before February 1983, you can share in a military pension only if it was included in the divorce decree. You would only receive a portion of your ex-husband's pension if he elects coverage for you. Whether you live in a community- or separate-property state has no bearing.

Military wives divorced in or after February 1983 can take advantage of the 1983 Defense Authorization Act. This federal law gave states the right to decide whether a military pension is marital property.

☐ **Resources**

You can get more information from the Army's Retired Pay Operation in Cleveland at 216-522-5301. For questions about active duty military pay, contact the Defense Finance and Accounting Service in Indianapolis. (You can reach the legal department at 317-542-2756.) You will need to supply your former husband's Social Security number.

R̸ Many divorced women reach retirement age unaware that they may be entitled to Social Security benefits based on their former husband's earnings. Others know they should get something, but cannot decipher the convoluted rules that determine who gets what.

What conditions must you meet to collect benefits based on your ex's earnings? First, your marriage must have lasted at least 10 years. Then, both you and your ex-spouse must be at least 62 years old. And, finally, the benefit checks cannot start until two years after the divorce. The latter provision was designed to discourage couples from divorcing solely to enable a dependent spouse to collect benefits while the other was not really retired.

The benefits payable to divorced spouses are not deducted from their former spouse's checks. They are separate benefits, equal to no more than half the amount the ex-spouse receives.

As a divorced spouse, your benefits are not affected if your ex-husband remarries. But if *you* remarry, you lose the right to benefits based on your former spouse's earnings—unless your second marriage also ends in divorce. If both of your marriages lasted 10 years or more, you can elect Social Security benefits based on *either* ex-husband's earnings.

If you are eligible for spousal benefits and your ex-husband dies, you have hit the daily double. As a divorced widow, you are eligible for 100% of your former husband's benefits, compared with 50% as a divorced spouse. You can collect as early as age 50 if you are severely disabled. You can even remarry without losing your divorced-widow benefits if you wait until after age 60 to tie the knot again.

Although the same rules apply to ex-husbands as to ex-wives, men are usually eligible for higher benefits based on their own earnings than they would receive if they applied for half of their ex-wife's benefits.

Dependent and disability benefits. A divorced mother or father who cares for children under age 16, or over 16 but disabled, is eligible for monthly mother's or father's benefits in the following situations (note that a marriage need not have lasted at least 10 years for payments to be made to a divorced person as a caretaker of children):

1. The divorced wage-earning spouse dies.

2. The divorced wage-earning spouse is severely disabled and is expected to remain so for at least 12 months, or indefinitely.

3. The divorced wage-earning spouse retires.

These benefits are payable no matter how many times the wage earner has married and how many other beneficiaries may also be eligible for payments based on the same earnings record.

☐ Prevention

When your family relationships change, it is a good idea to call or visit your Social Security office to find out how the change may affect present or future payment of your benefits.

AILMENT

I want to pay the least taxes in divorce.

℞ You will have a lot more assets to fight over if you learn and use the tax law wisely. Before you put the finishing touches to your settlement agreement, familiarize yourself with the following tax aspects of divorce:

Alimony.   Alimony is deductible by the spouse who pays it and taxable to the spouse who receives it. For this reason, it is usually in a divorcing couple's best interest to classify a transfer of assets as alimony, because a property settlement does not generate a tax deduction for either one of you.

Alimony payments need to continue for only three years to be deductible and can decline by as much as $15,000 a year.

You can label payments "alimony," but they must be for your ex-wife's (or, in rare cases, ex-husband's) support to create a deduction. Amounts clearly destined for the children will not qualify as alimony. For example, if alimony payments will decline when a child turns 18, the amount of the planned reduction is considered child support and is not deductible.

Property settlements.   Exchanges of property are treated as gifts, and neither spouse pays taxes upon divorce. But make sure you get extra assets to reimburse you for the taxes you will pay eventually if you accept highly appreciated property, such as stock, while your ex-spouse takes cash.

Child support.   Child support is neither deductible by the payer nor taxable to the one who receives it. The IRS is always on the lookout for child support disguised as alimony. If an audit determines that your self-styled "alimony" is really meant to support a child, no deduction will be allowed. Take care, therefore, not to lump alimony with child support in a settlement agreement.

Dependency exemptions.   No matter how much child support you pay, you may only claim exemptions for your kids if you have custody unless you can persuade the custodial parent to waive the right to the exemptions by signing IRS Form 8332. If you are the noncustodial parent, you must attach this form to your tax return every year you claim the exemption.

AILMENT

My ex-spouse has not paid the court-ordered child support.

R If your ex-spouse does not pay child support (or alimony), you can take your ex to court and get a judgment against the individual. The agreement to pay child support is a contract, even when it is not made a part of the divorce decree. A violation, then, is a breach of contract, and you can sue your former spouse, just as you can sue a builder who does not do the job the way it is stated in the contract. And a child support provision that is made part of the divorce decree becomes a court order. An ex-spouse who violates it is in contempt of court. That is a criminal offense for which your ex could go to jail.

In court, you must show that your ex knew of the court-ordered payment, had the money or the ability to earn the money, and willfully refused to pay it. You (or your attorney) can then ask the judge to put a lien on your ex's bank account, business, or car. If your ex then fails to pay up, you can ask the judge to have your ex's property seized. Or you can ask the judge for a wage assignment order that will force your ex-spouse's employer to garnish wages, that is, take the money out of your ex's paycheck. *Note:* Wage assignment orders must be reinstated each time your ex-spouse changes jobs.

(If you do not have a lawyer, go to your nearest child support enforcement agency and ask for help. Child support enforcement agencies are listed in the phone book and are often part of local district attorneys' offices.)

Do not worry if your ex tries to avoid paying by moving away. The 50 states and U.S. possessions have adopted the Uniform Reciprocal Enforcement of Support Act (URESA) to take care of the problem of runaway parents. Under URESA, you go to court in the jurisdiction where you got the divorce or where you and the children now live and tell the judge that your ex is not making payments. The court's judgment against your ex is forwarded to the new home state's court, and the judge there will order your ex to pay up. The judge can use the same methods described above—seizing property and garnishing wages—to get the money.

What if your ex-spouse goes into hiding? You can enlist the services of the federal and state governments to find the runaway parent. Under a federal law, P.S. 93-647, the federal government helps the states in locating runaway parents and forcing them to pay child support. This makes the government the bill collector of last resort.

Under the law, the federal Office of Child Support Enforcement administers a Parent Locator Service, a computerized system that helps locate parents who have eluded state welfare agencies. If you have a court order for child support, you can appeal to your state welfare agency for help. If the state is unsuccessful in tracking down your ex, you can use the federal Parent Locator Service to find your runaway ex. It takes from one week to two months for the federal system to ferret out a runaway parent. This service is open to both nonwelfare and welfare families.

The law also permits the garnishment of federal employees' wages and benefits, including military wages and benefits, Social Security benefits, and civil service retirement benefits. Most importantly, it makes the Internal Revenue Service your ally. Once your state welfare agency locates your ex, it can ask the IRS to use the same tactics it uses to collect back taxes to bag your child support.

☐ Prevention

So-called deadbeat dads often claim they stopped paying child support because the mother refused to allow them to visit their children. While the relationship between divorced parents is often bitter, denying your ex-spouse the chance to see his children merely punishes the kids. And from a purely practical standpoint, you will know less about your ex's job and financial condition if you are not on speaking terms.

AILMENT

I want to change my divorce agreement.

℞ Problems with support and living expenses keep coming up. However, an agreement usually stands unless there has been a "change in circumstances." Just because you suddenly realized that you made a bad deal does not mean you can plead duress, insanity, or bad advice to better the terms. Such efforts are generally unsuccessful. Courts do not like to change agreements.

However, a real change in circumstances can result in anything from a trade-off to a rise or decrease in alimony or child support payments. For example, if you have developed a heart problem and have required a quadruple bypass, resulting in enormous medical bills, you can probably petition the court and have the alimony you pay slashed anywhere from a couple of hundred dollars a week to nothing. Or perhaps 10 years ago you turned down alimony because you were a regional vice president earning $75,000 a year, but thanks to corporate downsizing, you are now waiting tables at Burger Shack.

Whatever the circumstances of your rise or downfall, you must apply to the court for a modification of your original maintenance provisions. That presumes you and your spouse have been unable to amicably discuss the problem and reach a fair and mutually acceptable agreement. The new court proceeding will once again require you both to disclose your finances. There will likely be a hearing. If you are the one seeking the modification, you must introduce evidence that *your* financial needs, employment, income, and other relevant factors have substantially enhanced or diminished your finances. You cannot go back to court because your ex-spouse is making more money, unless alimony was set artificially low at the outset because your ex-spouse was out of work at the time. *Note:* Many courts have held that inflation alone is not an adequate reason to change the original settlement. The theory is that inflation adversely affects both spouses. Remember, none of this applies if you have agreed to a lump-sum payment. That debt must be paid.

Unlike alimony, child support may be increased or decreased if either party's finances brighten or wane. The judge will take your children's needs into account before worrying about your own hardships, though.

If you can meet the burden of evidence, the court will order a modification of the original decree. This is allowed because divorce decrees, unlike other judgments, are never final, and the provisions concerning support, maintenance, custody, and visitation can be changed anytime circumstances warrant it.

Separation agreements play by different rules than divorce decrees and are much harder to modify without both spouses' written consent.

<table>
<tr><td>**CHAPTER**
EIGHT</td><td># Taxes</td></tr>
</table>

If there were a Museum of Financial Horrors, most of the exhibits would be in a chamber devoted to taxes. Audits, penalties, levies, seizures—taxes encompass a litany of monetary disasters that can even, in the stuff of nightmares, lead to imprisonment.

Of all the real and imagined terrors, the one that can give you truly chilling night sweats is the IRS. No matter how you feel about our nation's tax system, you are unlikely to be indifferent to the IRS. Even the most ardent supporters of taxation would admit that their feelings about the IRS hover between respect and fear. But if you have ever had a bad experience with the tax man, your feelings fall somewhere between fear and loathing.

No one wants to run afoul of the IRS. The potential consequences are too grave. Besides the sheer nuisance and time lost in the wilds of red tape and bureaucracy, there is the potential for harassment at the hands of government employees with almost unlimited power. And we know from our experiences with mindless computers how easy it is to become caught up in a surreal world of errors and mistaken identities that are impossible to unravel.

The tax ailments in this chapter are largely caused by problems with the IRS. Of course, there are other powers in the tax world besides the IRS. There are your state and local tax authorities, who hold an equal license to deprive you of your livelihood, your home, your life savings. In many ways, dealing with local tax agencies is just like dealing with the IRS, and you can apply many of the procedures and suggestions outlined here if you face audit or levy by your state. But because state taxes have 50 variations, you should also consult with a tax professional who is familiar with your state's tax laws if you get caught in a web spun by your local tax agency.

Although our annual rite of filing keeps income taxes ever in our thoughts, if you are a homeowner you need to focus on the property taxes you pay as well. The last section of this chapter, therefore, outlines what steps you need to take if your property tax assessment has risen faster than the actual market value of your home or other real estate. Paying too much property tax may not be as hair-raising as the specter of an IRS revenue officer on your doorstep, but over time, the financial drain can be as disastrous.

■ INCOME TAXES

AILMENT

I have not filed an income tax return in five years. Now I want to file, but I do not want to get into trouble.

℞ It is better to come forward and file your returns than to wait for the IRS to catch up with you. Voluntary filing will earn you more consideration from the IRS. If it wants to make an example of you, the IRS can pursue you to the point of criminal prosecution. Willful failure to file is a felony. The IRS does not often go to this extreme, however. To bring a case to trial, the IRS must prove that you did not file because you did not want the IRS to know how much you owed. Generally, to make this case, there must be a substantial tax liability. For this reason, the IRS will not prosecute for failing to file if the taxpayer is due a refund or there is little or no tax liability.

If you are expecting refunds, you should hurry up and file for them, so you can get your checks. You should also file your returns *immediately* if you have received a notice from the IRS collection division asking for your delinquent returns or proof that you have already filed. By complying right away, you rob the IRS of any claim that your nonfiling was willful (fraudulent). If you cannot meet the revenue officer's deadline for filing, ask for an extension of time. If you talk to the revenue officer, do not confess that you deliberately failed to file your returns.

If you expect to owe a lot of tax, find yourself a competent tax attorney. Explain your situation and let the attorney deal with the IRS as your intermediary. The tax attorney will contact your local IRS office and tell them that there is a client who has not filed, but who wishes to do so now. If one reason you have not filed is because you are missing income information, the IRS revenue officer will probably cooperate by providing your tax attorney with the income data entered under your Social Security number in the IRS computer. This will include W-2s; 1099s for miscellaneous income, interest, and dividends; and possibly information from 1098s showing mortgage interest you paid. The W-2 data will show how much federal tax was withheld each year.

Using your records and the information supplied by the IRS, your tax attorney will reconstruct your income and expenses and prepare a Form

1040. You may have to estimate the amounts you contributed to charity or spent on doctors and other deductible items.

If there is a balance due on the returns you did not file, the IRS will add up to 25% in late penalties, plus interest, to the amount you owe. But, if the IRS owes you a refund, you cannot be penalized. You may still be the loser, though, because you have only three years to claim refunds. Any money the IRS might have owed you for earlier years is forever lost. *Note:* Although there is a statute of limitations on receiving a refund, there is no statute of limitations on owing tax. You could file a return 10 or 20 years late showing a balance due, and you would still have to pay.

AILMENT

I cannot file my federal income tax return on time.

R No problem. You can get an automatic four-month extension of time to file your tax return by filing Form 4868, *Application for Automatic Extension of Time to File U.S. Individual Income Tax Return.* You do not even need a reason for being late. Remember, though, that an extension to file is not an extension *to pay*. You are required to compute your total tax liability, or estimate it as close as you can, and pay any balance due *with* Form 4868, which must be filed by the regular due date of your tax return (April 15 for most people).

When the automatic four months are up, you can get a second reprieve—but only if you have a good reason. To get extra time, you should either write to the IRS outlining the reasons you need an extension or file Form 2688, *Application for Additional Extension of Time to File U.S. Individual Income Tax Return.* The IRS requires that you first use Form 4868 before using Form 2688, unless your case is a "hardship." (What is a "hardship"? The IRS does not say.)

To obtain a second extension, you must give the IRS the following information:

- The reason why you are requesting the extension.

- How much additional time you need.

- The tax year to which the extension applies.

- Whether you have already filed another extension of time to file.

- Whether you filed your tax returns on time for the preceding three years and, if not, the reasons why.

- Whether you filed and paid in a timely fashion any estimated tax that may have been due.

As you already know, nothing is simple with the IRS. Most people would prefer not to answer all those questions and to say the heck with the whole thing. But if you end up owing a hefty tax liability and did not have an extension to cover you until you file, you could be hit with a large penalty for failing to file on time (including extension). Failing to pay on time will get you a penalty of one-half of one percent of the balance due for each month, or part of a month, that your tax liability remains unpaid. However, the maximum penalty is 25%. The penalty for filing late is 5% of the tax unpaid by the due date for each month, or part of a month, that the return is late, again up to a maximum of 25%. File more than 60 days late, though, and the penalty rises to $100 or 100% of the tax due, whichever is less. As we noted above: You do not have to pay this penalty if you request an automatic extension and properly estimate your tax liability on Form 4868.

Did you notice that the penalty amount is based on any tax you owe when you file? You can file months, even years, late and not be penalized if the government owes you a refund. In fact, in that case, the IRS does not care if you ever file at all. For that reason, you do not even have to go through the paperwork of asking for an extension if you are sure you are getting money back.

AILMENT

I have to file late and I am worried that I will have to pay a penalty.

℞ At the time you file your tax return, you can appeal to the IRS's better nature and ask for nonassessment of any penalties you would otherwise be liable for. The two penalties you want to escape by presenting evidence that you had reasonable cause are the failure-to-file and the failure-to-pay penalties.

There are several ways in which this can be handled. If you deliver your return to the IRS in person, your fate is in the hands of the taxpayer service employee (either a representative or a specialist) to whom you give your delinquent return. That IRS employee is required to determine if you had a reasonable cause for being late or if a penalty should be assessed. If the decision is made that reasonable cause does exist for nonassessment of a penalty or penalties, the employee should complete Form 4571, *Explanation for Late Filing of Return or Late Payment of Tax*, and attach it to your tax return. It also helps if you write down your explanation and attach it to Form 4571. Otherwise you can make an oral statement that the IRS employee will write on Form 4571. The representative or specialist must also make a note on your tax return that reasonable cause exists for nonassessment of the penalty. For Forms 1040 and 1040A, this is done by completing Form 4364, *Delinquency Computations*, and attaching it to the return. Watch the representative or specialist carefully to make sure this is done.

If the representative or specialist decides that reasonable cause does not exist and that penalties should be assessed, you will be told that you will have to pay the penalty. You will then have to file a claim of refund on Form 843, *Claim*, if you want to challenge the decision.

If you mail a delinquent return to the service center that shows you still owe tax, attach a letter explaining your circumstances for being delinquent and request that no penalties be assessed due to reasonable cause. You can also file Form 843.

If you think you will have more luck convincing the IRS not to assess penalties by talking with an IRS employee personally, you should file your tax return at your local IRS office with a taxpayer service representative or a taxpayer service specialist.

One person you should try to avoid meeting face-to-face is a revenue officer from the collection division. This will not be possible, however, if you ignore the four notices the IRS computer has sent you requesting that you file a delinquent return. At that point, your failure to respond will result in a taxpayer delinquency investigation (TDI). Once your TDI has been assigned to a revenue officer, the officer must either secure the delinquent return or discover if you are not required to file. The IRS expects the revenue officer to vigorously pursue your case. From here on, whether you are penalized is up to the revenue officer.

Of course, there is no law that says you must personally meet with the officer even after you have been personally contacted and directed to file the delinquent return with the revenue officer. You can bypass the officer and send the return directly to the IRS service center. When this happens, the IRS computer automatically sends a notice to the officer that the return has been filed and the case is closed. At that point, the officer does not care whether you had reasonable cause or even whether penalties should be assessed. The officer is usually happy, in fact, because the case is closed without expending more time.

AILMENT

I need to send in my tax return, but I cannot pay the amount I owe.

℞ You can ask for an automatic installment payment arrangement by attaching Form 9465 to the front of your 1040. On the form, specify the amount you propose to pay each month. You should get a response from the IRS accepting or denying your request or asking for more information within 30 days. You can get a copy of Form 9465 by calling the IRS toll-free at 800-829-1040.

Unless you owe $10,000 or more, you do not have to disclose your current financial status and include a full list of your assets and liabilities. There is another advantage: Again, if the liability is under $10,000 and if you stick to the terms of the payment schedule, no tax liens will be filed against your property.

However, there are some drawbacks to installment agreements as well. First, they are binding. Second, penalties and interest are due on the unpaid balance. When you file Form 9465, you are locked into a late-payment penalty of one-half of one percent a month plus interest on the unpaid amount. Taken together, the cost comes to 13% a year.

Or, you can pay off the IRS without an installment agreement. Rather than fetter yourself by attaching a 9465 installment agreement, try the following short-term fixes:

- Send in as much as you can with your return.

- Send more cash when you receive the first notice of tax due.

- Follow the payment up with some more money each time you receive another collection notice.

- With each notice, include a short note explaining why you cannot pay the full balance right now, such as illness or unemployment.

- In your note, reassure the IRS that you will continue to pay as much as you can.

Using this strategy, you can start by paying a fairly small amount for three to four months. With luck, you will be better able to pay off the balance after the first few months. If you file a 9465, you will be saddled with a strict payment schedule almost immediately.

Another option is to secure a loan from a friend or relative and to send in the full balance due with your return. It is better to borrow from almost any source than to be a debtor to the IRS.

AILMENT

I made a mistake on a tax return I already sent in.

R⁄ What you cannot do is wait to make your adjustments on next year's return. Income received or spent in a particular year must go on that year's return. You do not have to redo the entire return, however. Instead, get Form 1040X to make your corrections. (Call the IRS at 800-829-1040 to get Form 1040X.) If you are seeking a refund due to a net operating loss carryback, you may be able to use Form 1045 instead. Form 1045 is called a "quick refund" form, because the IRS must act on your claim within 90 days. You may have a net operating loss that can be carried back to an earlier year if you own a struggling business or were the victim of a large casualty.

Form 1040X is mailed to the IRS service center where you originally filed your return. Normally, it takes two to three months to process an amended return.

Note: Do not forget to amend your state tax return, too, if necessary. You will *not* need to amend the state return, for example, if the change is to income your state does not tax (such as U.S. government bond interest), federal withholding, self-employment tax, or credits your state does not allow.

The 1040X is a simple form that you can probably fill out yourself rather than spending from $75 on up to have a tax professional do it for you. If the mistake was caused by your preparer's error, however, the preparer should correct your return for free.

Form 1040X is a single sheet that must be completed front and back. The heart of this form is a comparison between the figures claimed on your original return and the corrected amounts. This recomputation of your tax liability is entered in columns A through C in the center of the form. Enter any changes to exemptions, including names and Social Security numbers, on the back of the 1040X.

For example, suppose you realize that you left $500 in bank interest off your return. Write the interest income you originally reported in column A. In column B, enter the increase in your income as a positive figure ($500). Add $500 to the amount in column A, and write the correct interest income in column C.

Note: Changes to income can have a domino effect. For example, don't forget to recompute taxable Social Security benefits, as well as deductions that are limited by a percentage of your adjusted gross income. In our example, increasing interest by $500 would reduce your write-off for medical expenses by $37.50 on Schedule A.

Explain the changes you are making on the reverse side of the 1040X. In our example, you might write, "Amendment to report interest income erroneously omitted from original return. Amendment to also reduce itemized deductions because of change in adjusted gross income."

Because the IRS decides whether to accept or deny a claim for refund based on your explanation, make your reason as clear and complete as possible, giving supporting facts, and, if applicable, your legal grounds for making the claim. If your refund is denied, your explanation may form the basis of an appeal. In that case, an incomplete reason may limit your legal argument in court. If your explanation will not fit on the back of the 1040X, attach additional sheets.

If you are changing your wages, attach the federal copy of your Corrected Form W-2 to the front of the Form 1040X. If you are amending to take itemized deductions, attach Schedule A. If you are increasing noncash contributions to more than $500, send along Form 8283. Also include any form used to compute a new credit or additional tax. If you are claiming a carryback, attach pages 1 and 2 of your 1040 for the year the loss or credit came from.

If you file a joint return, both you and your spouse must file a joint amended return. If separate returns were filed, you may not amend your spouse's separate return, unless you were named as fiduciary upon the death or guardianship of your spouse.

If you are divorced and are carrying back a net operating loss to a year in which you filed jointly, you may file a claim for refund with just your signature, and the refund check will be issued in your name alone.

In most cases, you have three years after the original return was due or two years from the date the tax was paid, whichever is later, to send in a Form 1040X. Failure to file a claim within this time keeps you from receiving a refund, no matter how valid your claim.

Exceptions: If your deduction or loss involves a bad debt or worthless stock, you have seven years to file a claim. Refunds based on your share of items from federally registered partnerships may be claimed within four years.

An amended return arising from a net operating loss must be filed within three years of the due date (including extensions) of the return on which the loss or credit was originally taken. If you use Form 1045 to carry back a net operating loss, it must be filed within one year after the end of the year in which a credit or loss arose. If you fail to meet this deadline, you must use Form 1040X.

Interest is paid on refunds made more than 45 days after your return was due (not counting extensions). If your amended return shows a balance due, however, you must pay the government interest. Interest runs from the due date of the return or the date the tax was paid, whichever is later, to the date your payment is received or to a date 30 days or less before a refund check is issued. The IRS will compute any interest on the balance due or overpayment and either bill you for it or include it in your refund.

No interest is paid on refunds resulting from net operating loss carrybacks if the refund is paid within 45 days after the claim is filed. Similarly, refunds arising from retroactive changes in the tax law generally do not pay interest.

AILMENT

My preparer made a mistake on my return, and I have been audited and billed for additional tax, interest, and a penalty.

℞ I hope you asked your preparer before hiring to promise to pay your interest and penalties if you were audited and the preparer had made an error. It would be better still if you had this commitment to pay in writing. In any event, write the preparer requesting that you be reimbursed for the interest and penalties. No preparer will pay your taxes for you; if the return had been prepared correctly, you would have paid the tax long ago. Attach a copy of the audit report, explaining the IRS's adjustment. Of course, if your preparer represented you in the audit, the preparer already knows about the problem.

Now, the best you can do is hope that your tax professional will do the honorable thing. If not, your only recourse is to sue in civil court. If the preparer is a member of a professional organization or the Better Business Bureau, you can also report his unethical conduct.

Use the sample letter on the next page to help you draft your plea to your mistaken preparer.

AILMENT

I want to minimize my chances of being audited by the IRS.

℞ The good news is that for most taxpayers fear of an IRS audit may be a thing of the past. Audit rates are down for all but the lowest-income taxpayers—1.67% of the 116,000,000 1040s filed in 1996 were audited.

With the odds of being audited so low, there is no reason to keep your deductions hidden in the shoe box where you stash your records. Even if you are chosen for audit, if you have kept good records you have nothing to fear. When you prepare your tax return, always give yourself, not the IRS, the benefit of the doubt. Interpret the tax law in your favor. If you do not practice legal tax avoidance, you are giving up any chance of saving hundreds or even thousands of tax dollars. You may as well file the Form 1040EZ and be done with it.

That said, there *are* ways you can avoid IRS scrutiny. Although there is no guarantee that you can avoid an audit completely, there are several actions you can take to minimize your audit risk, no matter what schedule you file, how much you earn, or even if you are on one of the IRS project

SAMPLE LETTER

Request for Preparer Reimbursement of Interest and Penalties— CP-2000 Due to Preparer Error

Date

Name of Your Preparer
Street Address
City, State, Zip Code

Dear Mr./Ms. Smith:

This is to inform you that I have received a notice from the Internal Revenue Service, assessing additional tax for 199X of $150, plus an accuracy-related penalty of $37.50 and interest of $28. Copies of pages 2 and 3 of this notice are attached.

The notice claims that $360 in interest/dividends from Perpetual Corporation was omitted from my return. I have reviewed my records and determined that this notice is correct. Because the Form 1099-INT/DIV from Perpetual was with the records I presented to you at the time of my interview, I believe the omission was due to preparer error.

or

The notice claims that $360 in interest/dividends from Perpetual Corporation was omitted from my return. The reason for this assessment appears to be a transposition error on your part. Instead of reporting $1950 in interest/dividend income, you mistakenly reported $1590.

I understand that I am responsible for the extra tax. However, I believe you should be liable for the penalty and interest resulting from your error. I am therefore requesting reimbursement of $65.50 penalty and interest.

If you have questions or require additional information, please let me know. Thank you.

Sincerely,

hit lists, such as the "underground economy"—home offices, small self-employed businesses, and rental real estate.

Verification. Make sure all third-party income and deductions reported to the IRS agree with your records and your tax return. Verify that:

- Forms W-2 from all employers match your reported salary.
- Forms 1099, showing interest and dividend income received from your banks and securities firms, match the amounts you received and entered on your return.
- Form 1098, mortgage interest statement from your bank or lender, matches your mortgage interest deduction.
- Other types of income reported on Form 1099, such as profits from bartering, unemployment compensation, and gambling winnings, are reported on the correct lines of your return.

If you find an error on any of these forms, contact the issuer and request a corrected version immediately. If possible, get the corrected form before you file your return.

If there is a discrepancy between the amount reported on your return and the figure shown on an information return, such as a 1099 or W-2, attach a statement explaining why the numbers do not match. For example, you and your sister may each be including half of the interest on a joint bank account. In that case, you would staple a statement to the back of your return, stating that you had "nominee income" and explaining that 50% of the interest is being reported on your sister's return (give her name and Social Security number).

Forms and schedules. Fill out the appropriate forms and attach required schedules. Here are some of the common forms the IRS expects to find on your return if you have certain items of income or expense.

■ Form 2119 (*Sale of Your Home*). When you sell a house, you receive a 1099-S (*Proceeds from Real Estate Transaction*) from the real estate broker or attorney, which shows the gross sale price of the house. If you do not file this form with your 1040, the IRS computer will spot the mismatch, leading the IRS to audit the sale of your home.

■ Schedule D (*Capital Gains and Losses*). If you sell investment rental property, your return must include a record of the sale on Schedule D. Failing to file Schedule D could lead to an audit because the IRS can easily match sales data reported on Form 1099-S against your return.

Auditors are also on the lookout for vanishing investments—those appearing on last year's return and not on the current year's. When property disappears, the IRS expects to see a Schedule D showing the asset was sold for a taxable gain or deductible loss. This applies to stock that was paying dividends one year, but inexplicably not the next, as well as to income-producing rental property.

■ Form 8283 (*Noncash Charitable Contributions*). If you make noncash charitable contributions in excess of $500, you must include Form 8283 with your return. If the noncash deduction exceeds $5000, you must also include a separate appraisal of the item donated.

Timing. File on time (including extensions). Filing late is not the way to avoid an audit. IRS computers review returns year-round, not only before April 15. Do not listen to tax professionals who claim that IRS workloads are set and returns are selected for audit by the end of August. This is a fallacy. A return can be selected for audit at any time. In fact, a return claiming unusually large deductions has a better chance of being noticed for audit if it comes in when the service center is receiving only 5000 returns a day than when it is being deluged with a million in April.

Pension distributions. Report all pension distributions, even if they are not taxable. When you receive a distribution from your IRA or pension plan (1099-R) and roll it over within 60 days to another qualified plan, it is not taxable income. Because it is nontaxable, you may think you do not have to include the item on your tax return. Do not be fooled. All distributions reported on Form 1099 should be reported on your return, even those that produce no tax. The 1040 has two boxes for pension distributions—one to show the total amount you received and another to report the taxable amount.

Form 8275. Do *not* fill out Form 8275 or 8275-R. The IRS says you should file Form 8275 or 8275-R if you knowingly take a position on your return that is questionable. But by using these forms, you are waving a red flag at the IRS, signaling that you are probably doing something wrong. In addition, the instructions for Forms 8275 and 8275-R require you to support your position by citing revenue rulings, revenue procedures, tax court cases, and tax law provisions. This means you need to hack your way through thousands of pages in our current tax code and court reports.

According to the IRS, there is a gain for your pains: If you attach Form 8275 or 8275-R to your return, and if the return is later audited and the issue decided against you, you will not have to pay any penalties. However, you will have to pay any additional tax, plus interest.

The fact is, you can take the same position regarding income and expenses, and rely on the same rulings or procedures, without attaching either of these forms to your return.

Other actions

- Be thorough. Remember to provide your complete address and Social Security number. Do not leave lines of the 1040 blank if the information applies to you. Sign and date the return. A joint return must be signed by both spouses.

- Be neat and legible. This is purely psychological, but it is true: Neat returns, especially computerized ones, are less likely to be audited because they simply look more accurate than handwritten or sloppy ones.

- Double-check your math to make sure it is correct.

- Avoid large refunds by adjusting your withholding allowances on Form W-4, filed with your employer.

- Report the name and Social Security number of all dependents.

- Report the name, address, and identification number of child care providers on Form 2441, *Credit for Child and Dependent Care Expenses*.

- Do not round off to the nearest $50 or $100.

- Show the IRS how honest you are by reporting small amounts of income the IRS is unlikely to find out about, such as jury duty pay.

- Do not volunteer information to back up your deductions.

- If you are self-employed, incorporate or form a partnership. The IRS focuses heavily on sole proprietors.

AILMENT

I received a notice from my IRS service center saying that I owe more tax.

R If the income reported on information returns is more than the income shown on a tax return, you will receive a notice of additional tax due. This notice is called a CP-2000, *Notice of Proposed Changes to Tax Return*, and some 3.5 million taxpayers receive them each year.

It sounds as if you are one of them. The first important point is that the CP-2000 is merely a *proposed* increase in your tax. It is not a bill. Therefore, you should not automatically assume the CP-2000 is right. Included with the notice should be a list of the payers, account numbers, and amounts of all income reported as paid to your Social Security number. You must check these carefully against your return and the Forms W-2 and 1099 you received to make sure the figures shown on the CP-2000 are correct. The IRS makes only a halfhearted effort to determine *why* your income figures don't match. Verifying the accuracy of the CP-2000 is up to you. In many cases there is a valid reason for any difference. For instance, bank errors frequently generate a CP-2000.

Do *not* pay any additional tax if the CP-2000 is incorrect. Instead, in a signed statement explain why you disagree with the proposed changes. Use the sample letters on pages 236–243 to help you draft your response. Attach your statement to page 5 of the CP-2000 and return it to the IRS. In-

---

SAMPLE LETTER

Form 1099 You Received from Payer Is Correct and Matches Your Return

Date

Internal Revenue Service
City, State, Zip Code

Re: Your Name
SSN: 123-45-6789

Dear Sir:

This is in response to your Notice of Proposed Changes to Tax Return (see copy of pages 2 and 3 attached). This notice is in error.

I received only $550 in interest income from Midland Bank, not $800 as you claim. Attached is a copy of a certified Form 1099-INT/letter from the bank showing the correct amount. This is the amount reported on my return.

or

I received only $550 in dividend income from Westport Corporation, not $800 as you claim. Attached is a copy of a certified 1099-DIV/letter from Westport showing the correct amount. This is the amount reported on my return.

Please adjust your records based on this documentation, and revise your notice to show no additional tax due. Thank you.

Sincerely,

SAMPLE LETTER

Payer Made an Error on Form 1099, and Your Return Is Correct

Date

Internal Revenue Service
City, State, Zip Code

Re: Your Name
SSN: 123-45-6789

Dear Sir:

This is in response to your Notice of Proposed Changes to Tax Return (see copy of pages 2 and 3 attached). This notice is in error.

Your notice claims that I owe income tax on $600 in interest/dividends from Knockwood Corporation. The actual amount of interest/dividends I received from Knockwood was $450. This is the amount reported on Schedule B of my return (see copy attached).

I have attached a certified copy of a corrected Form 1099-INT/DIV/letter from Knockwood Corporation, attesting that the correct amount of income should be $450.

Please adjust your records based on this documentation and cancel your notice of additional tax due. Thank you.

Sincerely,

clude any documents that support your explanation, as well as your telephone number during business hours. If there has been a bank or broker error in reporting your earnings, for example, send along a letter from the company confirming the mistake. If the interest is being reported on another tax return, provide that person's name and Social Security number.

If you cannot solve the problem by correspondence, you may request a meeting with an auditor or an appeals officer. The conference will be held in your local district office. Normally, you would take this step only if the IRS rejects your written explanation, but you might also want a meeting in person if you are unable to untangle or match the income attributed to you or if you have numerous documents to produce.

Of course, you may decide that the IRS is right after all. Perhaps you never received a Form 1099 for interest you actually earned, for example, or an item was left off your return through an oversight. In that case, you can put the CP-2000 behind you by signing the consent on page 5 of the

---

SAMPLE LETTER

Item Was Reported in Full but on More Than One Line or Schedule of the Return

Date

Internal Revenue Service
City, State, Zip Code

Re: Your Name
SSN: 123-45-6789

Dear Sir:

This is in response to your Notice of Proposed Changes to Tax Return (see copy of pages 2 and 3 attached). This notice is in error.

Your notice claims I failed to report $560 in interest/dividend income from Farflung Corporation. In fact, the amount was reported in full—$350 was reported as a capital gain dividend on line 14 of the Form 1040 and the balance of $210 was reported as an ordinary dividend on Schedule B. Copies of page 1 of my Form 1040 and of Schedule B are attached with the two separate amounts circled in red.

Please cancel your notice of additional tax due, or explain the reason for the discrepancy, if we have not identified the problem. Thank you.

Sincerely,

---

notice and by paying the amount due. Prompt payment will prevent any further interest from accruing.

Whatever your response, it should be made within 30 days. Use the envelope enclosed with the notice. If the IRS accepts your payment or explanation, it usually drops the entire matter without contacting you. If you do not receive a reply within two months, your problems with the IRS are probably over.

If you are agreeing to only part of the assessment, check box B. You are not required to send a check at this time. In fact, it is better not to. You cannot outguess the amount of compound interest, and it is easy to make a mistake in computing the extra tax. You want your correspondence with the IRS to end, not drag on indefinitely, and if you overpay, you can spend months trying to get a refund.

Instead, wait for the IRS to send you a revised bill. This generally comes

SAMPLE LETTER

Item Was Reported Elsewhere on Return

Date

Internal Revenue Service
City, State, Zip Code

Re: Your Name
SSN: 123-45-6789

Dear Sir:

This is in response to your Notice of Proposed Changes to Tax Return (see copy of pages 2 and 3 attached). This notice is in error in two respects.

Your notice claims that I failed to report $3000 in royalty income received from Spill Oil. This amount was actually reported on line 23, Form 1040, as miscellaneous income. A copy of page 1 of my Form 1040 is attached with this amount circled in red.

or

(Fill in the location of the income allegedly omitted and submit a copy of that page or schedule with your letter.)

Please adjust your records in accordance with this documentation and revise your notice to show no additional tax due. Thank you.

Sincerely,

---

in about a month. Then pay your tax with a check or money order. Do not send cash. Make your payment out to the Internal Revenue Service. Write your Social Security number (husband's number if a joint return), the tax period or year, and the type of tax ("income tax" or "Form 1040").

The amount of your payment will be the proposed balance due as shown on line 15, page 2 of the CP-2000 if you are not protesting the penalty. If you are enclosing a letter asking that the penalty be abated, your payment will be the sum of lines 10 through 13, page 2.

Staple your check to the middle of page 5 of the CP-2000 and mail in the envelope provided. Keep a record of your payment.

Do not expect a CP-2000 soon after you file your return. Matching millions of documents takes time. Current notices are for tax returns filed about a year and a half ago.

SAMPLE LETTER

SAMPLE LETTER

Social Security Number Is Yours, but You Have Changed Your Name

Date

Internal Revenue Service
City, State, Zip Code

Re: Your Name
SSN: 123-45-6789

Dear Sir:

This is in response to your Notice of Proposed Changes to Tax Return (see copy of pages 2 and 3 attached). This notice is incorrect.

Your notice claims that I owe income tax on interest/dividends reported under Social Security number 123-45-6789. I have remarried* and this income was reported on the joint return I filed with my spouse (SSN: 987-65-4321). A copy of this return is enclosed.

Please adjust your records accordingly, and revise your notice, showing no additional tax due. Thank you.

Sincerely,

*Note: You should immediately notify the Social Security Administration of your married name and ask to have your Social Security number reissued under your new name.

☐ Prevention

You cannot control the mistakes of others, but you can take steps to make sure a CP-2000 notice is not triggered by your own inaction or carelessness.

■ Do not file too early. Forms 1099 often straggle in after the January 31 deadline. If you jump the gun in order to get a quick refund, you may easily miss items of income.

■ Prepare your return from the Forms 1099, not your year-end statements or record of bank deposits.

■ Do your own Form 1099 match before mailing your return. Keep a list of all of your bank, credit union, or money market accounts,

SAMPLE LETTER

Social Security Number Is Yours, but Income Was Reported by Joint Tenant or Co-Owner

Date

Internal Revenue Service
City, State, Zip Code

Re: Your Name
SSN: 123-45-6789

Dear Sir:

This is in response to your Notice of Proposed Changes to Tax Return (see copy of pages 2 and 3 attached). This notice is in error.

Your notice claims that I owe income tax on $1200 in interest/dividend income from Windfall, Ltd. This income was earned on an account/ stock I own jointly with two of my aunts. All of the income was reported in my Social Security number because it is listed first on the account/stock. I have reported my one-third share ($400) on my return (see copy of Schedule B attached). The balance was reported by my aunts, Catherine Parnell (SSN: 679-24-3392) and Tessie Frizell (SSN: 711-45-2336).

For this reason, no additional tax is due. Please revise your notice accordingly. Thank you.

Sincerely,

---

stock holdings, and mutual funds. Compare this list to your Forms 1099 in early February and check each one off to make sure you are not missing any.

■ Notify the Social Security Administration if you change your name and it no longer matches the name on your Social Security card. The IRS and Social Security are as closely allied as Siamese twins. What Social Security doesn't know will hurt you with the IRS.

■ Have the payer correct its records if:

   ■ Income on a child's custodian account is being reported under your Social Security number.

SAMPLE LETTER

Social Security Number Is Yours, but You Received No Income (Payer or IRS Error)

Date

Internal Revenue Service
City, State, Zip Code

Re: Your Name
SSN: 123-45-6789

Dear Sir:

This is in response to your Notice of Proposed Changes to Tax Return (see copy of pages 2 and 3 attached). This notice is in error.

Your notice claims that I owe tax on $575 in dividend/interest income from Medallion, Inc. Although the Social Security number of the recipient shown on your notice matches mine, I do not have an account with/own shares in Medallion, Inc.

A letter from Medallion is attached, attesting to the fact that the corporation made an error on the Form 1099 sent to the IRS and that they paid me no income in 199X.

or

I have attached a letter from Medallion, attesting that they paid me no income in 199X and did not issue a Form 1099 for my Social Security number. Please review your records for a data entry error.

Thank you.

Sincerely,

- You divorce or your spouse dies and income on an account listed under your former spouse's Social Security number is now owned by you.

- You and a co-owner have agreed that the co-owner will report all of the income, but your Social Security number is listed first on the account or stock.

SAMPLE LETTER

CP-2000 Is Partially Correct

Date

Internal Revenue Service
City, State, Zip Code

Re: Your Name
SSN: 123-45-6789

Dear Sir:

This is in response to your Notice of Proposed Changes to Tax Return (see copy of pages 2 and 3 attached). This notice is in error.

(Insert appropriate paragraph(s) based on sample letters, explaining why the IRS is incorrect in adjusting your interest, dividends, or royalties.)

We do not dispute the inclusion of $785 in interest income from Excelsior Savings. This Form 1099 was apparently overlooked.

or

We agree that we inadvertently omitted interest income from Excelsior Savings. However, the actual amount received was $785, not $925, as your notice claims. A certified copy of the Form 1099-INT from Excelsior Savings is attached.

Please recompute the tax due on the additional interest income alone, and send us a revised notice. Thank you.

Sincerely,

AILMENT

The IRS has assessed an accuracy-related penalty against me.

R℞ The IRS routinely assesses what is called the 20% accuracy-related penalty anytime income is left off a return. This clearly violates the intent of the tax law, which meant penalties to be used as an object lesson in extreme cases. These days the IRS uses penalties "to enhance the revenue"—that is, to help balance the budget. Too often, the IRS gets away with it.

The accuracy-related penalty is supposed to be applied only when there has been negligence or a substantial understatement of tax. A substantial understatement occurs when the tax due on the CP-2000 is the greater of (1) $5000 or more or (2) more than 10% of your correct tax. This is pretty black-and-white, so there is not much point arguing if you overlooked enough income to generate a substantial understatement.

The negligence side of the penalty is where you stand a chance to win your case. Negligence can't happen by mere accident. It is intentional or the result of reckless or irresponsible behavior. Let us compare leaving income off your return to an auto accident. If you do not see an oncoming car because your view is obstructed by another car, you are not negligent. But if you do not spot it because you have been drinking or tried to beat the light at an intersection, clearly you are negligent.

Failure to report any amount of income is considered a strong indication of negligence. You can overcome this presumption, however, if you can provide clear and convincing evidence to the contrary.

What might persuade the IRS your omission was not reckless or intentional? There is no clear-cut answer. It is possible that the IRS might be swayed by the following:

- Your spouse, who normally prepared the return and kept all the records, died and you prepared the return on the basis of all the information you could diligently find.

- You were physically or mentally incompetent at the time the return was prepared.

- Your records were lost or stolen and, although you made a good-faith effort to reconstruct them, you apparently overlooked one or two items.

- Because you had several accounts with an institution and received more than one Form 1099 from it, you did not realize one of them was missing from your return.

- Because of a midyear merger or acquisition, it was unclear whether the Form 1099 you received from the successor institution included all of the income you earned, both before and after the takeover.

- You received a refund after making the same mistake in a prior year. (This is a safe admission if enough time has passed that the IRS can no longer take your refund back. The IRS has three years from the due date of a return to assess extra tax for that year.)

- You relied on the advice of a tax professional that the interest, dividend, or royalty was not taxable.

Claiming ignorance of the law is not normally a good excuse, unless a tricky or particularly murky area of the tax law is involved. The problem with omitting Form 1099 income is that the form itself tells you that the income is taxable.

Nor will the fact that you relied on a tax preparer to correctly complete your return excuse you from responsibility for negligence. You are required to inspect your return before mailing to make sure it is accurate. Of course, you may have recourse against your preparer for payment of the penalty in that case (see page 231).

Use the sample letter on page 246 as a guide in requesting that the IRS abate the penalty.

If your excuse for the error is not accepted, you will receive a second billing for the penalty. You may appeal or simply pay. However, if the IRS has been influenced by your explanation, you may hear nothing further after writing or you may receive a brief letter stating the IRS will not pursue the penalty; in either case, congratulations.

AILMENT

My tax return has been selected for audit.

R You have no doubt already received the audit letter inviting you to personally appear before an auditor. This appointment letter tells you to come in at a specified date and time. (If you operate your own business, a revenue agent may call and make an appointment to come to your place of business.) When you get your appointment letter, read it. It contains valuable information about who may represent you at the audit and briefly outlines your appeal rights. It also tells you which items are being audited. These are the issues you must produce records to support. These are not the only issues that may be audited, however. If the auditor suspects or uncovers an error or unallowable deduction during the audit, the auditor may expand the scope of the examination to include the new issue and ask you to send in additional records.

If your return is a nonbusiness one, you will receive information guides with your letter. These guides tell you what records are needed to verify the items being audited. If you have kept all the suggested records, you will have no trouble in the audit at all. Most people do not discover what records they need, however, until it is too late. If you do not have all the records you need, now is the time to try to reconstruct them—for example, by calling your doctor's office or mortgage lender.

If you filed a business return (Schedule C), you will not receive these information guides. Business owners must bring in all the journals and ledgers for their businesses as well as the original receipts and invoices,

---

SAMPLE LETTER

Request for Abatement of Accuracy-Related Penalty

Date

Internal Revenue Service
City, State, Zip Code

Re: Your Name
SSN: 123-45-6789

Dear Sir:

This is to request an abatement of the accuracy-related penalty of $234 assessed against us for failure to include interest income on our 1995 return.

We supplied our tax preparer with an itemized list of banks from whom interest was received in 1995. Hermitage Savings was on this list, and the preparer placed a check mark beside this payer, as if it had indeed been reported (see copy of list attached). Relying on this indication that the preparer had included each item on the list, we reasonably did not suspect any omission. Furthermore, this list, in itself, is evidence that we had no intention of omitting this income. In addition, we claimed Hermitage Savings interest in full on both our 1994 and 1996 returns, further proving that the omission in 1995 was merely an oversight, not constituting negligence.

Accordingly, we respectfully request an abatement of the $234 penalty.

Sincerely,

---

even though not all business expenses are being audited. They must also bring in bank statements for all checking and savings accounts to verify income.

A power-of-attorney form will also be attached to the appointment letter if you choose to have someone represent you. Should you bring in the professional guns or go it alone? By all means, discuss the audit with your accountant or lawyer beforehand. But there is no reason to bring either of them to the first audit session unless one of them prepared the return and the audit involves a complex issue you do not feel knowledgeable enough to deal with. You can always bring your preparer in to a later session or on appeal, if you and the auditor cannot reach an agreement. If the auditor wants to conduct the audit in your home or office, however, you may have a big problem, and your counsel should be present at all times.

The appointment letter tells you which year is being audited and gives you the address and phone number of the audit group handling your case. Do not hesitate to call the appointment clerk if you have any questions about what records to bring, if you need an extension of time to assemble your records, or if you want the audit transferred to an office closer to you.

If you cannot appear in person or do not want to spare the time, you may mail in your records. If you adopt this course, it is wise to let the appointment clerk know that you are going to handle your audit by correspondence, especially if your records will not arrive until after the appointment date. Send a copy of your appointment letter along with your records for identification and for help in locating your file. Keep the original letter and all other correspondence you receive during the course of the audit for reference in case you have questions or wish to supply additional information.

A word of advice about audit by mail: It is never as advantageous as coming in for an interview, and it is unwise if the issues are more complex than itemized deductions. When you mail in documents, the auditor is limited to those records alone. If they are not self-explanatory or do not exactly match the item you are being asked to prove, chances are you will lose the deduction, whereas if you or your representative were present, additional facts could be brought to light that would satisfy the auditor and win you the deduction. Remember, the auditor will not give you the benefit of the doubt. An auditor is permitted to evaluate oral testimony and allow a reasonable amount notwithstanding a lack of records. But you or your representative must be present to make an oral argument.

If you decide to risk mailing your records or simply have no choice, be sure to attach a thorough explanation of the facts pertaining to each expense and what each receipt is for. If you have no records at all to back up an expense, explain why, and the circumstances that make it deductible. This is the next best thing to oral testimony, although without records there is no guarantee your explanation will be given any weight. Include your phone number, in case the auditor wants to clarify any facts. The burden of proof is on you, however, so you cannot rely on the auditor to take the time or trouble to call you.

There is one exception to the axiom that once an audit is started it must go through. This is called the *repetitive audit*, and it is the IRS equivalent of time off for good behavior. If you have been audited for the same classified issues in either of the two preceding tax years and breezed through without changing your tax, you can avoid an audit this year.

Call the audit group before your appointment date and tell the clerk you believe yours is a repetitive audit. Your case will be suspended until the truth of your statement is checked and a decision is made whether to continue the audit. This is at the group manager's discretion. If even one issue is different or a deduction has substantially changed, you may have to go through another audit anyway. *Note:* Multiple audits of a Schedule C business are not considered repetitive—the IRS sees each year of a business as unique, so the issues are never the "same."

The audit interview. Be prepared to spend at least an hour and a half with the auditor if you filed an individual return and at least four hours if you filed a business return.

When you step through the door into the IRS waiting room, present your appointment letter to the receptionist, and take a seat and wait. If there is no receptionist, use the waiting room telephone to notify the group clerk that you have arrived.

What is the auditor doing while you are waiting? Possibly taking a first look at your file, because nonbusiness returns are often not assigned until the taxpayer walks in the door. The auditor will quickly scan to see what issues are being audited, how to pronounce your name, and what you do for a living. The experienced auditor will become familiar with your return as the audit progresses. If, however, yours is a business return, the auditor is already thoroughly acquainted with it, having analyzed it before your appointment letter was sent out and decided which issues looked promising.

How you react to the auditor can set the tone for the whole audit. A hostile attitude can prejudice the auditor against you from the start, making the auditor less patient, less sympathetic, and less open to your oral testimony. This is the last thing you need. Instead you should plan on being polite and cooperative.

Once the formalities are out of the way, your audit begins with the auditor asking you to present your documentation for each questioned item. The auditor will usually take each deduction, one by one, gathering all the facts and examining your receipts before moving on to the next. You may also be asked whether you have additional income, taxable or not.

The audit can be as thorough and rigorous as the auditor chooses to make it. In practice, the examination will be limited to the original issues and the documentation you were asked to bring to the interview. If additional information is needed, you will be given time to produce it.

Audit strategy. You should not wander into an IRS audit without a strategy. First, do not volunteer information. What you do not know about the tax law can hurt you. Begin rambling on about your daughter's overnight camp or Uncle Ernie, and you may stumble over the tax law: Your daughter's camp does not qualify as child care and Uncle Ernie made too much money to be claimed as an exemption.

Answer the auditor's questions, but do not feel you have to elaborate. Of course, you must give the auditor enough information to be convinced that you are entitled to your deductions. If your answers fail to satisfy, you will have to go into more detail until the auditor has all the facts needed. Find out exactly what information is still lacking, and stick to that subject.

Let the auditor take control of the audit and decide what issues to cover in what order and what questions to ask. If you let the auditor run the interview, there is less chance you will say something that will cost you money. Wait until the auditor has reached a final decision before raising your objections and arguments. There may not be any adjustments to get upset about.

As the audit progresses, try to get a feel for problems that may be brewing. Do this by asking if you have supplied enough proof for each issue and whether additional information is needed. Knowing where you stand gives you time to prepare a persuasive argument or a convincing explanation of why the deduction is reasonable.

The audit report.   When all your evidence is in, the auditor will decide whether you will be eating caviar or cat food in the near future. This determination may occur at the end of the audit interview or after you have provided additional information.

The audit can have one of three outcomes: (1) no tax due, (2) additional tax due, or (3) a refund. If the result is (1) or (3), you are a winner. But if the audit report shows you owe more tax, you have a decision to make.

The audit report is not a bill. Your auditor is merely proposing adjustments to your tax return. You do not have to accept them, so do not panic if the result is worse than you expected. You have 30 days after you receive the audit report to decide what action to take. During this 30-day period, you may do one of three things: First, you may submit additional information you believe might change the auditor's decision. The auditor will review this new data and will either mail you a revised report or letter accepting your return as filed, or send you a notice showing the same tax due as before, explaining why there has been no change.

If you have no other information to aid your cause, you may either agree or disagree with the audit report. If you decide to agree, sign one copy of the report and mail it back. If a joint return was filed, both you and your spouse should sign the report. Keep the other copy of the report for your records. You may send a check for the tax due with the signed report or wait for a bill from the service center.

The next **AILMENT** describes the appeals process if you decide to disagree with the audit report.

AILMENT

I want to appeal the result of my audit.

R You may believe that the auditor's report is unfair or incorrect. If you disagree with the auditor's findings, inform the auditor within 30 days of the date on the report that you want to exercise your administrative appeal rights.

The administrative appeals process consists of an "informal" level and a "formal" level. Neither level is open until your audit is complete. If an audit report was issued to you because you failed to provide requested information, you do not yet have the right to appeal. Only after the issues have been fully examined, based on your records, will you be granted an appeal.

At the informal level, you will meet your auditor's manager or a senior auditor. Either has authority to change the audit report after reconsidering the issues and the documents you provide. This change can be an increase in tax as well as a decrease, so be sure of the validity of your position before you charge in.

If you are dissatisfied with the outcome of the informal conference or if you wish to skip that level, you may request a hearing with the appellate division. Simply tell the auditor or group manager that you want a formal appeal. You do not have to put your request in writing.

There is one exception: If your audit was conducted by a revenue agent and the proposed deficiency is greater than $2500, you must file a written protest to appeal. The protest should state:

1. Your desire to appeal.

2. Your name and address.

3. The date and symbols on the letter sent with your audit report.

4. The tax year(s) involved.

5. A list of the audit adjustments you disagree with.

6. The facts supporting your position, plus a statement that to the best of your knowledge and belief and "under penalties of perjury," the facts are true.

7. The law or other authority you are relying on.

When your oral or written request is received, your file will be assigned to an appellate conferee, and an appointment letter will be sent to you.

At the formal conference, you will be allowed to present evidence on only the adjustments with which you disagreed. In arguing your position, you may give oral evidence or call witnesses on your behalf. You may also reintroduce the same documentary evidence you showed to the original auditor. New evidence may not be presented. Appellate conferees do not audit.

The conferee has broad powers to settle a case, and has two conflicting goals: (1) for you to pay the correct tax, but also (2) to keep you from going to court. To meet the latter objective, the conferee is willing to deal. Unlike the auditor, the conferee has settlement authority, and is permitted to consider and accept a settlement offer made by you if the proposed tax deficiency is less than $2500. The conferee may settle the disputed issues in your favor, even though the result has no legal basis at all. However, the conferee can use this settlement authority only when the outcome if the case goes to court is in doubt.

A settlement may also be reached through mutual concessions, each side giving a little until a reasonable compromise is reached. Sometimes, a settlement based on a percentage of the tax is proposed. The conferee will weigh the strength of the government's case relative to yours in deciding what concessions to make.

In other cases, if the conferee does not feel trial can be recommended, the conferee may concede an issue in full. But the conferee will settle based on the merits of the case, not merely to avoid a trial. Normally about 80% of all appeals are settled before trial.

If you agree to the conferee's proposal, you will be given a Form 870 to sign. If you and the conferee are unable to come to an agreement, a statutory notice of deficiency will be issued, and you will have 90 days to petition the Tax Court or pay the tax and file a claim. This latter route will lead you to the District Court or Court of Claims. (See the next **AILMENT** for information about taking your case to court.)

AILMENT

I lost my case at the IRS appellate level.

℞ Sometimes the only way to settle a tax dispute is to face the IRS in a showdown. And the easiest, handiest choice for a shootout is found in the United States Tax Court.

You do not even need a lawyer. The Court comes to you, too. Its 19 justices are like frontier circuit court judges, hearing cases in over 50 cities for your convenience and to spare you travel costs.

The Tax Court is not the only law around, though. You can head for U.S. District Court or the Court of Claims, too. There are a slew of reasons to pick one over the other, but most taxpayers prefer Tax Court because they can fight now and pay later. With the District Court or Court of Claims, you must ante up the tax and file a claim for refund.

You get to Tax Court by filing a petition. The petition must be filed within 90 days after the IRS has mailed you a statutory notice of deficiency (150 days if you are outside the United States). The day the notice was mailed is not counted, but the day of filing is. Do not turn your taxes into a cliff-hanger by waiting until the end of the 90-day period. Unlike many of us, the Tax Court still puts absolute trust in the U.S. mails. Your petition must be *postmarked* to be considered timely filed. Use certified mail and request a receipt. Do not use a private courier or facsimile machine.

What if you miss the deadline? You are denied your day in Tax Court. Set your sights on District Court or the Court of Claims instead.

☐ Resources

Before you file a petition with the Tax Court, send for a copy of *Rules of Practice and Procedure, United States Tax Court* (Superintendent of Documents, U.S. Government Printing Office, Washington, DC 20402).

AILMENT

The IRS has seized my property.

R̸ Although your situation is bleak, it is not hopeless. You have a right to redeem your personal property before it is sold. However, you must pay the tax and also all expenses of seizure, which could include storage charges and insurance. Real estate may be redeemed at any time within 120 days after the sale by paying the purchaser the amount paid for the property, plus interest of 20% per annum. You should call or visit an IRS office right away to pay the taxes in full, if possible.

There are also several other ways to obtain a release of seized property. These methods work on any type of seizure from bank accounts and paychecks to homes and autos. The IRS will release a levy or seizure under the following conditions:

■ *Hardship.* There is no tax authority for releasing a notice of levy because it is creating financial hardship for you and your family. But levies are released for this reason all the time. Because releasing a levy does not usually require the approval of a supervisor, collection employees often use their own judgment. By appealing to the revenue officer's sense of compassion, you may be able to get the levy of your bank account or paycheck released so that you can pay necessary living expenses.

■ *Bond.* A levy will be released if you deliver an acceptable bond to the IRS, conditioned upon payment of the delinquent taxes. IRS regulations outline what is meant by an "acceptable" bond.

■ *Payment of amount of U.S. interest in the property.* This condition applies to the seizure of a nonmonetary asset, such as a home or a car.

■ *Assignment of wages or installment payment arrangements.* You can get a levy released by signing a payroll deduction agreement or any type of installment payment arrangement.

■ *Extension of the statute of limitations.* Once tax has been assessed, the IRS has 10 years in which to legally collect the amount due. Revenue officers are under pressure not to let the 10-year statutory period expire without the tax being paid. When a statute has less than a year before expiring, an officer will try to get you to sign Form 900, *Tax Collection Waiver*, to agree to extend the time period of the statute. If you do not sign this waiver, a revenue officer will take any legal action possible to collect the tax before the 10 years is up. That includes seizing everything in sight, no matter how much hardship it causes.

On the other hand, the IRS may release a levy that has been made before the statute expires on the condition that before the property is released you sign the waiver form agreeing to extend the statutory period.

■ *Escrow arrangement.* Although seldom used, this arrangement benefits businesses with assets or inventory under seizure. Property is placed in escrow with a third party who takes control of it for the purposes of protecting the property and securing payment of the liability. The escrow arrangement works well where the IRS has a particular asset under seizure, such as an entire business, and the taxpayer cannot raise money to pay the taxes unless the property is released.

Note: The release of a levy does not prevent another levy in the future.

Unlawful sales. The IRS must follow certain procedures prior to the sale of the seized property. Unless these steps are taken, you may have grounds to set aside the sale as unlawful. Once the property has been seized, the IRS must provide written notice to the owner. Furthermore, the time, place, and manner of the sale of the property, plus a description of the property, must be published in a newspaper of general circulation in the county in which the property was seized.

The sale must take place not less than 10 days or more than 40 days from the time notice is given. (The sale may be adjourned for up to one month after the date in the original notice of sale if the district director feels that a postponement will serve the best interests of either the government or the taxpayer.) Furthermore, the sale must take place in the county in which the property was seized unless the IRS district director feels that it could get a substantially higher bid elsewhere.

The IRS is required to set a minimum price before the sale. If no person offers that amount at the sale, the property is deemed to have been purchased by the United States.

I owe so much tax that I will never be able to pay it.

℞ One remedy is to file for bankruptcy (see page 255). A less drastic action, if you can pay a part of the amount you owe, is to make the IRS an offer in compromise. This is an offer to settle your tax liability, including interest and penalties, for a smaller amount than you owe. If the offer is accepted and you pay the agreed-upon lesser amount, the IRS will close its books on this tax liability forever.

The IRS cannot refuse to consider your offer, but it is under no obligation to accept it, either. If the offer you submit is reasonable and it is not accepted, you must be given a chance to raise your bid. In effect, you are bargaining with the IRS to find a payment amount you both can live with. If the IRS rejects your offer, you should be sent a letter of explanation.

An offer in compromise must be submitted on Form 656, *Offer in Compromise*. Both you and your spouse must sign Form 656 if a joint tax return is involved. If you are claiming the amount cannot be collected (i.e., you see no hope of having enough money to pay the full amount), you must fill out Form 433, *Statement of Financial Condition*, as well.

The IRS will not consider an offer based on your financial condition unless it reflects the largest amount you can afford to pay. Form 433 asks you to list all your assets and liabilities, life insurance policies including cash surrender and loan values, the market value of your real estate, business inventory, furniture, vehicles, and securities, and any accounts or notes receivable. You must also list your income and expenses for the past two years.

In making your offer, you should start low and be prepared to up the amount if necessary. Offers that are small compared to the balance due may be justified in some cases. For example, you may be unable to return to work because of age or disability. Your offer should not be so ridiculously low that you do not seem to be bargaining in good faith. One guideline: Figure out the maximum you can afford to pay, then offer 20% of this amount initially.

Before accepting your offer, a revenue officer may require you to borrow money on assets that have some equity (such as your home), pay over loose cash you have in checking and savings accounts, sell stocks and bonds, and sell any "luxury" assets (such as an RV or boat).

The revenue officer may also ask you to pledge a percentage of your annual income for the next five to six years, refrain from claiming tax losses and bad debt deductions you would have been entitled to, and reduce the depreciation you will claim on business assets. The result: You will pay higher taxes in the future.

If your offer is accepted, you should be aware that interest will continue to accrue on any unpaid offer until it is paid in full. The IRS reserves the right to nab any future refunds, too, so long as the refund, when added to the amount of your offer, does not exceed the original amount you owed. Further, none of your payments will be applied to interest until all the taxes and penalties have been paid first. Finally, you agree to extend the statute of limitations for collecting your tax by at least a year (the statute is 10 years).

If you are offering to pay in installments, you must make each payment as agreed or the IRS can sue for the balance due on the offer or the liability that was compromised. It can also disregard the offer and take immediate collection action with notice.

When your offer has been paid in full, the federal tax lien against your property will be released. Having the lien still in effect will hinder your ability to get credit, but you can produce the offer in compromise to convince lenders that their funds will stay safe from the IRS as long as you meet the terms of the payment schedule.

What if your offer is rejected? The IRS will return the money you deposited. Your money cannot be applied to your delinquent taxes unless you agree in writing.

AILMENT

I want to discharge my taxes in bankruptcy.

Bankruptcy is certainly one way to spell income tax relief. Because of the financial and social ramifications of bankruptcy, however, you should explore other solutions to your tax liability first. For example, if you cannot pay your taxes in full, you can make an offer in compromise (see page 254) or try to negotiate an installment payment arrangement (see page 227). In fact, the threat of filing bankruptcy may sway the IRS into accepting an offer in compromise.

When it comes to discharging taxes in bankruptcy, timing is everything. You must meet the timing and other requirements of three rules before you are relieved of tax liability.

First, the bankruptcy petition must be filed more than three years after the due date of the tax return. For example, if you owe income taxes for 1994, and you filed your tax return on August 15, 1995, under an automatic extension to that date, the three-year rule will be satisfied on April 15, 1998. If you file your petition after April 15, 1998, your 1994 taxes can be discharged—but not your 1995, 1996, and 1997 taxes.

The bankruptcy petition also must be filed more than two years after you filed the delinquent return for which you are seeking a discharge. For example, you owe income taxes for 1994. You filed a late return on April 30, 1996. The two-year rule will the satisfied on April 30, 1998.

Your petition also must be filed more than 240 days after the date the tax was assessed. Normally, the balance due on a return is assessed right after the return is filed, but the date could be later. For example, the IRS could audit your return years after it is filed and propose an additional assessment. Also, if you submitted an offer in compromise within that 240-day period after assessment, the rule is extended while the offer is pending, plus 30 days. *Tip:* If a revenue officer offers you a choice of either making an offer in compromise or arranging an installment agreement, choose the latter. Unlike an offer, it does not suspend the 240-day period, although you will have to come up with some immediate money. But you may wind up paying less than you would under an offer.

A bankruptcy does not relieve you of all income taxes. Some taxes survive the discharge and can still be collected by the IRS. A discharge does not extend to the following taxes:

- A tax that is still assessable after the petition date. For example, this rule could apply if there is an open statute of limitations due to a substantial omission of income or if you have agreed to extend the statute of limitations.

- Debts based on returns that you were required to file, but did not.

- Debts based on fraudulent returns or willful attempts to evade tax liability. The burden of proof is on the IRS to prove fraud.

- The 100% penalty assessed on employers for failing to withhold and pay over payroll taxes.

Once taxes are discharged, the Bankruptcy Court can hold the IRS in civil contempt if it violates the discharge order. The IRS should honor requests to abate taxes. When you are in bankruptcy, an assessment can be made without allowing you the usual IRS conference procedures and right of appeal to the Tax Court usually available before assessment. In such a case, you may request a conference with your IRS district director to review the assessment before paying.

The discharge relieves you of personal liability for your taxes, but it does not release tax liens filed before you petitioned for bankruptcy. Thus, the IRS can still enforce its lien against property you owned before the bankruptcy or property that you fraudulently gave away to keep it out of their hands.

■ Property Taxes

My property tax bill is inflated.

R Local property taxes, which rose by 50% in some places between 1985 and 1990, may well be the fastest-rising tax you pay. More galling still, if your area's housing prices have turned soft, your tax bill may reflect your home's higher value of several years ago. Or the tax assessment, even if it's up-to-date, may simply be wrong. Nancy Freeman, president of Property Valuation Consultants in Joliet, Illinois, estimates overworked tax assessors set incorrect values 40% of the time, most often in the tax collector's favor. The assessments are typically 5% to 20% too high and cost homeowners $150 to $1000 in extra taxes each year.

If you believe your assessment is too high, you can appeal to have it reduced. Your success will be measured in hundreds, even thousands, of dollars. And your only cost could be a few hours of your time.

Asking for a new assessment on your home is a simple process that can be completed in one day. But do not expect an immediate reduction in your bill; you may face a long wait for a hearing.

Your home's assessed value. How can you determine whether your assessment is correct and fair? Start by visiting your local assessor's office and asking for a copy of the work sheet, known as the property record card, that was used to estimate your home's value. The identification number on your tax bill will help locate your home's assessment data card or printout. Also pin down the meaning of any abbreviations or codes on the card. Ask exactly how the municipality calculates your assessed value, working with the information on the card. Finally, ask for a list of all available exemptions, such as those for war veterans or homeowners age 65 or older, to make sure you received any you deserve.

Errors in appraisal. Check the property card for obvious errors. The data will include your house's age; square footage; number of rooms and fireplaces; the condition of your attic, roof, and garage; descriptions of the heating and air-conditioning systems; the type of construction; the size of your lot; and the quality both of your view and of the neighborhood. Make sure the card also notes any features that detract from your property, such as being located next to a freeway or an industrial park.

Errors often creep in because assessors rely on old property records and do curbside inspections. Mistakes can be as subtle as not accounting for the poor condition of your roof or a damp basement. Or they can be as glaring as math errors or a listing for a finished basement when your house has no basement at all. Such mistakes are often enough to upset the assessor's calculation of the home's worth. If property is valued at $100 a square foot in your area, and the card says your house is 34 feet across when it is actually 30 feet, the valuation will be too high.

If you find errors, you can usually win a tax reduction with one visit to the assessor's office. Similarly, it should be easy to lower your assessment if you discover you are not getting the benefit of some exemptions to which you are entitled, such as those for homeowners who are low-income, elderly, blind, disabled, or veterans.

Next, determine whether your assessment is fair. A two-step process is necessary. You must determine (1) the fair market value of your home and (2) your community's statutory or assessment ratio.

Fair market value.   Your assessment should be based on the current market value of your house. To estimate your property's market value, ask local real estate agents, banks, or the assessor for recent sales prices of three to five homes in your town that are comparable to your property in size and location. Ideally, the sales will have taken place no more than six months before your assessment.

To make sure the houses you cite are similar, compare their property record cards, if your assessor will let you see them, or look up their sales records in the county courthouse. Finally, drive past each house to verify that the exteriors and neighborhoods are comparable to your own. If not, adjust your house's market value accordingly. If your research shows the assessor's market value of your house is at least 10% out of line, you have an excellent chance of winning an appeal.

Once you know the sales prices of comparable homes, try to figure out why some of them may have sold for more than the assessment amount you are aiming for—is there a renovated kitchen, added bath, or swimming pool, for example? You may be able to check the details on property record cards.

Even if nearby houses have assessments roughly the same as yours, you might plead for a lower one. Some sample arguments:

- Although you spent a lot to build your home, its domed shape or unusual layout limits its resale value. To bolster your case, get an estimate of your home's value from an outside appraiser.

- Your appraisal is outdated. Since the assessor's last visit, a busy shopping mall opened nearby, a new fire station was built, or a voted-down school budget depressed property values.

One way to challenge comparable sales prices is to pay an expert to value your home. Because even a small savings is magnified with each passing year, spending $200 to $500 for an independent appraiser can be well worthwhile.

Assessment ratio.   The next step is simple in the 19 states where property is assessed at 100% of its fair market value. You merely check your property record card for your home's assessment, which is the same as its market value. Chiefly to make taxes more politically palatable, however, most communities practice fractional assessment—your house is assessed at some percentage, called the statutory or assessment ratio, of its estimated market value. Such partial assessment can trick you into thinking you are getting a tax break when you are not. For example, if your town uses an assessment ratio of 60% and your house is worth $100,000, it should be assessed at $60,000. But suppose it is erroneously assessed at $80,000. If you do not know your town uses fractional assessment, you may think your property is actually undervalued by $20,000.

Let us look at it another way. Say you believe your house is worth $150,000, your city has assessed it for $130,000, and your statutory ratio is 65%. Divide the assessment amount ($130,000) by the statutory ratio (65%). The result is $200,000. That is 33% more than your own $150,000 estimate. (Because the computations can be complicated, you may want to seek help from a clerk at the county board that oversees assessments.)

The math.   Now that you know your home's fair market value and the assessment ratio, you are ready to compute the correct assessed value by using the following formula:

$$\text{Fair market value} \times \text{Assessment ratio} = \text{Correct assessed value}$$

Your real estate taxes are too high if your property's correct assessed value is less than your home's official assessed value.

Sales ratios.   Another figure may factor in the equation—a sales ratio. That is how assessments compare to actual sales prices of properties that sold recently. A sales ratio of 90%, for example, means home values have declined by 10%. Ask the assessor for the sales figures used and your home's record card so you can check the math. For example, if your house is worth $225,000 and your town uses a sales ratio of 90% and an assessment ratio of 40%, multiply $225,000 by 90% to get $202,500. Then multiply that figure by 40% to arrive at your home's correct assessed value of $81,000.

If an assessment/sales ratio study has not been conducted recently, do a quick one by using the sales prices and assessments from the properties you tracked. Compute the assessment/sales ratio for each parcel, arrange the numbers in ascending order, and find the median.

Making your appeal.   Check with your assessor's office for limitations on your time to appeal. Many localities allow homeowners to appeal only within 14 to 60 days after assessment (or reassessment) notices are mailed out. After that period, you may no longer be able to request reconsideration of that year's assessment. If that time has passed, check your property record card for errors so they can be corrected before next year's assessment. Some states have a list of errors you are allowed to remedy even after you have received your tax bill.

There are several levels of appeal. The first is generally an informal meeting with the assessor. The next level is a formal hearing with the county tax assessor's office or tax assessment board, called a board of equalization in some places. The vast majority of cases are resolved here, but some states have a third level of appeal to a state board. Ultimately, if it is worth your time, you can go to court, accompanied by a real estate attorney.

First, call your assessor's office for a "decline in value" application. This is typically a one-page form, asking for your name, address, and the location and description of the property you are appealing, as well as the reason for questioning the assessed value. It also usually asks for your opinion of the property's value. If you will be meeting with the assessor in person, you do not need to send in evidence, such as multiple listings or information about comparable home sales, at this point. Attach a copy of your tax bill or assessment notice, however.

Once you file your application, including documentation on comparable home sales, all you have to do is wait. In some communities, the assessor's office will notify you whether they have accepted your revised home value without any need for you to appear. In most places, however, you usually start with an informal, oral plea before the local assessor. In a busy city like Los Angeles, it can take six to nine months to get your first appointment with the hearing officer. However, most disputes are settled in that one meeting. Be sure to bring along any useful documentation, even if you sent in this information before. For instance, if your property card has the wrong square footage, present your survey proving the correct figure.

If the assessor rejects your challenge, you can fill out an appeal form, usually available from the assessor, requesting a review of the assessor's decision by the local, county, or regional board of appeals, which is typically made up of three to five local businesspeople. Try to attend a board meeting in advance of your hearing to get a feel for the process. When you go before the board, take along your sales comparisons and other evidence supporting your oral arguments, such as recent appraisals, photographs, or floor plans. Give board members photocopies of your documents before you summarize your appeal orally. Conclude by proposing an alternative assessment.

If you are asked during the appeal if you would rather sell your house for the higher assessment or the lower one you are suggesting, do not get backed into a corner. How much you would accept for your house is not the point. What is relevant is whether your home is assessed fairly compared to similar houses.

The board generally hands down its decision within six weeks. If you lose, you can take your case to the state property tax board and, if necessary, to the state supreme court. Before you do, though, ask yourself whether the cost of hiring a lawyer—typically $250 to $1000—exceeds the tax savings you expect to win.

Warning: You need to continue making your property tax payments even when the assessment is under appeal. If you fail to pay the tax, you may be subject to late-payment penalties. If your assessment is lowered, you will receive a refund of the overpayments.

The best and worst cases for a reappraisal. Here are five arguments homeowners make in seeking a lower assessment and how effective each has been, according to assessors and real estate lawyers.

The Arguments	The Odds
Wrong or overlooked information.	A shoo-in.
Deterioration of the house.	Almost a sure thing.
General drop in housing prices.	A good bet.
Unfair comparison with other houses.	Do not count on it.
Older houses not revalued lately.	A long shot.

Retirement and Pension Plans

For most working people, retirement ranks just behind death and taxes as one of life's certainties. But how many of us are actually prepared for it? While 8 out of 10 middle-aged Americans think they can manage financially after they retire, the proportion of Americans ages 55 to 64 who think that they are not ready financially to retire has climbed to 28% of men and 33% of women, according to a 1996 Merrill Lynch survey conducted by the Wirthlin Group. (The error margin is five percentage points.)

The main worries are inflation and rising health-care costs, including fear that nursing home costs could ruin retirees and their families financially. Nine out of 10 Americans polled think they will need financial help in retirement from their children or the government. Worse yet, 83% fear their income will still fall short of their needs.

You cannot count on pensions and Social Security to bail you out, either. Not so long ago, companies rewarded loyalty with a handsome pension at retirement, based on salary and years of service and insurance by the government. You got a check each month for the rest of your life. For many workers, those days are over. This is especially true for employees of small businesses.

Employers are increasingly unwilling to assume the financial risks and regulatory hassles of the old-fashioned pension plan. Now they want *you* to shoulder the investment risks—and bear more of the cost, too. But the biggest potential for financial crisis comes from employers shifting to 401(k)s and other pension plans that require you to make the investment decisions. In effect, you may be among the many workers who, ready or not, have become their own pension-fund managers.

In this chapter, we offer the type of retirement savings advice employers used to regularly provide: how to avoid retirement planning mistakes, invest wisely for retirement, and make your savings outlast your lengthy old age. We also look at how you can keep your pension out of jeopardy, the best decisions for taking your pension payouts, and smart tax strategies to keep Uncle Sam from enjoying your savings.

Even if you have no pension, you will have the threadbare cushion of Social Security and Medicare. You can afford even fewer problems with these benefits if they form the best part of your safety net. In the last section of this chapter, we help you ensure you receive the correct amount of benefits and get the largest benefits to which you are entitled. We also explain how to enroll in Medicare and remedy medical costs that threaten your financial security.

Travel, sunny days in a retirement community, new hobbies and pursuits. We all dream about the stage of life when we can take it easy. But a happy and leisurely retirement does not just happen. Now is the time to lay the groundwork for the future. In this chapter, you will learn how to put a shine on your golden years. In the cures for pension and Social Security woes that follow, you will find answers that will keep the longest vacation of your life from becoming the biggest headache.

■ RETIREMENT

AILMENT

My company has made me a buyout offer, and I do not know whether to take it.

R Under ideal conditions deciding on early retirement will take extensive time and planning. But it sounds as if you may not have that luxury. If your boss has dropped an early-retirement offer on your desk, you probably have only a month or two to decide whether to accept or reject it.

In effect, a buyout offer is a "bribe" to leave a company that is downsizing. Buyouts often target middle managers or veteran workers earning high salaries and offer generous cash incentives for older employees to slip gracefully into early retirement. That prospect may be enticing if you just had a bad day at the office. But weighing such an offer can be maddeningly complicated. The career and financial stakes are enormous.

When evaluating an offer, you first need to answer two questions: Am I ready to retire? And, if I turn down the package, will I be laid off anyway? A buyout offer directed only at your department means the company has targeted it—or worse, you—for reductions, voluntary or otherwise. You may even be the intended victim of age discrimination. According to the American Association of Retired Persons, buyouts are commonly misused to rid a company of older employees.

If the offer cuts across company lines, you can breathe easier. The company is trying to reduce *numbers*, not eliminate specific individuals. However, if this is not the first buyout offer, find out what happened last time. Did the buyout achieve its goals or were workers let go involuntarily? If you will be axed if too few employees take the offer, you might as well let your company pay you to quit.

If an early-retirement package is appealing, you should thoroughly analyze it. Take the mountain of documents to your financial planner or accountant for help in assessing the pluses and minuses of the package. Expect to pay $100 to $200 an hour for 5 to 30 hours of work, depending on the complexity of the proposition.

Before you hire professional help, though, do a preliminary review of your own, following these guidelines:

Cash. Buyouts generally come in two forms. One is a hard-cash offer. You get a lump-sum severance amount, typically based on your years of service with the company and your salary. A common formula is to offer between a week's and a month's pay for every year worked.

You may also get a chunk of cash that amounts to a bonus for agreeing to leave. If you are not vested in your pension plan, that money can help make up for your loss in forfeiting part of the retirement benefits set aside for you. You also benefit if you are a short-timer who does not stand to get much under a pay-for-service formula.

Pensions. If you are vested and under age 55, a buyout offer might include the cash value of your pension. Employees age 55 or older may be tempted by a "sweetened pension," in which the company computes your benefit adding three to five years to your age or tenure. These sweeteners can boost your pension by as much as 30% over what you would have ordinarily received by retiring early.

Another type of sweetener forgives penalties for early retirement, wiping out, for example, the typical 5%-per-year cut in benefits for retirees who start taking benefits before age 62 or 65.

Are these sweeteners sweet enough? Companies like to compare their buyout offers to what you would get if you quit or were laid off that very day. However, assuming you are leaving of your own free will, the proper comparison is what you would get if you stayed on the job until your normal retirement age. Just a few extra years in a pension plan can increase the payout by 25% to 50%. Ask your company to work out the figures for you.

You should seriously consider seizing an offer, if it will pay you a pension equal to or greater than the one you would get by retiring at your normal retirement.

Health insurance. A 1986 law, known by its acronym of COBRA, requires an employer with 20 or more employees to continue your group health (but not dental) insurance coverage at *your* expense for up to 18 months after retirement, regardless of your age. Employer-provided coverage will probably be more comprehensive than a policy you could buy on your own, but also more expensive. Expect to pay $1000 to $2000 a year, depending on whether you cover dependents.

Increasingly rare are buyout offers that include an agreement to continue paying your medical insurance premiums when you retire. If you are one of the lucky ones, that coverage could be worth $1500 to $3000 or more a year. Be certain of the terms of the plan you are offered. Check whether the deductibles and benefits for an early retiree are the same as for employees. Warning: Most plans can be altered at your former employer's discretion if your employer reserves that right in writing; a few can even be canceled.

Life insurance. The most generous offers give early retirees the same life insurance coverage they had as employees. Without this option, you can generally convert from the company's group life policy to an individual policy costing, at age 55, about $400 a year per $10,000 of coverage. But making this switch could cost more than buying your own policy on the outside. Another carrot is little better than no insurance at all; you get a death benefit amounting to less than 50% of what you enjoyed as an employee. This benefit often shrivels each year, barely paying your funeral expenses if you live to age 70.

Beyond the money. Do not let dollar signs blind you to the goals you had before you heard the buyout offer. Deciding to leave your job, especially if you are in your fifties or sixties, is not trivial. You may never be able to find satisfying work this late in your career.

Even if a buyout offer arrives like an answered prayer, be sure you can afford it. Can you hang on until Social Security kicks in? Will your savings withstand the eroding effects of inflation? You will need at least 75% of your current income to maintain your lifestyle.

If you are younger, the buyout probably means a job change rather than early retirement. If so, is the severance pay enough to see you through until you get a new job?

Big decision, little time. No matter how pressured you feel to accept or reject the buyout offer, the law gives you about six weeks to ponder the deal. Employees offered early retirement are commonly asked to sign a waiver giving up the right to sue claiming age bias. If you are weighing such a waiver, the Older Workers Benefit Protection Act requires that you be given 45 days to make up your mind and 7 days after signing to have a change of heart. Of course, revoking the waiver could mean forfeiting all or part of the buyout package.

AILMENT

I want enough income to live on in retirement.

R Keep your money working. If you change companies or lose your job, resist the temptation to spend your retirement funds. Roll over your pension money, tax-free, into an IRA, and keep it earning.

How much to save. Even if you are on the leading edge of the baby boom, you still have time to lay the foundation for a comfortable retirement. The key, of course, is to get hopping while you still have time on your side.

If you have already reached your forties without setting aside a nickel for your retirement, you need to bite the bullet and save 15% of your income from now on. If that seems out of reach, remember the 15% figure includes your employer contributions to your retirement plan, if you have one.

Use the work sheet in Figure 9–1 to estimate how much you need to save to finance your leisure years. You will need at least 75% of your current earnings to maintain your standard of living, 80% or more if you want to live better. The good news is that Social Security and a company pension will provide at least some of the cash.

Social Security. It sounds like a hoax, but you really will be able to draw Social Security benefits. You may want to take this with a grain of salt, but the Social Security Administration projects that today's average 46-year-old will be paid slightly higher benefits (in today's dollars) than the average 65-year-old currently receives. If so, your future benefits will replace 42% of your wages if you are making around $22,000, and 27% of a $55,000 salary. Because a $55,000 salary buys the top benefit, the higher your earnings over that amount, the smaller the percentage of your income Social Security will replace.

For a gauge of your future benefits, call 800-772-1213 to request a copy of your Social Security earnings statement and benefit estimate (Form 7004).

Pension. If you work for a company with a defined-benefit pension plan, you can count on regular retirement checks based on your salary and length of service. A typical plan might provide an annual pension equal to 1.5% of your pay at retirement times the number of years you were on the job. Plug 30 years into that formula and you end up with 45% of preretirement income. Most plans are designed so that pension and Social Security benefits together replace 50% to 75% of salary for employees with 20 to 30 years of service.

If you have been climbing the job ladder by jumping from one firm to another, your pension will not be nearly as generous. Even if you stick with a series of jobs long enough to lock in full benefits at each (five to seven years, depending on the plan), your monthly pension income will be less than if you worked for just one employer. Assuming identical plans and salary levels, for example, a worker who changes companies at ages 35, 45, and 55, and retires at age 65, would receive a little less than half the pension earned by a less nimble employee who worked at one company for 40 years. Consider that when you entertain notions of job-hopping.

Ask your pension administrator for estimates of your pension's benefits depending on whether you leave the company today or stay until retirement.

Pension savings.   It is your job to make up the shortfall between your Social Security and pension checks and your targeted retirement income. Let us assume that you fill out the work sheet (Figure 9–1) and find out you will need $500,000 to close the gap. First, keep in mind that that is in tomorrow's inflated dollars. Half a million in 2018 is only about $228,000 today. Still, how can you amass that much?

Deferred-pay plans or 401(k)s.   If you are an employee, your best bet is a 401(k) tax-deferred retirement plan. Almost all large employers offer these plans, and 85% of the companies with defined-benefit pension plans also have a 401(k) or some other type of contributory savings plan, according to Hewitt Associates, a benefits consulting firm.

How does a 401(k) work? You agree to take a take-home pay cut by having your employer put part of your wages in a trust account for your benefit. You pay no taxes on this deferred salary, nor on the interest or dividends the account earns, until you tap the money in retirement. The popularity of 401(k)s is not hurt by the fact that many employers kick in from 25 cents to $1 for every dollar you save, up to 6% of your salary. Most plans let you save more than the amount that is matched, but your pretax contributions are limited by law to $9500 in 1997 (this amount rises in $500 increments with inflation). Matching contributions by your employer can bring the total up to the lower of $30,000 or 25% of your salary.

A 401(k) is not like a defined-benefit plan, where your employer promises to pay you a fixed pension amount. How well you do in retirement depends solely on how well your 401(k) investments perform. Again, it is a mistake to play it too safe. Two-thirds of all money in employer-sponsored plans is invested in guaranteed investment contracts (GICs) or other fixed-income investments. Their safety is illusory, however, because, with yields barely higher than money market mutual funds or Treasury securities, they do not protect you from inflation.

Ask your benefits officer for information on the track records of the various investment options for your 401(k). You should choose at least one stock fund. (For more information about investing 401(k) funds, see page 277.)

FIGURE 9–1   How Much You Must Save

1. Current annual income $_____

2. Annual income needed after retirement
   (75% to 80% of line 1) $_____

3. Annual Social Security income $_____

4. Annual pension $_____

5. Guaranteed annual retirement income
   (line 3 plus line 4) $_____

6. Annual retirement income needed from
   savings and investments
   (line 2 minus line 5) $_____

7. Amount you must save by retirement
   (line 6 times multiplier from column A) $_____

8. Amount you have saved already, including
   employer retirement plans $_____

9. What your savings to date will have
   grown to by the time you retire
   (line 8 times multiplier from column B) $_____

10. Amount of savings still needed
    (line 7 minus line 9) $_____

11. Amount of savings needed each year
    (line 10 times factor from column C) $_____

12. This year's contributions to your
    retirement plans $_____

13. Amount you need to set aside each year
    (line 11 minus line 12) $_____

IRAs. A 401(k) plan with an employer match is the best contender in your struggle for retirement wealth. But you are not necessarily down and out if your employer does not offer one or if you are self-employed. You can still win a few rounds with regular individual retirement accounts (IRAs), Roth (or back-ended) IRAs, self-employed retirement

FIGURE 9–1 Continued		
Expected life span after you retire	**Multiplier A**	
11 years	10.0	
15 years	13.1	
20 years	16.7	
25 years	19.9	
30 years	22.8	
35 years	25.5	
40 years	27.9	
Number of years before you expect to retire	**Multiplier B**	**Factor C**
5 years	1.104	.192
10 years	1.219	.091
15 years	1.346	.058
20 years	1.486	.041
25 years	1.641	.031
30 years	1.811	.025
35 years	2.0	.02
40 years	2.208	.017

plans, and variable annuities. And you can use them even if you have a 401(k).

The tax-deductibility of regular IRAs depends on whether you or your spouse has a retirement plan at work. If neither of you does, you can deduct your IRA deposits in full. But if either spouse is covered by a company plan, the deduction phases out by $1 for every $5 your adjusted gross income tops $50,000 on a joint return ($30,000 on a single return) in 1998. The deduction disappears completely when your income passes $60,000 on a joint return ($40,000 on a single return). (The phaseout range for joint filers increases to $20,000 from $10,000 after

2006.) In 1999 through 2002, the dollar level at which the AGI phaseout range begins for single taxpayers and joint filers will increase by $1000 each year. Thereafter, the increases accelerate (e.g., in 2003, the phaseout range begins at $40,000 for single taxpayers, and at $60,000 for joint filers). If you can deduct your contributions to an IRA, you should fund it to the max.

Even if your contributions cannot be written off, a regular IRA can still pay off, because there is no tax on the money your IRA earns until you withdraw the money. That can be like a dose of Miracle-Gro™ for your savings.

Contributions to a Roth IRA—limited to $2000 a year—are not tax deductible, but do earn nontaxable interest and can be withdrawn tax-free after age 59½ or to make a first-time home purchase. The Roth IRA promises greater long-term benefits than the regular IRA if your income tax rate stays the same or goes up when you withdraw your money. But if you expect your rate to be lower in retirement, you are better off with a deductible IRA. The Roth IRA is available to married couples with AGI of up to $150,000 and singles with AGI up to $95,000.

Self-employed retirement plans. When you are self-employed, or earn income from a sideline business such as consulting, you can sock part of those earnings into one of three plans: a Keogh, SEP-IRA, or SIMPLE plan. Contributions to any of these plans are tax-deductible and earnings are tax-deferred, which gives you the same double-barreled tax break as with a 401(k).

Keogh (or H.R. 10) retirement plans come in two models: defined contribution plans and defined benefit plans. The first concentrates on how much you can put into your plan today and the second on how much you will take out in the future.

With a defined-contribution plan, the amount of your contribution is based on your current net earnings, and your retirement benefits will depend on how much and how well you have invested. You may contribute 20% of your net earnings from self-employment, up to a maximum of $30,000.

The mechanics of defined-benefit plans are quite different. With these, you decide how much you want to collect when you retire, then calculate how much you will have to put in each year until then to get that defined benefit. You will need a pension plan specialist and an actuary to do the math if you choose a defined-benefit plan. The most you can collect if you retire at your Social Security retirement age is currently $125,000, or 100% of the average of your three best earning years in a row, whichever is less. Your Social Security retirement age depends on your year of birth, as shown on the opposite page:

If you were born	Your retirement age is
Before 1/2/38	65
Between 1/2/38 and 1/1/39	65 yrs., 2 mos.
Between 1/2/39 and 1/1/40	65 yrs., 4 mos.
Between 1/2/40 and 1/1/41	65 yrs., 6 mos.
Between 1/2/41 and 1/1/42	65 yrs., 8 mos.
Between 1/2/42 and 1/1/43	65 yrs., 10 mos.
Between 1/2/43 and 1/1/55	66 yrs.
Between 1/2/55 and 1/1/56	66 yrs., 2 mos.
Between 1/2/56 and 1/1/57	66 yrs., 4 mos.
Between 1/2/57 and 1/1/58	66 yrs., 6 mos.
Between 1/2/58 and 1/1/59	66 yrs., 8 mos.
Between 1/2/59 and 1/1/60	66 yrs., 10 mos.
After 1/2/60	67 yrs.

If you retire earlier, your $125,000 maximum benefit will be actuarially reduced.

Keoghs let you set aside a big chunk of cash. Your business may not have that large a profit margin, though. Or maybe you missed the December 31 cutoff for establishing a Keogh last year. In either case, you can still contribute to a SEP-IRA. With this self-employed version of an IRA, you can contribute and deduct 13.0435% of your net earnings, or $24,000, whichever is less. You have until October 15 (with valid extensions) of the following tax year to set up and contribute to a SEP-IRA.

Last and least, you may start a simplified pension plan called a SIMPLE if you have 100 or fewer employees. You can defer up to $6000 of your earnings each year into a SIMPLE. The investment options for SIMPLEs are the same as for 401(k)s. Your business cannot have a SIMPLE if it has another tax-favored retirement plan.

Deferred annuities. Variable annuities also offer the advantage of tax-deferred growth. You cannot deduct contributions, but there is no limit on how much you can invest. Variable annuities offer a choice of mutual funds, so your returns depend on which funds you choose and how well they perform. When considering a variable annuity, read the prospectus carefully for information about how the annuity works, including management fees, expenses, and annuity charges. *Note:* With sales commissions as high as 8%, annual expenses of up to 3%, and hefty surrender charges in the early years, you should not use a deferred annuity unless you have no other tax-deferred investment and will not need your money for at least a decade.

Other assets. If a dream retirement still seems unattainable, consider the other assets you will bring to retirement. Your home will likely be your biggest asset when you retire. A house that is worth $150,000 today will be worth almost $350,000 in 2018, assuming it appreciates just 4% a year. By that time, the mortgage probably will be paid off. Although it is an illiquid investment, your home could be a source of cash. For example, you could trade it in for a smaller house that requires less maintenance.

AILMENT

I am age 55 and counting down to retirement. Are there things I should be doing in advance to avoid costly mistakes?

 The following retirement planning timetable should be of help:

Age 55–59. Request your Social Security personal earnings and benefits estimate, to ensure its accuracy. Call the Social Security Administration at 800-772-1213, and ask for Form 7004.

Review the status of your company's pension plan regularly.

Revise your retirement income and expense projections, taking inflation into account.

Change the beneficiaries on your life insurance policies, if appropriate.

Join the American Association of Retired Persons to take advantage of their information and help (AARP, 601 E Street NW, Washington, DC 20049).

Gradually shift some of your retirement funds out of aggressive-growth stocks and funds into a more balanced mix of investments—for example, divided equally among the following four asset categories: growth stocks or funds (with a tilt toward blue chips rather than small companies), growth and income (or balanced) funds, bonds, and certificates of deposit with staggered maturities.

Use dollar cost averaging to ease out of your riskier holdings. Suppose you are 55 and have $200,000 in retirement assets, such as a 401(k) plan that you control, and that about $50,000 of that total is in aggressive-growth mutual funds. Over the next five years, while keeping the tax-deferred status of the money, you could shift $10,000 a year, or about $850 a month, into assets that are less volatile.

Use the same strategy if your current holdings are heavily weighted toward your own company's stock or that of any other single company. By diversifying into broad-based equity mutual funds, you can shelter your nest egg from a bad market fall.

If your current portfolio is performing well and you expect a sizable payout when you retire, you can afford to wait until you receive your lump-sum distribution to balance out your investments.

If you belong to an employee stock-ownership plan (ESOP), take advantage of a special federal law provision that lets you transfer out of your company's stock and into other investments beginning at age 55. You can diversify 25% of your account balance at first and another 25% five years later.

Age 60–64. If you are contemplating early retirement, evaluate the advantages and disadvantages. Try living for one month on your planned retirement income.

Once again, request a copy of your Social Security personal earnings and benefit statement. (Call 800-772-1213 and ask for Form 7004.)

Collect the necessary documents to process your Social Security benefits: both spouses' Social Security cards (or your numbers, if you do not have the cards), proof of both spouses' ages, and marriage certificate. You will also need a copy of your latest W-2 form when you apply.

Check how many years you have left to pay on mortgages and loans.

Prepare detailed cash flow projections from your estimated year of retirement until age 90, figuring in the effects of inflation.

Three years to go. Pick the right spot to spend your retirement money. If you plan to move, travel with a view to where you want to live, and try out your sunny location before you buy. Another thing to keep in mind if you plan to sell your house or relocate: You may be able to avoid paying taxes on up to $500,000 if you are married ($250,000 single) of home-sale profit. To qualify, you must have owned and lived in your house for at least two of the five years before the sale.

Figure your living expenses. Use a spreadsheet software program if you have a computer to create retirement budgets based on different assumptions. Start with your current expenses and then anticipate how those costs will change once you retire. In general, you can expect some costs—travel, entertainment, and health insurance, for example—to rise, while others—clothing, taxes, and perhaps housing—will fall. Keep in mind that active retirees are likely to spend more in the first five or so years of retirement than they will later on.

Budget for continued savings. You should strive to accumulate more wealth during the first seven or eight years after retirement, instead of dipping into principal.

Ask a financial planner to calculate how long your savings will last, or use a program such as *Retire Ready Deluxe ASAP* (DOS-compatible; $49.95 plus $4 for shipping from Individual Software; 800-822-3522). If your savings fall short of projected expenses, you may have to take on more investment risk in search of higher returns, postpone retirement, or plan on spending less after you are retired.

Make sure you have adequate umbrella liability insurance to protect your nest egg if you are sued.

Two years to go. Decide whether you are going to spend all day in a hammock or go back to work part-time to fill the hours. You may even need the income or want to build up a stronger financial fortress for the future. An increasing number of companies keep retirees on retainer for part-time work or special projects, so even if your retirement is not wholly voluntary, it pays to leave on good terms if you want future assignments.

Do not underestimate how hard it is to become a consultant or run a small business. If you intend to turn entrepreneur, enroll in a prebusiness workshop at a local Small Business Administration office.

Keep in mind that in 1997, Social Security recipients age 65 through 69 lose $1 in benefits for every $3 of annual earnings over $13,500; those under 65 can earn $8640 before losing $1 for every $2 of earnings above that amount. Earnings caps rise each year and disappear after you reach age 70.

Just before retirement. Zero in closely on what your retirement income and living costs will be.

Determine your exact pension benefits and decide whether to receive them as a lump sum and/or use them to purchase an annuity (see discussion on page 286).

Use all your benefits. This may be your last chance to use vacation time, take advantage of merchandise discounts for employees, or buy company stock at a reduced price.

Apply for Social Security benefits about three months before you want them to begin. Take a copy of your birth certificate and the number of your bank account if you would like to have your checks automatically deposited.

Track down pensions from former employers. Alert them of your retirement in writing about six months in advance, so they can start the necessary paperwork.

Set the peak retirement date. Ask your pension-plan manager to calculate your benefits based on different retirement dates. For example, by waiting until the end of the year, say, or your anniversary month, you could add a full year of service for the purpose of calculating your pension (see discussion on page 264).

Consolidate rollover IRAs with regular IRAs to cut down on paperwork and reduce fees. But keep nondeductible IRAs separate for tax purposes—payouts from nondeductible IRAs are not taxed.

Arrange for a continuation of your medical insurance coverage or, if you are age 65 or older, arrange for supplemental Medicare coverage (see discussion on page 297). Find out whether your company provides health insurance benefits for retirees or whether you can pay a monthly premium to stay with the group policy. By law, you are allowed to remain in your employer's medical plan for 18 months after you retire, but you have to pay the full cost of coverage, plus an administrative fee. After that, you can probably convert to an individual policy with your employer's carrier. However, such conversion policies usually offer bare-bones coverage at exorbitant prices. If you are healthy, shop for individual coverage on your own. Premiums for a couple in their early sixties are likely to run $400 to $700 a month. Even after you qualify for Medicare, you will need Medigap coverage (see page 306). If you are not in good health, think about postponing retirement until at least age 63½, when you can rely on the 18-month extension of your employer's group insurance until you are eligible for Medicare.

Consider long-term care insurance. If you can afford it and plan to buy it, do not delay. Long-term care insurance only gets more expensive and harder to qualify for as you grow older. A 65-year-old can expect to pay $1000 to $1600 a year for a policy that provides benefits of $100 a day for four years. For information and a list of companies that sell these policies, write for a free copy of *The Consumer's Guide to Long-Term Care Insurance* (Health Insurance Association of America, 555 13th Street NW, Suite 600 East, Washington, DC 20004; 202-824-1600).

Draft a durable power of attorney naming someone to handle your financial affairs if you become incapacitated.

Accelerate deductions if you will be dropping to a lower tax bracket after you retire. Take capital losses to offset other income, or make a sizable contribution to a charity this year instead of next year.

If you will be moving to another state, have an attorney there review your will to make sure it will still be valid. Also, set up a bank account in the new town before you move.

Sell a second car if you will not need it. In any event, alert your auto insurance company about your retirement. Your rates may go down because you will not be commuting.

Find out when your first pension check will be mailed. Arrange to have it deposited directly into your bank account.

☐ Resources

Free retirement planning help is available from a variety of sources. Some of it deals with how to find the right financial planner. The rest are workbooks and brochures to guide you through the retirement-planning maze.

The Institute of Financial Planners offers a free brochure titled, "How to Select a Financial Planner," as well as referrals to certified financial planners by ZIP code (3801 East Florida Avenue, Suite 708, Denver, CO 80210; 800-282-7526).

From the Better Business Bureau, you can get a brochure titled, "Tips on Financial Planners, No. 07-24-225." (Send a $2 check and a self-addressed, stamped envelope to the Council of Better Business Bureaus, 4200 Wilson Boulevard, Suite 800, Arlington, VA 22203; 703-276-0100). Specify the brochure number. Some tips on selecting a financial planner are also available on the BBB World Wide Web home page at http://www.bbb.org.

Retirement planners are also available from several mutual fund families: Dreyfus (800-782-6620), Fidelity Investments (800-526-7251), Everen Securities (800-472-3589), and T. Rowe Price (800-541-8460).

AILMENT

We want to buy a home in a retirement community without getting burned.

℞ The boom in so-called active adult communities—the Leisure Worlds and Sun Cities, for example—is a boon to healthy retirees who want to play and stay fit, while enjoying the company of other seniors. Buying into the right development can be a good investment, too.

You are wise to be cautious, though. A poorly planned development can tarnish your golden years. An underfinanced developer could go bankrupt before finishing the promised golf course or recreation hall. Substandard homes can plummet in value, wiping out a huge chunk of your nest egg.

First, check out the developer of the project. If the company is publicly held, ask for a copy of its latest annual report, plus the more detailed 10-K report that it must file with the Securities and Exchange Commission. If any item gives you a niggling doubt about the company's financial stability, ask your accountant or attorney for an opinion.

For both public and private companies, contact the state's department of real estate or similar regulatory body to see if any complaints have been filed against the builder. Also check the company's reputation with the area's Better Business Bureau. A developer who has completed several projects with few complaints more than likely builds quality homes and delivers on its promises.

If you are dealing with a builder new to the business, find out whether it has posted a completion bond guaranteeing that all the promised amenities will be installed. Also, check with local officials to make sure the builder has all the required permits for its highly touted facilities.

If you are buying a new home, request a home warranty policy insuring against defects. If the builder does not offer a warranty, make your purchase offer contingent on the home passing muster with a home inspector of your own choosing. This contingency clause will let you out of the deal without losing money if the builder refuses to correct any defects that turn up.

You should use the same contingency clause if you offer to buy a used home from a current owner in the retirement community.

Finally, ask homeowners how they like living in the complex and whether they are satisfied with how the developer has dealt with past problems.

Your last step before buying is to take a close look at the homeowners association. Get a copy of the group's bylaws. To avoid assessments you cannot afford, check to see if there is any limit on how much dues can be increased. Also get a copy of the association's most recent financial statements and operating budget. The association should have an adequate reserve to pay for any unexpected items, such as replanting storm-damaged trees, or such large future maintenance projects as repainting the clubhouse. The group should also be assessing a sufficient amount of dues to pay for ongoing repairs. If you cannot determine whether the association is healthy, have your accountant or attorney look over the paperwork.

Visit the area where you plan to retire at least twice so you can inspect all the developments in the vicinity. Compare both the quality and the quantity of the amenities before making your final decision.

☐ Resources

For specific information on places to retire, take a look at *Retirement Places Rated*, by David Savageau (Prentice Hall, $16.95), *50 Fabulous Places to Retire in America*, by Lee and Saralee Rosenberg (Career Press, $14.95), and *The 99 Best Residential & Recreational Communities in America*, by Lester J. Giese (John Wiley & Sons, $17.95).

■ PENSION PLANS

AILMENT

I want to invest my 401(k) and other retirement plan funds wisely.

℞ In recent years, corporations have switched in overwhelming numbers from defined-benefit plans, which pay a guaranteed monthly sum upon retirement, to defined-contribution plans, which put the burden on workers to set aside a portion of their salaries each paycheck and to decide how those funds should be invested. More workers over 40 are now covered by defined-contribution plans, the most common of which are 401(k) plans, than by traditional pension plans. That means your retirement destiny is in your own hands.

Obviously, controlling your financial future is no small matter. Because 401(k)s and other retirement plans let you invest pretax wages that accumulate tax-deferred earnings, you can amass tens of thousands of dollars before you reach retirement age. That potential becomes even greater if your employer matches your contributions.

That potential will go unrealized, though, unless you actively manage your fund's investments. You do not need to be a financial wizard. All you really need is common sense and the advice that follows. The first commandment is to contribute, contribute, contribute. Start young and invest as much as you can spare to profit from Uncle Sam's subsidy and the long-term power of compounding. If your company matches even a quarter of what you set aside, not contributing is like turning down a 25% return on your money market fund.

Where to put your money. With any long-term investment, you want diversification. That is why mutual funds, which hold from a few dozen to a couple of hundred stocks or bonds, fit the bill nicely. Large fund families also offer a range of stock, bond, and money market portfolios.

If you belong to a 401(k), the plan generally gives you the choice of investing in your own company's stock and a vehicle whose price doesn't fluctuate, such a money market fund or a guaranteed investment contract (GIC). Unfortunately, neither GICs nor a single company's shares offer much diversification. Despite this drawback, about 50% of all 401(k) money is invested in GICs, which resemble certificates of deposit except that they are issued by insurance companies, not banks. Because GICs are backed by the insurance company and come with no government guarantees, you should examine the insurance company issuing the GIC and ask yourself, "How solid is it?"

Another criticism of GICs is that they are income-oriented and thus not the best choice for younger workers. If you are years from retirement, you can do much better over time with growth vehicles such as a stock mutual fund.

Know your investments. Before deciding where to put your money, find out how the investments have performed. Call each mutual fund you are considering and request a prospectus. If you have a 401(k) plan that is managed in-house, the plan administrator should have this information. If not, call the investment firm that manages the plan. Many plans offer the same mutual funds sold to the public at large, so you should not lack for sources of information. Besides personal finance magazines you can subscribe to or buy at the newsstand, you can turn to *Morningstar Mutual Funds* (800-876-5005), a publication found at many libraries, and computer software, such as *Alexander Steele's Mutual Fund Selector* (310-478-4213).

Look for superior long-term records. Compare the 1-year, 5-year, and 10-year rates of return with averages for similar investments. Give bonus points to funds that consistently beat the market rather than racking up huge gains one year only to nose-dive the next. A good yardstick is to compare the fund's performance against the S&P 500 index.

If your 401(k) plan offers a guaranteed investment contract (GIC), ask your employer for the names of the insurance companies whose GICs are used in your plan's fixed-rate account. Then ask for ratings of their claims-paying ability by rating agencies, such as A. M. Best Company, Moody's Investors Service, and Standard & Poor's Corporation. Be concerned by a rating of less than A from Best, Aa2 from Moody's, or AA from S&P. If you cannot get this information from your employer, visit your local library's reference section to look up Best ratings, and call Moody's (212-553-0377) and S&P (212-208-1527) for free ratings. Many large companies buy GICs from several insurers and then offer 401(k) members a blended contract—a much safer tactic.

Do not sit still for a plan that does not offer options you like, that limits your choices to one or two investments, or that levies sales charges. Lobby for changes. If you have specific ideas, outline them in a note to your benefits manager. Persuade coworkers to join in your memo to lend it more weight. Most companies want their employees to be satisfied with their benefits, so they will sometimes make adjustments.

If you meet with resistance, try hiring a financial planner. Ask the planner to examine the plan and write a letter detailing its shortcomings and recommending alternatives. Then write to your employer, attaching the financial planner's letter. A complaint backed up by a professional opinion is more likely to get results.

Investment strategies. There is no one-size-fits-all investment mix. Whether you should put 20% or 60% of your pension money into stocks, for example, depends on a host of factors, including your age, finances, and tolerance for risk. So I am not going to tell you exactly how to slice up your investment pie. Instead, let us discuss basic strategies you can apply to your individual asset mix. First, do not use one strategy for your retirement accounts and a different one for your taxable investments. Think of them as one large mound of assets. Then evaluate whether you are too heavily weighted toward one class of asset or one style of investing. If so, use your retirement funds to diversify. For example, are your taxable investments top-heavy in bonds or certificates of deposit? Then use the 401(k) to invest in stock funds. Or if you have loaded up on high-tech stock elsewhere, put some of your retirement money into fixed-income investments and more conservative stock funds.

Or use your 401(k) to diversify among different sizes of companies, industries, or geographic areas. If the only stock fund offered in your 401(k) mirrors the S&P 500 stock index, use your taxable accounts or IRA to bet on start-ups or global funds, for example.

What if all of your assets are in your 401(k) or other retirement account? Then make sure it is invested in a balanced mix of stock and interest-bearing assets.

One popular Wall Street strategy you should avoid is market timing. This tactic embraces the obvious notion that you should buy stocks when the market goes up and switch into money markets when it goes down. Nailing market swings is hard enough under ideal circumstances. Within a 401(k), market timing can be almost impossible.

Dollar cost averaging. An attractive side effect of 401(k) plans is that by investing money gradually over the year, you benefit from dollar cost averaging. You are buying a fixed amount every month, whether the price of the shares you are buying is going up or down. Over the long term, you are likely to buy more shares at median prices, rather than at the top of the market. But dollar cost averaging works best with funds that have some volatility. With a low-risk fund that grows slowly, your $200 a month, for example, buys roughly the same number of shares every month as it seesaws between $35 and $38 a share. If you pick a roller-coaster fund instead, your $200 a month will have a better chance of buying at rock-bottom prices from time to time over the next 20 years.

Don't overdo your company's stock. No company is invincible. Stocks of such Gibraltarlike strength as IBM and Chrysler have plummeted at one time or another. Yet many plans match employee contributions with company stock. If yours does, beware of buying company stock with your own contributions, too. If your livelihood depends on the company and you have more than half of your assets tied up in the company's stock, you have entirely too many eggs in one flimsy basket.

Keep your balance. Once you have decided on the right combination of stocks and interest-bearing accounts or securities, maintain that allocation. At least once a year, shift your assets to restore the mix you wish.

Invest your age. When you are 10 or more years from retirement, your investments should tilt as heavily toward stocks as you dare. This is not reckless risk taking. True, stocks can be volatile over the short term. But they have almost always outperformed interest-paying investments over any given 15-year period. In any event, you can eliminate almost all of the risk by diversifying. Studies show that putting equal amounts of money into five stocks eliminates 80% of the risk. Increasing your holdings to 10 stocks wipes out 90% of the risk.

As retirement nears, shift gradually to more conservative investments. But don't forsake stocks altogether. You need their growth potential to defend against inflation after your paychecks stop. A rule of thumb: The percentage of your investments in stocks should equal 100 minus your age.

Tax matters. Choose heavily taxed investments for your 401(k). Because 401(k)s are tax-deferred, it makes sense to put these funds into investments that would otherwise be subject to tax. That includes stock mutual funds and such fixed-income investments as money market funds or corporate bond funds. Keep tax-exempt municipal bonds or low- or no-dividend stocks in your taxable accounts. You will pay little or no tax on the current earnings and only pay tax on any appreciation when you sell.

AILMENT

I am leaving my company and do not know what to do with my 401(k) plan.

R Beware. If you take your 401(k) money out of the plan, all of your pretax contributions and their earnings will be taxed in the year of withdrawal. If you are under age 59½ (age 55 if distribution is made after separation from service), you will be hit with a 10% penalty on the taxable amount, too.

There are ways to preserve your tax shelter, though. Your employer might let your money continue to grow in the company plan, or you could transfer it to the 401(k) of your new employer. You also have the right to move the money into an IRA.

If you opt for the IRA, ask for a direct transfer of your funds from the 401(k) to the IRA. If you take the cash yourself and personally roll the funds over into an IRA, 20% of your money will be withheld for the IRS. In order to avoid early-withdrawal penalties, you will still have to roll 100% of your nest egg, including the 20% you did not get, into another retirement account within 60 days of the distribution.

Here's an example: Suppose you have $200,000 in your 401(k) plan. If you don't ask for a direct transfer, you will get only $160,000 when you leave your job. The other $40,000 will be withheld for taxes. You can get your $40,000 back, but only if you put the full $200,000 into another retirement account within 60 days, assuming you can raise another $40,000. Then you must wait until you file your tax return next year to claim a refund of the $40,000 in withholding. If you roll over only the $160,000 you actually received, your $40,000 will be hit with federal and state income taxes, plus a 10% early-withdrawal penalty of $4000 if you are under $59\frac{1}{2}$.

If you are leaving your job because you have been laid off, you may not want to roll over money that you might soon need. But a rollover is usually preferable to losing 20% to withholding taxes up front. Money in an IRA is not untouchable. You can go to the bank and take some out the next day if you are willing to pay the taxes and penalty.

☐ Prevention

When you leave your job, take action to prevent the 20% withholding before you walk out the door. You will also have to do some research on your own to find the best place to put the money.

There are three ways you can avoid the 20% withholding:

■ *Leave the money alone.* The easiest thing is to leave the entire amount in your employer's plan. This option is required by law but employers sometimes neglect to mention it. An employer's plan offers advantages that some other plans do not: special 5- or 10-year averaging that can save a whopping amount of taxes and the ability to borrow against your assets. Before you leave your money where it is, find out the rules for getting your money out later. Under some plans, you cannot access your money until 60 days after your 65th birthday.

■ *Take your money with you.* Ask your employer to transfer the money directly to your new employer's plan. Of course, if you do not have another job lined up, or your new employer's plan has a waiting period (which they often do), this will not be an option.

■ *Set up a conduit IRA.* Ask your employer to roll the money directly into an IRA you set up at a bank or brokerage house just for this purpose. This conduit IRA will preserve your right to roll the money into another employer's retirement plan later. Do not put other retirement money in this conduit IRA. If you mix it with other retirement money, you lose the right to transfer the funds into a new employer's 401(k) later. That is because money in an IRA does not qualify for such favorable tax treatment as special averaging, nor can it be borrowed.

You really have no choice but to take your lump (minus the 20% withholding) if you want to use special averaging. If you are over 59½, this method of computing your tax on a large lump-sum distribution can lop staggering amounts off of your tax bill. Figuring taxes by using special averaging could result in a tax rate as low as 13%. Compare that to paying tax at your normal rate each year after retirement, as you withdraw your pension funds in installments. If you were born before January 1, 1936, you are eligible for 5- or 10-year averaging, whichever results in the least tax. But to use either 5- or 10-year averaging, you must take all of your cash out of your retirement plan in one year.

AILMENT

My employer is terminating its pension plan and buying annuities for the employees instead.

R You should be notified of the names of the insurance companies involved before the plan assets are transferred. When you receive such notification, read it carefully and, at your local library, check the ratings given to the insurers by at least two of the three major rating agencies: A. M. Best Company, Moody's Investors Service, and Standard & Poor's Corporation. If the ratings are below an A+ rating from Best and below a double-A rating from the others, complain to your employer. If the transaction proceeds anyway and you have the option of taking a lump-sum payout instead of an annuity, think about doing so. You may want to consult a financial adviser.

AILMENT

I worked for a company for 13 years and was vested in its pension plan before I quit to take another job. Now I have learned that the company has been taken over by another corporation. I want to find out what happened to my pension guarantee.

R The most common practice is for the acquiring corporation to assume the pension assets and obligations of your former employer. However, you could be rudely surprised at age 65 if you rely on that presumption. You need to do some detective work to verify where you stand.

You should have received some written notice from the company that bought out your former employer. If nothing reached you in the mail or you have misplaced it, call the human resources department of the acquiring corporation to find out the status of your pension. The pension plan in which you were vested may even have been terminated and its assets distributed among the participants, although you would presumably remember receiving your payout. But, by law, the company only has to make one try at contacting vested workers when a pension plan terminates. If you missed that communication, you might never know about the payout unless you get in touch with the company now.

Another possibility is that the pension plan has been spun off from the acquiring company's existing pension obligations into a separate entity. Again, you should have been notified of this at the time.

You can send general questions about pension rights to the Pension and Welfare Benefits Administration. Field offices are located in Atlanta, Boston, Chicago, Dallas, Detroit, Los Angeles, New York City, Philadelphia, St. Louis, San Francisco, and Seattle, as well as in Fort Wright, KY; Kansas City, MO; Miami, FL; and Washington, DC.

If you are not sure which company is responsible for paying your pension because of a corporate takeover, you can contact the federal government's Pension Benefit Guaranty Corporation (PBGC), which helps workers, their spouses, and other beneficiaries trace pension plans that have been closed, taken over by the federal agency, or otherwise transferred. Write to the Pension Benefit Guaranty Corporation, Missing Participant Program, 1200 K Street NW, Washington, DC 20005.

AILMENT

I want to make sure my defined-benefit pension is safe.

R℞ With a defined-benefit pension plan, the security of your retirement is entirely in your employer's hands. You are largely a spectator, but you can still take an active part in monitoring how well and wisely your employer is investing the pension funds entrusted to it. Money in defined-benefit plans should not be invested in highly speculative portfolios, for example, that trade in derivatives or commodities. Also, investments should be diversified to minimize risk, and expenses should be reasonable. To determine whether those standards are being met:

■ *Read summaries.* Read and keep the Summary Plan Description and any updates you receive from your employer, along with the Summary Annual Report (SAR). You should receive the SAR each year if you are in a plan that covers 100 or more people, and every three years if you are in a smaller plan. The SAR tells how much money is in the plan. Reading between the lines can provide extra information. For example, did your plan lose ground in a year when most investments were skyrocketing?

From the SAR, you should also be able to spot whether administrative expenses are extraordinarily high. Take, for example, the managers of a New York pension plan who spent almost three times the plan's average annual income decorating their offices. And the SAR will alert you to questionable financial transactions, such as loans of pension funds to company executives.

■ *Get the whole story.* To discover if any rules have been broken, the Pension Rights Center recommends that you request a copy of the full annual report, called Form 5500, from your plan administrator or from the Department of Labor. (Expect to pay copying costs.)

Form 5500 provides detailed data about how your pension fund has been invested and managed. Naturally, it is a complicated maze of technicalities. If you suspect mismanagement, but the form is undecipherable, ask a financial adviser to review it for you.

■ *Learn the rules.* Familiarize yourself with the Pension Benefit Guaranty Corporation (PBGC) rules. Chances are, you are at least partially insured by this federal agency if you are covered under a plan with fixed benefits and if you have worked long enough to become vested in the plan (typically 5 to 10 years). But some plans, such as those sponsored by religious institutions, are not insured at all. And some benefits, such as special early-retirement subsidies, may not be covered even in insured plans.

Although the PBGC provides some safety net, it is no substitute for your company's pension. There is a good chance you will not get as much through the PBGC as you would from your employer, assuming it stays solvent and continues to pay out pension distributions. The amount the PBGC can pay out is limited by law. A 65-year-old can receive a maximum of just $2166 a month from the PBGC. Younger retirees receive less.

☐ Resources

For an easy-to-read guide to pension management and to interpreting Form 5500, send $7.95 to the Pension Rights Center, Department K, Suite 704, 918 16th Street NW, Washington, DC 20006, and ask for *Protecting Your Pension Money.*

For more information about pension rights in general, send for *A Guide to Understanding Your Pension Plan* (document D13533), available free from the American Association of Retired Persons (AARP Fulfillment, 601 E Street NW, Washington, DC 20049; 202-434-2277).

Ailment
I want to make a claim for pension benefits.

℞ If you believe you are entitled to a benefit from a pension or welfare benefit plan, your first step is to file your claim in writing with your plan's administrator. Consult the Summary Plan Description you received from your employer for answers to any questions about how to file and how your plan processes claims. The Summary Plan Description, which is supposed to be written in easily understood language, tells what the plan provides and how it operates. It also must give you an accurate and comprehensive explanation of your rights and what you are entitled to under the plan.

If your claim for benefits is denied, you must be notified in writing of the reason, generally within 90 days after the claim is filed. You must also be told the specific plan provisions that caused your claim to be rejected and what additional information you can provide to make a successful claim. Finally, the notice of denial must inform you of your appeal rights.

If your claim is denied, but you still believe you are entitled to benefits, you can write to the plan administrator to request a copy of the complete plan rules. You may be charged a reasonable fee of up to 25 cents a page for the copy. Compare the plan rules with the plan provisions cited in the denial to find out whether the rules were correctly applied.

If you decide the denial was unjust, you have at least 60 days after the date on your notice of denial in which to appeal. A decision on your appeal generally must be made within 60 days, unless the plan provides for a special hearing or the decision must be made by a group that meets only periodically. You will receive a copy of the final decision that includes the reasons for the decision along with references to plan documents.

☐ Resources

You can get a free copy of the booklet *What You Should Know About the Pension Law* from the U.S. Department of Labor, Pension and Welfare Benefits Administration, Washington, DC 20210.

AILMENT

I have lost track of my former employer, but I think I am due a pension from a plan that has been terminated.

℞ Write to the Pension Benefit Guaranty Corporation at 1200 K Street NW, Washington, DC 20005. The letter should include your name, address, daytime phone number, Social Security number, date of birth, name of the employer, and, if possible, dates of employment and your employer's nine-digit employer identification number.

I have more than $100,000 invested in a tax-sheltered annuity. Before I turn 75, I must decide whether to annuitize or roll this money over into another account.

R It can be a tough decision. The answer depends on your income from other sources, your health and the health of your spouse, and whether you prefer a steady stream of income to the responsibility of managing a large sum of money.

First, get the numbers in black and white: What are the exact terms and payment options if you annuitize? The most common type of annuity, the joint-and-survivor annuity, pays a monthly check to the retired employee for life. After the employee dies, your spouse or other beneficiary receives a portion of the original benefit for life. You might be able to choose survivor percentages of 50%, 75%, or 100%, but the greater the percentage, the lower your monthly payments.

If you are married and your spouse agrees, you can select a single-life annuity with no survivor benefits. This may make sense if your spouse has his or her own pension or substantial income from other sources, or is not expected to live very long. Another possibility is to elect the single-life annuity and use the extra income to buy life insurance on the retired spouse.

Find out how big a check you will get under each of the available options.

An annuity frees you of the responsibility of managing the money, but your decision to annuitize is irrevocable. You also lock in a fixed rate of return, which is nothing to brag about in these days of low interest. If you are interested in an annuity, shop around to see whether you could use a lump-sum payout to buy a better deal than the one your company offers.

Another alternative is to take part of your distribution, perhaps 50%, as an annuity and the remainder as a lump sum. Investing the lump sum in a rollover IRA can help you keep pace with inflation, since very few annuities build in cost-of-living adjustments. Or you could roll over all of the distribution, even if you have to dip into it for current income, then flip the balance into an annuity if interest rates go up.

Note: If you opt for the lump sum, arrange for your employer to roll it directly into an IRA to avoid having 20% of it withheld for taxes (the price when the money passes through your hands). Follow the advice on page 277 for allocating the funds among investments with different levels of risk.

Finally, ask about a third option: systematic withdrawal. This would let you take the minimum payout required by the IRS. This amount is based on your life expectancy (as computed in IRS actuarial tables), but the remaining balance would go to your children as beneficiaries when you die. If your insurer cannot let you take systematic withdrawal and you do not want to annuitize (which is an irrevocable decision), you can roll your money over into an IRA. Or you can transfer your annuity directly to an annuity at another insurance company where you can postpone the decision to annuitize. Neither of these moves would subject you to taxes or penalties. But it could be costly if you are charged a commission.

AILMENT

I am about to retire and do not know whether to take my pension distribution as a lump sum or roll it over into an IRA.

R You do not say what age you are. To most people, retirement means taking leave of their jobs around age 65; not, however, to the IRS. The IRS has decreed that retirement age begins precisely at $59\frac{1}{2}$. Only then can you get at the savings built up in your tax-deferred retirement accounts, such as your 401(k), 403(b), IRA, or Keogh, without paying a 10% penalty in addition to ordinary income taxes on the withdrawal. Thus if you are still on the spry side of $59\frac{1}{2}$, you have to consider the early-withdrawal penalty in evaluating whether to take a lump sum.

Before you decide, let's take a look at both options:

Roll your money over. If you do not need the money immediately, you may roll over or transfer your distribution *tax-deferred* into an eligible retirement plan. That can include not only an IRA, but a new employer's 401(k) plan, if you are changing employment, or individual retirement annuities (other than endowment contracts). The rollover must be completed within 60 days of the distribution. Do not include your contributions to the plan in the rollover. You may elect a direct trustee-to-trustee transfer or roll over the distribution yourself. But be warned: If you receive the distribution, 20% will be withheld for income tax. To roll over the entire distribution, therefore, you will have to come up with the 20% withheld from your own pocket (see the discussion on page 280).

A lump-sum distribution rolled over into an IRA can later be transferred to another employer's qualified plan. The IRA must consist only of assets (or proceeds from the sale of assets) distributed from your first plan plus income earned on the account. You must make annual IRA contributions to another account.

You do not have to roll over your entire distribution. But only the amount rolled over is tax-deferred. If you make a partial rollover, you may not elect special 5- or 10-year averaging for the portion of your distribution that is taxed. Moreover, any amount of your lump sum that is not rolled over within 60 days is taxable.

Once made, a rollover cannot be revoked.

What happens when you eventually cash in that IRA or other qualified plan to which you rolled over? That is when there will be tax to pay. With luck, the tax will be less than you would have paid if you had taken your tax lumps in the year of distribution. But the decision to roll over can be more costly in two ways. First, you may be in a higher tax bracket when you later withdraw your funds. In addition, if your rollover is to an IRA, you lose the right to use 5-year averaging on the distribution. You must transfer your lump sum to a new employer's qualified plan to preserve the right to 5- or 10-year averaging. As we discuss in the next section, this special averaging can save a bundle in taxes.

Before electing a rollover, therefore, you should compute the current tax on your lump-sum distribution using 5- or 10-year averaging. Then compare this amount with an estimate of the tax payable on a future distribution. Take into consideration the fact that your funds will accumulate tax-deferred earnings if you choose a rollover. If you have no plans to use the funds until many years down the road (at age $70\frac{1}{2}$ or older), the advantage of a tax-deferred yield may be significant.

Take the lump sum.   Of course, you may plain need the money, perhaps to start a business, hang the tax consequences. In that case, keep your distribution and pay the tax. The same is true if you will have to withdraw the lump sum in the near future. If you decide that you cannot afford an IRA rollover, it may make sense to pay the tax bill now using 5- or 10-year averaging to reduce the taxes.

With special averaging, your tax liability is figured as if you received the money over five years instead of all at once. This method can have a big impact on your tax bill. For example, without special averaging, a married couple with $30,000 of ordinary income would pay $75,020 in taxes on a distribution of $250,000. With 5-year averaging, they would pay $59,218. The benefits of averaging dwindle, though, as distributions get larger. For any sum over $465,650, 5-year averaging gives you exactly the same tax as the normal tax calculation.

Generally, to use 5-year averaging: Your payout must represent your entire interest in the plan, you must have participated in the plan for at least five years, and you must be $59\frac{1}{2}$ or older.

Note: If you were born before January 1, 1936, you can average over 10 years, instead of 5. The basic rules are the same as for the 5-year method, except that your lump sum is taxed as if you drew it over 10 years. One twist: You must use the 1986 tax rates that went as high as 50%. Ten-year averaging saves you more tax than 5-year averaging on payouts of up to about $474,000. On the $250,000 payout in the aforementioned example, the couple's tax would be only $50,770 if they averaged over 10 years. With more than $474,000, you should use the 5-year method because you then get the benefit of today's lower tax brackets.

Another option available to seniors born before 1936 is a special capital-gains rate that can be applied to the portion of your lump sum that you accumulated prior to 1974. (Your benefits department can tell you exactly how much that is.) If you are eligible, you can declare that money to be capital gains and pay taxes on it at 20%, which is the current top capital-gains rate (10% if you are in the lowest 15% tax bracket).

To discover which averaging method will save you the most money, have your tax adviser run the numbers for you. This tax question is too tricky to answer any other way.

AILMENT

I am concerned that my company may go bankrupt, my pension checks may stop coming, or my lump-sum retirement payout may be less than my colleagues'.

℞ Your best source for pension help is the Labor Department's Pension and Welfare Benefits Administration. Field offices are located in Atlanta, Boston, Chicago, Dallas, Detroit, Fort Wright (KY), Kansas City (MO), Los Angeles, Miami (FL), New York City, Philadelphia, St. Louis, San Francisco, Seattle, and Washington, DC.

In addition, the Pension Rights Center has a national lawyer-referral service for individuals who need legal advice about pension issues. Write to Pension Rights Center, 918 16th Street NW, Suite 704, Washington, DC 20006, or call 202-296-3776.

■ SOCIAL SECURITY AND MEDICARE

AILMENT

I want to make sure the Social Security Administration has an accurate accounting of my employment and earnings history.

℞ Even if you are not near retirement, you should periodically check with the Social Security Administration to make sure that your employment and tax records are being correctly recorded. Social Security representatives recommend that every employee request an estimate of their personal earnings and benefits every three years.

These statements are available from Social Security at no charge by calling 800-772-1213. Ask for Form SSA-7004 or the Request for Earnings and Benefits Estimate Statement. You will receive a work sheet that you must complete and return in order to obtain an estimate of your potential retirement benefits.

You can apply by mail, but your documents will be safer if you visit your local Social Security office in person. If you want to mail in Form 7004, send it to Social Security Administration, Wilkes-Barre Data Operations Center, P.O. Box 20, Wilkes-Barre, PA 18703.

AILMENT

I was hurt in an accident, and my doctor says I will not be able to work for a while.

℞ You may be able to draw Social Security disability benefits. However, you must meet three stiff requirements to qualify. First, you must be physically or mentally unable to perform any substantial work. Second, your disability must be expected to last at least 12 months or reduce your life expectancy to less than 12 months. Third, you must have built up enough quarters of Social Security coverage—40 in the past 10 years, fewer quarters if you are younger than 31. If you apply for benefits at a local Social Security office, bring the same documents you would to get retirement benefits (birth certificate, latest W-2 form), plus addresses and phone numbers of your doctors and hospital.

AILMENT

I want to retire early, but I have dependents who might benefit from receiving Social Security survivor's benefits.

℞ If you stop working, perhaps by retiring young, the right of your dependents to receive survivor's insurance continues for a time, depending on your work credits, then lapses. However, there are ways of keeping your credits current with very little effort.

In 1997, only $670 in wages or self-employed income earned during an entire year is needed to entitle you to one quarter of work credit—$2560 is needed for all four quarters—a worthwhile reason for staying somewhat active.

Caution: The amount you have to earn keeps edging higher each year, because it is indexed to inflation.

AILMENT

I am a widow with children.

℞ You can get a widow's Social Security benefit at any age if you are caring for a child who is under 16 or disabled and entitled to benefits. Survivor's benefits on your husband's record are also payable to unmarried children under 19 who are attending elementary or secondary school full-time.

Your benefits will stop when you no longer have a child under 16 or disabled in your care. Usually, your benefits also will stop if you remarry before age 60. But benefits to your children continue as long as they remain eligible, regardless of whether you remarry.

AILMENT

I am a widow without children.

℞ Even without dependent children, you can receive widow's benefits when your husband dies, if you are 60 or older. The monthly amount will depend on your age when benefits start and the amount your deceased husband would have been entitled to or was receiving when he died.

Widow's benefits range from 71½% of the deceased husband's benefit amount at age 60 to 100% at 65. So, if you start receiving benefits at 65, you will get 100% of the amount your husband would receive if he were still alive.

If you are disabled, you can get widow's benefits as early as age 50, but your payment will be less.

Points to remember: If you are entitled to retirement benefits on your own work record, you can take reduced retirement payments at 62 and then receive the full widow's benefit at 65. Or, you can take a widow's benefit at 62 and get your full retirement amount at 65. Visit your local Social Security office for advice on which choice would be to your advantage. If you elect reduced widow's benefits between 50 and 62, however, your own retirement payment at 65 will also be lowered.

You will be eligible for Medicare at age 65, if your husband would have been entitled to monthly benefits or had worked the required length of time under Social Security before his death. Apply for Medicare about three months before you turn 65.

If you are 50 or older and become disabled while getting checks because you have young children in your care, contact Social Security about eligibility for Medicare. Even though you have not filed a claim for payments based on disability (because you are already receiving payments as a mother), you could be protected by Medicare, if you have been disabled for 24 months or longer.

AILMENT

I do not know whether to begin taking my Social Security benefits at age 62 or wait until I am age 65 or even older.

The answer, of course, depends in part on your finances, health, and frame of mind. If you have a tidy bankroll and a hankering for beaches, you may want to retire in your fifties. If you are still putting junior through college or think workaholics are too laid-back, you will probably still be punching a time clock into your seventies.

If you enjoy the coffee breaks but hate the commute, your decision may be influenced by how much Social Security you stand to collect at different ages. No matter when your biological clock tells you to quit, Social Security retirement checks are calculated on what is called your "full-benefit retirement age."

If you were born before 1938, your full-benefit age is 65. If you were born between 1938 and 1959, the age lies somewhere between 65 and 67, gradually increasing as you approach the later year. And, if you were born in 1960 or later, you have to keep laughing at the boss's jokes until age 67 to collect 100%. (See page 271 for your exact retirement age.)

As far as Social Security is concerned, you have three basic choices:

- You can retire at age 62, or at any point between then and full-benefit age, but your monthly checks will be reduced proportionately. Benefits are reduced by $6\frac{2}{3}$% if you retire at 64, compared with $13\frac{1}{3}$% if you stop working at 63 and 20% at 62 (the earliest possible age at which you can collect).

- You can retire at your full-benefit age, whether it's 65, 67, or sometime in between, and get checks for the full amount.

- You can keep working past the full-benefit age. Then, when you do retire, you will receive checks that are somewhat larger than normal.

Suppose that you decide to retire this year at age 62. Your Social Security check would be cut by 20%, so you would get only 80% of the amount that you would receive by retiring at age 65. The choice is not just between the two ages, 62 or 65-to-67. You can start drawing benefits at any point in time. At age $63\frac{1}{2}$, for example, a person whose full retirement age is 65 can retire with 90% of the full benefit.

Although you will draw this lower benefit for life, you will still be entitled to cost-of-living and other general increases in benefits.

But suppose that you will reach age 65 this year and do not want to retire. In this case, you will be entitled to a special bonus, called the delayed retirement credit. This bonus increases the benefit by 3.5% for each year in which you continue to work and do not receive benefits. The credit rises gradually until it reaches 8% in 11 years.

If you become disabled after you retire, but before you reach age 65, you can switch to receiving the disability benefits, which generally would be higher. Disability benefits end at age 65, but be aware that any month in which you receive disability benefits does not count as early retirement, so your subsequent retirement benefit would be higher.

Before you make your final decision, do some rudimentary math. For example, say you are entitled to an $800 monthly benefit at age 65. If you retire at age 62, that benefit would be reduced to $640 (80% of $800), a difference of $160 a month. Not taking into account cost-of-living adjustments, you would collect a total of $23,040 by the time you reached age 65. Again, not taking into account any annual adjustments, it would take 12 years for your benefits to catch up if you wait until age 65 to retire. If you invest the early payments and take those earnings into account, the break-even point is even further away.

Still, there are times when it pays to wait:

■ If you plan on working past age 62 and expect to make more than the earnings limit for Social Security recipients, you are better off delaying benefits. The annual earnings limit in 1997 is $8,640 for retirees under age 65 and $13,500 for those age 65 through 69.

■ Current tax law favors waiting to collect if your income (including half of your Social Security benefits) is high enough to trigger a tax on your benefits. If your income exceeds $32,000 on a joint return or $25,000 on a single return, from 50% to 85% of your benefits will be taxed. Instead of collecting early benefits, you would be better off using savings or investments for personal expenses. The advantages are twofold: By waiting you will get bigger checks, since the amount increases each month between ages 62 and 65. And drawing down your savings means less interest income to push your benefits into the taxable range.

In addition, you stand a good chance of living long enough to recoup the money you passed up by not retiring at age 62. As we saw in the example above, you break even after 12 years of higher benefits, or at age 77. According to life-expectancy data from the National Center for Health Statistics, the odds are in your favor. At age 62, white females are expected to live to age 83.1; black females, 81; white males, 78.9; and black males, 77.1.

AILMENT

I am retiring this year and do not know whether to apply for benefits at the beginning of the year or after I quit my job.

R Filing for Social Security benefits is as easy as making a phone call. It is the timing of the call that is critical: Benefits paid to two persons in the same circumstances can differ by as much as $10,000 in the first year—solely because of when the retirees ask for benefits to begin. This sobering disparity is due to a quirk in how the Social Security earnings test works. To understand and take advantage of the system, you need to know the rules.

Basically, if you continue to work after benefits kick in, you must keep your earnings below a certain level to receive full payments. If you are age 65 through 69, you lose $1 in benefits for every $3 of annual earnings over $13,500; under 65, you lose $1 for every $2 earnings above $8640. (The earnings caps rise each year, and there is no limit after age 70.)

You must let the Social Security Administration know in advance how much you expect to earn during the year so that any benefits forfeited under the earnings test can be withheld.

In the first year you receive benefits, the earnings test can be applied on a month-by-month basis, rather than on a yearly basis. That way, someone can start receiving full benefits right after retiring, even if earnings earlier in the year exceeded the annual earnings cap. Under the monthly test, benefits are reduced only if income during the month surpasses one-twelfth of the annual limit (that is, $1125 for someone who is age 65 through age 69).

Because of the earnings tests, most people assume they should apply for benefits to start when they retire from their regular jobs. But if you will be working part-time after retirement, that could be a costly mistake. You could be much better off filing for benefits *before* you retire.

If you are 62 or older (the minimum age for Social Security eligibility) and plan to work part-time after retirement, apply for benefits in January of the year you will retire. Even if you are unsure of your postretirement plans, there is no penalty for filing early. And you could hit the jackpot.

AILMENT

I do not know how to apply for my Social Security benefits.

R To schedule an appointment to apply for benefits at a nearby Social Security office, call 800-772-1213. You should apply three months before you want checks to start. When you go, bring along proof of age—a birth certificate or, if you do not have one, school records. You do not have to flash your Social Security card if you know your number. Be ready also to show your marriage certificate, evidence of military service, and most recent W-2 form (or tax return if you are self-employed).

If you present a voided check or deposit slip with bank or savings-account information, Uncle Sam will deposit your checks directly into your account. Each month's payment should arrive on the third day after the end of the month.

Warning: Act promptly when you start thinking about retiring or need disability income, even if you do not have all the necessary documents on hand. Get your application on record, then follow up with the documents. If you apply late, you may lose some benefits. The same is true when you want to apply for survivor's benefits. You should also file for benefits whenever there is any chance you have a valid claim. Do not assume that you are not eligible, or take someone's word for it.

☐ Resources

A free government booklet, *Retirement*, answers many questions about Social Security. Call 800-772-1213.

For addresses of your local Social Security offices, check in the U.S. Government pages of the telephone directory (sometimes under Health & Human Services).

AILMENT

I have never worked outside the home and am unable to collect Social Security on my own earnings.

℞ If you are married, you can qualify for spousal benefits, but you must wait until your spouse begins drawing benefits. However, once your spouse turns 62, you can register for Medicare coverage on your spouse's account. You can be covered by Medicare, even if your wage-earner spouse is not yet collecting benefits.

If you *had* worked and could claim your own benefits, you could begin drawing them as early as age 62. You could then switch to spousal benefits, if those were larger, when your spouse begins drawing Social Security. But if you begin taking your own benefits at 62, your benefit will be only 37½% of your spouse's, not 50%. If you wait until age 65 to begin drawing your own benefits, you could switch to full 50% spousal benefits at your spouse's enrollment.

You are entitled to either your own benefits or those as a spouse, whichever is greater. You are not entitled to both. The amount you actually receive will be determined at the time you apply for benefits.

☐ **Resources**

For more information about spousal benefits, order the Social Security Administration's free *Survivor's Benefits* pamphlet by calling 800-772-1213. Other pertinent pamphlets include *Understanding Social Security* and *Social Security, How It Works for You.*

AILMENT

My first marriage lasted 21 years. My second lasted 10. I do not know which ex-husband's Social Security benefits I can apply for or how much money I will be entitled to draw under each one's account when I reach retirement age.

R You can draw Social Security benefits under either ex-spouse's account. No doubt you will choose the account of the ex whose earnings were the highest and who is entitled to the largest benefits. But if you were still married to your second husband, you could not claim your first spouse's benefits, not matter how enviable they might be.

(There is one exception: If you remarried after age 60 and your former spouse has died, you may claim benefits on your deceased former spouse's account.)

A Social Security employee will help you get the information and benefits to which you are entitled. As mentioned above, you will receive 50% of your primary wage-earner husband's benefit, minus a certain percentage if you start drawing Social Security before you turn 65.

AILMENT

I am a widow who is collecting Social Security benefits on my deceased husband's account. Now I want to remarry.

R If you remarry after turning age 60—or age 50, if you are disabled—your widow's benefits will continue. After a year of remarriage, and if your new husband is collecting Social Security, you could then choose between keeping your widow's benefits and switching to spousal benefits on your husband's account. You will always be entitled to the higher of the two choices. If you are widowed a second time, and your marriage lasted at least nine months, you can choose between widow's benefits on either of your two husbands' accounts.

AILMENT

I do not know whether I should keep working after I start collecting Social Security.

R The financial question is how working after your normal retirement date will affect your Social Security benefits. This is only an issue in the age range from 62 to 70. If you retire in 1997 at age 62, you lose $1 of benefits for every $2 of earned income over $8640. If you are between age 65 and age 69, you can earn $13,500 before losing $1 of benefits for every $3 earned. These figures are adjusted upward annually. You can earn the limits in a single month, or spread them over the year.

These earned-income limits are applied to a family's total Social Security benefits, not just the wage earner's. Thus, if a husband or wife is drawing spousal benefits, those will be reduced as well, if the earned-income limits are exceeded.

This earnings limit applies only to earned income—W-2 wages or, if you are self-employed, your net earnings after subtracting operating expenses. Investment income, such as interest, dividends, rents, and capital gains, does not affect your Social Security payments. However, if you are a real estate dealer, farmer, or securities dealer, you may have to consider some of this type of income as earned.

And, if you are over age 70, you can bring home any size paycheck without having to surrender any benefits.

AILMENT

I want to sign up for Medicare.

R Generally, you can get Part A Medicare benefits if you are age 65 or over and can show you are eligible for Social Security (or Railroad Retirement) benefits on your own or your spouse's work record. In addition, you and your spouse qualify for Part A if you were a government employee whose work was covered for Medicare purposes.

Part A is also available to most individuals with permanent kidney failure, to those entitled to draw Social Security (or Railroad Retirement) disability benefits for more than 24 months, and to certain disabled government employees whose work has been covered for Medicare. If you are eligible for Part A, you can also enroll in Part B.

How to sign up for Medicare. If you are already collecting Social Security (or Railroad Retirement) when you turn 65, you will automatically get a Medicare card in the mail. The card usually shows the dates you are entitled to begin coverage under both Parts A and B. If you do not want Part B, you can refuse it by following the instructions that come with the card. If you are not receiving Social Security (or Railroad Retirement) benefits when you turn 65, you may have to apply for Medicare coverage. Check with any Social Security Administration (or Railroad Retirement) office to see if you are eligible. If you must file a Medicare application, do so during your initial seven-month enrollment period. That period starts three months before the month you first meet the requirements for Medicare.

For information about how and when to sign up for Medicare, or how to change an address or replace a lost Medicare card, contact any Social Security Administration office.

What Parts A and B cover. Before you decide to reject Part B, you should know what you are giving up. Medicare has two parts: hospital insurance (Part A) and supplemental medical insurance (Part B). Medicare pays only for care that it determines is medically necessary.

Part A. Part A helps pay for inpatient care in a hospital or skilled nursing facility or for care from a home health agency or hospice. If you are admitted to a hospital, Part A covers a semiprivate room, meals, regular nursing services, operating and recovery room costs, intensive care, drugs, lab tests, X rays, and all other medically necessary services and supplies. Covered services in a skilled nursing facility include a semiprivate room, meals, regular nursing services, rehabilitation services, drugs, and medical supplies and appliances.

Part B. Part B helps pay for doctor services (in the United States and abroad), outpatient hospital care, clinical laboratory tests, and various other medical services and supplies, including medical equipment. Covered services include surgical services, diagnostic tests and X rays that are part of your treatment, medical supplies furnished in a doctor's office, and drugs that cannot be self-administered and are part of your treatment.

AILMENT

When I enrolled in Medicare Part A, I did not sign up for Part B. Now I would like Part B coverage.

℞ You may still enroll in Part B during the annual general enrollment period from January 1 to March 31, and your coverage will begin on July 1 of the year you enroll. Your monthly premium probably will be higher than if you had enrolled in Part B at the same time you signed up for Part A. Generally, waiting to enroll in Part B costs you a monthly premium surcharge. The surcharge is 10% for each 12-month period in which you could have been enrolled but were not. However, you generally do not have to pay the surcharge if you delayed enrolling in Part

B because you were covered by a health plan where your spouse worked when you became eligible for Medicare. In that case, you can enroll in Part B during a special seven-month enrollment period. The period begins with the month the employer group health plan coverage ends or with the month your spouse stops working for that employer, whichever is earlier. In the case of certain disability beneficiaries, the special period begins when Medicare replaces the employer group health plan as the primary payer of the beneficiary's covered medical services.

AILMENT

I do not know whether I am covered by one or both parts of Medicare.

 Your Medicare card shows the coverage you have—hospital insurance (Part A) or supplemental medical insurance (Part B), or both—and the date your coverage started.

AILMENT

I am not entitled to Medicare based on my employment or the employment of my spouse, but I would like to buy coverage.

Individuals age 65 or over, who are U.S. residents and *either* U.S. citizens or aliens who have been lawfully admitted for permanent residence and have resided in the United States for at least five years at the time of filing, can purchase both Part A and Part B, or just Part B. The monthly premiums in 1997 are $221 for Part A and $43.80 for Part B.

AILMENT

I need help paying for Medicare.

If your annual income is at or below the national poverty level and you have limited financial resources, you may qualify for assistance under your state's Medicaid program in paying your Medicare premiums, deductibles, and coinsurance. To qualify, your income in 1997 must be less than $601 per month for one person or $806 per month for a couple, except in Alaska and Hawaii, where the limits are higher. Income includes Social Security benefits, pensions, and wages. Interest income and dividends may also count as income. In addition, you must be entitled to Medicare hospital insurance (Part A), and your financial resources such as bank accounts, stocks, and bonds cannot be more than $4000 for one person or $6000 for a couple.

If you think you qualify, contact your state or local welfare, social service, or public health agency, and ask about the Qualified Medicare Beneficiary (QMB) program or the Medicare Buy-in program. To get the telephone number for your state medical assistance office, call 800-638-6833. You can also get a leaflet explaining the QMB benefit by calling this number.

Even if your income is slightly above the national poverty levels, your state Medicaid program may pay your Medicare Part B premium. To apply, contact the same agency as for Part A, and ask about the Specified Low-income Medicare Beneficiaries (SLMB) program.

AILMENT

I do not know who to call with a question about a Medicare claim for doctor services.

R Call the Medicare carrier for the area where the service was provided. That carrier is responsible for processing the claim. The carrier's name and toll-free telephone number appear on the Explanation of Your Medicare Part B Benefits notice. They are also listed in the back of *The Medicare Handbook*. To receive a free copy of *The Medicare Handbook*, write the U.S. Department of Health and Human Services, Health Care Financing Administration, 6325 Security Boulevard, Baltimore, MD 21207-5187.

AILMENT

Medicare has not paid my claim in full.

R If you disagree with a decision on the amount Medicare will pay or whether services are covered by Medicare, you have the right to appeal for both the hospital (Part A) and medical (Part B) parts of Medicare. (Note that some appeal decisions are called *determinations*.)

The steps necessary to appeal are discussed in the following pages. You will also find detailed information about the appeals process in the notice Medicare sends you with its decision about your claim.

Appealing decisions made by hospitals, skilled nursing facilities, and other providers of Part A services. In many cases your first written notice will be from a hospital or other provider. This Notice of Noncoverage will explain why the provider believes Medicare will not pay your claim. Because this notice is not an official Medicare determination, you cannot appeal to Medicare. Instead, you must take the following steps if you disagree:

- Ask your provider to file a claim on your behalf to Medicare in order to get an official Medicare determination.

- You will then get a Notice of Utilization from Medicare. This notice is your official Medicare determination.

If you still dispute the decision, you can appeal by following the instructions on the Notice of Utilization.

Appealing decisions made by Peer Review Organizations (PROs).

PROs make decisions mainly about inpatient hospital care, ambulatory surgical center care, and care given by some HMOs. The PROs decide whether the care you got as a Medicare patient was medically necessary, of good quality, and provided in the most appropriate setting. To appeal a PRO determination, take these steps:

- Write to the PRO, and ask for a reconsideration. You have 60 days from the date you receive the determination to ask. (The PRO addresses and telephone numbers are listed in *The Medicare Handbook*.)

- If you are appealing a preadmission denial, ask for an expedited reconsideration. Your request for a review must be made by phone or in writing within three days of the initial determination.

- You will then get a letter from the PRO with the results of the reconsideration.

- The requirements for further appeal depend on the issue in question. The PRO's reconsideration determination will explain your appeal rights. In some cases, you can eventually appeal to a federal court.

Appealing preadmission hospital decisions.

If a hospital believes your proposed stay will not be covered by Medicare, it may decide not to admit you without consulting the PRO. If this happens, the hospital must give you its determination in writing.

If you or your doctor disagree with the hospital's finding, you can appeal. Here are the steps:

- Because the hospital's determination is not an official Medicare determination, you must ask the PRO to review it within 30 days from the date you receive the hospital's determination. A request for an immediate review must be made, by telephone or in writing, within three calendar days of the date you receive the determination.

- After the PRO reviews the hospital's decision, it will send you a determination.

- If the PRO takes your side and decides that Medicare will pay for your stay, the hospital is expected to admit you.

Appealing decisions of intermediaries on Part A claims. Appeals of decisions on most other services covered under Medicare Part A (skilled nursing facility care, home health care, hospice services, and a few inpatient hospital matters not handled by PROs) are handled by Medicare intermediaries. If you disagree with the intermediary's initial determination on your claim, you have the right to appeal, as follows:

- Contact the intermediary and ask for a reconsideration within 60 days from the date you receive the initial determination.

- Send your request directly to the intermediary or through the Social Security Administration.

- You will get a reconsideration determination from the intermediary.

- If you think the reconsideration determination is wrong and the amount in question is $100 or more, you can ask for a hearing by an administrative law judge. (You must make your request within 60 days from the date you receive the reconsideration determination.)

In some cases you may wish to take your dispute even further. In cases involving $1000 or more, you can eventually appeal to a federal court.

Appealing decisions made by carriers on Part B claims. You can appeal Medicare's adverse decision on a Part B claim. Details about the appeal process are printed on the Explanation of Medicare Benefits form you get from the carrier. Here is what you do:

- Write to the carrier and ask to review the determination. You have six months from the date of the determination to ask. Your request can be mailed or hand delivered to the carrier that processed your claim or to a Social Security office (the Railroad Retirement Board if you get Medicare through Railroad Retirement).

- The carrier will send you a written explanation of the outcome of its review.

- If you contest the carrier's determination and the amount in question is $100 or more, you can ask for a hearing before a carrier hearing officer. (You have six months from the date of the review determination to ask.)

You may combine reviewed or reopened claims if all the claims you want a hearing on have been reviewed by the carrier, and the request for a hearing is filed on time for each claim.

- Once you have a decision from the hearing officer, you can ask for another hearing before an administrative law judge, if the amount in question is $500 or more. (Your request must be made within 60 days from the date you receive the hearing officer's decision.)

  You may combine claims for the hearing before the administrative law judge if: (1) you have received a hearing officer's decision on all of the claims you want a hearing on, and (2) the requests for a hearing before an administrative law judge are filed on time for each claim.

- If you still need satisfaction, you can eventually appeal decisions involving $1000 or more to a federal court.

Appealing decisions made by health maintenance organizations (HMOs). If you have Medicare coverage through an HMO, your HMO usually decides questions of coverage, payment for services, the medical necessity, the appropriateness of setting, and the quality of your care.

When your HMO makes a decision to deny payment for Medicare-covered services or refuses your request for Medicare-covered supplies, you are given a Notice of Initial Determination. Along with the notice, your HMO must provide a full, written explanation of your appeal rights.

You can ask for a reconsideration, in writing, of your HMO's decision. You have 60 days from the date of the notice to ask. Follow these steps:

- Mail your request or deliver it to your HMO or to a Social Security office (or Railroad Retirement Board if you get Medicare through Railroad Retirement).

- Your HMO must reconsider its initial determination to deny payment or services.

- If your HMO does not rule completely in your favor, it must send your reconsideration request and its determination to the Health Care Financing Administration (HCFA) for further review and a determination.

- The HCFA will send you its reconsideration determination. If things are still not going your way, and the amount in question is $100 or more, you can ask for a hearing before an administrative law judge within 60 days of the HCFA's reconsideration determination. Your next and last stop is a federal court, but only if your case involves $1000 or more.

For more information.   If you want more information about your right to appeal and how to request it, call Social Security, or the Medicare intermediary or carrier in your state. (The number of the Medicare intermediary or carrier is listed on the notice explaining Medicare's decision on the claim. For information about your right to appeal a Peer Review Organization (PRO) decision, call the PRO in your state (PROs are listed in *The Medicare Handbook*).

Limitation on liability.   In certain cases, even if Medicare denies your claim, you will not be held responsible for paying the doctor or other health-care provider. These cases fall under the "limitation on liability" (or "waiver of liability") provision of Medicare law. This limitation on liability applies only when all three of the following requirements are met:

1. The services are furnished by an institutional provider such as a hospital, skilled nursing facility, or home health agency that participates in Medicare, or by a doctor or supplier who accepts assignment.

2. Medicare denied your claim for one of the following reasons:
   ■ The claim was for custodial care.
   ■ The treatment was not "reasonable and necessary" under Medicare program standards for diagnosis or treatment.
   ■ The claim was for home health services, if the patient was not homebound or did not require skilled nursing care on an intermittent basis.
   ■ The only reason for the denial is that, in error, you were placed in a skilled nursing facility bed that was not approved by Medicare.

3. You did not know or you could not reasonably be expected to know that Medicare does not cover the services you were given (for example, because you did not receive written notice).

This limitation on liability provision does not apply to Medicare Part B services provided by a doctor or supplier who did not accept assignment of the claim. However, in certain cases, Medicare law protects you from paying for doctor services that were provided on a nonassigned basis. If your doctor knows or should know that Medicare will deny a claim for a particular service because it was "not reasonable and necessary," the doctor must give you written notice—before performing the service—of why Medicare is not expected to pay. You must then agree in writing to pay for the services. If you never got this notice, you are off the hook for payment. If you paid, you may be entitled to a refund from the doctor. (The doctor's written notice is not an official Medicare determination. If you disagree with it, ask your doctor to submit a claim for payment to get an official Medicare determination.)

If you receive a bill from your doctor or another health-care provider for a service denied by Medicare, and you think the limitation on liability described above applies, contact your Medicare carrier for information on how to handle the problem.

AILMENT

I was billed for a Medicare service I did not get.

R If you believe a doctor, hospital, or other health-care provider has performed unnecessary or inappropriate services, or has billed Medicare for services you did not receive, you should immediately report this possible fraud to the Medicare carrier or intermediary that handles your claims. The carrier or intermediary will need to know the exact nature of the wrongdoing, the date it occurred, and the name and address of the health-care provider. Have this information ready when you call. (Telephone numbers of the Medicare carriers and intermediaries are listed on notices explaining Medicare's claim decisions. Medicare carriers are also listed in *The Medicare Handbook*.)

If the Medicare carrier or intermediary does not respond to your report of Medicare fraud or abuse, you may call the Health Care Financing Administration (HCFA) toll-free hot line at 800-638-6833. The hot line operator will refer you to a staff person at an HCFA regional office, who will ask for the following information:

- The wrongdoing you suspect, when it occurred, and the health-care provider's name and address.

- The name and location of the Medicare intermediary or carrier you reported it to, and when you reported it.

- The name of any carrier or intermediary to whom you spoke and what advice you were given.

AILMENT

My doctor has charged me more than the Medicare limit.

R A doctor or supplier who does not accept assignment must be paid directly. You are usually responsible for charges in excess of the Medicare-approved amount, because your doctor or supplier did not agree to accept this amount as payment in full. In a case like this,

Medicare will pay you 80% of the approved amount, after subtracting any part of the $100 annual deductible you have not met.

Even though a doctor or supplier does not accept assignment, there are limits on how much you can be charged for most covered services. In 1997, you cannot be billed more than 115% of what Medicare approves. Doctors or suppliers who go over this limit may be fined.

If you think your doctor or supplier has gone over the top, ask for a reduction in the charge. If you have already paid more than the charge limit, ask for a refund. If you are refused a reduction or refund, call your Medicare carrier and ask for assistance.

Special rule for doctors performing elective surgery. Medicare law requires doctors who do not take assignment for elective surgery to give you a written estimate of costs before surgery, if the total charge for the procedure is $500 or more. If the doctor did not give you this written estimate, you are entitled to a refund of any amount you paid over the Medicare-approved amount.

AILMENT

I want information about buying insurance to supplement my Medicare benefits.

℞ Contact any Social Security Administration office, state office on aging, or your state insurance department, and ask for a copy of the *Guide to Health Insurance for People with Medicare*. It describes Medicare's benefits and the types of private insurance available to supplement Medicare (so-called Medigap policies). This publication is also available by writing to the Consumer Information Center, Pueblo, CO 81009.

AILMENT

I am enrolled in a coordinated care (managed care or prepaid) plan that serves Medicare beneficiaries. This plan has refused to provide or pay for a service covered by Medicare.

℞ If the plan refuses to pay for any service, or refuses to provide a Medicare-covered service, you may appeal to the plan in writing. Under federal regulations, plans must follow special appeals procedures in the following situations:

- The plan has refused to provide a Medicare-covered service.

- You received a service covered by Medicare, and you or the provider billed the plan for the service and the plan refused to pay.

Consult the documents provided to you when you joined the plan for information about your appeal rights and how to file an appeal.

AILMENT
I need information about coordinated care plans that serve the area where I live.

R⁄ For a copy of *Medicare and Coordinated Care Plans*, write to the Consumer Information Center, Department 87, Pueblo, CO 81009.

Staff at the Health Care Financing Administration regional offices listed below can tell you if there are coordinated care plans in your area that contract with Medicare. This information is also available by calling 800-638-6833.

Boston: (For Connecticut, Maine, Massachusetts, New Hampshire, Rhode Island, and Vermont) Beneficiary Services Branch, 617-565-1232.

New York: (For New Jersey, New York, Puerto Rico, and the Virgin Islands) Carrier Operations Branch, 212-264-8522.

Philadelphia: (For Delaware, District of Columbia, Maryland, Pennsylvania, Virginia, and West Virginia) Beneficiary Services Branch, 215-596-1332.

Atlanta: (For Alabama, North and South Carolina, Florida, Georgia, Kentucky, Mississippi, and Tennessee) Beneficiary Services and HMO Branch, 404-331-2549.

Chicago: (For Illinois, Indiana, Michigan, Minnesota, Ohio, and Wisconsin) Beneficiary Services and HMO Branch, 312-353-7180.

Dallas: (For Arkansas, Louisiana, New Mexico, Oklahoma, and Texas) Beneficiary Services Branch, 214-767-6401.

Kansas City: (For Iowa, Kansas, Missouri, and Nebraska) Program Services Branch, 816-426-2866.

Denver: (For Colorado, Montana, North and South Dakota, Utah, and Wyoming) Beneficiary Services Branch, 303-844-4024, extension 1.

San Francisco: (For American Samoa, Arizona, California, Guam, Hawaii, and Nevada) Beneficiary Services Branch, 415-744-3617.

Seattle: (For Alaska, Idaho, Oregon, and Washington) Beneficiary Services Branch, 206-615-2354.

Estate Planning and Death

Of all the possible threats to your family's wealth, from inflation to bear markets to natural disasters, only one is certain to happen: your death. Despite this inevitability, many people make no provision for death. After all, it is easy to find excuses to put off estate planning. There is the hassle of finding a lawyer, the expense, and, worst of all, the cheerless contemplation of your own death. But none of these excuses justifies the price—in both money and frustration—that your loved ones will pay if you fail to put your affairs in order.

Death does not end your responsibility to your family and others. If you renege, your loved ones may truly need financial first aid. Now is the time to make sure the ones you leave behind will be financially secure. To accomplish that, you must arrange your financial affairs so there is sufficient income. Your estate must also be readily available—that is, not tied up in probate. Planning is also necessary so that federal and state taxes do not consume up to half of your wealth. Finally, a good plan will lighten the administrative load on the survivors. After all, they already have to deal with their grief.

By using a combination of wills, trusts, gifts, and insurance, you can pass on your estate with a minimum of red tape and without a penny of estate tax. This chapter will show you how to provide for your spouse and children, escape capital gains taxes, shrink your taxable estate, and avoid probate. With the right planning, you can arrange to die a financially flawless death. Once that planning is taken care of, you can devote yourself to living the perfect life.

■ GENERAL ESTATE PLANNING AND SETTLING

AILMENT
I want to avoid estate planning mistakes.

Rx Estate planning is a minefield where thousands of dangers are buried. We cannot discuss them all here, but we can look at 10 estate planning traps with the potential to do the most damage to your best laid (or delayed) plans. Check your estate plan against them.

Failure to make a proper will or to update it. Do you really want to surrender your right to distribute your property? If you die without a will, the state will choose your heirs for you. After scrambling all of your life to amass property, it would be a shame not to take time to protect and bequeath it. Once you draw up a will, review it periodically so that it will not be seriously outmoded at your death—one last affront to your good intentions.

Consider the consequences of dying without a will:

■ *The state will select your heirs.* Should you die intestate—that is, with no will—the courts will gladly step in and put your personal affairs in order. But the law's notion of who gets what after you're gone probably will not match your own. In most states, your property will be split among your spouse and children, often with one-half to two-thirds going to your offspring. Without even picking up a pen, you could be guaranteeing your spouse an impoverished old age.

■ *A probate court judge will name a guardian for your minor children.*

■ *The tax collector may get a large bequest.* When a will is part of a carefully drafted estate plan that includes trusts, a married couple can bequeath as much as $1.25 million in 1998 (rising to $2 million in 2006) to their heirs free of federal estate tax. Family business owners and farmers can exempt a higher amount.

■ *You will fill your state's coffers.* Only in a will can you name an executor to inventory your estate, pay your debts, file income and estate tax returns, and distribute assets to your heirs. If you push off with no designated executor, a judge may tap a public administrator for the task. Letting the state settle your estate can be like putting a bird dog in charge of your chickens.

Clearly, a will should be the foundation on which you build your estate plan, unless you use a revocable living trust as a substitute (see page 326).

Inflexible planning. Give your heirs enough leeway to meet emergencies or changing needs. It is very well to figure how much and how often your family should get income if you die. But the economy and your family's situation may change dramatically in the next 10 to 15 years. Rigid plans may force your family to eat cake when they cannot afford bread. For example, you may provide for your child's college education without permitting proceeds to be used for any other purpose. When you die, your family will not be able to touch the college fund, even if money is needed to feed and clothe your child until it's time for college 10 years from now.

Not enough liquidity at death.   If there is not enough cash on hand to cover last expenses, valuable assets, such as the family home or business, may have to be sold at once, often at a fraction of their value. The best solution is a life insurance policy that will automatically provide the required liquidity at death (see page 138). And the proceeds can be excluded from tax.

Failure to plan for disposal of a business interest.   Why let all your long hours and capital go to waste when you die? Astute planning can provide a guaranteed buyer at a guaranteed sales price—assuring that money will be on hand instantly when you die. Or if you want your heirs to continue the business, plan in a manner that will give them the best possible chance of succeeding.

Failure to integrate life insurance with other assets.   Have you accumulated a hodgepodge of insurance policies over the years? These policies may be out-of-date—for example, designating a deceased parent or a former spouse as beneficiary. Make sure you review your life insurance policies from time to time, and integrate them with other assets (such as Social Security benefits, stocks, and bonds) to form a cohesive plan. Choose policy settlement options that permit proceeds to be paid in monthly installments. Not only does this protect against spendthrift heirs, but it will increase the total amount of payments considerably—by as much as 35%.

Failure to tax plan.   It is often said, and even more often forgotten, that the government approves—or at least tolerates—the art of reducing your taxes *legally*. Yet the money squandered each year because of failure to use available tax saving strategies and privileges runs into the millions. It makes no more sense than throwing your paycheck out the window.

Neglecting to plan for retirement.   We mean what you want to do, where you plan to do it, and most importantly whether you will have enough money to make your dreams materialize. Studies show that most people reach retirement with lots of time, but few funds to fulfill their plans. The next pitfall is related to this situation.

Overdependence on government, business insurance, and pension plans.   These sources of income are attractive. But overreliance on them can have disastrous consequences. Suppose you change jobs but forget to convert your group life insurance, become uninsurable, and die grossly underinsured. Or suppose you reach retirement, receive only $300 a month from Social Security, find it inadequate (even with other income), go back to work, and in the process, lose most of your Social Security benefits because of the government's earnings limit.

Failure to keep priorities straight. As many financial planners advise, life insurance and an emergency savings account take precedence over other investments. "Get-rich-quick" schemes are likely to turn into "get-broke-fast" realities. Remember your responsibilities before you take risks.

Failure to plan your estate. This, of course, takes in everything we have already discussed. Still, it gets to the heart of the matter, because with proper planning and periodic reviews, there are no pitfalls to speak of. Remember, seeing your attorney once in a lifetime is not enough—it should be at least once a year. Of course, we are also presuming you will select other competent and qualified assistance.

AILMENT

My spouse died unexpectedly, and I do not know what needs to be done to settle the estate and manage the assets.

 After a spouse's death, the widowed spouse must take care of numerous financial details, including the following:

Within the first two weeks. Order a dozen (or more) certified copies of the death certificate from the county clerk's office or the funeral director. You will need them to claim death benefits and Social Security and to retitle joint assets, among other things.

Have your attorney review the will and file it in probate court.

Collect the documents needed to claim death benefits and to value the estate. These include bank, employee-benefits, brokerage, and mutual fund statements, your marriage certificate, and both of your birth certificates.

Apply for death benefits. Call your insurance agent, your spouse's employer, and your local Social Security office. Consider less obvious sources, too. For example, you may be able to claim life insurance benefits from your spouse's union or fraternal organization. Some of your spouse's debts, including the mortgage, auto loan, and credit card balances, may include an insurance rider that pays off the loan at death.

If you have trouble locating important documents, look for clues in your spouse's checkbook. An entry made out to an insurance company may signal a policy you did not know about. Check Schedule B of your spouse's last tax return for the names of banks, stocks, and mutual funds that produced income. If you believe your spouse may have life insurance policies that you cannot find, write to the American Council of Life Insurance (Policy Search, ACLI, 1001 Pennsylvania Avenue, NW, Washington, DC 20004), including a self-addressed, stamped envelope, and a request that member companies search their files. This service, which should take six weeks, is free.

Within the first months. It can take from four months to three years to collect your inheritance. In most cases, life insurance proceeds will arrive within a month. Deposit any excess cash you receive in the bank for at least six months. As insurance and other benefits come in, park the money in short-term bank certificates of deposit. That will buy you time to decide where to invest the money permanently.

Record your cash flow to help you determine where you stand financially. Compare your expenses with your income from all sources, so you will know whether to cut back or relax. Postpone major financial decisions, such as whether to sell your house, for at least six months to a year.

Within the first six months. Review your own will, and change beneficiaries on insurance policies or retirement plans that named your spouse. Also change names on joint billing accounts or credit cards. Reexamine your insurance needs.

If you are executor or administrator of the estate, notify creditors and satisfy genuine debts.

Between six months and a year. If you are executor or administrator, you must pay any taxes the estate owes. File the federal estate tax return, Form 706, within nine months of your spouse's death, if the estate is larger than $625,000 in 1998 (rising by about 4.5% each year until it reaches $1 million in 2006). You must also pay the estate's income taxes, due April 15, every year the estate is open.

AILMENT

My parents had a living trust. My mother, the surviving spouse, died last week. I was named in the trust instrument as the successor trustee, and I do not know what needs to be done.

 The following checklist should help you distribute your parents' assets and wind up the trust.

- Obtain the original of the trust document.
- Obtain certified copies of both your parents' death certificates.
- Draft an Appointment of Successor Trustee letter (see sample letter on opposite page). Sign this letter in the presence of a notary public.
- Review the trust. Notify all beneficiaries of your mother's death and their individual interests in the trust.

SAMPLE LETTER

Appointment of Successor Trustee

WILLIAM C. AND ALMA L. WYCLIFF
TRUST AGREEMENT
DATED SEPTEMBER 5, 1986

APPOINTMENT OF SUCCESSOR TRUSTEE

I, ELIZABETH J. WYCLIFF, the named successor trustee for the William C. and Alma L. Wycliff Trust Agreement, dated September 5, 1986, do hereby appoint myself, pursuant to the powers vested in me by said trust, as the Trustee of said trust.

Date: _____   _____
                        Trustee

State of California
County of Ventura

The foregoing was acknowledged before me this _____ day of _____, 1997, by _____.

[SEAL]

_____
Notary Public

- Inventory the assets in the trust.

- Notify property insurance companies and keep up coverage on all real estate.

- Notify all financial institutions holding trust assets, including banks, brokerage firms, and mutual funds, of your mother's death and your appointment as successor trustee. Take the original trust document to the bank, along with the death certificate(s), and close out bank accounts. Call mutual funds and ask what forms the company requires before it will distribute the trust assets.

- Collect any death benefits, such as life insurance or retirement funds, payable to the trust.

- An affidavit of death of trust beneficiary, along with a certified copy of the death certificate, must be recorded for each piece of real property. Then, record a new deed showing the new ownership. *Note:* If the property is being sold, a new deed does not have to be recorded.

- Meet with your accountant or attorney and assess the need for tax returns (income, trust, or estate).

- Pay valid claims against the trust.

- Once all taxes have been paid, distribute assets to the beneficiaries named in the trust. Obtain a receipt for distribution from each beneficiary.

AILMENT

I need to get sensitive information from my father's bank. He died recently and did not leave detailed records behind. I am worried that there may be bank accounts that will go unclaimed.

℞ Your bank should be able to tell you the procedure for getting the information you want. To give you an idea of what may be required, here is how the Bank of America handles such matters:

If you believe your father might have held an account or safe-deposit box at the Bank of America, you should contact the local branch office nearest to the deceased. You must wait at least 40 days after your father's death to request information. This waiting period is meant to prevent an unauthorized relative from raiding the account. It also lets payers who electronically deposit checks in an account reverse amounts unwittingly credited to the deceased after death.

You will need the name, Social Security number, and death certificate of the deceased. At this point, the bank will ask you to complete an "affidavit of decease" and have it notarized. In this affidavit, you swear you are your father's rightful heir and that his estate is not subject to probate, for example, because it falls below your state's probate exemption amount.

That done, the bank will tell you if your father had accounts at the bank and their size. You will also be told if he had a safe-deposit box there. The bank will allow you to remove items from the safe-deposit box and claim the cash accounts.

☐ Prevention

Once again, it must be emphasized how important it is to keep your financial affairs in order and to leave an inventory of your assets where it can easily be found by grieving relatives.

■ WILLS

AILMENT
I want to make sure my assets go to my children from a former marriage when I die.

R̸ There is only one way to make sure your property passes to your favorite heirs. Only a valid will can prevent loss, trouble, expense, and possibly undesirable distribution of your property.

Dying intestate is outrageously careless. But have no fear. Your state will step in and carve up your estate like a cantaloupe, giving slices away to your deserving—and undeserving—relatives.

Of course, your current spouse will get a share, to the extent that state law allows. Depending on where you live, your spouse will be entitled to from one-third to one-half of your estate. In some states, the surviving spouse's share is equal to a child's share. If you have three children, your spouse will get only one-fourth. The rest will be divided equally among your children, regardless of their ages or special needs.

The promises you make to your children will be empty if they are not backed up in writing. Oral expressions of intent made during your lifetime have no legal effect at all when you are dead. There are no exceptions to this rule.

Terms to come to. Do not list everything you own in your will because your holdings will change. Instead, inventory your assets and list their whereabouts in a separate letter of instruction that you give to your executor and loved ones.

Give percentages of your estate to your heirs, rather than fixed dollar amounts, because your assets may dwindle or grow over the years. For example, leave 50% of your property to each of your two children, instead of giving them each $50,000 of your $100,000 current estate. Remember, you cannot use your will to bequeath property that is jointly held—your share goes to your co-owner—or that has a named beneficiary, such as an IRA or life insurance policy.

You may, however, wish to earmark specific sums for relatives, charities, or your household help. For instance, you might write, "I give $5000 to my nephew, Tyler White." When making specific bequests, avoid confusion, spats, and hurt feelings by giving as detailed a description of each gift as possible. Do not write, for example, "I leave my best ring to my daughter Chelsea," but rather, "I leave my 14-carat diamond in the platinum setting to my daughter Chelsea."

You should list contingent beneficiaries in your will in case your first choices die before you do, cannot be located, or refuse to accept your bequests. And, to clean up loose ends, add a residuary bequest clause, spelling out who gets any loose property not specifically given to someone else.

Clauses that make your legacy conditional upon something that might ruin an heir's health, wealth, or happiness probably will not survive attack. You can leave your niece $10,000 for graduating from college, but not for marrying your business partner's son or serving in the Army. And refrain from any parting shots. A deadbeat cousin who is willed a tin cup, "so he can freeload off of someone else," may be able to sue your estate for slander and win enough to stop freeloading forever.

Use your separate letter of instruction to make gifts of smaller personal items. Such letters can be changed as often as you like and do not require legal help, witnesses, or notaries. Nothing causes as many fights within families as who gets what piece of china or other personal possessions. It also is a good idea to discuss your intentions with your family.

Letters of instruction are the proper place to express your wishes concerning organ donations and funeral arrangements. Make sure your doctor and family have copies; by the time your will is found and read, it may be too late to follow your wishes in these matters.

Also, include a statement revoking prior wills. If a court is presented with more than one document purporting to be your last will and testament, the one with the latest date will be selected as long as it was properly drawn, signed, and witnessed, unless it appears you did not draw up the document of your own free will.

Hiring help.   Do not practice false economy by drafting your own will. If your estate is simple—less than around $600,000 with no out-of-state real estate—hiring a lawyer will set you back a mere $75 to $200. Even so, it can be hard to resist the bargain lure of how-to books, software (such as Nolo Press's *WillMaker* and Parson's *It's Legal*), and even blank statutory will forms, which are available from state legislatures, bar associations, and office-supply stores in California, Maine, Michigan, and Wisconsin. (Other states have not passed laws yet authorizing the use of statutory wills.) It is best to resist such an impulse, because your homemade will can be made invalid because of a technicality. Remember, an invalid will is no different from no will at all. Besides, will forms cannot be customized to fit your particular needs. Michigan's version, for example, does not allow you to create a trust.

When your estate is large or complicated, legal fees can run into four or five digits. You can cap these fees somewhat by saving your lawyer time. Thus you will pay less by showing up with detailed, accurate lists of your assets, debts, and beneficiaries. You should also note who holds title to your property: you alone, you jointly with someone else, or a trust. Such lists, regularly updated and left with your lawyer, will also simplify your executor's task later on.

Of course, even estate-planning attorneys who are strongly opposed to do-it-yourself wills grudgingly admit that a self-drafted will can be better than none at all provided your needs are simple and you bone up on will basics. What is considered simple? If you are single or married without children and you do not have a lot of assets, you could use will forms or software to leave bequests (specific gifts), dispose of your residuary estate (everything else you own), and name an executor to carry out the will's instructions. If you are a parent with adult children, your needs are often uncomplicated, too, unless you plan to leave assets in trust for your grandchildren.

With will-writing software, you can name guardians for minor children and choose someone to manage their property until they become legal adults; or you can set up simple trusts to hold the assets until the children reach an age you specify. But there is great potential for error in creating these children's trusts. In addition, if you have more than $600,000 in assets, own real estate in more than one state, own a business, are remarried with children, or want to disinherit a child, you are skirting disaster if you draft a will yourself.

Note: Videotaping bequests has become a fad. While that may entertain your heirs, it is not a substitute for a written will. Videotaping the witnessing and signing can help thwart a will contest, though, if your disgruntled would-be heir claims you were clearly incompetent for leaving that individual out.

☐ Prevention

If you are an executive who is transferred or moves frequently to take new jobs, you have a special problem in planning your estate. Provisions in your will that were valid where it was drafted may not be recognized in another state. To prevent an invalid will, make sure your lawyer understands you are constantly on the move. That way, the lawyer can spell out provisions that otherwise might be assumed because of statutory or case law in the state where you currently reside.

For example, most states recognize a will as valid when it's witnessed by only two persons, but your new state may want three. Okay, generally, courts will admit a valid will to probate if it was valid in the state where it was drawn up. But why ask for problems when you can simply have three witnesses sign the document?

You can run into other gray areas involving such major issues as how the estate is to be divided and executors. For instance, a bequest to your children may include adopted children in one state, but not in another. Or, the time when a trust is distributed may vary, depending on when children reach majority in a particular state.

Nine states, mostly in the West, are community-property states. This means all property you acquired during your marriage, and while you lived in a community-property state, is owned by both of you, share and share alike. The proceeds of a sale of those assets remain community property, even if you later move to a separate-property (non-community-property) state.

But, if you move *from* a separate-property state *to* a community-property state, the personal property you acquired in your former home state keeps the status it had there—separate, tenancy in common, or joint tenancy. Because real property cannot be moved, ownership retains its original status.

Result: It is vital that you give your estate planner and your lawyer your complete family history, so they can give you a set of worry-free documents.

AILMENT

I want to cut my spouse and/or child out of my will.

R/ Before you put poison pen to paper, you should know that most state laws do not let you disinherit a spouse, and Louisiana is the one state where you cannot disinherit your kids at all. If you live in one of the nine community-property states, you can leave your half of the community property and all of your separate property to whomever you please. In the 41 separate-property states, for instance, your spouse is entitled to a portion, usually a third, of your estate. As a result, the most effective way to disinherit your spouse is by getting him or her to sign a prenuptial or nuptial agreement to that effect. Find a good lawyer to draft the document, though, because prenuptial agreements renouncing claims to an estate can be difficult to enforce.

Another way to express your hard feelings is to put the legal minimum in trust and to give your spouse access to only the income from that trust. After your spouse's death, the principal will go to your children or whomever you have specified.

AILMENT

I signed a joint will with my deceased spouse, and now I am remarried.

R/ Occasionally a husband and wife want to execute a joint will. This means that the wills of both spouses have exactly the same terms. The only difference is the signatures at the bottom. Besides being a valid will, a joint will is a contract between two spouses to leave their property to certain persons, usually relatives, as specified in the will. Joint wills are honored—and strictly construed—by the courts. When one spouse dies and the other remarries, the joint will is almost always still held to be in effect. At this point, you cannot change your mind about your bequests— you will be held to the terms of the joint will.

☐ Prevention

Do not use joint wills. Each spouse should execute a separate will.

AILMENT

I do not know whom to name as executor of my will.

℞ The executor you name in your will must combine diplomatic tact with executive skills. The executor's job is to wrap up your financial affairs. Assets that are part of your estate must be identified and valued (not included: trusts, life insurance policies, pension plans, and some kinds of jointly owned property). This often requires hiring and paying the fees of an appraiser, lawyers, accountants, and other professionals. The executor pays all of your debts, files tax returns, and distributes whatever remains to your heirs. Careful records must be kept, too, because most probate courts demand a detailed accounting of all money received, spent, or held by your estate.

Every estate must have an executor. If your will fails to name one or if that person fails to qualify (for example, because your choice predeceases you or becomes incompetent), the court will appoint an administrator to perform the executor's duties. When no relative or beneficiary can take the job, the appointee is likely to be a civil servant or even a creditor. Administrators and executors are typically entitled to a sliding scale of fees based on the value of your estate—on average 3% to 5% of your estate. Naming your executor, therefore, can be equal to a significant bequest, especially if an estate is large. The executor's fee on an estate of $100,000 might be $5000; on an estate of $500,000, it could be $20,000.

For this reason, you may want to name your spouse, if you have one, or the residual heir (who will receive all property you did not specifically give to others) as executor. Executors' fees are taxable as income. When family members act as executors, they usually waive the fee, so the amount is distributed as part of the estate and is received tax-free. If you are naming a relative as executor, you can save your heirs extra money by not requiring that the executor post a bond.

You can name anyone you trust as your executor. Most people prefer their spouse or a good friend, who may also be a beneficiary. But you can also choose a third party, such as a bank or lawyer. This might be done to ensure that your heirs are treated impartially or to benefit from experience in business or finance. If you have a large estate, you may need two executors: one person to interpret your wishes and another person or institution, such as a bank, to make business or investment decisions, pay taxes, and keep records.

Before naming your executor, make sure he or she is willing to accept the responsibility. You should also name one or two alternates who can act if your first choice is unable or unwilling to serve. You may want to go over your will with your executor ahead of time to clear up any possible confusion about your wishes.

AILMENT

I do not know when to change my will.

R̸ Estate planning needs to be revisited occasionally, at key times of your life, to make sure events have not upset your earlier arrangements. Here are seven reasons to change your will:

1. *When wedding bells ring.* Estate planning is more meaningful now. You must decide as a couple how you want your assets to be passed on. Whether or not you have children, separate-property states usually give a spouse one-third or one-half of an estate. If you die without children, your parents or siblings get the rest. If you want to leave all of your property to your spouse, you need a will. You cannot disinherit a spouse without his or her consent.

In community-property states, each spouse automatically owns one-half of all community property. Basically, that is property acquired during the marriage by means other than inheritance or gifts. You can leave your half of the property to anyone you want, including your spouse.

2. *When you become a parent.* The big question now is how your children will be cared for if both you and your spouse die. A will is imperative. You need to name someone to act as a personal guardian of your children. Consider using trusts, perhaps in your will, to handle assets that would go to your children (see page 332).

3. *For midlife planning.* Your assets are growing, so estate tax planning could save your heirs thousands in federal estate taxes. Act when you and your spouse have a combined net worth (including house, retirement plans, and insurance proceeds) of more than the amount each of you can bequeath free of the federal estate tax. This federal exemption amount is $625,000 in 1998 and rises by about 4.5% a year until it reaches $1 million in 2006. You should change your wills to make sure each of you owns enough assets individually to take advantage of your own $625,000 tax-free allowance, even if it means splitting jointly owned assets. A popular plan is to put assets valued at up to the federal exemption amount in a testamentary, "bypass" trust that benefits your spouse during his or her lifetime, then goes to your children. You can leave the rest of the estate to your spouse. (For more information about bypass trusts, see page 342.)

Update your will now, too, if there have been any family births, deaths, separations, or divorces that affect it. Do you need to change your appointed guardian, trustee, and personal representative, for example, because of death? Reevaluate specific gifts you are giving to people or charity.

4. *After a divorce.* In most states, a divorce automatically revokes the provisions of a will that apply to a former spouse. In some states, a divorce revokes the entire will.

5. *When tying the knot again.* To provide for your new spouse and still be certain your children are taken care of, talk to an estate-planning lawyer about a qualified terminable interest property trust—QTIP, for short. This trust can be set up in your will to give your spouse the income from the trust property and some rights to principal. But when your spouse dies, the assets go to beneficiaries you choose.

6. *When you retire.* If you retire to another state—or any time you move to another state—review your estate-planning documents to comply with your new state's legal requirements. Have you become a proud grandparent? Change your will to leave the next-next generation something.

7. *When a spouse dies.* Get a new will and, if needed, a revocable living trust.

Here are other occasions when you should update your will:

- If your net worth changes substantially (for example, you win the lottery).

- If a beneficiary dies before you do.

- If a change in tax law affects your estate or financial plan.

- When federal or state laws about trusts have changed.

- If you add or lose major assets (for instance, you start an art collection or you sell a vacation home you were leaving to your daughter).

- If you change your mind about how you want to divide your property.

Note: You do not have to write a new will every time you want to make small changes, such as substituting a beneficiary or bequest. These alterations can be done using codicils (see next **AILMENT**).

AILMENT

I want to change my will.

R You can modify your will by either adding a codicil or writing a new will. Whatever you do, do not scribble on your will yourself. You may unwittingly invalidate it and send your careful planning up in smoke. A codicil is really a formal amendment to a will executed with the same formality as a will. It leaves the original will intact, except for the specific change(s) you are making. A codicil should be drawn up by a lawyer, and, like the rest of the will, it must be witnessed. But if your codicils are complicated or begin to resemble the tail of a kite, it is better to revise the entire document to avoid any question of its validity.

In fact, if the original will is fairly simple, it might be easier just to make a new will.

☐ **Prevention**

If your original will is flexible enough, you can avoid the time and expense of constantly adjusting it. A good will accommodates your wishes in a wide variety of situations. A bad will is so detailed and rigid that any change of circumstances will make it difficult or impossible to administer and may result in unintended outcomes. For example, heirs may predecease you; your fortunes or the fortunes of others may wax and wane; your favorite charity may find its elusive cure or may be exposed as less than charitable. In drafting your will, try to anticipate and provide for unforeseen eventualities. For instance, name alternate executors and insert clauses that distribute a deceased beneficiary's share to surviving relatives.

AILMENT

I do not know where to keep my will.

R The obvious choice is your safe-deposit box. But putting your will in a bank safe-deposit box can cause delays because most banks seal the boxes at death and will not open them without a court order. Your spouse's safe-deposit box is a poor choice too, since the two of you may die together. You could keep a copy of the only will you wish to have probated in your safe-deposit box as a precaution. But the original signed will, as well as other documents you want your survivors to have immediate access to, should be kept at your lawyer's office, with a friend, at your business address, or in a home safe or fireproof box. In some counties, probate courts provide a will depository for a small onetime fee.

☐ Prevention

Do your heirs know where you keep your will? Or where you have bank accounts? Or your attorney's name and phone number? If the answer to any of these questions is no, you should prepare what is called a document locator. This is a detailed list of everything your surviving loved ones need to know. Without it, they might have to spend months—and hundreds of dollars in legal fees—ferreting out bank accounts, safe-deposit boxes, insurance policies, and other particulars of your finances. The following information is essential:

■ *Your advisers.* List the names, addresses, and telephone numbers of your accountant or tax preparer, insurance agent, stockbroker, attorney, financial planner, bank trust officer, employer, employee-benefits counselor, executor, and potential guardian for your children.

■ *Your debts.* Write down the names of your credit-card issuers, their addresses and phone numbers, and your card numbers. Also provide information about your mortgage, auto, and personal loans, including the phone numbers and addresses of lenders, loan numbers, terms, and rough balances.

■ *Your insurance.* Specify the amount, company names and addresses, policy numbers, beneficiaries, and location of policies for all coverages. Do not forget to include the same information for your group plans.

■ *Your personal papers.* Divulge where you keep your will, recent income tax returns, Social Security card, marriage certificate, military discharge papers, passport, business partnership agreements, house deed, mortgage, leases, and car titles.

■ *Your savings and investment records.* List names and addresses of all the financial institutions where you have savings or investment accounts. For each, specify the name(s) on the account, the account number, the type of investment, the date it was opened, and the approximate balance. Also, tell your survivors where to find account statements and passbooks, as well as stock, bond, mutual fund, or other investment documents.

■ *Your safe-deposit box.* Write down the bank and its address, who has access, where the keys are, and in whose name the box is registered. Also provide a complete inventory of its contents.

Update your document locator every year or so. Keep one copy at home, another in your safe-deposit box, and, if your children are young, a third with their potential guardian.

■ TRUSTS

Before reading about specific types of trusts that can fit your particular case, it is helpful to understand how trusts in general work. Quite simply, a trust is a legal entity that holds assets contributed to it by one person, called the grantor, for the benefit of one or more beneficiaries. The grantor sets down instructions as to how the trust should be managed and its income and principal paid out. This is done in a document called a trust agreement that is drawn up by an attorney. The grantor also chooses a third party, called a trustee, to hold title to the trust property and carry out the grantor's wishes.

To the uninitiated, trusts can seem discouragingly confusing, with dozens of different types, including ones with such improbable-sounding names as sprinkle and QTIP. Actually, there are only two basic types, testamentary trusts and living (sometimes called inter vivos) trusts. A testamentary trust is created in your will and takes effect at your death. A living trust operates during your lifetime.

AILMENT
I want to avoid probate.

R℘ Death shifts the burden of winding up your estate to those you leave behind. The wishes you expressed in your will must be carried out. To accomplish this, your assets must be identified and inventoried, debts and taxes paid off, and property distributed. The archaic legal procedure frequently used is probate. Because court supervision is involved, and court approval is sometimes required, probates tend to be cumbersome and expensive. Although the aim of probate is to prevent fraud in transferring your property and to protect your heirs from creditors' claims, few heirs need these safeguards. Probate becomes largely an unnecessary form-filing marathon. Additionally, probate is public. Your financial life and much of your personal life become public record.

Probate does have its good side. If you suspect there will be legal disputes about your estate, probate may be an effective way to resolve them. For example, you may anticipate conflicts between your ingrate beneficiaries as to their proper share of your obligations and assets.

But for most estates, the disadvantages of probate outweigh the advantages. Fortunately, with proper planning, simpler and less expensive techniques can be used to distribute your property.

Totten trusts and pay-on-death provisions. There is a special type of bank account that skirts probate, lets you use and control your money during your life, and lets you name the heir of your choice. Better still, it avoids the hazards of a joint bank account, where the other joint tenant can raid your funds before you die.

Just open an account in your name as trustee for your beneficiary. While you are alive, the beneficiary has no right to any money in the account. But after your death, the beneficiary can get ready access to the money by showing proof of identity and a certified copy of the death certificate.

Known as a Totten trust or "pay-on-death" account, this type of account lets you change beneficiaries at any time or destroy the trust simply by withdrawing the money and closing the account. Because you keep control, opening a Totten trust is not subject to gift tax.

The drawbacks? Your money will be deposited in a bank savings account or certificate of deposit—a safe, but low-interest-bearing investment. Note, however, that stocks, bonds, and other securities can also be designated as payable on death or POD. So, unlike securities held in joint ownership, you do not need another person's signature to sell, margin, or otherwise encumber your investments. Since securities held POD transfer to the beneficiaries upon death, they can ensure liquidity for your survivors during probate.

Another problem is that if a sole beneficiary dies before you do and then you die before designating a new one, the account will become part of your probatable estate. Finally, if your estate cannot pay all its debts or taxes, your executor can probably lay claim to the money from the account, even though it had already been distributed.

Joint ownership. In some cases, holding property as joint tenants (or as tenants by the entirety) is an ideal way to avoid probate. Because title passes automatically to your surviving spouse (or other joint tenant) when you die, jointly held assets bypass probate entirely.

Virtually any property with ownership documents can be held jointly, including real estate, securities, bank accounts, and personal property, such as automobiles or boats. As an estate-planning tool, however, joint tenancy can create estate tax problems for couples with sizable estates.

Here is how the problem arises. Say a couple jointly owns assets worth $825,000 and that both spouses die in 1998, when estates worth up to $625,000 escape federal estate tax. On the husband's death, his half of the joint property passes to his wife without penalty, because married couples may leave estates of any size to each other tax-free. When she dies, however, her estate will exceed the $625,000 exemption amount by $200,000, and $52,200 will disappear into the black hole of the federal budget. Had the couple held some of their property separately, they could each have taken advantage of the $625,000 federal estate tax exclusion.

Another shortcoming is that jointly held property cannot be placed in trust for a spouse. Because irrevocable trusts are the escape routes from federal tax when your estate tops a federal exemption amount ($625,000 in 1998, rising to $1 million by 2006), holding property jointly prevents you from using this valuable estate-planning device. (See page 327 for a discussion of irrevocable trusts.)

Joint tenancy can also create gift tax. Setting up a joint tenancy in real estate with someone other than your spouse will generally be treated by the IRS as a completed gift, and gift taxes will be due just a few months later, instead of when you die. Moreover, if you decide you want your joint tenancy property back, your joint tenant might refuse. Even if the other agrees, a second gift tax could be due when the joint tenancy property is transferred back to you.

Perhaps the biggest problem with joint ownership is that it gives another person a current interest in your property. With ownership rights, the other person can go to court to dissolve the joint tenancy and walk off with part of what was originally yours.

If you live in one of the nine community-property states, seek professional advice before making someone other than your spouse the joint owner of community property. In community-property states, all income earned and property acquired by a couple during marriage, except for individual gifts and inheritances, is deemed to be owned equally by each spouse. When the first spouse dies, half of that person's share of community property passes to the surviving mate, and the other half goes to heirs named in the decedent's will. The surviving spouse may or may not be among the named inheritors.

Do not confuse joint tenancy with tenancy in common, where each owner can usually transfer his or her share of the property at will and, at death, ownership goes to the decedent's heirs, not to the other owners.

If you have already created joint tenancies, it is not too late to change them. But do not try to undo them yourself. Hire a lawyer.

Living trusts.   There is another way to dodge probate that is more costly than joint ownership, but less likely to cause complications: Establish a revocable living trust. Unlike a testamentary trust, which is created in your will and takes effect upon your death, a living trust swings into action while you are alive.

Living trusts may be revocable or irrevocable. Revocable trusts are more popular because you continue to enjoy complete control over your property. You can spend the trust income, revise the trust's provisions, or terminate it. You can even act as your own trustee.

While you are alive, therefore, a revocable trust is no more than a legal fiction. Although you put title to assets in the trust's name, trust income is reported on your tax return if you or your spouse act as trustees. And the assets placed in trust are included in your taxable estate. Revocable living trusts avoid probate but not death taxes.

When you die, however, the trust comes into its own. In effect, it does the work of a will, distributing its assets to your heirs or staying in force for their benefit. A successor trustee of your choice will carry out your wishes, as expressed in the trust instrument.

An irrevocable living trust works exactly the same way upon your death. But when you establish an irrevocable trust, you no longer control the assets. Nor can you change the trust provisions. You give up all rights of ownership. For this reason, property in an irrevocable trust is *not* part of your taxable estate.

You and your spouse can each set up living trusts for your separate property. If most or all of your assets are jointly owned, however, you should probably use one revocable living trust for your shared property. Otherwise, ownership must be divided—a headache with assets such as real estate.

When you set up a living trust, sign a written trust document that explains how you want your property to be managed during your lifetime and how it should be passed on after your and your spouse's death. You keep the right to amend or revoke the entire trust. If circumstances change, you can usually change the document fairly easily. If you decide to revoke the trust, your trust property reverts—comes back—to you.

You will probably want to name yourself and your spouse as trustees of your trust. That way, you will keep complete control over your property and do not have to pay any trust management fees. Of course, you can name a bank or other commercial trustee, if you want, or share the trustee responsibilities with a commercial trustee. You will usually pay a commercial trustee an annual fee of 1% to 2% of the assets under management.

When the first spouse dies, the decendent's share usually remains in trust for the benefit of the surviving spouse. No probate of the trust assets is necessary. The surviving spouse usually then becomes the sole trustee of the trust, continuing to make decisions about how trust assets are managed and invested.

On the death of the surviving spouse, the property passes to the beneficiaries, according to the provisions of the trust. Again, no probate will be necessary.

If the trust involves a business, children or even a spouse might not know enough to take over if the grantor dies. Owners often put the stock of their businesses in trust with the current owner as trustee. When the grantor dies, a new trustee will take over running the business, but the profits will still go to the beneficiary.

Because the living trust avoids probate, it can save a substantial amount in administrative costs. It also lets you use certain techniques to avoid or reduce death taxes. Revocable living trusts are fully portable from state to state, too, where wills are not. And trusts can include language that lets your spouse or other heirs manage your finances if you become incapacitated.

Finally, a trust can be tough to contest. By the time a disgruntled relative finds a lawyer and files a civil suit, the money in the trust may already have been paid out to the beneficiaries. To pursue the case, the hapless relative would have to bring suit against each individual beneficiary, which is generally impractical. With a will, your assets could be frozen in probate for a long time.

What is the downside? For one, any appreciation in the assets of a revocable trust will be included in your taxable estate when you die. Also, general creditors can make claims against revocable trusts, since you controlled the assets up to the time of death.

What does a living trust cost? It usually costs more to have a lawyer prepare a standard trust and pour-over will than a simple will. (A pour-over will takes care of any assets you didn't transfer to the trust.) Fees typically range from $850 to $3500, depending on the complexity of the trust.

Probate or living trust?   Many people believe that probate is something to be avoided at all costs. But probate is not a bottomless pit. When your estate goes into probate, it does not mean that your heirs will never receive it. But probate is not free (executors and lawyers receive standard fees), and it is not quick (it can take up to a year or more), which are reasons why many people prefer to avoid it. Note, however, that two-thirds of the states have adopted the uniform probate code or similar legislation to make probate a simpler and less expensive process.

The best way to decide whether a living trust is right for you is to consult an experienced estate lawyer. In general, however, you are a candidate for a trust if one of the following applies to you:

■ *You live in a state where probate is costly and time-consuming.* Figuring probate costs is tricky. Court costs and fees for executors and attorneys vary widely from state to state. And states compute the size of estates in different ways. For example, some include the market value of a decedent's home; others do not. Thus, same-size estates could be valued for probate purposes at $600,000 in Texas, but $1 million in California. For help in estimating your estate's probate costs, consult the 50-state appendix in *Easy Way to Probate: A Step-by-Step Guide* (Random House, $10.00) by Kay Ostberg and HALT, a nonprofit consumer advocacy group in Washington, DC.

In general, say estate lawyers, probate is particularly costly in California, New York, and Pennsylvania, where total fees could top $35,000 on a $600,000 estate. By contrast, the fees for an identical estate in North Carolina, Texas, and Virginia would run less than $16,000.

■ *Your heirs are likely to prove litigious.* For example, you may plan to leave a large inheritance to your devoted companion, which could send your children through the roof. Irate heirs have rarely been able to overturn living trusts, so if your planned bequests are sure to rile, consider a living trust.

■ *You want privacy.* As your estate grows, so do the benefits of secrecy. You might not want the world to know that your spouse inherited $500,000 in securities.

■ *You fear becoming incompetent.* A living trust can let you avoid a conservatorship—that is, being placed under a court-appointed guardian—if you become unable to manage your own affairs. When setting up the trust, you can choose a successor trustee to manage your assets if you are physically or mentally incapacitated.

■ *Your property crosses state lines.* If you have real estate in more than one state, a living trust can spare your heirs the burden of multiple probates. For example, if you own property in three states, it may be necessary to open three probates (and enrich three lawyers). In some cases, a resident executor must also be appointed.

■ *A trust makes financial sense.* If setting up a trust will ultimately save your estate big bucks, take steps to stay out of probate. To find out how much a trust will save (or cost) you compared with probate, do the following math: Compute the likely cost of probate (usually a percentage of the value of your assets). Then subtract the following from the cost of probate: (1) how much the trust is projected to save in estate tax; (2) after-death expenses, such as legal and administrative fees (reduced by the tax saved from deducting these expenses); and (3) the difference in price between setting up a living trust and preparing a will. The larger your estate, the more likely a trust will cost less than probate.

One major inconvenience of a revocable living trust is having to transfer all of your assets to it. You must change the titles on stocks, bank accounts, and real estate to reflect the fact that your trust, not you, now owns the assets. If you establish a living trust but neglect to alter your title documents, the property in your name at your death will be subject to probate.

When you die, someone is going to have to put up with the nuisance and expense of transferring your assets. The question for you to answer is, who? With a living trust, you assume the costs and inconvenience. With a will, you leave it to your heirs.

☐ Resources

You may want to read more about living trusts in one of the many estate planning books available in libraries and bookstores.

You can also find more information on the subject in the following sources:

Neuberger&Berman has published a booklet that explains types of trusts and the pitfalls of not setting them up properly. To order a free copy of *Estate Planning through Trusts*, write to Neuberger&Berman Trust Company, 605 Third Avenue, New York, NY 10158; 212-476-9100.

Then there is one of Nolo Press's most popular self-help books, *Plan Your Estate with a Living Trust* ($19.95).

Whether you pick a will or a trust may ultimately depend on where you live. Your lawyer can advise you on probate in your state, or you can send away to HALT (1319 F Street NW, Suite 300, Washington, DC 20004, which offers guides on probate and trusts that detail each state's laws, including their taxes.

AILMENT

I want to set up a living trust for my IRA.

Your IRA is already a trust. As long as the beneficiary is not your estate, it will not go through probate. Just name an individual—or one of your existing living trusts—as beneficiary.

AILMENT

I want someone to be able to manage my money if I become incapacitated.

℞ You need a power of attorney. This is a legal document naming another person to act on your behalf, if you are away from home or become physically or mentally incompetent. A power of attorney is essential to a good estate plan. If you fail to plan for incapacity, your next of kin will not be able to handle your financial affairs until they get permission from probate court to act as your conservator or guardian. This can cost at least $300 to $500 in legal fees and take as long as three months.

Powers of attorney come in several types. Each is a two- or three-page document for which lawyers charge $75 to $150.

General power of attorney. A general power of attorney lets you name another person to act as your agent in business or financial matters when you know you will be away. It becomes void, however, if you are incapacitated. So it is useless as a precaution against the unexpected.

Durable power of attorney. This is the form to use in anticipation of serious illness, accident, or even disappearance. You usually sign it in conjunction with your will, but it goes into effect right away. It is called durable because it operates as long as you live, unless you revoke it. The person you designate can sign checks against your accounts, sell and buy securities and real estate, even run your business. Most durable powers of attorney are given to spouses, trusted relatives or friends, or the family lawyer. It is wise to choose a backup person in case your first choice becomes incapacitated, too, or decides not to act.

Whomever you choose, there is always a slight risk that the power will be abused. If you are worried that your assets could be embezzled or squandered, assign the durable power of attorney jointly to two people in such a way that neither can act alone.

Give the document to the person designated to act for you. There is no need to file it with a court.

Although the laws governing use of the durable power of attorney vary from state to state, all but Georgia, Louisiana, Oklahoma, and Wyoming recognize it. Most banks and brokerages will honor a durable power of attorney, but require you to execute their own separate power-of-attorney forms before they will let someone else transact business for you or admit them to your safe-deposit box. Ask your bank what procedures you need to comply with.

Springing power of attorney. This special version of the durable power of attorney springs into effect only if you are incapacitated. The person you designate cannot use it without a physician's statement attesting that you can no longer handle your financial affairs. The springing power of attorney is also recognized in most states. While it makes misuse of your assets more difficult, the springing power of attorney may be less acceptable at financial institutions. A bank or brokerage firm, for example, might refuse to accept a physician's statement that you are incapacitated unless it is ordered to by a judge.

Living trust. In some cases, you may want to combine a durable power of attorney with a living trust. This may be advisable if your assets are large enough to warrant professional management, if you are the head of a family business, or if you have no spouse or child who would be capable of managing your affairs. Banks and brokerage houses feel on surer ground with trusts than they do dealing with a power of attorney alone.

You may transfer all of your assets to the living trust or leave it empty with instructions for the person holding the durable power of attorney to pour your wealth into it if you are declared incompetent. Until then, you control the trust assets and receive the income. But the trust lets you name a successor trustee, such as a bank or trust company, to assume responsibility for your investments if you can no longer handle them.

You could pay a lawyer up to $3500 for setting up this kind of trust. If you want a bank to be the successor trustee, make sure it will act as trustee. Some big banks do not handle trusts with assets under $300,000.

Review durable powers of attorney and trusts at least every five years. File the documents with your personal papers or give them to the person designated to handle your financial affairs. Also store a copy in your safe-deposit box, making sure the designated agent or trustee has authorization to open the box.

AILMENT
I want my children to be well provided for if I die while they are still minors.

R With minor children, you almost certainly will want trusts set up for them upon your death, rather than leaving them property outright in your will. There are several reasons for this. Minor children cannot own more than a minimal amount of property in their own names. You must, therefore, name a guardian for your children's property, too. This includes the property you leave for their benefit, as well as their earnings or any other assets acquired by inheritance or gift. But appointing a guardian in your will is cumbersome and inefficient because the guardian, even if a parent, must often get permission from the court to pay the children's expenses from the legacy and must account for the assets' management. A boon for your lawyer, but not for your children. Moreover, the guardian must spend the money that you leave as state law dictates. Finally, if you leave property outright to minors, it usually has to be turned over to them at the age of 18, the age of majority in most states, when they are often too young to know how to manage their finances sensibly.

It is far better to create a trust to hold your children's inheritance. The trustee of your choosing will generally be free of court supervision and reporting requirements. Instead, the trustee will follow the instructions you put in the trust instrument. Also, with a trust, you specify the age at which your children come into their inheritance.

Your children's trust can be testamentary, that is, established by your will. Or you can avoid probate by creating a living trust for each child (see page 331). Trustees are usually given the power to spend any of the trust income or principal for your child's health, education, or living expenses. When your child reaches the designated age, the trust and the remaining trust property are distributed. For example, parents often stipulate that a third of a trust's assets should go to a child at age 25, with the other thirds distributed 5 and 10 years later.

Even if you rely on a trust to finance your child's upbringing, you should still name a property guardian in your will to supervise any property not included in the trust, such as a large gift your child receives after you die.

If the value of the property you leave your child is less than $25,000, a trust will not be economical. A more practical option would be to leave the property directly to your spouse (or the child's parent) or to your child under the Uniform Gift to Minors Act.

In creating a minor's trust, aim for flexibility. The trust should be planned as if you might die tomorrow, but it should not require frequent revisions if you do not. Try to take into account as many contingencies as possible: the death of one parent, the death of both parents, and even the death of one or all children. The provisions of the trust regarding how the trust income and assets are to be used should be as general as possible, too. You should give the trustee considerable discretion in making payments, because no matter how carefully you plan, you cannot anticipate every situation that may arise. Your trustee's discretionary powers should include the right to tap trust principal in case of an emergency.

If you have more than one child, decide whether you want different trusts, or different provisions, for different children. Many parents believe the best approach is to divide property equally among children in separate trusts and have each trust distributed when the child reaches a certain age. Other parents believe such trusts may not achieve true equality, because one child may develop greater needs after the trust is established. For example, a young child will need more financial assistance to get a bachelor's degree than an older sibling who is already in college. One way to rebalance the equation is to provide for a "pot" trust, in which assets are placed in a single trust and distributed as needed (for education or other needs specified in the trust), until all children are old enough to have completed their educations. At that point, the trust will be divided equally.

Another option: a so-called sprinkling provision, which lets the trustee allocate income and principal to beneficiaries based on their changing needs. If one child marries money, while another is permanently disabled in an accident, for example, the trustee can give the less fortunate heir a bigger share.

If your child is disabled, you may need to include special provisions in your trust (see page 334).

It is not unnatural for parents to want control over their children's lives, even after death. For example, if you struggled up from poverty and want your offspring to learn the value of work, too, you could say that a percentage of trust income should be used for necessities, while the rest can be withdrawn only to launch a business. You can even include incentives in your trust document, such as a clause that entitles your child to more of the trust income when earning a bigger salary. Spendthrift clauses that prohibit a beneficiary from assigning future trust income to creditors are also popular.

If you try to be too dictatorial from the grave, though, your child may be able to successfully challenge your trust's provisions in court. Court decisions vary from state to state, but trust instruments that prohibit a child from marrying are usually easy to overturn.

AILMENT

I have a handicapped child who will inherit my property.

R Not surprisingly, the problems of providing for disabled children are quite complex, and wills and trusts intent on caring for them must be designed carefully. For example, if you want to leave all or part of your legacy to a disabled beneficiary, do not give the beneficiary control of the inheritance. Doing so may disqualify the disabled child from federal and state social service programs. Worse, Medicaid or Social Security Supplemental Security Income benefits may be cut off until the legacy has been used up.

To sidestep this trap, your assets should be used only to provide luxuries, not to pay for basic support. One solution is to bequeath your estate to an obliging relative or friend in your will, along with a letter instructing that individual to spend some of the money on your disabled heir. Your child will still be eligible for public assistance, and your assets will be out of the state's reach. Unfortunately, if your informal trustee selfishly decides to keep all of your money, your child has no legal recourse.

You can protect against an unscrupulous relative or friend by using a testamentary trust. But then you have to guard against institutional predators. Social service agencies have successfully gone to court and seized the assets in trusts set up for disabled beneficiaries to reimburse the cost of services. Both sides have won some legal scuffles, so it is imperative to have your trust drafted by an attorney who is familiar with your state's case law. Call your state or local bar association for a referral to an experienced lawyer.

You can probably keep the government at bay if you use the right legal language. First, state clearly in your trust instrument that trust income should be used to supplement, not replace, public assistance. Emphasize that intention by including a sprinkling provision in the trust instrument that gives your trustee power to distribute income and principal, not only to your disabled child, but to other beneficiaries as well. And direct that the principal will be given to other relatives or to a charity when the trust ends.

In instructing the trustee, devote attention to the problem of escalating health-care costs and what might happen if and when trust payouts fall short of medical needs. Address the issues of how, when, under what circumstances, and at what rate the principal can be invaded and used up. You will need to name a personal guardian, in addition to a trustee, although the same person can serve as both.

Finally, consider an escape clause that calls for the trust to terminate if it is challenged in court. Again, the principal should not go to your disabled child, but to other beneficiaries. During your lifetime, ask these secondary beneficiaries to look after your child, using some of the assets they will inherit if the trust terminates. Be wary of putting this request in writing, though. It may give your state legal grounds for challenging your child's right to receive government benefits.

AILMENT

I do not know whom to name as my trustee.

R Most people appoint themselves as the initial trustee. If you set up a marital trust for jointly owned property, you and your spouse can serve as cotrustees. You will, of course, need to also name a successor trustee to take over when you die.

Your trustee can be any competent person of legal age or an entity such as a partnership or corporation. If you have a modest-sized estate, it can probably be managed by your surviving spouse or a relative or friend. Because the trustee will be managing your assets, it does help if the person you appoint has a working knowledge of finance and tax law. The advantage to naming a trusted individual is that such a person probably has a good feel for what you would want, will be more flexible than a corporate trustee, and will usually minimize or waive fees.

However, large estates with complicated assets may require professional management. So may trusts that are expected to last for more than five years. Banks and trust companies provide this service for an average fee of 2% of the trust's assets. On the plus side, corporate trustees have an indefinite life, so you do not need to worry about the trustee dying. They are not managing trusts in their spare time. And they usually have access to good investment and tax advice and recordkeeping services. Experts agree that mismanagement and fraud are far more common with individual than with corporate trustees. If you are considering using a corporate trustee, pay a visit to its trust department. Meet some of the trustees, ask about investment philosophy, and get a feel for the place.

Keep relations and rivalries among your heirs in mind. Putting your son in charge of his sister's income could spark resentment or worse.

Make sure you select at least one alternate trustee so that if one dies, goes out of business, or resigns, there will still be someone to carry on.

You may want to give someone the power to change trustees if yours performs poorly. Otherwise your heirs may have to sue to remove the trustee, an expensive ordeal. Giving removal power to your beneficiary can create a sticky tax problem, though. If your heir can change trustees at will, especially if the trustee has the power to invade principal, the IRS might reason that the money is not really in a trust at all. Because the heir can shop around for the right trustee, the IRS could impose both income and estate taxes as if your property had been bequeathed outright.

AILMENT

I have several thousand dollars' worth of Series EE U.S. Savings Bonds. I would like my two daughters to get these bonds when I die.

R̸ You can ensure that your savings bonds are transferred to your daughters by having them reissued to show yourself as the owner and your heirs as the beneficiaries. To have the bonds reissued in this manner, request Form PDF-4000 from the Federal Reserve Bank of Kansas City (P.O. Box 419440, Kansas City, MO 64141-6440; 816-881-2000). Send the completed form and the bonds to the Federal Reserve Bank of Kansas City. The maximum number of names that can be registered on a bond is two (two co-owners or one owner and one beneficiary). So you may want to divide your bonds between your two daughters.

■ ESTATE TAXES

AILMENT

I do not know whether my estate will owe tax when I die.

R̸ The federal estate tax is imposed on the value of your estate before it is distributed. Many states have estate or inheritance taxes as well. If you are not on your guard, the tax bite can be vicious. The maximum estate tax is 55% on taxable estates of more than $3 million. For smaller estates, the looting is less dramatic. But each tax dollar saved can be more critical to the heirs of a modest estate than it is to wealthier families.

Not every estate is taxed. You can dodge the federal estate tax bullet entirely by making sure the value of your taxable estate is less than the federal exemption amount. In 1998, you can bequeath up to $625,000 tax-free. This amount rises by about 4.5% each year until it reaches $1 million in 2006. If your joint estate will clearly be worth less than the federal exemption amount, you can skip this **AILMENT** entirely. If you are married, each of you may exempt $625,000. This means that you can leave a combined wealth of $1.25 million to your heirs tax-free in 1998.

But even if your estate is relatively modest now, bear in mind how easily your net assets could grow to be worth well over $1 million by retirement. Just the increase in your home's equity, inflation, and a bull market could bring you up to that. That is all the more true if you have company profit-sharing plans or stock options. And if you own a small business, you can make the jump even faster. Note, however that family business owners and farmers benefit from an extra exemption—$675,000 in 1998, declining to $300,000 in 2006. The value of the business or farm must exceed

50% of the value of your estate, and you must have been active in the business for five of the eight years before your death. Your heirs must also continue to manage the business for five years. If an heir calls it quits, the IRS can come back and impose estate taxes on the family business portion of your estate.

Before you can assess your tax peril, you must estimate the value of your taxable estate. The math is elementary. Add up your gross estate, than subtract allowable deductions and exemptions.

You can estimate your federal estate tax liability by filling out the worksheet (Figure 10–1). First calculate the present value of your gross estate (line 1) by adding up these assets:

- Stocks, bonds, real estate, and cash.

- Household furnishings, motor vehicles, jewelry, and collectibles.

- Proceeds from your life insurance policies and annuities (including the cash surrender value of a policy you hold on your spouse).

- Retirement plan benefits, including IRAs and employer-sponsored pension and savings plans.

- Gifts you have made with strings attached. For instance, if you gave your vacation house to your daughter, but kept the right to use it whenever you liked, the IRS will consider the house to be still yours.

- Property in a revocable living trust.

- Assets over which you hold general power of appointment. For example, say your mother gave you the power to sell her home after she dies. Because you are authorized to sell the property to anyone, including yourself, the IRS considers the house yours, even if you never touch it.

- Your share of jointly held property. One half of the value of property held in joint tenancy with your spouse is included in the estate of the first spouse to die. The total value of property you own as a joint tenant with someone other than your spouse is included in the estate of the tenant who dies first, unless the survivor can prove having put up part of the purchase price or the property was received by gift or inheritance. If you purchased the property together, the portion you paid for is part of your estate.

If you and your spouse live or have lived in a community-property state, all income earned and assets acquired by the two of you while living in that state, except for individual gifts and inheritances, are considered community property, and half of it is included in each spouse's estate.

FIGURE 10–1   Federal Estate Tax Worksheet

1. Gross estate $_____

2. Outstanding debts $_____

3. Administrative and funeral expenses _____

4. Adjusted gross estate (line 1 minus lines 2 + 3) _____

5. Marital deduction (bequests or gifts during your life to your spouse) _____

6. Charitable bequests _____

7. Taxable gifts made after 1976 _____

8. Taxable estate (lines 4 + 7 minus lines 5 + 6) _____

9. Federal estate tax before credits (find the amount on line 8 in column A of the table below and read across to column B) _____

10. Federal credit against gift and estate taxes* 192,800

11. Federal estate tax less federal credit (subtract line 10 from line 9) _____

12. Maximum credit for state death taxes (column C) _____

13. Estimated federal estate tax (line 11 minus line 12) $_____

*The federal gift tax credit is $202,050 in 1998; $211,300 in 1999; $220,550 in 2000 and 2001; $229,800 in 2002 and 2003; $287,300 in 2004; $326,300 in 2005; and $345,800 in 2006.

Next, add up your outstanding debts (line 2), including mortgage balances, other loans, liens on your real estate, income and property taxes, and credit-card balances. Also, estimate funeral expenses and the cost of settling your estate (line 3). Court costs and attorney's, executor's, accountant's, broker's and appraiser's fees can claim 5% to 10% of your gross es-

	B	C
A Taxable Estate	Federal Estate Tax before Credits	Maximum Credit for State Death Taxes
$ 50,000	$ 10,600	$ 0
100,000	23,800	0
200,000	54,800	1,200
300,000	87,800	3,600
400,000	121,800	6,800
500,000	155,800	10,000
600,000	192,800	14,000
700,000	229,800	18,000
800,000	267,800	22,800
900,000	306,800	27,600
1,000,000	345,800	33,200
1,200,000	427,800	45,200
1,500,000	555,800	64,400
2,000,000	780,800	99,600
3,000,000	1,290,000	182,000

FIGURE 10–1 Continued

tate. To find your adjusted gross estate (line 4), subtract your debts (line 2) and final expenses (line 3) from your gross estate (line 1).

You can leave your entire estate to your spouse tax-free because of something called the marital deduction (line 5). You might want to have your spouse fill out a photocopy of this worksheet to see if estate tax will be due when your spouse dies.

To determine your taxable estate (line 8), add any taxable gifts made after 1976 to your adjusted gross estate (line 7 plus line 4) and subtract your marital deduction (line 5) and charitable bequests (line 6). You can make tax-free gifts of up to $10,000 a year each to as many people as you like (married couples may jointly give as much as $20,000). After 1998, the $10,000 annual exclusion for gifts will be indexed annually for inflation.

Prior to 1982, the annual gift limits were $3000 for individuals and $6000 for married couples. To determine the amount of taxable gifts you have made, check copies of old gift-tax returns that you filed.

Now use the table on page 339 to estimate your tax bill. There is *no* estate tax due if your estate is $625,000 or less in 1998. For estates above $625,000, brackets range from 37% to 55%. If your taxable estate totals $800,000 (column A in the table), federal estate tax before any credits are applied would be $267,800 (column B). You are entitled to a $202,050 federal credit against gift and estate taxes (line 10). (If you have paid any federal gift tax after 1976, subtract that too.) Fill in the remainder on line 11. Finally, on line 12, you can deduct a $22,800 credit for state death taxes (column C) to find the federal government's share of your estate—in this case $42,950 (line 13).

AILMENT

I want to minimize the size of my taxable estate and thereby reduce my estate taxes.

R Death may be certain, but there is no reason estate taxes have to be. In fact, you can escape the federal estate tax entirely by making sure that the value of your taxable estate is below the federal exemption amount. The amount you can bequeath tax-free is $625,000 in 1998. This amount rises about 4.5% a year, until it reaches $1 million in 2006. That does not mean, however, that you can avoid the tax just by giving away all but the federal exemption amount on your deathbed. The federal estate and gift taxes are unified, meaning that the value of taxable gifts as of the time you made them will be added to the property you hold at death in calculating your estate tax liability. (To estimate whether your estate is likely to incur federal tax, fill out the worksheet on page 338.)

Fortunately, the estate tax law is riddled with dozens of loopholes. With proper planning, your children—and grandchildren—can mourn your loss in luxury.

Gifts. You can give as much as $10,000 a year each to as many people as you wish without triggering the gift tax (married couples can jointly give up to $20,000). After 1998, the $10,000 annual exclusion for gifts will be indexed annually for inflation. You can also make tax-free gifts of any amount to charities and unlimited payments to health-care and educational institutions to cover a relative or friend's medical or tuition bills.

Gifts can be an important part of an estate plan. Start now with a dozen children and grandchildren, and you can transfer a lot of wealth before you die. Add some friends and other relatives and you could easily give away more than $1 million tax-free over many years.

If you exceed the $10,000 exclusion, you have a lifetime credit equivalent to a $625,000 exemption from the gift/estate tax in 1998 (rising gradually each year to $1 million in 2006). That $625,000 will go a lot further now as a gift than it will as a bequest 25 years hence. After all, a logical gift is an asset that may well appreciate, such as a growth stock or undeveloped real estate. Such a gift will not hurt your pocketbook much and could even fall under the annual exemption. But if you continue to hold onto the asset, it could trigger a huge tax later on. Finally, contrary to assertions in government tax publications, the gift tax rate is not the same as the estate tax rate. It is lower.

Installment transfers. Instead of giving your property away, you can sell it to your children or other heirs. You must report the sales proceeds as current income on your tax return. However, taxes are deferred because you do not recognize the income all at once, but rather as payments are received. That means the income from later payments could be taxed at a lower rate if your tax bracket goes down—when you retire, for instance.

From the buyer-beneficiary's perspective, installment payments can be set at an amount that matches the income earned by the asset purchased. This will cover most or all of the yearly installments. For instance, the buyers might derive $900 annually in dividends on a stock they are paying $1000 a year for. That way, the beneficiaries do not have to make big cash outlays to buy the assets.

Some clients like to combine installment sales with the gift exclusion. If the yearly installment comes to less than $10,000, you can forgive the balance due, making it your annual gift. (The $10,000 annual gift tax exclusion is indexed for inflation after 1998.)

Share ownership. Another way to avoid estate taxes is to divide the ownership of real estate into two parts. When you purchase a condominium, say, you can split ownership into a "lifetime interest," which you buy, and a "remainder interest," which your child buys. The IRS requires that the child put up the money, although gifts from grandparents could boost the child's purchasing power. Your life expectancy according to IRS actuarial tables determines how the ownership is split—80% to 20%, for example. When you die, the lifetime interest is legally dissolved, and your child assumes full ownership tax-free. Hire an attorney to draft the required documents.

Marital deduction. An even bigger bonanza is the so-called marital deduction, which lets you give during life or bequeath at your death as much as you want to your spouse tax-free as long as your spouse is a U.S. citizen. (If your spouse is not a citizen, consult a tax adviser.) The write-off has its limitations, though: If your spouse ends up with more than the federal exemption amount ($625,000 in 1998, rising gradually each year to $1 million by 2006), you may only postpone the estate tax until your spouse's death.

Bypass trust. One way to solve that problem is through the use of trusts. For example, a bypass trust (sometimes called a family or credit-shelter trust) lets both partners in a marriage take advantage of their separate federal estate tax exemption to pass as much as $1.25 million to their heirs tax-free in 1998. Under this arrangement, you bequeath assets worth up to the federal exemption amount tax-free to the trust. The rest goes directly to your spouse, and because of the marital deduction, that bequest also escapes taxes.

For the rest of your spouse's life, the trust's income can be collected, and usually up to $5000 or 5% a year of the principal, whichever is greater. (However, it generally is not advisable for the spouse to receive payments from the trust unless needs cannot be met from the spouse's own resources, since this reduces the tax savings.)

After your spouse's death, your children or other heirs become the trust's beneficiaries. But because the trust was not under your spouse's control, the assets do not count toward the spouse's taxable estate. Furthermore, any income or appreciation on trust assets also will be exempt from your spouse's estate taxes, providing it was kept in the trust rather than distributed. And as long as your spouse's own assets are less than the federal exemption amount ($625,000 in 1998, rising gradually each year to $1 million in 2006), your estate makes the entire trip from you to your spouse to your children free of estate taxes.

To reap these tax savings, bypass trusts must be included in a couple's wills or trusts before either spouse dies. But they do not become funded until the first spouse dies. Because you generally have no way of knowing which spouse will die first, each spouse's will should provide for the bypass trust. Note that these trusts *cannot* be funded with joint property or property that is designated to pass to a beneficiary other than the bypass trust. Thus, in arranging the trust, you may have to divide up your joint property and retitle your assets.

If the expected tax benefits of the trust are eliminated by unforeseen events, such as a change in the tax law, the trustee can be authorized to distribute all of the trust's assets to the beneficiaries. The surviving spouse can even be named as a trustee, although care should be taken to avoid having the trust become part of the spouse's taxable estate. (For the same reason, you should be careful about naming other trust beneficiaries, such as children or other family members, as trustees.)

Other trusts. You can multiply your estate tax savings by setting up other trusts in conjunction with a bypass trust. These include the "QTIP trust" and the "general power of appointment trust." If you have a large estate, you should consult your tax attorney to determine whether you can benefit from using these trusts.

If you want the final say over who receives your assets, consider a qualified terminal interest (QTIP) trust. Under this trust, your spouse must receive all of the trust income for life. The principal goes to your choice of heirs after your surviving spouse dies. QTIPs are commonly used to prevent a spouse from cutting off children from a prior marriage.

With a general power of appointment trust, you put your assets in trust for your spouse, but appoint an adult child, say, as trustee. Your spouse is the sole beneficiary with a general power of appointment—that is, your spouse decides who ultimately inherits the property. This somewhat obsolete form of trust is used most often when a spouse is incapacitated or otherwise unable to manage property.

Generation-skipping trust. If you have grandchildren, this type of trust may be attractive. The trust income generally goes to one of your children. After your child dies, the trust dissolves, and any remaining assets go to one or more of your grandchildren. The assets of the trust are included in your estate. The big tax savings comes when your child dies. Generation-skipping trust assets of up to $1 million ($2 million for married couples) are exempt from estate tax. After 1998, the $1 million generation-skipping transfer tax exemption will be indexed annually for inflation.

AILMENT

I want to minimize the income taxes my heirs will pay.

R̸ You can arrange to have those assets subject to income tax distributed to your heir who is in the lowest tax bracket. Other assets not subject to income taxes can be designated for heirs in higher tax brackets to equalize the true inheritance value of your estate among the heirs. A trust arrangement can also be written to equalize the effective distribution.

What assets are subject to income tax when they are bequeathed at death? U.S. Series E or EE savings bonds, IRAs, and other tax-deferred assets, such as annuities, are subject to income taxes because this income has never been taxed while you were alive. Such bequests are technically known as "income in respect to decedent," or in the jargon of accountants, "hot assets."

Special tax rules apply when savings bonds are transferred to your heirs at death. The person responsible for your final return (usually the executor or administrator) may elect to do one of the following: The first possibility is to include all of the interest earned on the bonds before your death on your final income tax return; the person inheriting the bond would then include only the interest earned by the bonds after your death. Alternately, the executor can pass the accrued interest on to your heir, who will pay the tax on all of the interest earned by the bonds both before and after your death, when the bonds are cashed in or matured. This election also applies to accrued interest on Series E or EE bonds that has been deferred by trading the bonds in for a Series HH bond.

AILMENT

I want to defer federal estate taxes on a closely held business.

R You can defer federal estate taxes on a closely held business for up to five years after the regular date for estate tax payments under an obscure provision of the tax law. When the five years are up, the tax must be paid in 10 or fewer equal installments. A special 2% interest rate is available for the first $458,000 of deferred tax. Note, though, that interest for the first five years must be paid annually.

To qualify an estate for these breaks, the decedent must have been a U.S. citizen or resident at time of death, and the value of the business interest must be more than 35% of the adjusted gross estate. Adjusted gross estate is the value of the gross estate minus deductions for expenses, debts, taxes, and losses. If the business is a farm, it can include interests in residential buildings and related improvements on the farm.

The law defines an interest in a closely held business as one of the following:

- An interest as sole proprietor in a trade or business.

- A partnership interest in a trade or business, if the partnership has no more than 15 partners or 20% or more of the total capital interest in the partnership is included in the decedent's gross estate.

- Stock ownership in a corporation, if the corporation has no more than 15 stockholders or 20% or more of the total capital interest in the corporation is included in the decedent's gross estate.

To defer the tax, the estate's executor must attach a notice of the election of this provision to an estate tax return that is timely filed.

AILMENT

I want to set the value of my closely held business for estate tax purposes.

R Use a buy-sell agreement to fix the value of your business interest for estate tax purposes. Under such an arrangement, the stockholders or partners agree to buy, at a specified, predetermined price, the shares of any one of them who dies or wants to get out of the business.

If it is a valid business arrangement, the option or contract price will set a tax value that the IRS will accept, even if the fair market value of the stock when you die is higher.

To guarantee that funds are available for the buyout, insure each shareholder's or partner's life with the business named as the beneficiary and the proceeds earmarked for the purchase.

In setting the buyout figure, a qualified appraisal is essential. The pros in business valuation are the large accounting firms, investment bankers, and independent valuation experts. If you hire a business appraiser, pick a member of either the Institute of Business Appraisers (IBA) or the American Society of Appraisers (ASA). Ask about their credentials, experience, the outcome of any dealings with the IRS, and whether they have appeared as an expert witness in litigation. Do not use your company's accountant, because it is not an unbiased opinion.

Your expert should look to such factors as the nature and history of your business, its earning capacity, the value of goodwill or other intangibles, the economy, and the market price of stocks in comparable companies.

Index